Cambridge Studies in Social Anthropology

General Editor: JACK GOODY

BUDDHISM AND THE SPIRIT CULTS IN NORTH-EAST THAILAND

OTHER TITLES IN THE SERIES

BUDDHISM AND THE SPIRIT CULTS IN NORTH-EAST THAILAND

S. J. TAMBIAH

Professor of Anthropology
Harvard University

CAMBRIDGE UNIVERSITY PRESS

CAMBRIDGE

LONDON   NEW YORK   NEW ROCHELLE
MELBOURNE   SYDNEY

Published by the Press Syndicate of the University of Cambridge
The Pitt Building, Trumpington Street, Cambridge CB2 1RP
32 East 57th Street, New York, NY 10022, USA
296 Beaconsfield Parade, Middle Park, Melbourne 3206, Australia

© Cambridge University Press 1970

Library of Congress catalogue card number: 73-108112

ISBN 0 521 07825 3 hard covers
ISBN 0 521 09958 7 paperback

First published 1970
First paperback edition 1975
Reprinted 1977 1980

Printed in Great Britain at the
University Press, Cambridge

PREFACE

From 1960 to 1963 I spent three happy and rewarding years in Thailand as a UNESCO 'expert' attached to the International Institute for Child Study (now called the Bangkok Institute for Child Study). The Institute was sponsored by UNESCO and the Government of Thailand. The greater part of my time was devoted to participating in a programme of multidisciplinary research on problems wider in scope than the name of the Institute implies. The project that engaged most of my time and effort was the study, with the assistance of Thai colleagues and other UNESCO experts, of three villages in their regional setting. The villages were situated in the Central Plain, the North-east, and the North. My share of the work was wholly devoted to anthropological investigations relating to kinship, economy and religion. The material presented here pertains to the north-eastern village and its region and was collected in 1961–2 (and subsequently in the course of two long vacation trips made from Cambridge in 1965 and 1966). I express my grateful and warm thanks to two successive enlightened, energetic and stimulating Directors of the Institute, Professor Hugh Philp and Dr Lamaimas Saradatta, for supporting the study in every way, and to my other colleagues in the Institute, particularly Mr Tahwon Koedkietpong and Mr Aneckun Greesang, whose field assistance, co-operation, and friendship were invaluable in collecting, translating and interpreting the information. Much insight was also gained from my association with Mr Anders Poulsen, who has provided most of the plates that adorn this book. I hope that by dedicating the book to the Bangkok Institute for Child Study I can pay at least a fraction of my debt to my colleagues in Thailand, to UNESCO, to the Government of Thailand (particularly the Ministry of Education) and, most importantly, to the villagers and monks of Baan Phraan Muan who taught us something of their culture with patience, kindness and accommodation.

I came to Cambridge in September 1963 and it was there that much of the material was analysed and written up in first draft. In my writing I have received much intellectual stimulation and guidance from my friends and colleagues, particularly Edmund Leach (who has taught me most of the anthropology I know) and Professor Meyer Fortes.

I am also deeply grateful to the Center for Advanced Study in the Behavioral Sciences for affording me leisure, library facilities, editorial and secretarial assistance in order that I could complete the book. The meticulous and creative editorial assistance of Miss Miriam Gallaher is

Preface

remembered with admiration. Thanks are also due to the secretarial staff in the Bangkok Institute, and in the Department of Anthropology at Cambridge, for typing assistance given at various stages of preparation. I thank my wife, Mary Wynne, for her patient and skilful editorial and bibliographical assistance and moral support.

The text contains numerous names and concepts which originate in the Sanskrit and Pali languages: their orthography follows the normal conventions of romanization but omits all diacritical signs. There are even more numerous references to Thai words, especially in the north-eastern dialect, for which no proper system of transcription into the roman alphabet has as yet been devised. I have therefore transcribed these words as best I could, omitting all diacritical marks.

Cambridge   S.J.T.
October 1969

CONTENTS

TABLES

ILLUSTRATIONS

PLATES

FIGURES

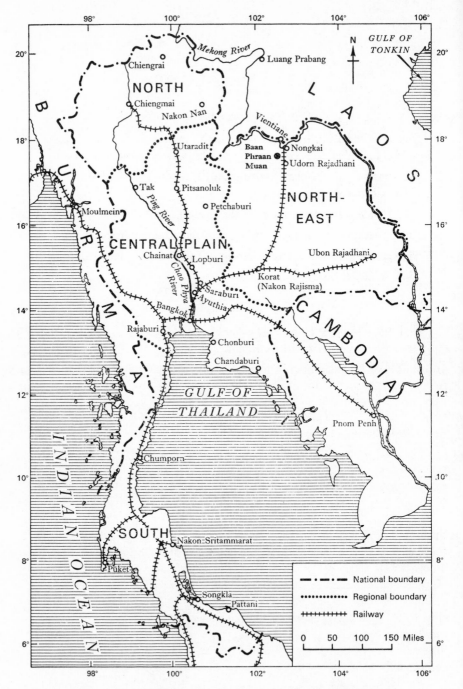

Fig. 1   Map of Thailand, showing natural regions and place-names

1

INTRODUCTION: THE PARTICULAR
AND THE GENERAL

A Thai village is not an island by itself; it is part of a wider network of social relationships and it is embedded in a civilization.

Following the method of study usually employed by anthropologists, I describe the religious practices and rituals of the people in a small-scale universe studied at first hand. But my objective in writing the book is not simply to give an ethnographic description of the exotic religious customs of a strange village in a remote corner of the world; it is to use the particular to say something general. By this I do not mean that the village in Northeast Thailand which I describe is 'representative' of every other village in the country or some such atomistic statistical assertion, but that insofar as this village is embedded in a civilization and has participated in history and has shared cultural elements with other villages, the structural properties and the processes that characterize its present religious system may reveal features which are of general import. What I have in mind is nicely stated by Postan (in his *Inaugural Lecture*, 1939, p. 34) provided we substitute 'anthropological' for 'historical': 'Microscopic problems of historical research can and should be made macrocosmic—capable of reflecting worlds larger than themselves. It is in this reflected flicker of truth, the revelations of the general in the particular, that the contribution of the historical method to social science will be found.'

The procedure by which I identify and describe religion is primarily through ritual. Essentially I devote most of this book to dissecting and then relating four ritual complexes that are enacted in a Thai village. They are: rites performed by Buddhist monks and therefore labelled 'Buddhist'; *sukhwan* ritual, concerned with recalling the escaped spirit essence of persons and performed by village elders; the cult of the guardian spirits or deities of the village which has its own officiants (the *cham* and *tiam*); and rites addressed to malevolent spirits that cause individual illnesses, of which spirit possession is the most dramatic. These four complexes dominate the religious field but do not exhaust it.

The anthropologist faces certain problems of contextualization and delimitation in dealing with these ritual complexes. For example, the Buddhist rites along with the institution of monkhood and the major religious concepts that go with them, which are observed in the village today, have a wider generality in both time and space. There is a history of Buddhism from its origins in India until the present, and there is the spatial existence of Theravada Buddhism (which primarily concerns us here) not only throughout Thailand but also in the neighbouring countries of Ceylon, Burma, Laos and Cambodia. These projections in time and space also apply to much of the other ritual complexes, though not with the same depth in time and spread in space as manifested by Buddhism. What are the implications of this immense backdrop to the anthropologist's stage?

It could be said that the requirements of my exposition are three-dimensional: to present the religion as a synchronic, ordered scheme of collective representations; then on the one side to demonstrate how the system of religious categories is woven into the institutional context and social structure of the contemporary villagers; and on the other to relate the same system to the grand Buddhist literary and historical tradition.

Let me deal with each of these aspects in turn.

It is right and proper for the anthropologist to assert that his first and foremost task is to document the religion as the present-day subjects live it and to understand it in terms of the subjects' own intellectual, moral and affective categories (and thereafter to seek to construct a scheme of interpretation which reveals the principles underlying the ideology and behaviour he has witnessed and recorded).

In order to present a synchronic picture of village religion I have in this book tried to see how the four ritual complexes are differentiated and also linked together in a *single total field*. In respect of each ritual complex —and of all four together—I try to elucidate how religious ideas and constructs are ordered, what the symbolism and message contents of the rites are, how the officiants are distinguished, and so forth. The focus is on the contrastive features of the four cults or complexes as collective representations, and in displaying these features I use four concepts: opposition, complementarity, linkage, and hierarchy.

The framework and conceptual tools for my structural analysis of ritual derive from many anthropologists (chief among whom are Radcliffe-Brown, Lévi-Strauss, Leach, and Turner) and from other fields of relevance to our subject (such as linguistics and information theory). In two respects I can claim to have gone further than the previous contributions on ritual. First, I have argued that, since much ritual includes the recitation of words, we should perceive ritual as consisting of both 'word and deed'; in any case since in Thai rituals the use of sacred words is an important component, I have tried to interpret their role and the manner in which they are integrated with ritual action.

The particular and the general

A second deviation from the beaten path consists in the attempt to see myth and ritual as two closely related domains and to examine their dialectical relationship. Since Malinowski's 'charter theory of myth' we have had virtually no ethnographic analysis, let alone a fertile theoretical formulation, of the relation between myth and ritual. Lévi-Strauss has a marginal interest in the problem, but he has progressively become concerned with myth as an autonomous realm of thought.

The relation between a collectivity of rituals seen as a system in its own right (in terms of the arrangement of categories and symbols and officiants) and the social structure and institutional environment of the people who practise the religion is another matter. This has been in the past, and still remains, an anthropological task *par excellence*. It is the kind of special illumination that an anthropologist can provide by virtue of his approach and method of study. In order to see this particular linkage between ritual and society, it might at times be salutary for the anthropologist working in South-east Asia consciously to ignore the connections between his field data and the philosophical, doctrinal, and literary aspects of civilization, so that he can all the better understand the nexus between religious action and social context. This perspective is arrestingly conveyed by Leach's phrase 'practical religion', by which he means not theological philosophy, often greatly preoccupied with the life hereafter, but religion which is 'concerned with the life here and now', religion whose components are meaningful not only because of internal coherence but also 'because of their practical integration with the secular life of the religious congregation' (Leach 1968*b*, pp. 1–3). This mode of elucidation is the second major interest of this book.

The third dimension is the relation between religious belief and ritual action observed in the field and the corpus of Buddhist literature composed from classical times, that is, between the religious events of the present and the grand historical events of Buddhist civilization. The study of religion from this perspective is quasi-anthropological, in the sense of demanding the skills and knowledge of other disciplines (e.g. Indology and History of Religion) in addition to one's own.

Anthropologists have in recent years wrestled with this problem, especially in respect of India. One school, stemming from Redfield and his associates, formulated the question in terms of the relation and the processes of interaction between two levels or entities—between the great tradition of civilization and the little tradition of the village. This formulation and others which have replaced it—such as Higher Sanskritic Hinduism versus Lower Popular Hinduism—have been mistaken in two important respects: first, insufficient regard was paid to the fact that the

3

great literary religious tradition is itself varied and has been both cumulative and changing; secondly, it has for some curious reason not been seen that contemporary live religion, even that observed in the village, incorporates a great deal of the literary tradition. *Brahman* priests, Buddhist monks, ritual experts and scribes in some measure deal with literary and oral knowledge transmitted from the past and which they themselves systematically transmit to their successors. And for the common people at large such texts and knowledge have a referential and legitimating function, even if they themselves have no direct access to them.

Thus in this book, wherever I have engaged in relating the present to the past, I have used two concepts to describe the connection: *continuities* and *transformations*. By continuities I mean the *persistence* of certain structures or customs from the past into the present; and by transformations I mean *systematic changes* in forms over time, both in the historical past and between a structure in the past and that currently observed in the village. A simple example is the institution of monkhood: there are certain aspects of it which have been transmitted unbroken from the classical past, and there are others that have shown systematic transformation. Or again, a myth recorded in the village may have its classical literary version (continuity); but the same myth seen in conjunction with a contemporary ritual may show a new relation (transformation) not present in the classical form.

Although one of my aims is to relate wherever helpful the religious forms of the present to the literary and historical past, I should make it clear in order to avoid misunderstanding that such relating is not systematically followed, nor done in the manner of an Indologist, philosopher or historian of religion. I do not examine the *history* of a doctrine for its own sake, or that of a myth or religious institution. This is the province of a specialist of a different kind. My primary reference point is always contemporary village religion. Some aspect of it may be viewed in relation to a classical institutional form and its changes, or may be illuminated by consulting an older literary formulation, or its meaning enlarged by a representation in classical architecture and sculpture. Thus the history of and changes in Buddhist monastic life have interested me because they illuminate monastic life in the village today; and the many facets of the serpent symbol which appears in village myth are better discerned, and an expansion of meaning accomplished, when its appearance in classical architecture is scrutinized. It is only in this manner that I relate the present to the past; the piecemeal nature of the past as it appears in this book springs from the problems dictated by the events studied in the village.

A few words now on the logic of the sequence in which chapters are presented. After some thought, it occurred to me that the most effective strategy of presentation is to begin with the *duality* of village religion as a contrapuntal theme—its present intactness and its historical roots—and to suggest indirectly how the past lives in the present and the present can at the same time be seen as a transformation of the past. The opening chapters reveal the dialectical play between the present and the past.

Thus Chapter 2 introduces the village of Phraan Muan and its region as it is today, and then in the second half paints a historical backdrop, which tells us something of the grand historical events which must have affected the region in which Phraan Muan exists.

Chapters 3 and 4 inject the contrapuntal theme in a slightly different way, with Chapter 3 outlining the Buddhist cosmology as it has been presented in Buddhist literary works, and Chapter 4 dealing with the major religious categories of thought in village religion. I also introduce the point—which will be illustrated in later chapters—that although the classical cosmology may not be *verbalized* in the village it nevertheless makes its appearance in village *ritual*.

Chapters 5 and 6 are intended to be *historical* introductions to early Buddhist monasticism, and to the classical conception of a monk's way of life and its relation to the way of life of a layman. Chapter 7 provides the comparison and contrast by plunging us directly into the institution of monkhood in contemporary village life. Thereafter the subsequent chapters unfurl the many features of village religion in their variety, intricacy and colourfulness—like a long Japanese scroll.

Although most of the time I deal with one tiny spot in the backwoods of Thailand, I want it to be remembered that this spot and the whole country in which it is located exist in a wider region of South-east Asian societies which share many things in space and time. Therefore wherever a comparative point can be appropriately made to aid understanding I do so by referring to Burma, Ceylon, Cambodia or India. The value of such a wide-ranging view (combined with a meticulous attention to detail) was seen in the late seventeenth century by De la Loubère, who so perceptively wrote about Siam:

But if... I do yet enlarge on certain matters beyond the relish of some, I entreat them to consider that general expressions do never afford just ideas; and that this is to proceed no farther than the superficial knowledge of things. 'Tis out of desire of making the Siamese perfectly known, that I give several notices of the other kingdoms of the Indies and of China: for though vigorously taken, all this may appear foreign to my subject, yet to me it seems that the comparison of the things of neighbouring countries with each other, does greatly illustrate them. (De la Loubère 1693, p. 2.)

2

THE STAGE AND ITS SETTING

THE VILLAGE OF MUAN THE HUNTER AND ITS REGION

Baan Phraan Muan means the village of Muan the hunter. There is a myth which has wide circulation in the region where this village is located. It not only gives us some idea of the verbal play in which Thai people take pleasure and excel, but also relates a number of villages distinguished by name into a wider regional complex. The villages in the legend exist; so does the swamp. They lie in a region extending from Udorn to Nongkai on the Thailand–Laos border (see Fig. 2).

This is the story of an ox called Hoo-Saparat. A rich merchant (*seethii*) who lived at the spot which is now the swamp (*byng*), called Chuan, owned a pregnant cow. The rich man asked his servant Siang to take the cow out to graze. The cow disappeared. Siang and others tried to track it and the place where they did this was called the village of *Noon Duu* (which means 'upland' and also 'to look' (*duu*)). The cow wasn't found there and its tracks were followed until it was found at the village of *Pakhoo* (*pa* = meet; *khoo* = ox). The ox was then taken to graze at the village of *Naam Suay* ('beautiful water'). The herders stopped to eat and the cow disappeared again, because it wanted to find a place to calve. Siang then went to see a hunter called Muan to ask whether he had seen the cow. Muan was not able to help. Muan lived in the village that was called Baan Phraan Muan (village of Muan the hunter). The tracks of the cow were discovered again and followed; the cow was eventually found and its legs were securely bound at the village of *Ngua Khong* (*ngua* = ox; *khong* = 'rope to bind legs'). The cow calved at this place, and Siang took the placenta to wash at the village of *Naam Kun* (*naam* = water/pond; *kun* = not clear/muddy). The cow and calf were taken back to the owner who lived in *Byng Chuan*.

There is another version of the myth which gives the central role to Muan, the founder of our village: it was he who successfully traced the lost cow of the *seethii* and received recognition for it.

The village of Phraan Muan is located in North-east Thailand between Udorn, the administrative capital of the province bearing the same name, and Nongkai, the border town on the Mekong River, which separates Laos from Thailand. It is about seventeen kilometres from Udorn, and has to be reached along a feeder road that branches from the main road linking the two towns.

The village is the last unit in a formal administrative hierarchy. Udorn

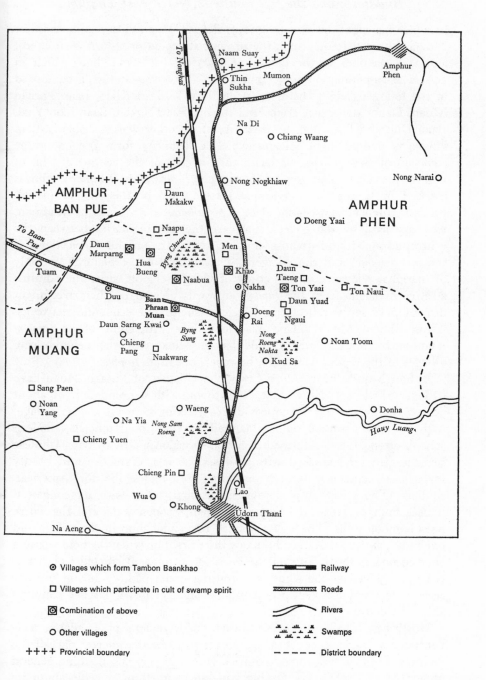

Fig. 2 Baan Phraan Muan and its region

7

province has eight districts (*amphur*); Phraan Muan village is in Amphur Muang (the district in which the provincial capital of Udorn is situated), and is a member of the commune (*tambon*) of Baan Khao, which in 1961/2 had a population of 8,000 persons. This *tambon* in turn is composed of the following eight 'hamlets' or 'villages'—Baan Khao, Baan Phraan Muan, Daun Marparng, Baan Hua Bueng, Baan Nakha, Baan Ton Yaai, Baan Duu and Baan Naabua (see Fig. 2). In other words, Phraan Muan village is one of eight villages which collectively form the commune (*tambon*) of Baan Khao, which in turn is part of the central district of Udorn province. The *tambon* has a chief headman (*gamnan*) who is assisted by a headman (*puyaibaan*) from each of the villages (*baan*). Phraan Muan village has an elected *puyaibaan*. Both kinds of headman, who are paid by the government, are the intermediaries between the central administration (whose chief representative at the district level is the *nai amphur*) and the villagers. The administrative hierarchy is only of marginal relevance in this study of village religion, since the administrative divisions from the *tambon* upwards created by the government do not necessarily reflect the villagers' social and economic networks. Thus, Phraan Muan village has close links with some of its *tambon* members but not with others; and it has close links with other neighbouring villages of the region which are, however, not in its *tambon*.

Although quite near Udorn town, the villagers of Phraan Muan have had very little contact with it. The town, with a population of about 30,000 in the early sixties, provided a striking contrast to the village, with its administrative offices manned by uniformed officials, modern schools attended by uniformed children, shops owned by thriving Chinese businessmen (and stocked with radios, TV sets, cosmetics and beauty magazines), cinemas, beauty parlours, and nightclubs for American soldiers. The village was depressing at first sight, with its congested houses built on stilts; the better ones had wooden walls and the worse ones bamboo walls. There was in 1961 one small shop in the village and one radio; and most of the adults saw their first film when the field workers showed one to them. During the rains, deep mud obstructed travel, but the eye rejoiced at the sight of sprouting green paddy; during the dry season, dust and heat kept people indoors and the brown parched countryside provided no visual relief.

North-east Thailand, like the other major regions of Thailand, concentrates on agriculture; it is also reckoned to be the poorest part of the country. Both these features require a gloss which says something general about the society we are dealing with and something specific about its north-eastern region.

8

The stage and its setting

There is an old tradition in Thailand, which, true or not, conveys a distinctive feature about that country. It is said that each free man had the right to cultivate up to twenty-five *rai* (about six acres) in order to maintain his family. The people of Thailand were in the past, and still remain, a nation of small farmers, the vast majority of whom are engaged in growing one crop—rice.

Rice is the chief crop of Central, North-east, North and South Thailand, the four main regions of the country. There is a dramatic difference in the scale on which it was grown between before 1850, when Siam, as the country was then called, had little contact with the West, and after 1850, when as a result of the Bowring Treaty, there was an explosive expansion in rice-growing ensuing from Siam's participation in world trade, the expansion of which in turn was, partly at least, related to developments in steam transport and the opening of the Suez Canal. There was a tremendous increase in the volume of rice exports, especially between the 1870s and 1930s, and one writer describes the change thus: 'This 25-fold increase—over the probable maximum volume at the time of the Bowring Treaty—which took place while the population roughly doubled itself, represents the major economic change in Thailand since 1855.' (Ingram 1955, pp. 39–40.)

This economic expansion may have stretched the social structure but certainly it did not burst it. In fact, it emphasized even more than before that the Thais had an entrenched preference for rice-growing and for living in village settlements. Furthermore, the economic expansion and prosperity, rather than changing traditional religious orientations and practices, may well have reinforced some of them, notably the belief in the ethical virtue of merit-making and the scale on which it was practised. The economic change was thus accomplished, with a change neither of technology nor of social rules and religious orientations. It was, however, achieved in an uneven fashion within Thailand. Until about 1900 it was the Central Plain of Thailand that showed the greatest expansion in rice cultivation, but from 1905 onwards the outer provinces of the North and North-east showed significant advances, especially with the construction of the railway. By 1935 the North-east was responsible for 20% of the country's total rice exports (Ingram 1955, p. 47).

But although the North-east, like most other parts of Thailand, participated in the process which broadened the peasant's economic horizons, it was—and is still—beset with its own peculiar chronic problems. Its soil is not so fertile as in the North or the Central Plain; whereas the North is greatly helped by irrigation systems, and the Central Plain by a system of canals in a flat terrain, the North-east depends entirely on monsoon

9

rain by and large unaided by the artifices of water-control and irrigation. Thus the North-east, while it distinguished itself by showing a marked increase in the area cultivated in the last few decades, is also the region where yields declined most sharply—a commentary on the marginal nature of the lands brought under cultivation and the inadequacy of water supply. (Yet, by some curious twist of nature in this dry area, there are some three or four swamps and ponds in the vicinity of our village which are remarkable landmarks and exemplifications of the value of water.) The data reported in the *Census of Agriculture* for 1963 (when rearranged according to the Ministry of Agriculture classification of the four major regions) show that the average holding in the North-east is 21·6 *rai*, which compares favourably with 25·9 for the Central Plain, 23·0 for the South and 8·6 for the North. But the yield in the North-east is the lowest: 169·2 kilograms per *rai*, as compared with 216 for the Central Plain, 210 for the South and 302·5 for the North, which enjoys irrigation. (Wijewardene in Silcock (ed.) 1967.)

Phraan Muan village is thus representative of its region in that it is poor. It depends on one rice crop a year, and its yields are controlled by the volume of rainfall it receives. Rain is notoriously unreliable in both timing and amount, and the hazard of crop loss due to drought is endemic. This, combined with poor soils, gives much lower rice yields than in the Bangkok Plain. During the dry season village wells and ponds dry up and villagers have to go some distance to draw muddy, slimy water. It is not to be wondered then that water should occupy villagers, not only in their economic activities but in their rituals and myths as well.

I shall proceed now to give a picture of the social structure of the village in terms of the ecological categories and principles of classification employed by the villagers themselves.

The word *baan* has many ranges of meaning. First of all it means a house; it also represents a compound cluster (*baun baan*); it also means 'hamlet' or 'village' in its widest extension (in the sense of a settlement composed of houses), and for major subdivisions of it (e.g. 'large' or 'small' hamlets).

The settlement pattern of Baan Phraan Muan is clustered, like that of other villages in the region. The nucleus is a dense settlement called *baan yaai* (big hamlet) intersected by narrow lanes. The branch dirt road that leads up to the village, and goes beyond to Tambon Baanpue, separates this settlement from the *wat* (cluster of buildings forming the Buddhist temple). Lined along the road, opened ten years previously, are houses that have overflowed from the main settlement and comprise *baan naui* (small hamlet). This settlement contains primarily young families who could not find space in their parents' compounds in *baan yaai*. All villages in the region are clustered and are separated from one another by distances of three to four kilometres or more. The village is thus a distinct ecological entity. The settlement itself is comprised of separate categories: *baan* (hamlet or village) is distinguished from *wat* (temple); the fields (*naa*) surround the *baan*; at the edges of the fields are swamps and ponds (*byng*) which are a distinct category of nature, for they provide fishing and symbolize perennial water; and finally forest (*paa*), now more or less cut down, separates one village from another.

In a sense the major ecological and social distinction within the village (*baan*) is that between the *wat*, where the monks live, and the houses of lay villagers (*baan*).

The most conspicuous physical feature of the village is the cluster of buildings comprising the *wat*. The components are a large wooden *sala* (preaching hall), a small dilapidated *bood* (the chapel, where ordination takes place and where monks hold certain services, such as confessions, to which laymen are not admitted), and the *khuti* (monks' dwellings). The *wat* compound is large and bounded by a fence with two gateways. The village school is held in the *sala*, and this fact alone makes the *wat* a focal point in village life and a source of ear-splitting noise, caused by children both at work (largely repetitive learning) and at play. In addition to its serving as school and place of religious worship and instruction, the *sala* is also the village hall and large meetings of a secular nature are held there. The *wat* is thus the focus of village devotional and recreational activities, the two of which merge in certain collective rites distributed over the year. But despite the children and their schooling, the monks lead a segregated life in their *khuti*, which stands at the farthest end of the *wat*, away from the village. The place of the *wat* in the village cannot be expressed in a simple dichotomy: if the *wat* is distinct from *baan*, it is also the central architectural complex in the village; if the monks are segregated from village life, village life in its collective aspect is acted out in the precincts of the *wat*. The *wat* belongs to the village; it was built and is maintained by the villagers; its inmates are of village origin— though in a formal sense one should say that the *wat* belongs to the *Sangha* (the order of monks) and its ecclesiastical organization.

The settlement can be said to be composed of the following inclusive groupings: the family, the household, and the compound. Not only is the smaller contained within the larger, but all three are dynamically inter-related in terms of the domestic and compound cycles.

In 1961 there were 149 households and 182 families in the village, with a total population of about 932. The age distributions (rough estimates) were as shown below.

TABLE 1. *Age distributions of the population of Baan Phraan Muan*

10 years and under	221
11–20	249
21–30	152
31–40	104
41–50	93
50+	99
No information	14

A brief account of residence and inheritance customs is a necessary preliminary to the understanding of household and compound structure.

Ordinarily a newly married couple lives uxorilocally for a few years in the house of the wife's parents as members of the same household.[1] A change takes place when the next sister gets married; the older sister and her family may either build a house for themselves in the parents' compound, or move out altogether and live neolocally. This residential change is usually synchronized with other changes: no more are the couple part of the parental household, economically dependent on them and also contributing their labour to the parental farming enterprise. The wife's parents informally transfer some land to the couple so that they can farm independently, and also establish themselves as a separate household. (Legal possession of this land takes place later, usually in the form of intestate succession.)

Traditionally in Baan Phraan Muan (and its region), sons either settled uxorilocally and worked land inherited by their wives or, equally frequently, cleared new forest land to make their own farms (*jab jawng*) and lived neolocally after marriage. This pattern of transmission of property through females and uxorilocal residence, combined with pioneering settlements, was in vogue as long as land was freely available; today with scarcely any new land available for development, the inheritance ideology is distinctly manifesting bilateral features. This trend will probably become marked in the future; present figures, however, still show a statistical emphasis on female rights to land.

Table 2 gives a synchronic cross-section of household composition in a sample of 80 households. It shows that 65% were elementary families (with or without odd relatives) and that 26% were multiple extended families composed of parents and usually their unmarried children plus families of married children among whom *daughters* predominate. A dia-

---

[1] In a sample of 106 married couples the proportion that took up uxorilocal residence soon after marriage was 85%, virilocal 9·4%, neolocal 4·7%, other 0·9%.

TABLE 2. *Household composition (sample = 80 households)*

Elementary family			
Parents + unmarried children	46		
Parents + unmarried children + odd relatives	5	52	(65 %)
Husband and wife + odd relatives	1		
Extended family			
Parents + unmarried children + married daughter's family	17		
Parents + unmarried children + married son's family	3	21	(26 %)
Parents + married daughter's family	1		
Limited extended family			
Widowed parent + married daughter's family	4	(5 %)	
Other			
Families of two sisters	2		
Polygynous family (two wives)	1	3	(4 %)

chronic picture of Table 2 is that a married daughter (sometimes a married son) lives for a short period with her parents in the same household, and then sets up a separate establishment in the compound (or elsewhere) when the next sister marries, until finally the youngest sister marries and lives with the parents as the stem family and will succeed to the parental house. At the next stage a widowed parent may well become the dependant of the stem family, and on his or her death the cycle starts again.

It is clear then that the domestic cycle is linked with the compound cycle. The local word for compound is *baun diawkan* or *baun baan*. If there is more than one household within a fenced compound, typically the most senior male, or if he is dead then his spouse, is the point of reference for purposes of identity; for example *baun baan* Phau Tu Phan means compound of grandfather Phan, and the constituent households are described as living within a common fence (*'juu nai wua diawkan'*).

At any particular point of time the compounds may show varied composition. For instance, the composition of the main hamlet (*baan yaai*), which had ninety-nine households, was as follows in 1961/2.

There were eight compounds of multiple households, two to six in number, whose key linking numbers were close kin who referred their residence rights to a common ascendant or set of them. In these compounds there was usually a core of females who provided the kinship and inheritance links, but there were also instances of brothers only or siblings of both sexes and their descendants. In *baan yaai* thirty households formed these eight compounds.

There were also 'pseudo' compounds composed of two or more non-kin households who had either inherited their site from unrelated sources or had themselves acquired the residential site. Common fence here signified friendship and neighbourliness, but not common ownership. Property rights were held separately. A slightly different situation is that of two kinsmen who, having left their own parental compounds for lack of space, acquire adjacent plots intentionally or accidentally, and decide to maintain a common fence, though their properties are separate. *Baan yaai* had some thirty-three such households forming 'pseudo' compounds.

The third type is the 'single household' compounds. There were in *baan yaai* thirty-six such units, and about six of these were households of parents and married children. These compounds will in time turn into multiple household compounds, that is, the first and third types belong to the same compound cycle.

The cycle may be formalized thus:

1. a fully developed compound would consist of the parental household (which would include the prospective stem family) and households of married children, usually daughters;

2. when the parents die the link between sisters, or more rarely between brothers and sisters, will be the link between households;

3. in the next generation, classificatory siblingship (*phii-naung*) (especially matrilateral first cousinship) and more remote ties will link the constituent households.

In short, there is in the village a tendency toward co-residence, in compounds, of married female siblings and classificatory *phii-naung* (matrilateral parallel cousins), owing to the custom of uxorilocal residence and the inheritance of residence rights in compounds by daughters rather than by sons. Thus is the domestic cycle meshed with the compound cycle.

The implications of these inclusive groupings of family, household and compound for religious activities will occupy us in later chapters. A stem family or a junior dependent family will not usually be reckoned as an independent unit for ritual activities—such as making a contribution to a collective Buddhist festival or to a communal propitiation of the guardian spirit. Nor will it be an independent unit in the reciprocities of gift giving and labour services in rites of passage such as marriage and death. A household which is autonomous in the compound with respect to its domestic economy and ownership of paddy stocks, and which participates as an independent contracting unit in reciprocal economic services and dyadic contracts, will also be reckoned as an autonomous unit for ritual activities and enjoy the privileges and shoulder the duties thereof.

The normal acting unit or grouping in the village is a 'household'. Co-residence in compound involves reciprocities between households in economic and ritual matters, but these shade off into the reciprocities of wider kinship, neighbourliness, and village membership. It is true that individual afflictions, life crises and rites of passage are first and foremost the concern of the patients' or celebrants' family and household, then of the surrounding circle of close kin and finally of distant kin and neighbours and friends. But it is my view that it would be a mistake and a relatively barren inquiry to search for the nexus between ritual concepts and religious symbolism, and the social structure in Baan Phraan Muan, in terms of *social groupings* alone or even primarily in terms of them. The essential structural ideas bearing on ritual are coded in terms of *principles of social classification* as portrayed by the kinship terminology, rules of social distance symbolized in marriage rules, the ordering of generations, and the topology of social space embedded especially in the physical divisions of the house and compound. I shall examine these features now.

Although residential and inheritance patterns have a matrilateral colouring, kinship is bilateral and ego-oriented. This, combined with a tendency towards village endogamy as an empirical fact, produces important results. Table 3 shows both high village endogamy and the greater tendency for women to have origin in the village than is the case for men. Among 87 married couples living in the village, 56 (64%) of the husbands were born in the village, but 78 (or nearly 90%) of the total 87 wives were born in the village. For most people the number of kinsmen in the community, both cognatic and affinal, is therefore large. In fact, the entire village population consists of a social universe that is subject to a common scheme of social categorization *which contains or includes the particularities of ego-oriented reckoning within the generalities of the society or village-wide categorical scheme*. It is important to grasp this integrating principle.

TABLE 3. *Birth-place of married couples living in Baan Phraan Muan*
(sample = 87)

Birth-place of husbands		Birth-place of wives			
		Baan Phraan Muan	Same *tambon*	Same district	Elsewhere
Baan Phraan Muan	56 (64%)	48 (85·7%)	4 (7%)	2 (3·6%)	2 (3·6%)
Same *tambon*	8 (9·5%)	8 (100%)	—	—	—
Same district	10 (11·5%)	10 (100%)	—	—	—
Elsewhere	13 (15%)	12 (92·3%)	—	—	1 (7·7%)
	87 (100%)	78 (90%)	4 (4·6%)	2 (1·9%)	3 (3·5%)

The ordering of persons in this system is along two axes—the vertical generational (which defines respect and authority relations) and the lateral 'sibling' (which defines sexual accessibility and approved marriage). Both axes embody concepts of social privilege and obligation.

The following is a formal picture of the village-wide status categories which divide the village into hierarchical segments. I do not propose to go into details of kinship terminology. In terms of village usage and categorization the important point is that certain kinship terms for consanguineal kin over three generations are applied right through the village, thus dividing the population into generational categories.

1. *Pu-ya-ta-yai* (fafa-famo-mofa-momo). This is a collective concept used for the four grandparents as well as all 'grandparents' in general. Each term can be used singly to refer to the particular grandparent (e.g. *pu = fafa*). The villagers use this collective term to refer to ancestors and to dead elders to whom merit is transferred in merit-making rites.

2. *Phau-mae* (fa-mo). In the narrow sense these terms refer to own father and mother. They are used as a collective expression to refer to both parents together. The terms father and mother are, however, used widely to refer to persons of the parental generation and appropriate sex. Thus *phau-mae-phuu thaw* are 'persons of father–mother status'. These are all the elders in ego's village. The accent is on generation and age, which call for respect on the part of *luug-laan* (described below), and carry the right to assume leadership roles in the village and to call upon the labour power of junior generations. The most commonly used term for persons of this category is *phuu thaw* (old persons); in their role as intermediaries, mediators and arbitrators they are called *thaw kae* (old old).

3. *Phii-naung* (elder sibling–younger sibling). This, again, can be used singly of a particular individual and collectively to refer to a category of persons. In everyday usage the sex of a sibling is not specified in address; in terms of reference sex can be specified by a suffix. Once again the terms are used not only for full siblings, but also for all males and females of ego's own generation. Rather than specifying sex it specifies relative age. As a collective term, *phii-naung* refers to kin of one's own generation, villagers of one's own generation, and, in its widest extension, all ego's kin (*yaad-phii-naung*).

4. *Luug-laan* (child-grandchild, nephew). The rules of usage are similar to those already described. *Luug* in its kinship frame of reference is own child or children; it is extended to all members of the junior generation. *Laan* is grandchild; in its wider extension it means persons of the second descending generation. Thus this collective category lumps both descending generations together.

The stage and its setting

These hierarchical social categories are a significant pointer to the social structure of the village community. In the grandparental generation each of the grandparents is specified by sex and type of link in the collective term; in the parental generation the terms for father and mother make up the category. In one's own generation, not the sex of siblings but their relative age is conspicuous in the collective category. In the case of *luug-laan* category, both descending generations are grouped together irrespective of type of link, sex and relative age.

In the sphere of ritual activities examined in this book, the reciprocities and exchanges considered are those between *phuu thaw* (or *phau-mae-phuu thaw*) and *luug-laan* (children and grandchildren).

The conspicuous feature of kinship relations in Baan Phraan Muan is the phrasing of obligations and relationships in the idiom of four terms: grandparent, parent, sibling, and child-grandchild. These terms imply asymmetrical and reciprocal behaviour. There is no particular complex of behaviour attributes associated with, say, mother's brother as distinct from father's brother, father's sister as distinct from mother's sister. Close kin are naturally more important than more distant kin, but which of the close kin (outside ego's families of procreation and orientation) depends on situational circumstances and not on jural norms. The wider grouping that assembles at ritual occasions is the bilateral kin, plus affines, the representation again being flexible and the operative factors situational. Fellow community members also assemble and play roles, for the village conception of reciprocity extends to all its members. They, too, can be comprehended within the collective generational and age categories deriving from the terminology of kinship.

The lateral axis differentiates persons in ego's own generation. Kinsmen in one's own generation (including affines) divide into two categories (*phii/naung*: older/younger siblings) and the concept *yaad phii-naung* is used in its widest reference to mean 'kinsmen'. While marriage across generations and which breaks the rule of 'relative age' (the rule that the husband must be older than his wife) is prohibited, especially if the partners are close kin, marriage and sex regulations are usually formulated in terms of the lateral *phii-naung* own generation series which is differentiated into the following named sub-categories. All sub-categories incorporate the relative age distinction.

1. *Phii kab naung* (blood brothers and sisters; siblings). Sex relations (*see*) between siblings is forbidden. If they engage in them, they must be forcibly separated. Marriage (*aw kan* = 'to take') between them is impossible. These attitudes are axiomatic and are therefore not the focus of verbal elaboration. Thus, in short, sex and marriage are prohibited with *phii kab naung*.

2. *Luug phuu phii naung* (first cousins). Sex relations between first cousins are forbidden; once again, if they engage in them, they must be forcibly separated. Marriage is forbidden because they are descended from a common ancestor (*haam gaad sum diawkan*). Village attitude is that such unions are 'impermanent and against custom' (*bau yuen pid booran*) and denies that stable and prosperous marriage is possible between first cousins. It is axiomatic that a marriage ceremony cannot take place (*tham pithii baw dai*), and that if two first cousins live together and refuse to be separated, they will be disinherited and disowned. Villagers appear to observe these rules strictly. No marriage between first cousins was encountered.

3. *Phii-naung* (classificatory siblings/second cousins). Second cousins are not separated from third cousins by means of a special term, but they comprise a special category in regard to sex and marriage—a transitional ambivalent category.

Sex between second cousins is not a serious matter if of temporary duration. But in this village since sex usually follows courtship, and courtship is a prelude to marriage (in fact ideally there should be no intercourse before marriage), sex relations between second cousins carries the possibility of marriage.

Village attitude to marriage of second cousins is ambivalent. *Tham prapheenii haam tae aw dai khaw chaub ragkan*—'custom forbids but they can marry if they love each other'. They can be married ceremonially in the orthodox fashion, but if second cousins break the relative age rule (i.e. the woman is an 'older sibling of the man'), they have to go through a certain ritual to overcome the effects of incest. In normal usage a husband can be referred to by his wife as *phii* (older sibling) and can refer to his wife as *naung* (younger sibling). Thus a marriage that contravenes relative age distinctions creates unacceptable linguistic asymmetry between husband and wife. There are cases of second cousin marriage in the village but they are infrequent.

4. *Phii-naung: yaad haang*. The second term means distant relatives. Persons of third cousin range and further distance fall into this category. Marriage is recommended or approved within this range; and sex relations without marriage are not prohibited.

5. *Khon oeuen*: 'other people' are non-kinsmen. Typically they are persons of other villages in the region. It is possible to marry them, thereby converting non-kin to kinsmen.

6. Finally, we come to the unknown 'outsider' who marks the limit of sex relations and marriage. He stands at the edge of the social universe, rather than signifying a special forbidden category. Witchcraft is attributed to remote villagers. Outsiders are also those from the urban world to

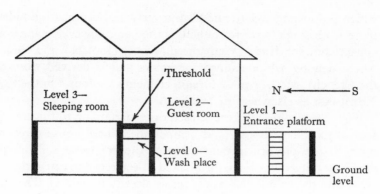

Fig. 3*a* Profile of house, showing levels

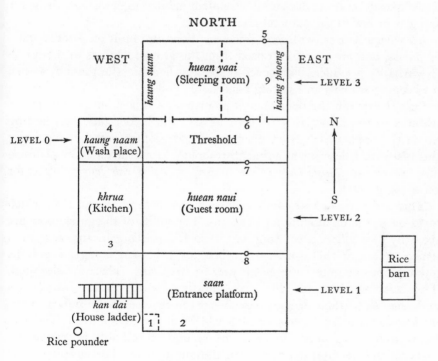

1. *Haan naam*: covered water pots for drinking
2. Water pots for washing feet
3. Fireplace
4. Water pots
5. Pillar called *saaw haeg* (1)

6. Pillar called *saaw khwan* (1)
7. Pillar called *saaw khwan* (2)
8. Pillar called *saaw haeg* (2)
9. Shelf with Buddha statue

Fig. 3*b* House plan (living space on raised floor)

which power and wealth and also poverty and degradation belong. While there is no single term for outsiders they are, however, named as groups: Cheg (Chinese), Kaew (Vietnamese), Khaeg (Indians), and Farang (a word which denotes white-skinned foreigners and is derived from *farangseed*, the French). Most of these foreign elements are found in the towns of the North-east as elsewhere in Thailand.

Now I shall present a set of categories pertaining to the arrangement of space in a village house (and compound). These house categories which refer to the physical arrangement of the rooms and floor space carry social meanings which are formulated in reference to categories of persons, especially the lateral *phii-naung* series already described. They also derive meaning from certain other features of social structure: the custom of initial uxorilocal residence and the frequent habitation of married daughter and son-in-law in the parental house.

All village houses, with very few exceptions, are built on wooden stilts or pillars, and are therefore raised from the ground. Access to the house (*baan*) is by a ladder. The space under the floor on the ground is used for keeping animals and storing household goods.

Fig. 3*b* sets out the floor plan of an orthodox village house. The major features of the layout that concern us are: the ladder (*kan dai*) leading up to the *saan*, which is an unenclosed and roofless entrance platform; this platform I describe as a first 'threshold'. From the entrance platform one enters the *huean naui* (little house) or *bawn rab khaeg* (place for receiving guests).

This guest room is roofed and has walls, except on the side which gives on to the open entrance platform. The limits of the guest room are fixed by two pillars *saaw haeg* and *saaw khwan* (*haeg* means 'first' and *khwan* refers to the 'spiritual essence' of a human being). From the guest room one enters the *huean yaai* or *baun naun* (place for sleeping). This sleeping room, too, has two important named pillars: *saaw khwan* and *saaw haeg* (their arrangement being the reverse of the pillars in the guest room, so that both *saaw haeg* will be at the extremities). The area between the two *saaw khwan* is the second 'threshold' in the house, marking the sleeping quarters from the guest room. The sleeping room is internally divided into *haung phoeng* (room of parents) and *haung suam* (room for son-in-law and married daughter), but this room has no actual partition, only an invisible one. This invisible partition is the third 'threshold'.

To the left of the guest room is the kitchen (*khrua*) and adjoining it the washing place (*haung naam*), which is an open platform on which are pots of water used for bathing and for cooking. It is a place for cleansing, and is used by members of the household only.

The stage and its setting

All the floors of the named divisions are on different levels. The washing place (*haung naam*) is the lowest in level (level o). The entrance platform (*saan*) is at the next level (level 1); the kitchen is on the same level. The guest room (*huean naui*) is higher (level 2), and the sleeping room (*huean yaai*) is the highest level (level 3). These levels o–3 are not accidental but are symbolic of the various values assigned to the divisions of the house.

The directions and cardinal points I have indicated in the diagram have symbolic values. Ideally, a person entering the house would face north and the entrance platform is at the southern end and the sleeping room at the northern end. The directions can be reversed. Never must the sleeping room be placed in the west. The kitchen and the washing place are also always on the western half of the house. The four directions have these values: east is auspicious, represents life, is sacred (the Buddha shelf of the house is always placed in the easterly direction), and is the direction of the rising sun. East is also, when one faces north, the direction of the right hand and represents male sex. West is inauspicious, represents death, impurity, and the setting sun. It also represents the left hand and the female sex. North is auspicious and is associated with the elephant, an auspicious animal because of its size, natural strength and its associations with royalty and Buddhist mythology. South is of neutral value.

Social values are attached to the divisions of the house. Our ultimate interest in this phenomenon is that rituals held in the home such as mortuary rites, *sukhwan*, exorcism, depend for part of their meaning and effectiveness on the exploitation and manipulation of the social meanings attached to house categories.

The compound fence (*wua*) marks the boundary of private property. Outsiders are not expected to enter the compound without invitation.

Saan (the entrance platform), reached by climbing the ladder, is a threshold. It gives entry into the house proper, and is a place for washing one's feet before entering the house. Pots of water are placed on the floor (the boards of which are loosely spaced to permit water to flow through), and persons coming from the outside are normally expected to cleanse their feet. Only persons who are invited or are socially admissible can mount the ladder and step on the *saan*. '*Khon ouen*' or 'other people' are those who are normally excluded from entering the house, unless invited.

The kitchen (*khrua*) is not a particularly private or sacred place. Cooking, however, is normally a female task. Hence it is predictably placed in the west and to the left.

The wash place (*haung naam*) adjoining the kitchen is a platform with water jars. It is used for washing and bathing by family members only;

it is considered unclean, but the dirt is 'private' and pertains to the family.

The *huean naui* is the place for receiving and entertaining guests (*baun rabkhaeg*). Typically these guests are second and more distant cousins, neighbours and friends from the same village, and other nearby villagers. People in these categories (*phii-naung/yaad haang*) are eminently marriageable and are permissible sex partners. They are forbidden to enter the sleeping quarters (*huean yaai*), unless they enter into a marriage relationship with a member of the household. They are divided from the sleeping quarters by a threshold space represented by the two *khwan* pillars which stand between the rooms.

The sleeping room or 'large house' (*huean yaai*), the most sacred place in the house, is divided into two by an invisible partition. The *haung phoeng* (the parents' room) is always the eastern half, the *haung suam* (the room for son-in-law and married daughter) the western half. Thus the relation, parents/*versus* son-in-law and married daughter in the house, is expressed by values associated with east and west.

When the house is located in the ideal direction (*huean yaai* at the northern end), *haung phoeng* is, for a person facing it, on the right and *haung suam* on the left. We have seen that right in village formulation is auspicious and also associated with male; left is inauspicious and associated with female. (Thus in any assembly of both sexes, men ideally sit on the right and women on the left.) There are always two doors leading into the *huean yaai*—one into the *haung phoeng* and the other into the *haung suam*.

To describe now the significance of the *haung yaai* as a totality in relation to the other house categories: apart from the members of the household (normally parents, children and son-in-law) for whom the *haung yaai* represents sleeping quarters, *only* siblings of parents (*phii kab naung*) and first cousins (*luug phuu phii phuu naung*) are allowed to *enter* the *haung yaai*, though not to sleep in it. These two kin categories, we have seen, are considered so close that sex and marriage with them are forbidden.

These restrictions which apply in everyday life are not operative on ceremonial occasions such as death, marriage, ordination and a merit-making ceremony in the house when monks are invited. On such occasions the ritual proceedings take place inside the sleeping room (*haung yaai*) and all guests can enter. Ritual occasions temporarily obliterate the restrictions of everyday life; marriage, for example, recreates and adds to the social structure of the house; death disturbs and diminishes it. These same rituals, however, in some of their sequences exploit the house categories to convey meaning, as we shall see in subsequent chapters. By way of example, let me cite here a sequence in the marriage ceremony which refers back to the house categories.

The most conspicuous social feature of the division in the sleeping quarters (*haung yaai*) between the parents' 'room' and the son-in-law's 'room' is that a son-in-law must not enter the sleeping quarters through the doorway of the parents-in-law; furthermore, once inside the room he must never cross over into their 'room'. This taboo does not bear on children of either sex, including the married daughter. There is only one occasion on which the son-in-law ever enters through the doorway of his wife's parents. At his wedding ceremony, he is ceremonially led through that door by the ritual elders (*thaaw*) for the ritual of *sukhwan* (binding the soul essence to the body). This symbolizes that he is accepted into the house by the bride's parents and that he is legitimately allowed into the sleeping quarters as a son-in-law. There is no reciprocal taboo on parents-in-law crossing over into the *haung suam*. The taboo on the son-in-law represents an asymmetrical 'avoidance' with all its sex and incest connotations.

To sum up: in this account of social structure I want to emphasize these features of the village as a community; it is a distinct ecological entity, it manifests a high degree of endogamy, and the structure of its kinship is bilateral. For most people the number of kinsmen in the community, both cognatic and affinal, is large, and the village scheme of social categorization emphasizes the asymmetrical relationships between the superordinate senior and subordinate junior generations into which the total community is divided, rather than differentiated and strongly defined dyadic relationships within demarcated kin groups. Marriage should, in theory, be outside the second-cousin range. The marriage of first cousins is prohibited. Kinship terminology is consistent with the bilateral kinship system. Authority exercised by, and respect owed to, elders is buttressed by their position in the household and compound complexes, and by the fact that property transmission is gradual. The spatial layout of the village house is an instructive map of social relations which is incorporated into and expressed in rituals.

Finally, a few comments on the economy of the village: we have noted that rice cultivation is the basic activity. A remarkable feature is that there is no marked economic differentiation in the village, a feature which comes into focus in a comparative context when distributions for Phraan Muan are compared with those reported for villages in the Central Plain (e.g. Sharp 1953). There are differences between households in land ownership, but they are not steep.

Tabulations of rice land ownership, based on tax records (1962) for nearly the whole village (129 households were listed), gave these figures: 16 (12·4%) were reported as landless, and only 14 (10·8%) as owning more than 40 *rai*; the mean ownership was 16·5 *rai* and the median 13·5 *rai*. The mean size of a rice farm holding (i.e. figure arrived at after excluding the landless) was 18·82 *rai* and the median 15·5 *rai*. (Note that other categories of land are excluded in this calculation.)

Now it is well known that land ownership data are notoriously difficult to interpret accurately. Our previous discussion of inheritance customs and the nature of the domestic and compound cycles in the village should warn us against too readily accepting the 'landlessness' of young couples (who are prospective heirs or are informal tenants of their parents/parents-in-law) at face value, and also against giving too much weight to the supposedly large holdings of elderly parents (who in fact have informally divided up their land among their heirs). If there are such inaccuracies in the gross figures cited above, their correction would merely add more weight to my assertion that Baan Phraan Muan shows little economic stratification. There is very little renting in or renting out of land, and landlord–tenant categories are not important in village economy. There are differences in house types but here again standards of living are markedly egalitarian, though without doubt at a low all-round level. The hierarchy in the village is primarily of a generational nature rather than a creature of economic maldistribution.

Although rice is the staple crop, most of what is produced is consumed locally. Small amounts are sold, but villagers depend primarily on the manufacture of palm sugar in the dry months for selling in the market for cash. The sale of pigs, poultry, locally woven cloth and mats, and locally caught fish brings in additional money. Young men of the village readily work on road construction for wages during the dry months, and this is an important source of money income. These men usually return to the village; the drain of young men to urban centres which is a marked feature in the North-east is as yet of small importance in this village.

It would seem that the village is more involved in trade relationships now than it was in the past. Salt was produced in the village by boiling saline soil; it still is, but not enough to satisfy needs. Cloth is widely woven by women, but today manufactured cloth is preferred. The trade contacts are mainly in the direction of Nongkai and over the border into Laos, not with the town of Udorn. The largest items traded are palm sugar, pigs and rice.

It is not only trade relationships that take villagers outside. A certain proportion of marriages are with men and women in other villages and this produces some mobility, especially among the men. Annual temple fairs attract residents of nearby villages. The younger men nowadays travel during their dry-season work.

Although, by and large, the social life of the village is inward looking, and the village is a sharply perceived social universe, what was expressed in the myth reported at the beginning of this chapter should not be forgotten: that Baan Phraan Muan is in the pathway of various networks—trade, marriage, religious participation, cultural transmission—of varying extension from region to national polity.

It is also a part of the wider stream of history.

THE CARAVANS OF HISTORY

The village of Phraan Muan is in North-east Thailand and is situated a few miles from the western bank of the Mekong River. The geographical location of the north-eastern region is such that from the beginnings of Siamese and Laotian history it constituted an outlying 'frontier' province which was frequently forced to change its political affiliation. It passed into and out of the control of waxing and waning kingdoms whose capitals were Wiangchan and Luang Phrabang; Chiengmai, Ayudhya and Bangkok; Angkor and Pnom Penh. In terms of modern political entities, we can say that the North-east was a frontier region to which there were multiple claimants, namely Cambodia, Laos, Thailand, and sometimes even Burma.

Precisely because of its frontier location, the north-eastern region appears to have had a colourful and chequered political and religious experience. I can only roughly paint here the outlines of the caravans of history that have passed through its territories. This sketch should be regarded as a backdrop to the contemporary scene which is our real focus of interest. But it is a peculiar kind of backdrop: it both does and does not give context to the present in the same way the medieval English village can be said to provide background for the observation of contemporary village life in East Anglia. In any case, the historical sketch that follows will make plausible the backward glances into the past that will be made at various points in this book.

It is probable that the Thai have been in mainland South-east Asia for a long time; they made their first appearance on stage in political garb, however, only in the thirteenth century when suddenly Thai principalities and kingdoms mushroomed. Rather than talk of the invasion of the Menam basin by the Thai, it is perhaps more correct to view their political emergence less as the result of sudden mass influx than as the consequence of progressive migration over time and the gradual engulfing of the Mon–Khmer and Tibeto–Burman speaking sedentary valley populations.

The fact that the emergence of the Thai as political collectivities took place in the thirteenth century is important. In this century revolutionary changes shook the politics of mainland South-east Asia and sounded the death knell of the older Indianized Mon and Khmer polities. At this time was felt the thrust of the Mongols southwards, especially under and after Kublai Khan who ascended the Chinese throne in 1260; the Thai may have felt added pressures to move southwards themselves by virtue of this thrust. Whatever the strength of this push, the Thai in fact took control of such small principalities as Lamphun, Sukhothai, Lavo (Lophburi), Swanalok, which were then under Mon or Cambodian control.

Before this political dominance of the Thai manifested itself, the territory which is presently called Thailand was, up to the thirteenth century, in the divided possession of the Mons who controlled the upper Menam and the Khmers who dominated the lower Menam and the upper Mekong (in which region our north-eastern village is located).

The Mon dynasty which controlled the upper Menam was based at Haripunjaya (Lamphun); it was a champion in the twelfth century of Buddhism (of the Theravada kind). The history of the Mons in Thailand, of course, stretches farther back; the Mons of southern Burma adopted Buddhism at an early date, expanded into the central valley of the Menam, and set up the famous kingdom of Dvaravati (third to seventh centuries); they left numerous Buddhist monuments and images; and upon the historic ruins and location of the Mon capital was to grow up much later the Thai city of Ayudhya.

The religious components of the Khmer civilization, one of the greatest of further India and which controlled lower Menam and upper Mekong, were somewhat different from those of the Mon. Khmer culture had been heavily influenced by Sanskritic brahmanical forms, especially Saivism and, to a lesser extent, Vaishnavism. Apart from this, Khmer civilization had by the eighth century also been affected by Mahayana Buddhism through the Srivijaya and Sailendra dynasties of Sumatra.

Whatever the particular differences between the Mon and Khmer civilizations, they had a much more general characteristic in common which Coedès has aptly conveyed in the appellation 'Indianized Kingdoms of Southeast Asia'. Historians of further India assert that the great kingdoms of South-east Asia, both on the mainland and in the Indonesian Islands, were the product in earlier times of Indian cultural 'colonization', which did not mean military occupation or political domination by the parent Indian states. 'Indianization', says Coedès (1968), 'must be understood essentially as the expansion of an organized culture that was founded upon the Indian conception of royalty, was characterized by Hinduist or Buddhist cults, the mythology of the Puranas, and the observance of the Dharmasastras, and expressed itself in the Sanskrit language' (pp. 15–16).

Although these indigenous Indianized Mon and Khmer civilizations lost their political control over Thailand, they left behind them cultural imprints which became the legacy and heritage of their successors.

Let us therefore return to the Thai on the eve of their political appearance. They had for a long time been established in Yunnan which lay within the orbit of Chinese civilization; according to Eliot (1954, Vol. II, p. 81), it is likely therefore that they were aware of Chinese Buddhism. Placed on the route from India to China, the Yunnan Thai must also have had contact with Indian culture and Buddhism stemming from Indian centres. But perhaps more importantly, the Thai of upper Menam obviously were influenced by the Hinayana Buddhism of their Mon masters. Nor must we overlook the influences radiating from Burma: King Anawrata of Burma captured Thaton in A.D. 1057, and from there he carried to his capital at Pagan a number of monks of the southern school together with the Pali Canon (Wells 1960, p. iv). He became an ardent Hinayanist and spread the faith in the wake of his military excursions. 'After the reign of Anawrata Pali Buddhism was accepted in Burma and in what we now call the Shan States as the religion of civilized mankind and this conviction found its way to the not very distant kingdom of Sukhothai' (Eliot 1954, p. 82).

In Siam the first Thai breakthrough was in the form of the displacement of the Mons of upper Menam by the Thai chief of Chiengrai, who founded the kingdom of Lan Na with its capital at Chiengmai (A.D. 1296). But more importantly, the kingdom of Sukhothai arose vigorously farther south, having displaced the Khmers, with all the vitality of a new bloom. The most famous of Sukhothai's kings was King Ramkamhaeng, who claimed in an inscription that the borders of his domain were Luang Phrabang in the north-east, Sri Dharmaraja (Ligor) in the south, and Hamsavati (Pegu) in the west.

From our point of view what is of prime importance is that Sukhothai enthusiastically espoused and was transformed by Sinhalese Pali Buddhism (with which, as we have seen, it had already made contact *via* the Mons and Burmese).[1] Sinhalese Buddhism had undergone a phase of revival and efflorescence in the twelfth century under Parakrama Bahu I; from Ceylon it had penetrated into the Mon polities of Burma and from there it radiated all over the Indo–Chinese peninsula. It is possible that Ligor

---

[1] Wood (1924, p. 7) is of the view that the Thai people as a whole espoused Hinayana Buddhism after their migration into Thailand.

in Southern Thailand was another centre of Pali Buddhism, which was brought to its shores from Eastern India and Ceylon.

The famous Sukhothai inscription of Ramkamhaeng states that the court and the inhabitants were devout Buddhists and that they observed the season of *Vassa* (rain retreat) and celebrated the festival of *Kathina* with processions, concerts and readings of the Scriptures. In the city were to be seen statues of the Buddha and scenes carved in relief, as well as large monasteries (Eliot 1954, p. 81).

The significance of this religious espousal of Pali Buddhism—especially in the form that was propagated from Ceylon—cannot be exaggerated either for Thailand or for that matter for South-east Asia. Coedès (1968, p. 253) evaluates the event thus:

In the twelfth and thirteenth centuries the common people received a new contribution from India in the form of Sinhalese Buddhism. The penetration of this new faith to the masses cannot be doubted: in Cambodia, Siam, Laos, and Burma, Buddhist cosmogony and the doctrines of retribution for one's acts and of transmigration have been deeply ingrained in the humblest classes by the teachings of the Buddhist monks.

In accepting this formulation one should not confound the popularization of Pali Buddhism with the spread of the 'pure' religion of the Pali Canon, for even in Polonnaruwa, the seat of Sinhalese Buddhism, Mahayanist and Hindu influences were present (Rahula 1956), and in Thailand the cross-currents of the Mon–Khmer civilization were too rich and varied to permit a puritanical narrowing of cultural traditions.

The kingdom of Sukhothai was superseded by the kingdom of Ayudhya, which was founded farther south in A.D. 1350. The waning of Sukhothai also coincided with the rise of Thai–Laotian polities in the north-east, which event has a direct implication for our area of ethnographic interest.

It is not at all clear from the available evidence whether or not the Sukhothai kingdom actually controlled the eastern provinces of present-day Thailand; King Ramkamhaeng's claim lacks independent confirmation from Vietnamese or Cambodian sources. It is certain that up to the twelfth century, at least, Khmer domination extended up the Mekong to Wiangchan, and that even with the possible loss of Wiangchan to Sukhothai the Khmers remained for a long time—at least well into the fourteenth century—masters of the country situated downstream from the great bend of the Mekong River. In the light of this we might say that the region around our village of Phraan Muan was subject to both Khmer and Sukhothai influences concurrently, although we do not know who exactly was its political overlord.

The stage and its setting

The situation suddenly changed radically, for in the fourteenth century there was a political explosion from the locally established Thai. The Thai principalities of Muang Chawa (modern Luang Phrabang) and of Wiangchan joined hands and drove the Cambodians south, thereby claiming the regions populated by the Thai. No doubt the birth of the first Laotian state was facilitated by the fall of Sukhothai. The kingdom of Lan Chang (Wiangchan) was probably founded in 1353 by Fa Ngum four years after the submission of Sukhothai to Ayudhya.

Laotian historical tradition actually begins with the legendary Khun Borom who led the first Lao-Thai into the area; Fa Ngum is an historical successor of the line said to have begun with Borom, and he is thus described as reclaiming his paternity. According to the Laotian chronicle *Nithan Khun Borom*, Fa Ngum was brought up at the Cambodian court, was taught there by a monk of Theravada persuasion, and when he came of age, the King of Cambodia not only gave his daughter in marriage to him, but also provided him with an army to reconquer the kingdom of his fathers. It appears that Fa Ngum captured Luang Phrabang and Wiangchan, and even advanced on Lan Na and the Korat plateau; and that the other Thai principalities, including Ayudhya, were forced to negotiate with him and seek his friendship (Coedès 1968).

Three essential features may be inferred from this account: the Laotian kingdom of Wiangchan was a power in its own right; it was culturally influenced by Khmer civilization; it also, like other Thai polities, espoused the cause of Sinhalese Buddhism. 'The accession of Fa Ngum is important not only because it marks the establishment of a state destined to play a major political role in the central Indo-Chinese peninsula, but also because it resulted in the introduction into the upper Mekong of Khmer culture and of Singhalese Buddhism through the intermediary of Cambodia.' (Coedès 1968, p. 225.)

Contemporaneous with the Laotian kingdom of Lan Chang was the powerful and politically even more important kingdom of Ayudhya on the lower Menam. This kingdom too was raised on twin pillars which carried the weight of the total culture. These were a keen sponsorship of Theravada Buddhism, which represents the carrying on of Sukhothai traditions, and, at the same time, an enthusiastic acceptance of certain Khmer cultural elements and patterns which constituted a reversal of earlier Sukhothai orientations. While in the Sukhothai era the Siamese showed a marked and perhaps deliberately antagonistic contrast to the then dominant Khmer civilization, notably in political organization and art, in the Ayudhya phase they borrowed in an uninhibited manner from Cambodia its political institutions, vocabulary, system of writing and art forms (which the Siamese genius transformed). In the initial stage of political upsurge, the Siamese needed to establish their identity through differentiation; once established, they wanted now to be as great as the Khmers, and succeeded. In this sense Ayudhya became the true heir of Khmer civilization in its elaboration of divine kingship adapted to Buddhist Canons, in its transformation of Khmer and U Thong art styles, and in its literary efflorescence.

Now to return to the Laotian kingdom of Lan Chang ('country of a million elephants'). From the mid-fourteenth century to the mid-sixteenth century it flourished and established its identity. While no doubt heavily influenced by Ayudhya, it threw out another arm to link up with the kingdom of Lan Na (Chiengmai), which in turn had important links with Burma, both as a victim of its aggression and as a receiver of its religious influences. During this period Wiangchan had important diplomatic contacts with Lan Na; Laotian princes married Chiengmai princesses and a Laotian prince once even successfully claimed the throne of Lan Na.

But in the sixteenth and seventeenth centuries the scourge of the various Siamese and Laotian kingdoms was Burma. From around 1550–1650 the Burmese successfully invaded Chiengmai and occupied Lan Na; they then successfully extended their control over Wiangchan and the North-east. By the eighteenth century the Laotians were able to reassert their independent political existence, but at the cost of fragmenting into the two independent kingdoms of Wiangchan and Luang Phrabang. The strong links with Chiengmai, however, continued. It is by virtue of this historical connection with Chiengmai that the Udorn region of North-east Thailand (where our Phraan Muan village is located) manifests a religious and linguistic feature which distinguishes it from Central and Lower Siam: the sacred Buddhist writing of North-east Thailand and Laos is in a script called Tham, which is a Shan script influenced by Mon writing (see Tambiah 1968c). For Central Thailand the corresponding script is the Korm (Khmer) script, which traditionally, since the days of Ayudhya, has been the script in which Buddhist literature was written there.

The next historical landmark in the fortunes of North-east Thailand and Laos was the late eighteenth century. The Burmese at the height of their power had invaded and laid waste in 1767 the city of Ayudhya. The Thai soon afterwards, in an upsurge of new-found vigour and solidarity under Phaya Tak Sin, recovered Ayudhya and pushed the Burmese back. The Burmese had also occupied Luang Prabang in 1752 and imposed their protection on it. The success of the Thai against the Burmese also meant the extension of their umbrella of influence over the Laotians. The Thai in fact took Wiangchan in 1778, and held it until

1782 when the first king of the present Chakri dynasty handed it back. The Thai, now based in Bangkok, also exerted influence over Luang Phrabang, which was reduced to the status of a dependency.

Thus it could be said that from the last quarter of the eighteenth century until the end of the nineteenth, both North-east Thailand and the Laotian kingdoms came under the cultural and political influence of the Central Thai of Siam. But already the European colonial powers were opening their voracious jaws at the borders of Siam. In 1893 the Franco–Siamese Treaty was signed by which Siam agreed to withdraw from the left bank of the Mekong and to recognize Laos as a French protectorate. North-east Thailand, the site of Phraan Muan village, finally passed into the undisputed political control of Thailand.

I have presented in brief outline some of the grand events that were staged on location in North-east Thailand, as well as others which, by virtue of their happening in its vicinity, must have affected it. North-east Thailand, the home of 'Laotian' Thai, was originally a part of and influenced by Khmer civilization; it was affected by Burmese politics; it was later a part of the Wiangchan kingdom, which was a counterpart and equal of the Thai polities of Chiengmai and Ayudhya. It is difficult to say who at any particular period owned the region in which today lies the village of Phraan Muan; it is less difficult to guess what were the cultural and religious elements deposited in it by the parade of historical events.

It is not my intention at all to explain the religious institutions of the villagers, as I observed and studied them in 1961–2, in terms of the deposits and debris of history. I am not interested to trace the path along which a particular item travelled from one date to another date. The outline has been given to sensitize the reader to the historical backdrop, and to make him appreciate that when, in elucidating a feature or a pattern in the village, a comparative reference is made to India, Burma, Ceylon, Cambodia or Laos (or rather, to some place or event in these countries fixed in time and place) it is not at all arbitrary but can be illuminating. For while the features that compose the culture of the village of Phraan Muan were in a sense 'arbitrarily' deposited by history, a major task of the anthropologist is to see the logic and structure behind the manner in which these elements combine today to form a coherent whole. In elucidating this, the coherent structural patterns of a previous historical era or a contemporary neighbouring society can be appropriately invoked to appear before us to aid our understanding in terms of similarity or contrast. It is in this sense that I shall invoke the past whenever so warranted.

3

COSMOLOGY

Rather than begin the exposition of Buddhism by discussing 'doctrine' I shall begin with 'cosmology'. But what is the difference between doctrine and cosmology, and how are they connected? And why do I choose the unorthodox path?

Bishop Copleston, who in some respects was a more sympathetic commentator on Buddhism than most of his Christian contemporaries, gave an unexpected answer to a question he posed: to what extent does the content of the Pali Canon serve for a description of Buddhism in Ceylon today (i.e. 1890s)? He first divided the contents of the classical literature into two groups: that which dealt with 'the moral system [and] the human life on which it rests', and that which was composed of 'the legendary histories and the theories of cosmogony and geography'. He then gave this answer: 'The whole being divided into these two groups, we may assert that the first, the moral, is held now with little alteration; but that the second, the mass of legends and cosmogony, has been so greatly developed and raised to so much greater prominence, as to make the later Buddhism differ widely from the Pitakas' (1892).

Curiously, the first half of the answer, though unorthodox, is probably true; and the second half, which is conventional, is unduly exaggerated. Where the Bishop was right in a novel way—against those who saw a vulgarization of doctrine over time, and in repudiation of the arrogant claim of some nineteenth-century European scholars that the Sinhalese 'have been content to relearn their own religion' from them—was that the major concepts and assertions of the Buddhist doctrine cannot drastically change. Where the Bishop exaggerated in a conventional manner was to think that a vast gap separates the wild jungle of cosmology and mythology from the ploughed fields of doctrine: such a view is possible only if it is thought that doctrine and cosmology have no affinity or similarity of message contents whatsoever.

There are many versions or Canons of the Buddhist Scriptures—such as the Sanskrit Canons, Chinese and Tibetan Canons, etc.—but I am concerned here primarily with the Pali Canon, or more accurately with that particular recension of the Scriptures of the ancient sect of Vibhajjavadins that was set down in writing at the Mahavihara monastery in Anuradhapura

32

in Ceylon around 20 B.C., and was accepted as the true scripture in Burma, Siam and Cambodia.

The Pali Canon, known as *Tripitaka* (three baskets), consists of *Vinaya Pitaka* (which includes the core *Patimokkha* rules of discipline); Sutta Pitaka (the sermons and discourses of the Buddha); and Abhidhamma, which is later than the Sutta and consists mostly of a complex arrangement and commentary on the discourses.[1]

It is clear that the components of the Pali Canon were not composed simultaneously. Lines of growth are visible in the *Vinaya* and the Sutta. According to Sinhalese tradition, however, the Canon was fixed at the Third Council held in the reign of Asoka (*c.* 272–232 B.C.). The author of *The Questions of Milinda*, which book was composed by the beginning of the Christian era, knew the Canonical books by the names they bear now. Thus apparently nothing discredits the conclusion that the Pali Canon was substantially fixed in Asoka's time, so far as the *Vinaya* and the Sutta discourses are concerned. Thus it can be said that, despite the accretion of commentaries which, in any case, must refer to the original 'text', doctrine as such has been transmitted in the southern school relatively unchanged.

In contrast it is said that Buddhist mythology and cosmology have grown lush and unrestrained like a wild creeper. It is, however, interesting to note that the seeds of the full-blown beliefs, myths and cosmologies of a later period are found in the Pali Canon. The *Vinaya* and Sutta Pitaka have many references to supernatural beings and occurrences. The Khuddaka Nikaya of the Sutta collection contains the *Jataka* stories in verse form which are the kernel for the later prose elaborations. Similarly the skeleton of the pantheon and the framework of the cosmology are clearly perceived in the *Vinaya* and Sutta[2] (e.g. Atanatiya Suttanta (Rhys Davids, Part III, 1957, Ch. 32)).

With the passage of time, the elaborations in the realms of cosmology and mythical history have been fantastically ornate. The life story of the Buddha has been enlarged and embellished with many incidents unknown to the Pitaka: 'The details of the Buddha's birth and of his renunciation,

---

[1] The *Vinaya Pitaka* includes, in addition to the *Patimokkha*, the *Mahavagga* and *Cullavagga* (which deal with the rules of admission to the order, give the occasion and circumstances when the Buddha made the rules, and give biographical details of the Buddha). The Sutta Pitaka is divided into four prose collections called the *Nikaya* (Digha, Samyutta, Majjhima and Anguttara) and a fifth section mostly in verse form (Khuddaka Nikaya); this last includes the Dhammapada, the Thera and Theri-gatha (devotional songs) and the *Jataka* stories in verse form. See Eliot (1954) for information on the contents of the Canon.

[2] In a subsequent chapter we shall see that the *paritta* (verses chanted for protection) also have their final authority or source in the Canonical literature.

of his visit to his mother in heaven, and of his visits to Ceylon, came actually to take precedence, in interest and in the poetical wealth laid out upon them, over the more authentic incidents in the *Vinaya* (Copleston 1892, p. 422). The theory of a succession of previous Buddhas, which had its nucleus in the Canon, was developed in time into elaborate accounts of their lives. Perhaps the most important elaboration in respect of congregational interest and usefulness for *bana* instruction are the 550 birth stories of the Buddha, the *Jataka* collection. Finally there has been the 'boundless field' of cosmogony/cosmology which, with its cycles of ages, multitude of universes, concentric circles of oceans and cataclysmic cosmic changes (both big bangs and steady states), has appeared at first sight to be mere fantasy run wild and away from religion.

But is Buddhist cosmology (and its related mythology) really simply 'the systematizing of the imaginary' which is the 'besetting intellectual sin of India' and the Orient? Is it quite unrelated to the doctrinal and ethical ideas of Buddhism as most commentators appear to think?

The *Encyclopaedia Britannica* describes cosmology in the broadest sense of the word as 'that branch of learning which treats of the universe as an ordered system'. The name is derived from the Greek *kosmos* ('order', 'harmony', 'the world') plus *logos* ('word', 'discourse'). 'Cosmology is that framework of concepts and relations which man erects...for the purpose of bringing descriptive order into the world as a whole, including himself as one of its elements.' It describes the world in terms of space, time, matter, motion and causality. (The related questions of inner nature and purpose are usually relegated to the branches of cosmogony, ontology, eschatology, etc., but I shall include them here under the cosmological rubric.)

I would like to suggest that, contrary to the normal practice of ignoring Buddhist cosmology or relegating it to footnotes, it be seen as providing a nice entry into the universe of religion. It has many facets: it first of all gives a picture of the universe in terms of space, time and matter; secondly, it translates this physical universe into a *pantheon* of deities, humans, animals and demons to which can be attributed ethical and moral qualities; finally, the cosmology gives a dynamic picture of the nature, workings and purpose of the universe in terms of the motion of the personifications in the pantheon, this motion up and down (and bursting out of the universe altogether) being conceived in terms of ethical and spiritual force and energy. Thus it might be said that the cosmological scheme says figuratively and in terms of metaphorical images the same kind of thing which is stated in abstract terms in the doctrine. The basic doctrinal concepts of Buddhism such as *karma* (ethical causation), *samsara* (cycle of rebirths), *nirvana* (final extinction), *dukka* (suffering), etc., which are alleged to explain man's predicament and to direct his religious action, are also embedded in the cosmology (and its associated pantheon).

But what is the advantage of the aid of cosmology in studying religion? In this monograph I approach religion through ritual and I would like to suggest that there is a close connection between cosmology and ritual. Cosmological and supernatural categories are embedded in the rituals I shall describe; they chart the geography and define the architecture of sacred space and are expressed in the material symbols that are manipulated in the rituals. In the rituals we see cosmology in action.

If one may allow oneself the luxury of some aphorisms, it may be said that ritual is for the practical man what philosophy is for the thinker. If the saint and the ascetic act upon themselves—their minds and bodies, and inner states—the layman acts upon the world with the external things of the world. For the layman ritual acts are outward symbols of interior state; the ascetic on the other hand performs disciplinary acts directed inwards upon himself so that he can gain mastery over the outer world.

For all the reasons set out I shall not tread the conventional path by starting with the definition of basic ethical and doctrinal concepts of Buddhism, but rather describe first its cosmology and the implications thereof.

The cosmology that I present is an abbreviated version of ideas that are prevalent in Thailand, Burma and Ceylon and are reported by several writers (e.g. see De la Loubère 1693, Alabaster 1871, Hardy 1880, Yoe 1896, Monier-Williams 1890). No villager in Baan Phraan Muan is able to present the details of the total picture in the way I do. But fragments of and allusions to the traditional cosmology appear in many myths and rituals, and the ritual experts in the village can in such contexts expound relevant portions of the lore to the inquirer. Parts of the cosmological scheme will come to life in some of the rituals and myths documented in later chapters.

Thailand itself is the home of a cosmological treatise written in 1345 by the heir apparent to the throne of Sukhodaya (who later became King Lut'ai). This work entitled *Trai bhumikatha* ('The History of the Three Worlds'), while written in Siamese, was entirely based on Pali works (Coedès 1957). It brought together, however, various fragments and passages in a single work which appears to have been the first systematic treatise on Buddhist cosmology. It not only contained the traditional cosmology but also used it as a vehicle for moral dissertations and to present a picture of monarchy conforming to Buddhist ideals.

Again, in 1776, Phya Tak, who recovered Thailand from the Burmese, compiled a standard Siamese work on Buddhist cosmology. It was called

Traiphoom, ran to sixty volumes, and was no doubt based on classical sources (Thompson 1941, p. 624).

Although the Buddhist cosmology in its broad outlines shows much similarity to the Hindu version, it expresses variations and systematization in terms of Buddhism's own religious world view. Hence it should be treated in its own right.

According to Buddhist cosmology, there are innumerable world systems or galaxies. Each system has its own sun and moon, and its earth containing continents and oceans, with a mountain in the centre called Mt Meru. Upwards from the mountain extend the heavens, downwards the hells. These world systems are periodically destroyed and re-formed in cycles of vast stretches of time (*kalpa*)—in modern astro-physics this characterization would be called the theory of the pulsating universe.

The world system consists of thirty-one planes of existence divided into three major categories: *kama loka* (in which there is form and sensual desire (pleasure and pain)); *rupa loka* (in which there is form but no sensual enjoyment, only a kind of intellectual enjoyment); and the *arupa loka* (in which there is no perceptible bodily form and no sensation). The order in which they are presented here is hierarchical from the lowest to the highest. We may note that the scheme is based on a progression from corporeality to incorporeality, from body to intellect.

These three major planes of existence subdivide into the thirty-one more specific planes in a complex manner. And in order to describe the ordering we must start from the centre of the world system.

Mt Meru stands in the centre of the earth, and it is the pillar of the world. Between Meru and the great rocky circumference which is the wall of the earth are alternating concentric circles of seven mountain ranges and seven oceans. A last (eighth) great ocean adjoining the rim contains four continents at the cardinal points; the southern continent is Jambudvipa (which is ours). It is the most sacred in the time cycle in which Gotama Buddha was born.

'KAMA LOKA'

The *kama loka* plane of existence expresses the cosmology that is directly relevant for our study. This plane of bodily form and sensual feelings is divided into eleven *loka*: six are heavens inhabited by gods (*deva loka*); five are worlds, four of which are inhabited by human beings, animals, ghosts, and demons. The fifth world consists of eight major (and other subsidiary) hells, situated in the interior of the earth, in which intense torment and pain are experienced.

Cosmology

The six heavens ('deva loka')

The first heaven is below the summit of Mt Meru and is the residence of the four guardians of the world (*lokapala*). The second heaven (*Tavatinsa/Tawutisa*) is on the summit of Mt Meru, over which presides god Sakka or Indra. These two heavens must, in fact, be taken together because Indra presides over the four guardians, and together they impinge on the world of men and animals. In myth and ritual Indra always appears as the presiding deity.

Around and just below Indra's abode at the summit of Mt Meru are the four mansions of the world guardians.[1] The palace to the east is that of Dhrita-rashtra (Dhratarashtra), King of the *Gandharvas* (choristers and musicians) who guard the eastern domain of the world and minister to the pleasure of all gods. They wear white garments and are mounted on white horses and wield swords and shields of crystal. On the south is the palace of Virudhaka (Virudha) whose attendants are the *Kumbandas*, monsters of immense size and ugly form. They wear blue garments, are mounted on blue horses, and their swords and shields are made of sapphire. They guard the southern division of the world. The palace of Virupaksha stands in the west and he is the King of the *Nagas*. Their colour is red; they wear red garments, ride red horses, carry weapons of coral and flaming torches. They are the guardians of the western portion of the world. The northern division belongs to Kuvera or Vaisravana (Vessavano), who rules over the *Yakshas*; they are adorned in golden garments, ride horses that shine like gold, etc. The *Yakshas* in the classical descriptions are not as malevolent as they have come to be in modern Ceylon. (See Hardy 1880, pp. 45–7). The Thai represent them in their temples as enormous and horrible, though recognizably human in form.

In Buddhist mythology the *Yakshas* and *Nagas* appear frequently. In Ceylon the *Yakshas*, ruled over by Kuvera the god of wealth, have been elaborated on and transformed into the much-feared malevolent demons. In Thailand, on the other hand, it is the *Nagas* who have a special place.

The *Nagas* will figure importantly in this study of Thai religion. A brief introductory note on them is therefore appropriate. They are thought to reside under the rocks that support Mt Meru and under the waters of the earth. Their bodies take the shape of serpents. They enjoy the status of 'demi-gods', and in Buddhism are usually represented as favourable to the religion and its adherents. At the same time they are considered

[1] In Thai the four guardians (*thao lokaban*) are called: Thataret, Wirulahok, Wirupak, and Wetsuwan.

37

to be formidable enemies when their wrath is aroused. They are associated with rain and fertility.

Beyond and higher than the second heaven of Indra are four other heavens that fall within the definition of *kama loka*. Of these, only one need be mentioned here, the fourth called *Tusita* in which resides the all-compassionate *bodhisattva* (Buddha-to-be) Maitreya, awaiting the time when he will come down into the world of men as the next Buddha and saviour. The *Tusita* heaven is regarded as the most delightful of the heavens, in which all desires are satisfied. In it grows the *kalpavriksha* tree (in Thai, *Karaphruk* or *Kamaphruk*), which produces fruits of gold, silver, jewels, etc., that gratify all desires. The tree appears frequently in Thai rituals and will greet us with its promises at many places in this book.

The five worlds

The four lower worlds of men, animals, *asuras* (demons), and ghosts (*preta*) stand in contrast to the heavens. While life in the heavens is unadulterated pleasure, the lower worlds are increasingly painful. Human beings and animals as forms of life are self-evident and require no commentary at this stage, but the others do.

The *asuras* are in Buddhist (and Hindu) mythology the arch opponents and enemies of the gods. They are demi-gods themselves and are of the underworld, living under Mt Meru. They have had repeated contests with the gods of Indra's heaven, and the great representation of this contest is the churning of the ocean for the nectar of life which the gods successfully took away from them. This story is represented in both Hindu and Buddhist architecture, notably in Cambodia at Angkor. The *asuras* were finally subdued by Indra, and it is the task of the four guardians to continue to ward off their attacks. Rahu and Ketu are the much-feared *asuras* which swallow the moon and cause eclipses. The *asuras* as the classical opponents of the deities have found other expressions in contemporary South-east Asian countries: *devas* versus *yakka* in Ceylon, versus *nats* in Burma, versus *phii* in Thailand.

While the *asuras* are a permanent category of supernatural being, the *pretas* are of a different status. They are ghosts of dead humans who had recently inhabited the earth. They are condemned to live in a kind of hell or may wander about on earth, haunting the places they formerly lived in. Although in themselves not harmful to man, their appearance and attributes are disgusting. They are of gigantic size, they have dried up limbs, loose skin, enormous bellies. They continually wander about, consumed with hunger and thirst, yet are never able to eat or drink because of their small mouths, constricted throats and the scorching, boiling heat that emanates from their bodies.

Some writers have seen in *pretas* the inversion of the Buddhist monk (Yalman 1964). It is also apposite to point out that the *preta* condition of perpetual hunger and thirst may possibly signify the extreme punishment for withholding food from monks and for being stingy in merit-making. Despite their sinful condition, it is felt that relatives can and should transfer to the *pretas* some of the merit accruing from their merit-making acts (such as donating gifts of food and other items to the monks).

Finally, the eight major hells of the fifth world are fiery places of intense misery and pain. One has only to see the murals on the walls of Buddhist temples in Thailand and Ceylon to understand that hell is no mere abstract concept but is imagined in all its horror and sadism. In heaven handsome men and women embrace and walk around in a garden of wishing trees (*kalpavriksha*) studded with diamonds and other gems; in hell one burns in raging fire and one's sides are pierced with weapons by demons. A Siamese law book (*Book of Indra*) gives the following description of heaven (Alabaster 1871, p. 294):

There is a celestial abode in the Dewa heavens, an aerial dwelling covered with gold and gems, with roofs shining with gold and jewels, and roof points of crystal and pearl; and the whole gleams with wrought and unwrought gold more brilliant than all the gems. Around its eaves plays the soft sound of tinkling golden bells. There dwell a thousand lovely houris, virgins in gorgeous attire, decked with the richest ornaments, singing sweet songs in concert, with a melody whose resounding strains are never still. This celestial abode is adorned with lotus lakes, and meandering rivers full of the five kinds of lotus, whose golden petals, as they fade, fill all the air with sweet odours. And round the lakes are splendid lofty trees growing in regular order, their leaves, their boughs, their branches, covered with sweet-scented blossoms, whose balmy odours fill the surrounding air with heart-delighting fragrance.

THE 'RUPA LOKA' AND 'ARUPA LOKA' ('BRAHMA LOKA')

Whereas the six lower *deva* heavens belong to the domain of form and sensation (*kama loka*), there are twenty other, higher heavens.

The next level upwards is that of the *rupa loka*, consisting of sixteen heavens where there is form but no sensual enjoyment. Beyond them are the four *arupa* heavens with no form at all. These last are of minimal significance in village myth and ritual.

This brief outline of classical Buddhist mythology contains a number of significant ideas that are essential to the understanding of Buddhism as a religion that is not only thought but also lived. One vital conception is that all the orders of being described are fundamentally homogeneous or of one kind. There are six forms of existence—god, demon, man, animal, ghost, soul in hell—whose distinctions are only of temporary duration and through which all human beings (except those who have entered the path leading to salvation) may at one time or other pass. The god may be reborn as demon and an animal as man, etc.; a change of condition is a realistic possibility depending on one's *karma* and ethical status. At any one point of time, the stratification is a statement of a gradient of pure bliss and tranquillity enjoyed by the gods to black torment suffered by those in hell. The gods, especially those in the six lower heavens, exist in subtle corporeal forms. Although they are not omnipotent, they are capable of beneficial acts towards human beings. They, too, are subject to the universal law of dissolution and rebirth. They appear in the cosmology mainly as protectors of the faith, ready to help believers or to testify to the true doctrine. In turn, the other orders of existence can descend or go upwards. The ghosts and demons are not perpetually condemned; they may harm men but they are also subject to the law of rebirth and can change their status for the better.

This is essential for grasping the Buddhist notions of 'this world' and the 'other world', *laukika* and *lokottara*. All the levels and forms of existence so far described belong to 'this world': the heavens, the earth, and the hells; gods, men, beasts, and demons. Canonical Buddhism's conception of 'otherworldliness' is *nirvana*, the salvation of extinction from rebirth and existence. Otherworldliness does not simply mean concerns which transcend the present existence, or rebirth, or existence in the heavens of *devas*, but a liberation from sentient existence. *Lokottara* means 'hypercosmical'. I emphasize the point because some anthropologists have mistakenly assimilated 'rebirth' and the 'next' life to the notion of 'otherworldliness'.

A second fundamental idea embodied in this cosmological scheme is that, in the dynamic hierarchy of sentient existence, it is man in his human condition living on this earth who is the fundamental acting agent. It is said that in order to attain *nirvana* any order of being, even a god, must be born of a woman in a human status in his last life. Central to the Buddhist doctrine is that to be born as a human being is a privilege because it offers the only opportunity for betterment and final liberation through one's decisive effort. It is in a human status that new *karma* and increment to it can be made. A god can merely enjoy the fruits of previous *karma* and must be born a human to ascend higher.

A transformation of this relation is expressed again in respect of a layman (i.e., one who is not a monk) reaching *nirvana*. While normally it is a monk alone who may reach the final state, should a layman be on the threshold of *nirvana* he should either become a monk or immediately pass into the state of death (*parinibbana*). Thus the whole cosmological system focuses on man as the moral agent, and it holds the possibility of a complementary relation between man and god on the one side, and between man and the dark agents on the other. Man can transfer the fruits of his merit to them; in turn, he can be affected for good or evil by them. The way is thus open in ritual action for manipulating the categories and achieving a change of moral state.

While the total cosmological scheme is integrated in this manner, the scheme also contains a tension or inconsistency or opposition of ideas. This tension derives basically from the philosophical and doctrinal formulations and can be simply put thus: if the doctrine of *karma* gives an explanation of present suffering and squarely puts the burden of release on individual effort, then the doctrine that supernatural agents can cause or relieve suffering and that relief can come through propitiating them contradicts the *karma* postulate. Some writers (e.g. Spiro 1967 concerning Burma) see this tension as a basic inconsistency between Buddhism and supernaturalism (or animism). While I recognize that this categorical opposition is present in Thailand, I see it as one which operates within a total field that expresses other relations as well of complementarity and hierarchical ordering between Buddhism and the spirit cults. To emphasize one aspect at the cost of others seems to me to be a partial analysis; to go further and assert that there are, in fact, two contradictory religions in uneasy co-existence appears to me to be a misunderstanding.

While we must await the presentation of the Thai data in later chapters to see that another way of looking at the religious system is possible, I should like to make a point regarding analytical orientation which may have a bearing on the question.

Some analysts may take as their point of reference the postulates of doctrinal Buddhism as the essence and reality of Buddhism, and therefore also the base line for studying popular Buddhism. This orientation dictates its methodology and shapes the final conclusions, for the analyst accordingly seeks to see how 'non-doctrinal' facts are adapted, modified and rationalized in relation to the 'doctrinal' ideas. The question is thus prejudged. Another method is possible and it is more open. While being mindful of the doctrinal and mythological heritage, we can pay attention to the total array of religious ideas and rituals as they present themselves and see the internal relations and distinctions in this total field. The doctrinal approach is especially mischievous if, as in Spiro's study of Burmese supernaturalism, the Buddhism contrasted with the *nat* cults and exorcism rituals (which are analysed in detail) is not that of the ideas and activities of the village Buddhist temple and its monks or the rituals performed by monks (which are conspicuous by their virtual absence in his book), but a set of tenets drawn almost exclusively from doctrine stated in the Canonical texts. Furthermore, it is not at all clear whether the alleged inconsistency of the two religions is a product of the anthropologist's own understanding of what true Buddhism really is, or is an irresolvable incompatibility reflected in the ideas and actions of the actors themselves. The Burmese evidence is unclear; at best it would appear that sophisticated Burmese are at one level aware of a contradiction, but it is startling to read that 'None of the villagers, however, showed any awareness of the basic inconsistency...' (Spiro 1967, p. 46). However, one should not throw out the baby with the bath water. Distinctions, oppositions, complementarities, linkages and hierarchy do exist in the arrangement of ideas, ritual idiom, techniques and roles of the practitioners, and the behaviour of villagers according to context and situation; an exploration of these is a major task of this book. The anthropologist must find a new way of relating the past to the present, classical dogma to present ideas.

THE BUDDHA, 'BODHISATTVA' AND 'ARAHAT'

Those who have broken through the various orders of sentient existence and have reached (or are about to reach) the liberated state are the Buddhas and certain lesser others who have entered the path to *nirvana*.

Three kinds of persons who have attained a supreme religious state appear significantly in ritual and worship. They are the Buddha, who has reached *nirvana*, the *bodhisattva* who is an embryo Buddha or a Buddha-to-be, and the *arahat*, an ascetic who has entered the path and is credited with miraculous powers.

The Buddha

The achievement of Buddha-hood was not unique to the historical Gotama. According to Buddhist tradition there have been several Buddhas in the past, and some twenty-four have appeared in the preceding cycles of time. In the present aeon or *kala*, Gotama was the fourth to appear. He was preceded by Kakusandha, Konagamana and Kassapa.

In the Mahapadana Suttanta (Rhys Davids, Vol. III, Part II, 1910, Ch. 14) Gotama Buddha is said to have related the histories of the last seven Buddhas, starting with Vipassi and taking in the four Buddhas of this aeon including himself. In this account the following features are of

particular interest because they are reflected in one way or another in
the religious life of Thai villagers:

the Buddha manifests the remarkable faculty of remembering past
births, which is attributed to his clear discernment of truth through
personal effort and is also a revelation from the gods;

a Buddha, before he makes his appearance in human form, exists as
a *bodhisattva* in the heaven of delight and at the proper time descends into
his mother's womb mindful and self-possessed;

in the biography of Vipassi—which was later transferred to the Buddha
himself—it is stated that he was born of royal status, endowed with the thirty-
two marks of the Great Man, and that there were two careers open to him:

If he live the life of the House, he becomes Lord of the Wheel, a righteous
Lord of the Right, a ruler of the four quarters, conqueror, guardian of the
people's good, owner of the Seven Treasures...But if such a boy go forth
from the Life of the House into the Homeless state, he becomes an Arahant,
a Buddha Supreme, rolling back the veil from the world (*ibid.* p. 13).

Thus it is stated that a world conqueror and a world renouncer are two
sides of the same coin;

the biographies also state, in terms of a time scale, the progressive
shortening of human life and by implication also its degradation. Thus
while the length of life at the epoch in which Vipassi was born was
8,000 years, in this aeon the length of life diminishes successively from
4,000 years at the time of Kakusandha to 100 at the time of Gotama.

This fateful decline, however, is counteracted by the idea that a Buddha
appears from aeon to aeon under similar circumstances to preach a similar
faith, which hopeful message is represented most importantly for contemporary villagers in the beliefs centring around Maitreya, the next
Buddha to come.

The most important Buddha is, of course, the historical Gotama who
embodies the idea of all Buddhas. And the orientations to this Buddha
in popular Buddhism are complex and paradoxical.

One puzzle is the relation between the Buddha and the gods in the
Buddhist pantheon. The *Pitaka* (Pali Canon) characterize the Buddha
as omniscient and pure but do not suggest that he is a god; however, they
do represent him as instructing the *devas* and receiving their homage.
Two transformations took place in institutionalized Buddhism which
can be expressed in terms of the pantheon.

If a Buddha cannot be called a Deva rather than a man, it is only because
he is higher than both. It is this train of thought that lead [sic] later Buddhists
to call him Devatideva, or the Deva who is above all other Devas... (Eliot
1954, p. 340).

Buddhism and the spirit cults in North-east Thailand

A parallel change took place in respect to the gods. The Canonical doctrine of the *Dhamma* had very little to do with the *devas*, in the sense that the truths of religion did not depend on them although their existence was granted; for example, when the Buddha preached in Magadha the local deities were not considered the personifications of cosmic forces or the revealers of truth. (In the Kevaddha Sutta, for instance, the Buddha belittles Brahma and the gods as being ignorant of the answers to certain basic metaphysical problems; the Digha Nikaya also contains the ironical account of the origin of gods as being a progressive descent from superior worlds, while the gods (especially Brahma) have illusions of being the creators.) The critical change incorporated in the cosmological scheme is the conversion of deities into protectors of the faith, who take their place in the *karmic* scheme. In the *Jatakas*, for instance, Indra (who, in the Hindu Vedas, is a demon slayer) is depicted as the heavenly counterpart of a pious Buddhist king, protector of the religion whose throne grows hot when a good man is in trouble. From being autonomous powers gods had now become mediators.

Another puzzle—which is probably of more direct concern to us—is the dual orientation to the Buddha. On the one hand, the Buddha, a human being, is dead and has reached *nirvana*. This being so he cannot directly affect human beings or influence their future status, because salvation is a personal quest. On the other hand, the Buddha has been credited with supernatural powers—when alive he had extraordinary markings and qualities, and after his death his relics, *mahadhatu* (which significantly include jewels, ornaments and the holy texts) have spiritual power; so do consecrated images. Thus these objects are conceived as 'magical power stations' and have been associated with rain-making ceremonies in Ceylon (Geiger 1960) and Thailand (Wales 1931).

The following facts drawn from the literature on Buddhist traditions might help in the solution of this problem. A passage written by Hardy (1860) vividly describes the worshipper's relation to the Buddha; the description is as valid today as it was for the last century; it could apply equally well to Ceylon, Burma, or Thailand.

The people, on entering the wihara, prostrate themselves before the image of the Buddha, or bend the body, with the palms of the hands touching each other and the thumbs touching the forehead. They then repeat the threefold formulary of protection, called *tun-sarana*, stating that they take refuge in the Buddha, in the Dharma, and in the Sangha, or they take upon themselves a certain number of the ten obligations, the words being first chanted in Pali by a priest, or in his absence by a novice. Some flowers and a little rice are placed upon the altar, and a few coppers are thrown into a large vessel placed to receive them... (p. 209).

44

Cosmology

The problem of the inconsistency of worshipping an extinct being and of soliciting the aid of an external agent in a religion which doctrinally maintains that salvation is the product of a personal quest and striving is a classical one. It was one of the dilemmas dealt with in *The Questions of King Milinda*, written at the beginning of the Christian era.

The question posed by King Milinda to Nagasena was that if the Buddha accepts gifts he cannot have passed entirely away, he must be still in union with the world. On the other hand, if he has escaped from all existence and is unattached to the world, then honours could not be offered to him.

Nagasena's answer, if sophistic, is yet fascinating, for it invokes some incisive analogues. The Blessed One is set entirely free and therefore accepts no gift. Nevertheless, acts done to him, notwithstanding his having passed away and not accepting them, are of value and bear fruit. If gods or men put up a building to contain the jewel treasure of the Buddha's relics, the devotee attains to one or another of the three glorious states by virtue of the supreme good which resides in the jewel treasure of the Buddha's wisdom.

A great and glorious fire that has died out would not accept any supply of dried grass or sticks; but men by their own effort can produce fire. A great and mighty wind, were it to die away, cannot be produced again; but men, oppressed by heat or tormented by fever, can produce wind by means of fans and punkahs. The broad earth does not acquiesce in all kinds of seeds being planted all over it; yet it acts as a site for these seeds and as a means of their development.

The message conveyed by this argument is that the Buddha's attainment is symbolized by the relics, that when men pay homage and give gifts to the Buddha, goodness is caused to arise within them, that in fact the symbols of the Buddha act as a field of merit and men by their own ethical efforts can plough, plant and produce fruits in it.

What is lacking in Nagasena's argument is any statement of the spiritual power emanating *per se* from the sacred objects which commemorate the Buddha. According to popular tradition, the Buddha told his disciple Ananda that the objects that may be properly worshipped are relics of his body, things erected in commemoration of him (e.g. images), and articles he possessed, such as the alms bowl, girdle, bathing robe, etc. The sacred bo tree under which he attained understanding has come to be an object of reverence. So have the sacred books which contain the doctrines that the Buddha taught.

All these objects are called *cetiya* on account of the satisfaction they produce in the mind.

Buddhism and the spirit cults in North-east Thailand

The religious monument that has attracted special comment by writers (e.g. Leach 1958, 1962; Yalman 1964) is the *dagoba* (*dhatu garba* = relic womb), which brings together and transcends the polarities of death and life, impurity and purity, dissolution and fertile creation.

Similarly, it could be argued that certain religious objects and persons bring together and synthesize the notions of spiritual and political sovereignty. These notions are eminently symbolized in the person of the king as *chakravartin* (universal ruler) and as *bodhisattva* (Buddha-to-be). The relation of the sacred tooth relic in Ceylon and the Emerald Buddha image in Thailand to the institution of kingship (and statehood) under the umbrella of Buddhism is well known. Perhaps less well understood is the symbolism of Buddha's footprint on the top of the mountain (e.g. Adam's Peak in Ceylon, Phrabat in Thailand, and Mt Popa in Burma). Just as the cult of the spirit of the mountain was traditionally associated with political unification and centralization under a king, so does the footprint on the mountain top declare that the people and the territory in question are the inheritance of the Buddha. These associations lead us back to the sacred mountain of Meru at the centre of the universe, often artificially reproduced in the centre of the royal cities of South-east Asian kingdoms.

So we return to the puzzle: What is the ordinary Buddhist's orientation to the Buddha and his material embodiments and symbols? It is unconvincing to say that what has been described are aspects of 'magical Buddhism' which are 'meaning-raising devices' (Ames 1964). This interpretation is that of a theologian and not of an anthropologist. More convincing are interpretations which see the resolution of the polarities of pure–impure, death–fertility in the relics of the Buddha. This is for me a starting point for unravelling the problem of conversion and transfer. If by one criterion the pure entities are remote and inaccessible, and if by another, relics and texts (and jewels and gold) are invested with power, it is the final bringing together of *power plus purity*, the inaccessible and the accessible, as constituting a primary problem in religious technology, that has to be explained.

The 'bodhisattva'

The traditions relating to *bodhisattva*, those who are on the threshold of becoming Buddhas, are manifold. One destined to be a Buddha must finally be born as a man, so the *bodhisatva* does not tarry for long in the heavens of delight.

The *bodhisattva* who stirs the imagination and holds the greatest promises for the Thai villagers is Maitreya, the next Buddha who will arrive to bring salvation to the world. Maitreya is revered by all Buddhist sects as the coming saviour, and his name signifies one who is full of love toward all beings.

It is believed that the Buddha himself elected Maitreya as his successor and that Maitreya now resides in the *Tusita* Heaven (*Dusit* in Thai), the heaven of contented beings, from where he watches over and promotes the interests of Buddhism. He awaits the time when he will appear on earth as Maitreya Buddha.[1] Tradition has it that the Buddha predicted that his teachings will last for 5,000 years, at the end of which they will no more be respected or even remembered because of the world's corruption and degeneracy.

According to the *Vinaya*, the Buddha had fixed a time limit of 500 years starting from his death during which the Law would last. The same period is confirmed by Nagasena in his dialogues with King Milinda. It appears that Buddhagosa in the fifth century A.D. extended the duration of the message in this world to 5,000 years. He foresaw five successive steps of retrogression, at intervals of one thousand years: first, the disappearance of the acquisition of the degrees of sanctity, then of the observance of the precepts, of the knowledge of the Scriptures, of the exterior signs of religion, and lastly of the corporeal relics of the Master which would be gathered together and cremated at Bodhgaya (Coedès 1964). Apparently this prophecy motivated, at various critical dates in the reigns of famous kings, the holding of convocations, writing of Scriptures and revival of religious enthusiasm. The most recent manifestation in our time was the 2,500th year (Buddha Jayanthi). The Siamese cosmological treatise, the *Traibhumikatha*, was produced long ago under similar inspiration.

To this pessimistic prophecy, however, Buddhist tradition has joined an optimistic messianic one. Maitreya, the next Buddha, will descend at the end of this decline. Religion will wax again, *arahats* will arise, men will be freed from toil and care, hunger, old age, and sickness. We shall see later that Buddhist ritual in the village dramatizes with great expectations the coming of the next saviour. It is therefore relevant to compare Maitreya with the Buddha. The Buddha belongs to the past; his teachings exist but he is extinct; it is possible that he is not in direct contact with this world. Maitreya lives in heaven, is interested in the present order of things as well as in the future, and his descent into the world from heaven is imagined to bring collective salvation and benefits to those

---

[1] The *Tusita* is the fourth heaven in the 'sensual' *deva loka*. Alabaster (1871) makes the interesting statement that when he asked the Siamese why the embryo Buddha occupies a low sensual heaven instead of the highest heaven of the *brahmas*, he was told that since the term of life allotted to one in the *brahma loka* is vast beyond imagination, the coming of the next Buddha would be delayed if he were to live there (p. 177).

who will be fortunate enough to see him at that time in the status of human being.

However, it is not in the countries of Theravada Buddhism but in those in which the Mahayana form prevails that the concept and cult of the *bodhisattva* has been greatly elaborated. There *bodhisattvas* abound—the most glorious of whom are Manjusri, Avalokitesvara and Vajra-pani. They are imagined to be permanently in the celestial worlds in benevolent relationship with humanity. Mahayana Buddhism, it would seem, has systematically incorporated the existing gods into its pantheon and transformed them into benevolent mediators and future Buddhas who will not necessarily descend to earth as human Buddhas.

These Mahayanist developments are echoed in the so-called Hinayana countries, which have at various times been fertilized by Mahayana influences. We have already noted that Sinhalese, Burmese and Thai kings were elevated to the status of *bodhisattva*. In certain situations, messianic Maitreya status may be claimed by charismatic leaders of popular rebellions against established kingship (Mendelson 1963). In Ceylon the protective guardian god Natha has been identified with Maitreya, and others like Saman and Skanda are regarded as *bodhisattva* whose role is to guard and protect both the Buddhist religion and the secular kingdom. Parallels can be found in other societies; but insofar as we are concerned with religion in the Thai village of Phraan Muan it is sufficient to remember that it is Maitreya alone who enjoys the adulation and the anticipations of a *bodhisattva*.

The 'arahat' and his miraculous powers

While the Buddha is a personage of the past who has reached *nirvana*, and Maitreya is the coming Buddha, the *arahat* is a lesser personage of both the past and the present,[1] who is inferior to the other two but is nevertheless on the path to salvation. The attributes of an *arahat* are of interest to us because they have relevance for understanding certain village rituals, especially those connected with healing and exorcism. Their bearing on these rituals nevertheless is not readily apparent.

Buddhism poured new content into an old word. The term *arahat* was previously applied to persons with honorary titles and of worldly position who were entitled to receive gifts, and also to ascetics who subjected themselves to self-mortification (*tapas*). The Buddhist conception applied more narrowly to the ascetic man of religion who has entered the

---

[1] According to the post-Canonical Buddhist writers, *arahats* belonged to the past and the world has been bereft of them for over 2,000 years. But with the coming of the Messiah Maitreya there will be *arahats* again.

Ariyan path and has reached its end, and consequently possesses the knowledge of emancipation. By the exercise of meditation (*dhyana*), the performance of certain ceremonies, and the observance of the prescribed course of moral action, the *arahat* has entered the path of salvation and his mind is therefore free of desire for, and cleaving to, sensuous objects, and free of the accompaniments of sorrow and pain. At his death he reaches the state of *nirvana*.

Now the notion of *iddhi* (or *siddhi*) is ancient in India, and Buddhism accepted and confirmed its existence and reality. The mystic powers of *iddhi* are not miraculous in the Western sense of interference by an outside power to contravene known laws of nature, but are special powers in conformity with nature possessed by certain people who are able to accomplish acts beyond the powers of ordinary men. Typically they are gained by ascetics.

The Buddhist suttas enumerate the *iddhi* powers in several places. For instance in the Samanna-Phala Sutta the Buddha enumerates the five modes of mystical insight that an *arahat* possesses:

the practice of *iddhi*—'being one he becomes many, or having become many becomes one again; he becomes visible or invisible; he goes, feeling no obstruction, to the further side of a wall or rampart or hill, as if through air...he walks on water without breaking through, as if on solid ground; he travels cross-legged in the sky...even the moon and the sun, so potent...does he touch with his hand...' (Rhys Davids, Vol. II, 1899, pp. 88–9);

the heavenly ear—the ability to hear sounds, both human and celestial, whether far or near;

knowledge of others' thoughts;

memory of his own previous births;

the heavenly eye—the knowledge of other people's previous births.

What is of special interest in respect of the concerns of this book is the relation between the achievement of *arahatship* and the possession and employment of these mystic powers. In the Samanna-Phala Sutta the Buddha has listed 'The Fruits of the Life of a Recluse' and in this list the mystic powers of *iddhi* rank high, superseded only by the higher achievement of the destruction of ignorance, rebirth and the sure knowledge of emancipation.

Thus a remarkable feature of the *arahat* is that in the course of his mental and spiritual progress he naturally attains extraordinary powers. But in the Kevaddha Suttanta (Rhys Davids, Vol. II, 1899, Ch. II) the Buddha is said to have taken a definite stand regarding their exercise. On being urged by Kevaddha, a young householder, to perform mystic wonders so as to make the people of Nalanda more devoted to the Exalted One, the Buddha, while conceding that he has himself realized the powers of *iddhi* (the 'mystic wonder' and the 'wonder of manifestation') asserted strongly that he loathed their practice, and that a greater and better wonder, which he had realized and recommended, was the wonder of education, that is, the system of self-training which culminated in *arahatship*.

The doctrinal position thus is that while it is inevitable that, at an advanced stage in his progress, the searcher attains mystic powers—which are in fact a mark of his progress—the exercise of these powers is dangerous both for the monk, who may be seduced into a vain magical mastery of the world, and for the laymen, because it may cause confusion in their minds and give opportunity for unbelievers to degrade the mystic powers of the recluse and equate them with the efficacy of base charms. The Buddha therefore forbade the monk to exhibit his powers before non-initiates, and the following stricture is embedded in the Canonical Law of the *Vinaya*: 'You are not, O Bhikkus, to display before the laity the wonders of *iddhi*, surpassing the power of ordinary men. Whosoever does so shall be guilty of a wrong act' (*dukkata*).

While Buddhist commentators and expositors state the above as the Buddha's position on this issue, a measure of ambiguity and contradiction is introduced in the Patika Suttanta (Rhys Davids, Vol. IV, Part III, 1957, Ch. 24), which belongs to the same historical period as the suttas already cited. In this dialogue the Buddha claimed to have worked wonders of an amusing and magical nature to vindicate his superiority over other ascetics.

I am not concerned here with sifting out the true doctrine but to pinpoint a phenomenon dealt with in classical Buddhist doctrine and which serves as a point of reference for certain kinds of cults and practitioners one meets in the field today.

The powers of *iddhi* (*itthibat* in Siamese) as set out above are not peculiar to Buddhism alone; they are for the most part stereotyped and occur in all the ascetic and mystical literatures of India (Eliade 1958).

The supra-normal powers of the *arahat* thus have an indirect bearing on contemporary religion in so-called Buddhist countries. Strictly speaking, in the Buddhist discussion of the problem, it is by virtue of mental discipline and by undergoing an inner transformation that the monk gains the mystic powers, and it is because their indulgence and exercise would stall his progress to the final goal that Buddha forbade their display as *dukkata* (evil deed). To make false profession of the attainment of *arahatship* is one of the four crimes that result in permanent exclusion from the priesthood.

But the possibility of acquiring mystic powers is not denied. And the way is therefore open for someone to take to the ascetic and meditative discipline in order to acquire them. An example that springs to mind is the Burmese *weikza*, who is regarded as possessed of supernatural powers, long-lived and on the path to *nirvana* (Mendelson 1963). The possibility is also there for someone to use the vehicles of inner transformation—chants and spells— without actually undergoing the mental transformation in the Buddhist meditative sense. Thus come about hierarchical distinctions between ritual specialists and practitioners in respect of their ethical status and endowment with spiritual power (*rit* in Siamese). The actual results of these possible developments we shall see later in Chapter 18, which deals with exorcism.

THE BUDDHA AND MARA

The parade we have so far witnessed of the grand Buddhist protagonists will be seriously unrepresentative if we do not also give a place, if not of honour then of a conspicuous nature, to Buddha's great antagonist, Mara. This demon antagonist appears in village myth and ritual frequently, for he is to the Buddha as *baab* (demerit) is to *bun* (merit).

Mara is generally regarded as the personification of death; he is the Buddhist counterpart of the principle of destruction. In more philosophical terms he can be equated with the whole world of sensuous existence and the realm of rebirth, as opposed to liberation and *nirvana*: for such a world is under the sway of desire and death. And in the thought of the *Pitakas* there is a clear connection between desire and death. For the world built on desire waxes and wanes, flourishes and decays; hence the ruler of worldly desire is also god of death. But Mara is not the ruler over hell. The function of judgment and punishment is assigned in the Buddhist pantheon to Yama, the god of the dead.

The Buddhist texts refer extensively to the various encounters between the Buddha and Mara the tempter; Mara's temptations also extended to monks, nuns and laymen in order to lure them from the path. In the Padhana Sutta Mara is represented as visiting Gotama on the banks of the Nerañjara, where he was practising austerities, and tempting him to abandon his endeavour. But the most important encounter—greatly elaborated in later books and chronicles, and constituting today a lively part of village lore—is the attack on and temptation of the Buddha by Mara, as the Buddha sat under the bo tree immediately before his enlightenment. This encounter not only is recalled in some village rituals but also gives mythological legitimacy to a ritual act performed widely and habitually—*yaadnam*, the pouring of water on the ground when transferring merit. I shall relate the bare details of this great encounter between good and evil in Buddhist folklore:

When Gotama sat under the bo tree engaged in his final effort to attain Buddhahood, Mara, whose nature is sinful, determined that he must at once destroy the man who was about to pass beyond his power. He first sent his three daughters Raka (*raga* = love), Aradi (*arati* = discontent), and Tanha (*trichna* = desire), beautifully bedecked, to tempt him. Gotama drove away these women who wanted to chain him in the fetters of concupiscence. Then King Mara, in fury, assembled his generals and his fearsome army and decided to make war on the *bodhisattva* so that he might flee in terror. At Mara's approach all the *deva* gods, the *Nagas* and other spirits who had gathered round the *bodhisattva* to pay him homage and sing his praises, took unceremonious flight, except the earth goddess. Mara employed all his miraculous powers to hurt the *bodhisattva*—from the brandishing of weapons by hideous forms, the causing of thunderstorms and violent gales, to the final hurling of his powerful thunderbolt, which however stood over the Buddha like a canopy of flowers. Undaunted, Mara challenged the Buddha to prove that the seat, the throne on which the Buddha sat, was his by right. Mara proved his own claim to that throne by calling on his generals to affirm his might.

Here we must let Alabaster (1871, pp. 154–5) present to us his translation from Siamese sources:

The Grand Being reflected. 'Truly here is no man to bear me witness; but I will call on the earth itself'...Striking forth his hand, he thus invoked the earth: 'O holy earth! I who have attained the thirty powers of virtue, and performed the five great alms, each time that I have performed a great act I have not failed to pour water upon thee. Now that I have no other witness, I call upon thee to give the testimony. If this throne was created by my merits, let the earth quake and show it; and if not, let the earth be still!'

And the angel of the earth, unable to resist his invocation, sprang from the earth in the shape of a lovely woman with long flowing hair, and standing before him, answered:

'O Being more excellent than angels or men! it is true that when you performed your great works you ever poured water on my hair.' And with these words she wrung her long hair, and a stream, a flood of waters gushed forth from it.

Onward against the host of Mara the mighty torrent rushed...and his whole army fled in utter confusion, amid the roarings of a terrific earthquake, and peals of thunder crashing through the skies.

The Thai villagers of today, whenever they have done an act of merit which is rewarded by blessings chanted by monks, transfer some of this merit to the dead, to the gods, to other humans, by pouring water upon the earth, thereby calling upon the goddess of the earth, Nang Thoranee, to witness the act.

4

PRIMARY VILLAGE CONCEPTS

The previous section on cosmology and Buddhist traditions was designed to serve a dialectical function in relation to the ethnographic data. The classical ideas will sometimes guide the ordering of the ethnography, just as much as the categories and relations that emerge from the ethnography will sometimes serve to clarify the classical formulations.

In this chapter I deal with primary concepts that emerge from the observation of thought and deed in the village.

'Bun' and 'baab' (ethical norms) and their implications for merit-making

Bun (merit) and baab (demerit) are verbal categories frequently used by the villagers. These concepts—especially the former—constitute the major ethical notions by which villagers conceptualize, evaluate, and explain behaviour. They derive, of course, from philosophical Buddhism, but village formulation deviates from the strict doctrinal one and must be understood in its own terms.

The words tham bun (to make merit) and aw bun (to take merit)—used as equivalents—refer to the giving of gifts to the Buddhist monks and the Buddhist wat. The second expression highlights the Buddhist attitude that merit is made not by giving per se but is 'acquired' by the willingness of the monks to receive. (The sociologist may phrase the transaction thus: the gift-taker in this context is superior and is capable of transferring some kind of spiritual grace to the giver.) The concepts 'make merit' and 'take merit' express a double relationship in which the transaction is given a particular ethical twist.

Performing acts of merit and avoiding acts of demerit are directed to the achievement of certain results. The value of merit-making is discussed by villagers under two aspects: first, it is said that one's fund of merit accumulated in this life will ensure a rebirth blessed with happiness, prosperity and wealth. (The achievement of salvation or final extinction (nirvana) is not usually stated as a goal nor for that matter does it have any personal relevance for them.) While merit-making is thus given ideological direction in terms of somehow immunizing the consequences of death and ensuring a prosperous rebirth, villagers also say that it has certain consequences in this life: the giving of gifts to monks produces

53

a happy and virtuous state of mind. This is no doubt a 'vague' formulation, but we should not disregard it because of its vagueness. (Virtue and purity are by their nature somewhat diffuse, easily contaminated and relatively powerless. At the same time they are also considered the best ethical preventive against misfortune.)

A characteristic of this morality is that one's actions are graded as meritorious or sinful and one's fate after death is said to depend on the final balance of pluses and minuses. Villagers say that, if a man has a large balance of merit over demerit, his *winjan* (soul) will go to *sawan* (heaven) and when his merit is exhausted he will be reborn on this earth (*log*); if he has committed both *bun* and *baab*, he will first go to hell (*narog*) and stay there until his demerit is expiated, then he will go to heaven to enjoy his merit before being reborn; if his life was wholly sinful, he will be committed to hell or will wander a long time on earth as a disembodied spirit (*phii*) before he can be reborn.

From the doctrinal point of view the quest for salvation is a strictly individualistic pursuit. In the village context, merit-making as the principal religious activity is certainly seen as having consequences for individuals. But the social unit engaging in merit-making need not be the individual— it may be a family, a household or a kin grouping, or even the entire village. Individuals then may act as representatives of other individuals or groups, or may make merit on behalf of another person or other persons, although part of the merit accrues to the actors themselves. Thus transfer of merit is not only thought possible, but is also highly institutionalized.

The nature of merit-making acts, their occasions, scale, content and grading, and the results sought, constitute a major problem for exploration in this book. But enough has been said already about *bun* and *baab* as ethical concepts for me to mark out some interpretative points which I think deviate from the conventional analyses of Buddhism. Although these points anticipate some of my conclusions, I need to state them here in order that the reader may appreciate my later elaborations.

My first unorthodox point is to question the idea that Buddhism is concerned with non-empirical ends and expresses only symbolic or ultimate values. I do not question the fact that some aspects of Buddhistic behaviour —or for that matter of any other system of 'religious' behaviour—do have this dimension. But the ethic of *bun/baab* as formulated by villagers appears to me to have 'empirical' objectives—that is, certain practical results are sought. Seeking a prosperous rebirth is an empirical objective of a deferred nature. The feeling that engagement in merit-making results in a felicitous state of mind is more immediate and direct, and it

Primary village concepts

needs to be highly emphasized that this is a psychological state much coveted by Thai villagers.

A related point to consider is the appropriateness of overstating the dichotomy this world/other world, and associating Buddhism exclusively with the second category. It is certainly true that doctrinally Buddhism is concerned with the problem of death and its aftermath; that the Buddhist monks signify withdrawal through their monastic life, and in their 'parish' role act as mediators between death and rebirth. But it needs also to be emphasized that merit-making is, in part, expressly directed to hastening rebirth and also to securing a better rebirth than the existing one. This orientation may also be interpreted as asserting that human life is not finite, it does not end with death, but belongs to a rebirth cycle. The preoccupation is with death, but death that can be converted into life. In this connection we should keep in mind that popular thought conceives of human states in heaven or hell as transitional phases, leading to the subsequent reality of human life in this world.[1]

It was sometime after I had formulated this view that I read a passage in Max Weber (Gerth and Mills 1946) which puts the argument cogently in respect of the followers of contemplative asceticism. Weber points out that even the sacred values of a religion orientated to a 'beyond' as the locus of definite promises are preferably not to be interpreted on that account as being 'other worldly'. Or rather, other-worldly sacred values are by no means values of the beyond. 'Psychologically considered, man in quest of salvation has been primarily occupied by attitudes of the here and now; for the devout the sacred value, first and above all, has been a psychological state in the *here and now*' (p. 278). The Buddhist monk in search of *nirvana* seeks the sentiment of cosmic love just as the puritan *certitudo salutis* is the feeling of a permanent state of grace.

To restate what seems to be an essential feature in religious behaviour: in Buddhism, as in many other religions, there is, to use a Durkheimian phrase, a double relation and the linking up of contraries. A series of dichotomies, for example this world/other world, living humans/ancestral spirits, body/soul, permeates religious thought. Religious action is oriented to influence the relationship between these oppositions, so that living human beings can experience prosperity and continuity of social life. Thus ideas such as better rebirth, or union with the inaccessible pure

[1] There is possibly a paradox here that merit-making should be directed to hastening rebirth, since this means cutting short the time spent in heaven that is earned by merits! The theological answer is that it is only through human existence that one can increase one's merit and go forward in one's ethical quest. For the ordinary man there is the additional fact that it is life on earth alone that is experientially known and that life in heaven is an 'unreal' projection.

divine, or immunization of the potency of the supernatural impinging on humans, are expressions of this desired mediation attempted through ritual action. Whether we call this 'empirical' is not the issue, but whether its characterization as 'non-empirical' is valid or meaningful.

Bun is not only predictive of future rebirth status—where its value is highly uncertain. Its explanatory power lies in interpreting present status and present circumstances. This is its convenience as a theory of causation. But the paradoxical fact is that in a Thai village (as in Buddhist Ceylon) there exist also other theories of causation of human circumstances, such as planetary, demonological or even divine intervention. As Obeyesekere (1958) has argued, these frames of explanation are not mutually inclusive, with *karma* or *bun/baab* being an ultimate formula.

What is the behavioural relationship of this general but diffuse theory of ethical causation to merit-making? We shall see later on that merit-making acts are categorized and form an elaborate scheme; yet the results of *bun*, to the acquisition of which they are said to be largely oriented, are not readily evident in everyday life. *Baab*, on the other hand, while not clearly categorized—and indeed certain moral precepts whose contravention causes demerit are often broken with impunity—has clearly evident results in everyday life in the form of illness, death, misfortune and the pervasive existence of evil spirits.

The puzzle, then, concerning the concept of *bun* and the objective of merit-making is something like this. Merit-making is a pronounced religious activity, yet the results of *bun* are vaguely formulated as a desirable state of mind or a better rebirth. In this life a human being is highly susceptible to misfortunes caused by powerful and immediate external agencies. Yet in the final hierarchy of judgment *bun* and Buddhist preoccupations occupy the highest place and are given precedence even as the source of ultimate (though not necessarily accessible) power.

This puzzle can of course be expressed in terms of a certain widespread arrangement of ideas. Purity, whether personified or an impersonal quality, is relatively inaccessible, is powerless, and is unstable because it is easily contaminated; impurity is the direct opposite. The same can be said of virtue/sin, happiness/misfortune, and similar conceptions. The concept of *bun/baab* can be fitted into the same scheme of thought.

Bun, as defined in popular thought and action, is attained through liberal gifts to the monks and the temple. To a sociologist, then, it is one type or category of gift-giving and its essence can be inferred by comparing it with other types of material transactions. The idiom in which such transactions are dressed and the objects or values exchanged tell us about the relative positions of giver and receiver and the nature

56

of the communication between them. The seemingly unilateral nature of merit-making highlights the ethical value put on voluntary giving at a cost to oneself. How does this ethical force released by the giver influence his moral state? And why is this pattern of giving placed on a higher level than other exchanges?

Another feature of merit-making is that although the actors make merit, as individuals or families, either on their own behalf or in order to transfer merit to some other person or persons, the merit-making occasions *par excellence* are the collective calendrical rites held at the temple. That is to say, merit-making, although particularistic in intent, is usually done in a collective context. Such occasions are by far the most conspicuous religious activity in the village. In this sense merit-making as a collective ethic directed to a community institution—the *wat* and its monks—provides occasions for residents of a village to assemble periodically. The village as a territorial community is clearly manifest on these occasions.

These collective merit-making occasions are also characterized by a festival spirit, fun and recreation. It is necessary to bear this robust aspect of Buddhist worship in mind and to account for it, for a narrow treatment of Buddhism as concerned with the other world and preoccupied with death makes it seem to impose a rather grim and morbid concentration on 'existential anxieties'. How is it that sermons and chants on *nirvana*, salvation through wisdom, or acts of superhuman charity and denial of the world can be accompanied by gay processions, dancing and gambling?

'Khwan' and 'winjan' (*spiritual essences of individual human beings*)

Whereas *bun* and *baab* are concepts ultimately derived from the Pali Scriptures, we now come to two sets of 'cultural doublets' (as Michael Mendelson has put it) which are intriguing because they consist of one term derived from Pali (or Sanskrit) and the other from the Thai language.

In the *winjan/khwan* doublet, the former derives from the Pali concept *vinnana* (consciousness), while *khwan* is a Thai word connoting some kind of spirit essence or soul. The same pair is found in Burma in the form *winyan* versus *leikpya* (the butterfly soul which, like the Thai *khwan*, leaves the body easily).

The second doublet is *thewada/phii*, where the first is derived from the Pali *devata* and the second is indigenous. (The Burmese counterparts are *devata* and *nat*.)

In a historical reconstruction one might be tempted to say that the 'borrowing' culture retains both the borrowed and the indigenous concepts, unwilling to let one interpretation go in favour of the other. But as an anthropologist I am impressed by the meaningful opposition of ideas provided by these terms and their structural role in the field of contemporary religious ideas as a totality.

The concepts of *khwan* and *winjan*, both expressing the notion of spiritual essences connected with the human body, are difficult to define and describe.

Taking *khwan* first: some writers have rendered it as 'life soul'; others as 'benevolent guardian spirit of an extremely ephemeral essence'. The villagers' characterization of *khwan* subsumes a number of ideas: the *khwan* resides in the human body; it is attached to the body and yet can leave it. The causes and consequences of the *khwan's* departure are formulated in a circular manner: the *khwan* takes fright and leaves its owner's body (*chao khong*) when he is frightened, sick or in trouble, or *caj bau dee* (mind not good). The very act of its fleeing the body in turn exposes the owner to suffering, illness and misfortune.

The flight of the *khwan* itself cannot be seen; it can only be inferred from its effects. But in some instances the evidence is more direct. 'Supposing you are in one place and someone sees you elsewhere, then your *khwan* is wandering and must be instantly recalled.'

The *khwan* is one entity; it is also fragmented into thirty-two separate essences associated with different parts of the body. (No villager can list the body parts where they reside.) But the rites for recalling the escaped *khwan* treat the totality, that is, the separate essences as a unity.

Animals have *khwan* too: the animal that occupies the villagers' minds when they say this is the buffalo used in agriculture. The rule that is usually enunciated is that any being which has a *winjan* also has a *khwan*. (But yet *khwan* is also attributed to paddy—however, in this instance, the spirit of paddy is personified.)

The *khwan* must be understood in relation to *winjan*. The *winjan*, also a spiritual essence, resides in the body. But it is different from *khwan*. The *khwan* can leave the body temporarily, thereby causing illness, but it can be recalled and mental and physical health thereby restored. At death the *khwan* leaves the body for good, followed by the *winjan*. The *winjan* leaves the body only with death. In fact, death is described as the escape of the *winjan* from the body. After death, people are not concerned with the *khwan*, only with the fate of the *winjan* and its subsequent transformations.

It is apparent that there is a complementarity and opposition implied by this pair of concepts. The nature of the spiritual essences and their relationship are seen better in the rites addressed to them. These will be discussed later in Chapter 13. At this stage let me formulate the relationship in this way:

Primary village concepts

Khwan is associated with life and the vicissitudes of life; *winjan* is associated with death and the vicissitudes after death. Both are spiritual essences that animate life; the *khwan* actively and the *winjan* passively, or rather the former as a variable substance, the latter as permanent. Their roles are reversed after death. The *khwan* dies for good (or becomes passive), but the *winjan* disengages itself from its mortal coil and leads a separate existence. If I may hazard the description of these concepts in terms of psychological states in the English language, *khwan* relates to morale (the Thai explanation of why *khwan* rites are performed is to confer 'good living and strength') and *winjan* to mind or consciousness (*cit caj*).

The Thai villager thus conceptually distinguishes two spiritual essences. This duality does not fit into the simple 'body/soul' dichotomy; if we are to fit the Thai notions we can say that two aspects of the 'soul' are distinguished. While the villager makes the conceptual distinction, he becomes highly inarticulate and vague if the anthropologist strives to make him verbalize their respective properties. From the observer's analytical point of view, the distinction becomes sharper when he analyses the rites associated with *khwan* and *winjan*.

'Thewada' and 'phii' (two opposed supernatural categories)

As verbal categories the words *thewada* and *phii* are habitually used by villagers to refer to certain supernatural agents or personifications. The two categories are in their general reference opposed: the *thewada* (*devata*) are divine angels, benevolent in nature, and living in heaven (*sawan*); the *phii* are malevolent agents, either free-floating, localized in the world of human beings, or condemned to hell (*narog*).

This way of stating their characteristics immediately raises the question of how *thewada/phii* concepts are linked with human ethical status—*bun/baab*—and life/death. Now, in general, it is said that the *winjan* of every individual turns into a *phii* at death. *Phii*, then, are after-death phenomena. Villagers say that those persons who have lived a meritorious life go to heaven, but this heaven is quite different from the heaven in which *thewada* reside. A human being can never become a *thewada*; he can go to heaven and he can then be reborn; *thewada* are never reborn. This statement is quite different from the doctrinal position in Buddhism. Humans who have lived a life of *baab* are condemned to hell or become malevolent spirits living (disembodied) in this world. It would seem then that if *phii* are pictured as after-death human phenomena, there is a basis for their differentiation into kinds of *phii*, with characteristics ranging from benevolence, prestige and responsible power to malevolence, notoriety and caprice.

59

Buddhism and the spirit cults in North-east Thailand

The basic opposition between *thewada* and *phii* emerges in village ritual. *Phii* can punish people and cause illness or misfortune. The help of the *thewada* is necessary to diagnose the malevolent agent and, depending on the category of *phii*, either to placate him or exorcize him. Thus the village diviner (*mau song*) always begins by inviting the *thewada* (*pao-sakke*) to appear in his divining device and 'force' the *phii* to appear. In this instance the *thewada*, as good agents, are helping man to circumvent misfortune. Normally, because *thewada* are opposed to *phii*, they do not appear in the propitiatory or placatory rites addressed to the latter and conducted by a specialist (*cham*). But they make their appearance again in rites of exorcism as the enemies of afflicting malevolent spirits.

In ordinary village formulation the *thewada* constitute a relatively un-differentiated category of divine benevolent agents. The classical cosmology stated earlier postulates the existence of twenty-six heavens subdivided into three kinds of *loka*. By and large such fine gradations are ignored in the village. The accent is not on formulating a pantheon of hierarchically ordered and named individual gods. To be sure, on specific ritual occasions, or in reciting portions of mythology, the names of distinguished deities occur, for example Phra In (Indra the ruler of the second heaven), the guardians, Phra Prom (Brahma), and others characterized specifically as 'female' such as Nang Thoranee, the goddess of the earth. (For instance, Indra, King of the second level of heavens (*Dawadung*) with his three-headed elephant *Erawan* and his host of angels appears frequently in Thai legends, and it is to his inspiration that the Thai attribute the *Lak Inthapat*, an old law book.) But these personages are not ordered on a cognitive map; rather they are activated by ritual or mythological context and therefore I shall follow the thought patterns of the village and elucidate the attributes of these personages when I deal with specific myths or rituals. In ordinary dialogue the *thewada* belong to a single undifferentiated category. From a comparative point of view this orientation of the Thai villagers of Phraan Muan is dramatically different from that, say, of the Sinhalese villagers, for whom a hierarchy of gods and their individuality is a *sine qua non* of thought relating to the supernatural world (Obeyesekere 1966; Yalman 1964).

There is one noteworthy divergence between the village and the classical formulations of gods and godlings and malevolent spirits. In the classical and doctrinal tradition both the deities and the inhabitants of the heavens, and the demons and victims of the hells, are subject to rebirth and the vagaries of *karma*; their status is not permanent. For the villagers, however, the *thewada* are a permanent heavenly category of non-human origin. In contrast the *phii* are visualized as beings who were formerly human—

60

the most elevated of them in the imagery of prestigious, powerful or respected elderly human beings, the most malevolent as manifestations of humans who have died violent deaths. Unlike the undifferentiated *thewada*, the *phii* as a general category are highly differentiated and their attributes extend from benevolent and disciplinary guardianship to extreme capricious malevolence. The first type may then enjoy an elevated title (e.g. *Chao Phau* = respected father) which makes them a mixture of both *thewada* and *phii*. While in a general sense they are opposed, the border line between *phii* and *thewada* may in actual fact be vague. This need not necessarily mystify us because hierarchical positions and comparisons are usually relative.

The incorporation of *thewada* into Buddhism and their role in expressing Buddhist aspirations and ideals finds conspicuous demonstration in myths and rituals current in Phraan Muan village. I have already described the myth associated with the *bodhisattva* Maitreya who now lives in Tusita heaven as a deity and will in time descend to earth as the next Buddha and saviour. Some aspects of this myth are dramatized in *Bun Phraawes*, which is the village's grandest annual festival.

Another legend which is known but not ritually dramatized in the village (but is performed in Central Thailand) is that of the Buddha's descent from heaven after preaching to his mother. The Buddha's mother died seven days after his birth and thereby she was deprived of hearing the truth from the lips of her own son. The Buddha, in compassion for her, ascended in three steps to reach Indra's heaven to which his mother had been transported, and there preached to her and the gods for three months. Indra then devised three ladders to facilitate the Buddha's return to earth. The centre ladder was made of seven precious substances— gold, silver, coral, ruby, emerald and other gems. The Buddha descended on this. To its right was a ladder of gold on which Indra descended, blowing the conch and accompanied by his retinue of gods. To its left was a ladder of silver by which Brahma and the other Brahma gods descended, holding an umbrella over the Buddha. The three ladders appeared to the people of the earth as three rainbows.

There are many other legends of the presence of the gods at sermons given by the Buddha, and of their acclamation of the truth he preached. The presence of *thewada* in rituals conducted in the village today thus harks back to classical traditions.

5

THE INSTITUTION OF MONKHOOD
IN HISTORICAL PERSPECTIVE

Buddhism has had a rich and extensive history, and its historical development has profoundly affected it as a religion. In becoming an established mass religion it made adaptations to the political and social environments in which it found itself. Thus for instance in many of the areas it spread to, it became an 'established' religion: it validated and complemented the institution of kingship and to some extent influenced the ideology of statecraft. Buddhism and kingship had a close complementary relationship in Ceylon, Burma and Thailand, all of them countries of Theravada Buddhism.

Moreover, Buddhism went through both sectarian differentiation and missionary phases outwards from India. The major split was that between the Mahayana and Theravada schools.

Thus a single original tradition has had variant developments in different societies. A contemporary student of Buddhism may therefore consider the feasibility of thinking in terms of Sinhalese Buddhism, Thai Buddhism and so on, although he has to keep in mind that there is a universal Buddhist tradition which has become particularized in different societies.

The approach of the anthropologist studying Buddhism as a popular religion at the village level may differ radically from that of philosophers and theologians. While granting that one cannot fully understand the role of a monk in village Buddhism without also understanding the place of the monk in pristine or doctrinal Buddhism, the anthropologist will also try to see how the institution of monkhood—the principles of recruitment, the interaction of monks with their lay congregation, the ritual services the monks perform—is directly integrated with village social structure and interests. While noting that there is a core of generalized religious concepts and idiom which derives from the grand Buddhist tradition and which has currency in village thought and religious action, he will concentrate on how these concepts have been transformed and worked into the texture of village life to produce not so much a vulgarized or distorted or debased religion but a live, ordered and meaningful entity.

Let me begin by contrasting some developments in Hinduism and Buddhism, for, after all, Buddhism had its origin in India.

Monkhood in historical perspective

The Buddhist monk is in some respects like the Hindu *sannyasin* in that he renounces the world and removes himself from society, its affiliations and its obligations. The *sannyasin* is outside the social structure; his quest in the Indian context is an extreme statement of an individual pursuing his own salvation (Dumont 1960).

Max Muller in his *Hibbert Lectures* contended that the brahmanical 'ascetic' (*sannyasin*) was the model for the Buddhist and Jaina counterparts. Dutt (1960) contests this viewpoint and argues that the ancient *parivrajaka* ('wanderer') tradition was the seed bed which gave rise to all the wandering sects. The resolution of this particular problem is not of concern to us here. It is relevant to note that *sannyasin* means one who renounces or casts off (the world), *bhikkhu* means one who is without possessions and lives on alms. Other closely associated concepts are *nirgrantha* (without ties), *vairagi* (free from affections). All wanderers may be described as those who go forth from home into homelessness (*parivrajya*). But in time the different wandering sects created their own traditions of contemplation and organization, and came to terms in different ways with the surrounding society.

In caste-bound, status-bound, purity-bound India the *sannyasin* is casteless, neglectful of normal rules of social distance and pollution, and is at the same time a revered holy man. The *sannyasin* by renouncing the world and going forth into homelessness broke Vedic tradition, especially all those rules that applied to the householder (*grahastha*). He did not sacrifice, and wore no token of Vedic culture such as the sacred thread or the symbolic tuft of hair on the head. In a sense therefore the householder and the renouncer were polar opposites.

But in time certain important developments took place in Indian society which produced resolutions of this dichotomy and tension. It is a common event in India that all reforming sects are over time incorporated into the Hindu complex and assigned a place inside it. In respect of the *sannyasin* the great resolution was the incorporation of the life of the wanderer and renouncer as the final stage in the theory of the four *asramas* (progression of life through four stages). The incorporation was legitimated in the later *Upanishads* which describe an initiatory ritual into the *parivrajya* (going forth) condition: the initiate ceremonially disowns Vedic social and religious practices by rejecting the sacred thread and tuft of hair, by stretching his legs over the sacrificial utensils, by throwing the wooden utensils into the fire, etc. He is considered, however, to take the fire, which he no longer will tend, into himself or into his belly (Dutt 1962). Thus the stages of indoctrination and the life of a householder proclaimed in the Vedas were not only preserved but declared essential prior stages in the life cycle.

Equally important was the change wrought within the *brahman* caste itself. The Vedic *brahman* and his successor of later times were different beings. The *brahman* has over time come to champion some of the values of the *sannyasin*: he has espoused the values of *ahimsa*, he and his gods have become vegetarian. Thus paradoxically the *brahmans* have become the repository and guardians of important *sannyasin* values *while remaining in the world within the caste system*, in fact at its apex. They are the purest and most prestigious caste(s) with monopolistic access to the auspicious sacred, and they represent the *élite* moral values of Indian society which many castes of lower status do not practise or cannot approximate in their conduct.

It seems to me that the development of monkhood in Buddhism has been in some respects the reverse of that undergone by the *brahmans*. Buddhism in its pristine aspect was in many ways a revolutionary religion, especially when viewed in relation to the caste system of India. Some have argued that Buddhism was in part a *kshatriya* reaction (which originated in the less *brahman* dominated regions of North-east India) to Brahman supremacy and ritual formalism (Thomas 1951, p. 3). The Buddhist texts portray certain contradictions but on the whole it is not a distortion to sum up the situation thus.

It is not so much that Buddhism had a social ideology that fulminated against caste but that it tended to leave caste alone. Caste status was explained by the theory of *karma*, but the Buddha placed morality and virtue above formal caste status (Rahula 1956, pp. 233–6). At best Buddhism provided an ethical interpretation of the caste system: the virtuous outcaste was superior to an immoral *brahman*, and no one is a *brahman* in the moral sense by virtue of birth ascription alone.

Perhaps more important was that pristine Buddhism advocated and practised an open recruitment to its ranks and caste was considered irrelevant to salvation. Monkhood was not defined by caste status, and the monks could not form a caste stratum. The rule of celibacy further meant that the monks could not renew themselves through physical reproduction as a social stratum or group.

A revolutionary aspect of the Buddhist *bhikkhu*, when compared with brahmanical practice, was that as a mendicant he must accept without discrimination cooked food given by any devotee. This is a dramatic rejection of the orthodox rules of commensality. According to the teaching of the *Vinaya* (disciplinary code) and the suttas, *bhikkhus* are prohibited from accepting raw rice.

Moreover Buddhism brought together all strata of society on an equal footing as a congregation at the place of worship or instruction, thereby again taking a stand opposed to brahmanical doctrine which insisted on participation graded by caste status and the exclusion of the lowest castes from its temples.

In one respect the *brahman* and the *bhikkhu* are thoroughly opposed. It is true that the rules of the *Vinaya* lay great stress on personal etiquette, decorum, personal cleanliness and propriety of demeanour, but Buddhism is dramatically anti-brahmanical in enjoining contemplation of and contact with death as a major preoccupation of the monk. The accent is on visiting graveyards, confrontation with death and corpses, meditation on death to understand the transitoriness of life and body. The wearing of *pamsa-kulina* rags gathered from graveyards is an extreme gesture of this absorption with death. Thus Buddhism encouraged the cultivation of equanimity in respect of that very situation which is considered to confer the most severe form of pollution in Hindu society—death. The ritual role of the *brahman* priest is by contrast eminently auspicious and pure and concerned with the changes and progress of life itself. And when *brahman* priests participate in mortuary rites, they do so not at the first impure and malevolent stage soon after death but in the second, post-cremation phase when the soul of the dead is transformed from the unclean *pret* (ghost) to the revered *pitr* (ancestor).

Thus in all these respects the wandering *bhikkhu* was a contrast to the *brahman* priest and more akin to the *sannyasin*. He is in the classical tradition of one who sets forth from home into homelessness. There is no need here to document from the texts that an eremitical life was recommended to the *bhikkhu*—that his 'four resources' should be mendicancy, clothing in cast-off rags, forest life, and using urine as medicine. The famous dictum in *Mahavagga* is 'ma ekena dve agamittha'—'let not two of you go one and the same way'.

But texts of the same period also relate that householders gave alms to the *Sangha* (the order of monks), that monasteries and dwelling houses for monks had been established. The four resources became optional. And by the time *The Questions of King Milinda* in the second century B.C. was composed, the resolution was that although the eremitical ideal was upheld, monastic life was taken for granted and recognized as a fact. Thus in his works on the history of Buddhism in India, Dutt (1960; 1962) puts great emphasis on the change in the life of the *bhikkhu* from a wandering to a settled monastic life. This transformation was accompanied by the rules, practices and rituals of settled monastic life which I shall briefly outline later.

I would argue therefore that when Buddhism became an institutionalized religion, the Buddhist monk had to make a passage that was the reverse of the one made by the *brahman* (who while remaining in the caste system appropriated some *sannyasin* values). The monk, while standing for a way of life set apart from that of the householder, nevertheless had to have regular ritual and material transactions with the laity. It is this same organized relation, which presupposes and makes possible a separate monastic communal life distinct from and contrasted with lay life, that also largely distinguishes the life of the *bhikkhu* from that of the wandering, individualistic (and at best loosely organized) *sannyasin* in India.

The distinction and relation between monk and householder is a focal point in the organization of Buddhism as a mass religion. And as might be expected, the texts portray a tension of ideas concerning this distinction. We can begin to explore this tension with the conception of the Buddha himself. The founder of Buddhism, having realized the highest truth, did not become as might have been expected the 'silent one' but passed on to the higher stage of attainment as the *Samma Sambuddha*, teacher of all men, a role that was prompted by the miseries of all unenlightened creatures and the upsurge of compassion in his heart for them. The Buddha converted his own spiritual cognition into a message (the *Dhamma*) which after him was to be preached by the *Sangha* (the order of monks). The Buddha-to-come, Maitreya, is conceived in the same way.

Now, contrasted to the notion of the Supreme Buddha as *sattha* (teacher) is the conception of the Pacceka Buddha who is inferior in that he is the solitary saint (compared to a rhinoceros) who has attained perfection by himself and for himself alone. The Pacceka Buddha is never co-existent with a supreme Buddha, and he makes his appearance only during the period intervening between the attainment of *nirvana* by one supreme Buddha and the advent of the succeeding Buddha. He reaches *nirvana* without having risen to supreme Buddhahood.

This asymmetrical evaluation of the compassionate teacher and the lonely saint was reflected in the controversies resolved by the *Sangha* in early times in Ceylon. Rahula (1956) reports some of them. In the first century B.C. (which period is considered as the most important for the shaping of Buddhism in Ceylon) there was a debate among several hundred monks who assembled at a conference to decide whether the basis of the *sasana* (religion) was learning or practice. It was decided that learning was the basis of the *sasana* rather than practice, and the *Dhamma-kathikas* (preachers or teachers learned in the *Dhamma*) succeeded in silencing the *Pamsukulikas* (who wore robes made of rags). Learning was declared necessary and sufficient for the perpetuation of the religion. Thus out of such controversies in institutionalized Buddhism grew two vocations which were not so distinguished in the original texts: the vocation of books (*gantha-dhura*) and the vocation of meditation (*vipassana-dhura*), the former being considered the more important (Rahula 1956, pp. 158–60).

The issue came up again later in slightly different terms: whether the *bhikkhu* should concern himself with social service and humanitarian activities (i.e. parish role) or only with his personal salvation. Rahula says that opinion was divided; he cites the story of Cullapindatiya Tissa to throw light on this issue (pp. 192–3). The gist of the story is that the monk Cullapindatiya Tissa did not visit and sympathize with a female *upasika* (devotee), who ministered to his needs, when misfortune befell her in the form of a fire that burnt her house. He merely turned up the next day at mealtime to receive alms.

The question raised by this story is of the greatest importance for this book. Should the monk consider himself only concerned with his salvation and therefore accept gifts from laymen without any corresponding obligation (*mutta-muttaka*), or should he be subject to the obligations of *dhamma-dana* (gift of spiritual service) which is aptly phrased in a fourteenth-century Sinhalese exposition of the *Dhamma* (*Saddharmalankaraya*) as follows: 'Render help in return by spiritual gifts to lay people who always support you with material gifts'?

Rahula reports that the *Majjhima Commentary* which cites the story praised the attitude of the monk, but that majority opinion disagreed.

In both Ceylon and Thailand the established view was and is that the *Sangha* has ritual and spiritual obligations to the laity. The recommended ideal is for monks to be *gramavasi* (residing in towns and villages and engaging themselves in educational and religious activities) rather than *vanavasi* (residing in the forest and engaged in meditation with no obligations to the laity). In the latter category are included *tapassi* (hermit or ascetic monks) and *pamsakulikas* (monks who wear robes made of rags) who, whenever they make their periodic appearances, face hostile rejection by the established *Sangha*. Such forest dwellers also pose an interesting problem (Obeyesekere 1968): the laity are apt to consider them holy and to pursue them with gifts, making their escape from the world and the adulation of the masses difficult if not impossible.

According to the monastic rules set out by the *Vinaya*, the *bhikkhu* is advised to assist his parents when they are in need of material help and to give them medical attention when they fall ill. Although his initiation into monkhood and his secluded life signify his departure and separation from his home, withdrawal does not mean that it is wrong for him to maintain close relations with his parents.

These developments in the dialectic of ideas and practices in institutionalized Buddhism diverge from the theory of monkhood as understood in philosophical Buddhism, which sees monkhood as an initiation that offers a man a way out of reciprocity, a way for a man to become entirely himself living in but not dependent on society. Here the meditating monk becomes the model of non-reciprocity, of spiritual enhancement through personal effort, of the liberated and non-attached being who may receive but need not give.

Monkhood came to have a different societal relation when its way of life was regularized in monastic communities which had systematic transactions with the laity. Here too the paths of the layman and the monk were considered quite different, as in the Canonical literature. It was recognized that the householders had a strong craving for and attachment to their lands, wealth, wives and children, and servants, that they neither understood nor accepted the idea of the renunciation of their possessions. Thus Rahula, himself a *bhikkhu* and an historian of ancient Ceylon, states that lay religion in ancient Ceylon was based on the fundamental conception that the monks were expected to show the laity not 'the way to emancipation' but 'the way to heaven'.

The aims of making merit on the part of the laity—from the peasant to the King—were security and safety and prosperity in this world and the next. The values sought were wealth, health, long life, intelligence, power, high caste and beauty. The layman saw the monk as a mediator and a vehicle in this quest. The *Sangha* was called in Ceylon *punnak-khetta* (merit field) in which one sowed seeds of merit and reaped a good harvest. But to achieve this end an unblemished *Sangha* and virtuous monks were necessary, and the distinction between monk and layman must be preserved. These are *sine qua non* of Buddhism.

FROM EREMITICAL TO CENOBITICAL LIFE

One last feature remains to be briefly outlined in this historical introduction. That is the shift in the life of the majority of monks from a wandering to a settled life and its organizational accompaniments.

This change is significant for two reasons. First, in the India of early times there were many kinds of wandering sects, and certain particular features in their communal life distinguished the communities of Buddhist monks from others. Secondly, these communal practices were set out as basic regulations that were enshrined and became the charter for future monks. Buddhism is not indigenous to Ceylon or Burma or Thailand, though it took root there and over time developed features specific to each environment. But there are not only general doctrinal principles

68

but also rules of discipline and set communal ceremonies which are considered an essential part of the orthodoxy, and these receive validity precisely because of alleged unchanged transmission of Pali texts from the time of the founding of the religion.

Most of the formal regulations pertaining to monastic life in Thai villages today derive their basis from this heritage. They are not indigenously contrived and nothing in village social organization will explain the disciplinary code, or the ordination procedure, or the substance of the Pali chants recited by monks. Yet these features, stemming from the grand tradition, are woven into the texture of village life and have associated features and elaborations which constitute the foci of anthropological investigation.

A legitimate inquiry for an historian—which I am not—would be to trace how a wandering sect became a settled order, and in the case of the *bhikkhus*, how the *Sangha* which is unitary on conception became plural monk-communities, which lived virtually as autonomous corporations supported by the state and lay donors.

The *Vinaya* texts, as for example the *Mahavagga* (Rhys Davids and Oldenberg, Part 1, 1881), provide some crucial indications of the features emphasized and elaborated in early Buddhism. The *Mahavagga* is divided into the following four sections which deal with rules and injunctions that still remain essential features of monastic life in Theravada countries.

First *Khandhaka* (The Admission to the Order of *bhikkhus*): this contains the rules of admission to monkhood and the *upasampada* (ordination) procedure (which are followed to this day), and lists the duties of a monk toward his *upagghaya*, preceptor, etc.

Second *Khandhaka* (The *uposatha* and the *Patimokkha*): this section emphasizes the importance of the monks coming together half-monthly to recite the penitentiary confession of *Patimokkha* (which I shall deal with in detail in the next chapter). A vital clue as regards the decentralized nature of monastic communities is reported in this section in these terms: the Buddha is supposed to have ruled that the 'complete fraternity' which should recite the *Patimokkha* is 'one residence' (i.e. a monastery), thereby emphasizing the autonomy of the fraternities.

Third *Khandhaka* (Residence during the Rainy Season, *Vassa*): in this section is stipulated that the retreat for three months during the rainy season is obligatory. Great emphasis is placed on the fact that a monk may not absent himself from his *Vassa* residence for more than seven days. He may legitimately leave the residence if his parents are sick, if his fellow monks or nuns require his attendance, or if he is needed to officiate at merit-making activities of laymen, but he must return within the stipulated period.

Fourth *Khandaka* (The *Pavarana* Ceremony): at the conclusion of the *Vassa* residence the monks are exhorted to hold *Pavarana* which involves the following: 'Every Bhikkhu present invites his companions to tell him if they believe him guilty of an offence, having seen that offence, or having heard of it, or suspecting it' (Rhys Davids and Oldenberg 1881, p. 328). The object of the exercise is that it would result in the monks living in accord with each other.

Thus we see in the *Mahavagga* that regulated ordination, recitation of the *Patimokkha* on *uposatha* days, the observance of *Vassa* residence, marked at its conclusion by the *Pavarana* rite, were considered the basic features of classical established monasticism. The story of how these practices were developed, partly as a basis of differentiation from other sects, and how they led to a change from eremitical to cenobitical life is not known in detail.

The differentiation and routinization of the life of *bhikkhus* probably is best seen in the rain retreat (*Vassa*), which was a custom among wanderers of all sects. This general custom was apparently individuated and specialized by the Buddhists (Dutt 1960; 1962). The rainy season became an occasion for the *bhikkhus* to live together in a congregation of fellow monks. The rule in the past—and which prevails to this day—is that *Vassa* residence be taken on the day after the full moon of *Asalha* (or a month later) and be concluded three months later. During this period the mobility of monks is restricted.

Eliot (1954, pp. 245–6) describes the early practices thus: 'The year of the *bhikkhus* was divided into two parts. During nine months they might wander about, live in the woods or reside in a monastery. During the remaining three months, known as *vassa* or rainy season, residence in a monastery was obligatory.' *Vassa* was the time when people had most leisure so

it naturally became regarded as the appropriate season for giving instruction to the laity. The end of the rainy season was marked by a ceremony called *Pavarana*, at which the monks asked one another to pardon any offences that might have been committed, and immediately after it came the *Kathina* ceremony or distribution of robes. *Kathina* signifies the store of raw cotton cloth presented by the laity and held as common property until distributed to individuals.

Over time this temporary residence changed into permanent residence, and the *Vassa* itself became a marked phase of retreat and intensified religious activity in the routine life of monastic communities. The original settlements during the retreat were of two types—the *avasa* situated in the countryside and built and maintained by the monks, and the *arama* located in a town or city as a private enclosure within the grounds of a lay donor and patron. Later on established monasteries came to be designated as *arama* or *vihara*. The critical and essential features of monastic life—as it is lived today in a Thai village *wat* (the name for the temple complex, derived from *avasa*)—are thus contained in the original regularization and routinization of the rain retreat (Buddhist Lent), and codified in the *Vinaya* texts. Notable among them is the fixing of boundaries —*sima*—for the residence. This stating of the limits according to a set procedure was an essential requirement for a body of *bhikkhus* to live together. Today in Thailand the *sima* stones have to be installed, according to set procedure and with consent from the higher authorities, to define the boundary of the *uposatha* hall (*bood* in Thai)—which is the most sacred component of the temple complex and in which ordination, recitation of the *Patimokkha* (disciplinary rules), and other prescribed acts take place.

The concept of *sima* therefore requires elucidation. In a politico-territorial sense it defines the boundaries (the widest margin of influence) of a political state, or smaller administrative unit. In the case of the localized community of *bhikkhus* I would suggest that its significance is somewhat different: it separates out and encloses a sacred space of a *limited* extent *vis-à-vis* the vast secular space of the village and town inhabited by the laity. It is fully evident in rural Thailand today how important is the ecological separation of *wat* (with its widest boundary enclosing the total complex of buildings and its inner boundary enclosing the sacred *bood*) from the *ban* (village settlement), which parallels the separation of monk from villager (*bhikkhu* from *grahapati*). It is the *bood* that best symbolizes this distinction—for in it alone can ordination take place (in the presence of laymen) and certain recitations be conducted (from which layman are vigorously excluded because these spiritual exercises relate to the vocation of the monk). Before laymen can enter the *bood* they must remove their footwear, and a candidate for ordination has to worship the *sima* stones to mark his entry into the sacred space and life.

If the *Vassa* retreat is a critical marker in the annual cycle of activities, then it is to be expected that its beginning and its conclusion should, as in the past, receive special recognition. The ordination ritual (*upasampada*, meaning 'exceeding gain or advantage'), which we have previously noted is a formalized ceremony of admission to monkhood, is in contemporary Thailand (as in Ceylon) usually timed to take place in the month preceding the rain retreat. The vast majority of ordinations take place at this time, and this again is an old custom. The ceremony assigns certain material obligations to lay sponsors and ritual roles to the assembled monks. The end of the retreat is marked by the *Kathina* ceremony, which in its classical sense means the distribution of robes by the lay donors to the monks for their use in the year commencing after the retreat.

While these rituals imply a regular relation of monks with a continuing congregation, what activities have marked off the monks as following a vocation set apart from their congregation? For one, the recital of the *Patimokkha* by the full assembly of monks living as a community semi-monthly on the sacred *uposatha* days (at full moon and new moon) is an imperative act. It is said to be the outward token of the inner bond of the *Sangha*. According to Dutt the *Patimokkha* recital was originally the renewal of fellowship and unity as a body after a long period of dispersal by the members of a sect. In settled monkish communities the ritual became a recitation of the list of transgressions against the collective *Sangha* life, and an expression of the unity of the monastic community undivided by schism. Later with the elaboration of the *Vinaya* (the disciplinary code of 227 rules) the *Patimokkha* recital became the main item in the liturgy of the *uposatha* service.

The special characteristic of the decentralized and locally limited brotherhood of *bhikkhus* is best represented by the concept of *sanghakamma*, transactions of the *Sangha*. These transactions are held in 'full and frequent' assemblies according to carefully defined procedural rules. An act of ordination, adjudicating on infringements against the disciplinary rules of the order, settling schismatic disputes, etc., are examples of the matters of concern to the assembly. The basic idea behind the notion of *sangha-kamma* is that a democratic community takes decisions on matters of concern. Since these decisions are taken by all the members together in assembly, members are equal and are expected to abide by the decisions of the majority.

According to Buddhist tradition the Buddha on his last missionary tour told his disciple Ananda that after his decease the *Dhamma* (doctrine) alone should bind the *bhikkhus*, and that he repudiated the idea of a successor who would be their leader or head. Thus it is said that in the early *Sangha* there was no hierarchy and locus of authority; while the elders and older monks deserved respect and privilege in etiquette, they could only advise and instruct, not legislate or compel. The elders (*theras*) did not possess episcopal authority; at best they were the chief teachers of the order.

The absence from the beginning of a firm hierarchy of positions and consequently of authority relations is so conspicuous and intrinsic a feature of the Buddhist *Sangha* that it needs to be firmly underlined.[1] In earliest times the want of a central authority in the *Sangha* was shared with brahmanism. However, in theory, the members of the *Sangha* were not 'priests' or 'mediators'; they joined a confraternity to lead a higher life which could not be achieved within the ordinary society. This openness and voluntariness of the vocation was expressed in the mode of recruitment. Subject to certain conditions, any free man was admitted; and there were two simple ceremonies for admission—the novitiate and the higher ordination (*upasampada*). The monk took no vows of obedience and was at perfect liberty to return at any time to the world of lay life.

The tradition of *sanghakamma* in full assembly and the *Patimokkha* confessional (and other customs), although at one level diacritical and ideological markers of the monastic way of life, were in actual practice fluid in interpretation and thereby somewhat 'anti-structural'. The way in which the *Patimokkha* confessional service was actually conducted in the past (and is conducted today) is instructive. The *Mahavagga* (Rhys Davids and Oldenberg 1881, pp. 242–5) records the procedure thus: 'He who has committed an offence, may confess it; if there is no offence you should remain silent...if a Bhikkhu, after a three-fold proclamation, does not confess an existing offence which he remembers, he commits an intentional falsehood.' Thus the practice is that the list of offences is read out and the brethren are asked three times after each item whether they are pure in this matter; 'only if a monk has anything to confess does he speak. It is then in the power of the assembly to prescribe some form of expiation. The offender may be rebuked, suspended or even expelled. But he must admit his guilt. Otherwise disciplinary measures are forbidden' (Eliot 1954, Vol. I, p. 244). Eliot sums up the organizational structure of the pristine monastic communities thus:

The Buddha's regulations contain no vow of obedience or recognition of rank other than simple seniority or the relation of teacher to pupil...In the *Sangha*, no monk could give orders to another: he who disobeyed the precepts of the order ceased to be a member of it *ipso facto*, or if he refused to comply with the expiation prescribed. Also there was no compulsion, no suppression of discussion, no delegated power to explain or supplement the truth. (p. 247.)

This ancient tradition that Buddhist monastic communities are democratic, self-governing organizations has relevance and a large degree of application to the contemporary *Sangha* in Thailand (and Ceylon), although the historical facts are complex. A true estimation of the persisting underlying organizational principles can only be arrived at after considering the relationship of Buddhism and the *Sangha* to kingship and the state;

[1] See relevant quotation from Thomas (1951), below, p. 80.

73

the administrative requirements stemming from the ownership of land and other endowments; and the size of the monastery itself, which is partially related to its location in urban or rural environments and to the kind of patronage it enjoyed or enjoys.

It would take us too far from the interests of this book if we considered these questions in detail, so I shall make only a few simplified statements. Buddhism in the so-called 'Theravada' countries came to have a recognized relationship with the state. By and large the theory of kingship and the rituals associated with it in Burma, Thailand and Cambodia were influenced by Indian brahmanical ideas. But there is a striking difference in that, unlike in India, the *brahmans* were confined to the court and were not a general caste or stratum in the society. Dumont has asserted that in India, *dharma* (morality), as represented by the *brahmans*, was superior to *artha* (power), as represented by the *kshatriya* ruler; morality legitimated power; *dharma* and *artha* in turn stood opposed to the inferior domain of *kama* (economy). In 'Theravada' countries there was no such *dharma* of the *brahmans* acting as a check on kingship.

A conception of *anacakra*, royal power, as opposed to *buddhacakra*, the spiritual power of the *Sangha* deriving from its inner discipline and the vocation of the monks, prevailed in Theravada countries. The king was indeed the protector, defender and patron of the *Sangha*, and at the very apex of the society there was a fusion of politics and religion, spiritual and secular power, to a degree perhaps unknown in India. Just as the status of *Chakravartin* (world ruler) was equated with that of Buddha (the idea being that a world conqueror and world renouncer are alike), so did the kings claim the title of embryo Buddha (*bodhisattva*), and the relics of the Buddha became the symbols of kingship and political autonomy. In this capacity, the king gave patronage to Buddhism: he built monasteries and temples, and endowed them with land. But he interfered little with ecclesiastical matters, and wherever monasteries were endowed with property they enjoyed autonomy in administering them, as well as judicial and fiscal exemptions and other immunities. In the heyday of such thriving monastic communities the differentiation of roles, the division of labour and bureaucratization of organization was complex (e.g. see Rahula 1956 for ancient Ceylon); but in contemporary Ceylon, the monastic bodies enjoying landed property (the Malwatte and Asgiriya chapters of the Siyam Nikaya) show a much looser and decentralized organization, more in line with the classical theory of localized communities and also with anthropological expectations of what might be expected in a society with certain types of kinship and caste institutions (e.g. see Evers 1967). Ceylonese 'sects' which arose in the nineteenth century, and which do not enjoy such landed property, are even more fragmented and decentralized (Ames 1963) and have resisted any interference by political authorities in respect of a more 'rational' and country-wide organization.[1]

Thailand in some ways exemplifies this decentralizing tendency. Land endowment to the monasteries by the king and laymen was customary, and the monasteries apparently enjoyed immunity of control from royal officers (Wales 1965). Today the association of royal temples with property is by no means great or spectacular. While some monasteries enjoy traditionally derived property, royal patronage consists of the *wat* having no more than a special status, with some superior-titled monks getting allowances from the state, and the prestige of royal presentations of robes and other gifts at the *Kathina* ceremony at the end of the Lenten season. Thus monastic communities enjoy in most matters a great autonomy. Their internal structure is loose. The only recognized position is that of the abbot (*chao wat*). In large monasteries there may be informal positions of deputies and assistants, or even groupings of monks into divisions (*gana*) with their heads. In small monasteries—especially in village *wat*—there is scarcely any formal hierarchy of office below the abbot. However, the assemblage is not altogether one of equals. The distinction between novice and monk, the distinctions of seniority of service, the relation between ordainer (*upacha*) and ordained, pupil and teacher, senior monk and junior monk attached to him, etc., are all important for the internal ordering of the monastic community.

What I have tried to say so far is that at the macro-level the relationship between king (and his administrative machinery) and the Buddhist *Sangha* (itself fragmented into separate communities and sects) was in the main one of patronage and protection without interference.

But the nature of this association has to be modified in two directions, although the essential point remains intact. There is evidence for ancient and medieval Ceylon that the *Sangha* had some influence on kingship and politics: kingship and the polity were infused with Buddhist meaning and identity, the coronation ritual over time shifted (in part at least) from a brahmanical to a Buddhist form, and various kings ceremonially dedicated their kingship and their realms to the *sasana* or even to the *Sangha*. Apart from these ideological and ceremonial features, it appears that the *Sangha* even played politics in earnest: it sometimes determined the succession to the throne, and its various sects competed for royal favour and patronage. (See Rahula 1956, Ariyapala 1956, Geiger 1960, Paranavitana in Ray (ed.), Vol. I, 1959, Ch. 9.)

However, the evidence, especially in modern times, shows a more

[1] An authority on this problem is Arnold Green, whose writings are as yet unpublished.

pronounced counter-tendency for the king and the political state to
influence the *Sangha*.

There are known instances in Ceylon, Burma and Thailand when the
king, as defender and protector of the religion, has 'purified the religion'—
such as settling schismatic disputes and rival claims of sects, or, when the
order of monks was in danger of dying out or was debased, re-establishing
it through new ordination succession (usually through the agency of
monks invited from other Buddhist countries). Not unrelated to these
reforms were moves made to ensure a *Sangha* loyal to the king and willing
to act in support of the regime.

The successful unification of a territory and the expansion of frontiers
by a king, with the increase of royal power through greater centralization
of control, has been paralleled in attempts to introduce some kind of
national hierarchy and unification in the Buddhist *Sangha*. Ceylon in
the eighteenth century under King Kirti Sri provides an example. Thailand,
which never became a colony, is an example in recent times, and its
achievement on a *formal* level is quite complete. There exists in Thailand
today a national ecclesiastical hierarchy which is largely the creation of
the central political government and in fact reflects the institutions and
divisions of civil and territorial jurisdiction. One should not underestimate
the importance of this official hierarchy for the organization and activities
of the *Sangha* as a whole. The hierarchy of officers and organs, and the
country-wide network of educational establishments are significant avenues
of social mobility and channels for the acquisition of prestige and power
in a political sense (see Appendix to this chapter).

Nevertheless, it is important to note that at the base of the system
are a multitude of local *wats* supported by lay congregations, headed by
abbots chosen by them (though ratified by the ecclesiastical superiors), and
in the main run as relatively autonomous monastic communities in close
integration with the villages or towns which maintain them. Important
connections between these localized *wats* produce regional networks which
are not the product of the official *Sangha* organization. This book is
concerned with the village *wat*, its monks, and its lay supporters in terms
of this latter perspective.

A different perspective, also important, looks at the various kinds of
links, including those in the official (formal) organization, which produce
a network of social relations, channels of mobility, levels of differentiation,
and a distribution of power at the level of the total society. This theme
is proper for a different and more ambitious work on Thai religion.

Monkhood in historical perspective

APPENDIX TO CHAPTER 5

A NOTE ON THE HIERARCHICAL STRUCTURE OF THE 'SANGHA' IN THAILAND

According to Wales (1965), in Thailand a national organization of the *Sangha* directly related to the political authority of the king and his administration only became established in the first reign of the present dynasty (which started in 1782).

Information concerning previous centuries is uncertain and does not indicate a national religious hierarchy. In thirteenth-century Sukhodaya, the office of *Sangharaja* is mentioned; in sixteenth-century Ayudhya, the administration of the order was for the first time divided into Northern and Southern divisions in the reign of Maha-dharmaraja. But De la Loubère (1693), who gives valuable information on the late seventeenth century, makes no mention of a hierarchy, only of heads of monasteries enjoying separate jurisdictions; there appears, though, to have been a respect hierarchy based on the distinction between abbots of royal *wat* and ordinary *wat*, with the head of the palace *wat* being the most respected of them all. De la Loubère deserves to be quoted in full, for his remarks throw light on the situation two centuries later.

Every convent is under the conduct of a superior called *Tchaou-Vat*,[1] that is to say, Lord or Master of the convent; but all the Superiors are not of equal dignity: the most honourable are those which they call *Sancrat*,[2] and *Sancrat* of the Convent of the Palace is the most reverend of all. Yet no superior, nor no *Sancrat*, has authority or jurisdiction over another...

The missionaries have compared the *Sancrats* to our bishops, and the simple superiors to our curates...None but the *Sancrats* indeed can make *talapoins*, as none but bishops can make priests. But otherwise the *Sancrats* have not any jurisdiction nor any authority, neither over the people, nor over the *talapoins*, which are not of their convent; and they could not inform me whether they have any particular character which makes them *Sancrats*, save that they are superiors of certain convents designed for *Sancrats*...

The King of Siam gives to the principal *Sancrats* a name, an umbrella, a sedan, and some men to carry it; but the *Sancrats* do not make use of this equipage, only to wait upon the king, and they never are *talapoins* that carry the sedan. The *Sancrat* of the palace is now called *Pra Viriat*. (p. 144.)

Definite information concerning political penetration into *Sangha* affairs comes to us from the reigns of Rama I (1782–1809) and the suc-

---

[1] *Chao-Wat.*

[2] *Sangharaja*: De la Loubère means by this term probably the abbots of royal *wat* who are given special titles.

ceeding monarchs of the Bangkok Period. A reorganization and revival appeared necessary after the ravages of the Burmese wars which destroyed the Ayudhya kingdom. The 'purification of the religion' went hand in hand with ensuring the loyalty and co-operation of monks. The decrees called *Kathmay Brah Sangha* dealt with details of monastic discipline and directives to lay officials to see that the disciplinary rules were implemented.

It was in the reign of Rama IV (Mongkut) (1851–68), who was himself previously a monk and who founded the Thammayuttika Sect, that a complex organization of the entire *Sangha* was instituted (see Wales 1965 for details).

A basic distinction was that between 'royal' monasteries and 'ordinary' or 'commoner' monasteries. The heads of the royal monasteries (*raja gana*) were appointed and installed by the king at the beginning of every reign. Each head was assisted by two officials also royally appointed. In contrast the heads and other officials of the ordinary monasteries were appointed by the people or by nobles who founded and supported the institution.

On top of this ground-level structure was erected the hierarchy. From the heads of the royal monasteries the king appointed four ecclesiastical officials (*Cau Gana Hyai*), each of whom with his assistant administered the four great departments into which the Order was divided: the Northern and Southern Divisions of the Mahanikaya Sect, the order of hermit monks who were distinguished from the scholar monks (*gantha dhurah*) although they belonged to the same Mahanikaya Sect, and lastly, the newly constituted Dhammayutika Sect (founded by King Rama IV).

The question is, how did the king (or rather the relevant governmental agency such as the Department of Religious Affairs) select monks for appointment to the ecclesiastical offices. One device was the holding of religious examinations under royal auspices and administered by the heads of royal monasteries. Degrees of *parian* for Pali studies were granted together with monthly payments from the treasury. (The hermit monks did not sit examinations and were thus excluded from high ecclesiastical office.)

Combined with the examination system was the ranking of ecclesiastical offices according to *sakti na* grades, as in the case of lay civil and military officials. The *sakti na*, as applied to civil and military hierarchies, was an index of the prestige of office and endowments that went with it. By applying the same system to the religious hierarchy, the higher ecclesiastical officers and monks who were holders of office or aspirants to it were brought in line with national structures of power and respect.

But it is clear that one ought not to exaggerate the relevance of this centralization and hierarchization for the multitude of small village and other *wats* founded and supported by the laity. The *Sangharaja's* jurisdiction over monks and monasteries was weak and ill-defined. He had everything to do with national projects such as revision of doctrinal texts, and little to do with the administration of individual monasteries. Thus breaches of discipline were ordinarily judged by heads of monasteries; some were adjudicated by the courts under the charge of the four departmental heads. In the case of serious crime the monk was unfrocked and handed over to a special secular court.

These administrative arrangements which took shape in the reign of Rama IV were the basis for further changes leading to the contemporary hierarchy in Thailand. An Act relating to the administration of the Buddhist *Sangha* was passed in the reign of Rama V in 1902; subsequent Acts of 1941 and 1963 have further modified and elaborated the system evolved in the previous century.[1]

The formal hierarchy as it exists today copies the pattern of the civil (territorial) administration and the high level (executive and legislative) institutions at the political centre (see Blanchard 1958). The king is in theory the final authority in all *Sangha* affairs. The *Sangha* is related directly to the government through the Department of Religious Affairs in the Ministry of Culture. This ministry disburses funds, administers temple properties, and issues legal directives. The ecclesiastical head of the Order is the Sangharaja (Prince or Patriarch of the Church), chosen by the king from the executive council of the Order. This body is a Council of Ministers chosen by the Patriarch with the consent of the Minister of Education. They are drawn partly from the legislative body (*Sangha Sabha*), also appointed by the Patriarch, and partly from the general body of monks. The administration is divided into four departments (Administration, Education, Propagation, and Public Works), each headed by a member of the Council of Ministers. These heads choose their own departmental subordinates. Quite separate from the departments are the various levels of ecclesiastical judicial courts whose members are appointed by the Patriarch in consultation with the Legislative Assembly.

Below these central ecclesiastical institutions are the territorial divisions. In descending order they are: nine regions, each headed by a commissioner; seventy-one provinces, each headed by a provincial head; districts in the charge of district heads; communes headed by commune heads; and finally the basic unit, the *wat* or monastery in charge of the abbot. Each superior level office controls the promotions of the next inferior grade.

[1] This is a description of the pre-1963 situation. The 1963 Act concentrated power in the hands of the Sangharaja and the Council of Elders (*Mahatherasamakhom*).

Buddhism and the spirit cults in North-east Thailand

The abbot of the local temple is ratified in office by his superior, but is initially chosen by his local congregation.

According to the promotion system, monks who wish to climb up this hierarchy are partly dependent on the passing of examinations, which are of two sorts: the *Nagtham* divided into three grades, and the more prestigious *Parian* grades (Pali studies) made up of six grades. Monasteries function as the educational establishments for the training of monks, and are subject to complex differentiation in size, prestige and financial endowment relative to their educational activities, especially in respect to Pali studies. In Bangkok there are two universities for monks. One could therefore speak of a national educational network which is important for the mobility of monks academically and administratively.

There is an honorific ranking system of monks which is dependent partly on scholarly attainments, and partly on administrative status backed by patronage. The titles, especially the superior ones, are usually attached to 'royal' *wats* and range from *Phraa Khruu*, various grades of *Phraa Raja Gana*, to the top level *Somdet* grades.

ADDITIONAL NOTE TO PAGE 73

Thomas (1951, pp. 22–3) succinctly describes the situation thus: 'Within [the *sima*] boundary each assembly was self-governing. There was no hierarchy, but seniority was reckoned by the number of years from ordination, nor did a central authority exist to check any tendency to change or development in new directions.'

6

THE RULES OF CONDUCT FOR MONKS, NOVICES, AND LAYMEN

As we have seen, early Buddhist tradition emphasized it was the *Dhamma* (doctrine) and the rules of discipline (as contained in the *Patimokkha*) that should bind the community of monks, who were recommended to decide on issues and exercise discipline in democratic collective assembly with full appreciation of the individuality and moral responsibility of each monk.

The shift from eremitical to cenobitical life was no doubt historically important. Whereas the poetical books of the *Tripitika*, especially the Songs of the Monks and the Nuns, are a panegyric on solitary meditation in the midst of nature's beauties, in the *Patimokkha* we breathe the atmosphere of conventional monastic establishments.

However, monastic life was still decisively different from the domestic life of a married householder. From one perspective the logical opposite of home is homelessness (the wanderer's life); but it is equally true to say that collective life among members of the same sex (as in monastic life) is also the logical opposite of family life, which is based on the difference between and therefore the symbiosis of the two sexes. Monasteries are also distinctive by virtue of being 'total institutions' in Goffman's sense (1961), that is, establishments whose encompassing or total character signifies a barrier to social intercourse with the world outside.

The paradoxical feature of the Buddhist *Sangha* is that, while its organizational form is anti-hierarchical and antagonistic to specifying status positions with associated competencies, the disciplinary rules which the monks have to follow are spelled out in such fine nagging detail. One answer to this paradox is that a de-emphasis on social structure and an emphasis on individual responsibility through the internalization of ethical rules is a consistent characteristic of salvation seekers who have renounced organized society. But the actual situation, as we shall see in this chapter, is more complicated.

The disciplinary rules find their most detailed expression in the Canonical text called the *Vinaya Pitaka* (especially the *Maha* and *Cullavaggas*). What is the relation between the *Patimokkha* and the *Vinaya*?

The *Patimokkha*, we have already seen, is a liturgical formulary or manual which states the rules governing the conduct of monks. The *Vinaya* contains the same precepts but they are accompanied by a vast quantity of explanatory matter. Some scholars believe that the *Patimokkha* manual is the original and the *Vinaya* an amplification of it. Rhys Davids and Oldenberg (1881, pp. ix-x) assert that the *Patimokkha* 'is one of the oldest, if not the oldest, of all Buddhist text-books; and it has been inserted in its entirety into the first part of the *Vinaya*, the *Vibhanga*'. Pachow (1951) confirms this view, considering the *Patimokkha* to be the oldest text in the *Vinaya Pitaka*. The method of amplification in the *Vinaya* proceeds thus: 'First, in each case there is a history of the circumstances under which the Buddha propounded the rule. Then comes the rule, and then the verbal glossary and commentary. Then follows an immense number of illustrations, cases in which, as it is stated, doubt arose whether a monk was guilty or not...' (Copleston 1892, p. 197). The Theravada tradition is that the *Vinaya* regulations are in a chronological sequence because they were pronounced by the Buddha himself as each incident or dispute arose in time.[1]

Since the core precepts are contained in the *Patimokkha* I shall use one version of the former to make a content analysis of the rules. There are in fact many versions of the *Patimokkha* (see Pachow 1951, 1953 for details).[2] I shall use here an English translation from a Pali version published in Thailand (Nanamoli Thera 1966).[3] The following are the traditionally recognized groupings of the rules.

1. *Parajika*, 'the four causes of defeat', crimes which are punished by expulsion from the Order.

2. *Sanghadidesa*, thirteen cases which entail the 'initial and subsequent meeting of the community', that call for suspension, penance and reinstatement by an assembly of at least twenty monks.

3. *Aniyata*, the two 'indefinite cases' that involve expulsion, suspension, or expiation according to circumstances.

4. *Nissaggiya Pacittiya*, thirty cases which entail expiation and forfeiture of articles (which monks have improperly taken or used).

---

[1] According to Theravada tradition the *Vinaya* rules were propounded by the Buddha, and the rules were collated at the First Council at Rajagriha soon after his death, with some modifications included after the Second Council at Vaisali in the fourth century B.C.

[2] The word *Pratimoksa* (in Sanskrit) has been differently interpreted in the texts: one acceptable meaning is 'towards deliverance'. There are a number of texts of the *Patimokkha* belonging to different schools with differences in the number of rules and the verbal content. It cannot be said that the texts were written at one point of time. Each also appears to have undergone changes with time.

[3] This is substantially the same as the translation published by Rhys Davids and Oldenberg (1881). Since there are minor differences, I prefer to use here a document actually used in Thailand today.

5. *Pacittiya dhamma*, ninety-two offences which entail expiation only.

6. *Patidesaniya dhamma*, four cases that must be confessed.

7. *Sekhiya*, seventy-four rules concerning observations and proprieties that must be recited.

8. *Adhikaranasamatha*, the 'seven cases of settlement of litigation', that is, the rules to be observed in conducting judicial investigations concerning the conduct of monks.

Rather than follow this classification or list the rules in detail I shall follow a different scheme, using my own labels to bring out the areas and order of emphasis portrayed by the rules.

(A) The four *parajika* offences, few in number, entail the extreme punishment of expulsion from the Order. Two offences are 'crimes against society' in general, which are not peculiarly religious in that most governments punish them. These crimes are: (1) theft of such nature that kings would punish by arrest and execution, imprisonment or banishment; and (2) homicide or inciting (or aiding and abetting) another to commit suicide. Some texts phrase (1) above as taking anything not given, even a blade of grass, an injunction which takes a serious view of any kind of theft.

If we then leave aside these two, the two remaining relate to sexual offence, namely a monk having sexual intercourse 'even with a female animal', which undermines the vocation of monkhood, and to crime against Buddhist doctrine by falsely claiming the superior state of a Noble one's (i.e. *arahat's*) knowledge and extraordinary qualities.

(B) It is in the classes of crimes other than the extreme *parajika* offences that we distinctly see the order of emphasis and weighting. The crimes which evoke the assembly of monks, suspension of the offender, his penance and reinstatement are concerned with two areas only: *sexual offences* which are short of intercourse but express lust or intention of lust; and offences detrimental to *monastic community life*. The sexual offences, which are meticulously enumerated, are of the following types: intentional ejection of semen (which certainly includes masturbation); any form of bodily contact with a woman; verbally suggesting or inviting sexual intercourse; receiving a robe from an unrelated *bhikkuni* (nun); and acting as an intermediary in marriage, concubinage or other sexual arrangement. The last offence indirectly points out that the vocation of monkhood is antithetical to and separated from marriage, the crucial institution of the life of a householder. 'A wise man should avoid married life (*abrahmacariyam*) as if it were a burning pit of live coals' (Dhammika Sutta).

On a par with these sexual offences are the following which deal with

83

relations between monks in collective monastic life and with the basis of monastic life itself. They are: falsely accusing another monk of one of the four major crimes (*parajika*); attempting to cause schism of the community either singly or in a group, resisting admonishment by fellow monks concerning the rules of discipline; not getting the assembly of monks to select or ratify the site of residence. It is also specified that the residence itself should be of a type which causes no harm to creatures and has a surrounding walk (for meditation and also, I may say, for separating spatially and symbolically the habitation of the monk from that of the layman). A final injunction is against a monk corrupting families by giving them gifts and thereby living on intimate terms with people of a village or town, a relationship which would attack the basis of monastic life.

(C) The third level of offences in the hierarchy—requiring expiation with forfeiture of the possessions in question—focuses on two themes which may be described as firm rejection of the way of life and occupations of the householder, and a careful enumeration of the improper ways of accepting and soliciting gifts from laymen, ways which in turn manifest the sin of avaricious acquisition and accumulation of possessions. What is noteworthy about these precepts is their manifestation of the double relation that on the one hand the monk's way of life is a rejection of the layman's, and on the other, that indeed a monk is in an elaborate relation of gift-acceptance from the layman.

The monk should not solicit robes from a layman except under certain stipulated conditions; he should not accept robes in excess of his needs; without being invited to do so, he should not instruct the giver how the robe should be made or what quality of robe should be purchased on his behalf.

The injunctions against the handling of money and against directly engaging in trading transactions are conspicuous. A monk should not directly accept from a donor the price of a robe, but may direct the donor to entrust the money to the monk's steward, who is expected to hold it in trust. A monk should not pick up or cause to be deposited for his personal use gold or silver.

Furthermore, possessions that suggest a life of luxury or of aesthetic pleasure are denied a monk: items listed are silk rugs, felt rugs of black wool (the latter should be disfigured by adding other colours), etc. The possession and eating of rich foods (such as ghee, butter, honey, molasses) outside of specified circumstances (usually relating to sickness) is also punished by expiation and forfeiture. Other, less serious venal offences, such as using a bed or chair upholstered with cotton, and asking for and eating rich foods, call only for expiation.

The rules of conduct

(D) The rules at the next level are the largest in number, ranging over many spheres, and together make up the cluster of attributes that ordinarily characterize a monk. Infringement of these rules requires only simple expiation (through confession and absolution). The behavioural areas are distinguishable as follows.

Sexual improprieties: these improprieties relate to conduct that may give a second or third party the impression of immorality, or may lead the monk to the actual commission of an offence. Thus a monk must not be found seated alone with a woman; he must not intrude upon and sit in the bedroom of a man and his wife if one or the other objects; he must not sleep under the same roof with a woman (even if they are physically in different places). Rules regarding proper behaviour with a *bhikkhuni* are listed: a monk should not give a robe to a *bhikkhuni* who is not related (except as an exchange); he should not 'exhort' *bhikkhuni* without the permission of other *bhikkhus*, and never after sundown. He should not sit with a *bhikkhuni* or go on a journey with her (or any other woman) by appointment.

Separation from the layman and his way of life: A monk may not sleep more than two or three nights in the company of a layman. He should not dig the earth, or cause it to be dug, nor should he damage plants. This injunction virtually rules out the monk's engaging in agricultural work.

Perhaps even more telling is that a monk may not rehearse the *Dhamma* word by word (with text and commentary) with one who has not been admitted to the Order. The discrimination against a woman—presumably on the grounds of her inferior chances of salvation and her dangerous sexual attributes—goes one step further. A woman may not be taught more than five or six sentences of the *Dhamma* without an intelligent man being present. Furthermore, a monk may not make the claim to a layman that he has attained a 'superior human state'.

Behaviour towards fellow monks: expiation is required if a monk hits another monk, makes a threatening gesture towards him, provokes him, eavesdrops when other monks are disputing, etc. A monk is urged to put away furniture after use, not to deny a fellow monk room to sleep, and to desist from other acts which might endanger the physical safety of his brethren. Other offences against the Order are fully admitting a person under twenty years of age to the Order when his age is known, and disparaging the training precepts and the law that the Buddha taught.

Food: restraint in the consumption of food is much elaborated upon. The well-known rule is that the monk should not consume food between noon and the following morning. Other rules specify that a *bhikkhu* (unless sick) may not eat more than one meal at a place of food distribution, should not receive from lay donors cakes and sweets in excess (which in any case he should share with other *bhikkhus*), should neither ask for nor consume superior foods, etc.

Non-violence: the last major category of rules relates to the theme of non-violence and *ahimsa*. It is important that a monk's way of life be sharply distinguished from activities that lead to the taking of life; this theme is also strongly emphasized in the Jaina religion and ranks very high in the brahmanical code. The rules, which form an interconnected cluster, are: drinking wines and spirits ('maddening', hence conducive to violence), depriving any living creature of its life, using water with knowledge that it contains living things. A rejection of the military code is expressed in the injunction that a monk should not visit an army in full array without suitable reason; and if he does so with good reason, he should not visit the battlefield or witness an exercise or parade.

(E) The final set of some seventy-five rules is merely recited in the form 'I shall' and 'I shall not'. As a rough classification, these rules elaborate on the proper demeanour and manners of a monk and the proper demeanour and respect a layman should show a monk when the latter is expounding the doctrine to him. Under the former are minute specifications about the proper manner of wearing the robe, of sitting and walking, of tranquil body posture, of eating without noise and greed, of accepting food, etc. The proper etiquette a monk should expect from a layman is carefully stated. A monk should not expound to a man who has an umbrella (or stick) in his hand, or wears shoes, or wields a weapon, or is in a vehicle, or is lying in an easy chair, or has his head covered, or is sitting while the monk is standing. Some of these disrespectful gestures do not apply to a sick person.

The reader will have noted that the '227' rules are wide in range, uneven in the topics they relate to, and that many are concerned with minute details of conduct. Rather than accounting for this content in terms of a collection of historically disparate elements brought together in an accidental or arbitrary manner, it is more revealing to view the rules as representing those aspects of conduct that have come to be emphasized and considered important in monastic life. The minute enumerations are an index of behavioural emphasis and preoccupations.

The hierarchy of emphasis judged in terms of seriousness of offence may be briefly summarized as follows.

If we exclude the grave social crimes (theft and homicide), the major emphasis is put on sexual offences and on those that would undermine the life of a monastic community. The eschewing of sexual activity (the ideal of celibacy) (*brahmacharya*) is not only a major requirement for emancipation from suffering and desire, but is in a sense a prime index of the salvation quest. Moreover, it is clear that the salvation quest in organized Buddhism is to be undertaken in a community of fellow monks, the lonely seeker being exceptional.

Next priority is given to formulating the ethics of taking gifts from laymen and to vigilance against the temptations of money, wealth and possessions. The meticulous ethics of receiving gifts is also an indirect statement of how necessary this material dependence on the layman is if the monk is to follow his quest.

A lesser category of offences has a wider span, elaborating on the themes already stated. It deals with minor sexual improprieties, and with restraint in the acceptance and consumption of food; it emphasizes the separation of the monk's way of life from that of the layman, both physically and occupationally; it also emphasizes that the full doctrine cannot be transmitted to the layman but is a preserve of the monks; and it develops the theme of non-violence and the abhorrence of military pursuits.

Finally we have the rules of conduct which are simply recited. They relate to the demeanour of the monk, and to the demeanour of the layman appropriate for being taught the Law.

From the standpoint of a numerical measurement, we see that the less serious offences are more numerous in kind than the more serious. This of course may be true of any hierarchy of offences. But the meticulous listing of details of behaviour relating to the minor offences is indicative not only of what most monks are in danger of committing but also of the kind of outward form of conduct which is taken to symbolize and express the *bhikkhu's* special mode of life.

The *Patimokkha* defines the basis of monastic life and the proper conduct of a monk. In this sense it is a kind of charter or constitution (although it does not by itself exhaust the techniques and methods of the salvation quest). If we accept it as a yardstick in this limited sense, then it is revealing to make a digression and contrast the *Patimokkha* with the charter of one tradition of Christian monastic life, for this contrast will help to bring out the special features of Buddhist monachism.

It is not to the 'desert monks'—the Egyptian and Syrian monks of the early centuries A.D., who in isolation were concerned with the individual soul in its interior life—that I wish to refer, but to *The Rule of Saint Benedict* which provided the basis for Christian monastic life for some five hundred years (*c.* A.D. 650–*c.* 1150).

The Rule is a relatively short piece of writing. And yet it has liturgical and penal provisions, formal precepts and practical advice, and legislation on every department of monastic life, as well as spiritual instruction. What is of especial interest is the kind of monastic life envisaged by *The Rule*, in both its internal structure and its relation to the world at large. The monastery, which *The Rule* describes,

is a unit, completely self-contained and self-sufficient, both economically and constitutionally. A community, ruled by an abbot elected by the monks for life, is supported by the produce of its fields and garden and has within the wall of its enclosure all that is necessary to convert the produce into food and to make and repair clothing and other articles of common use (Knowles 1963, p. 4).

Its inmates were to serve God and sanctify their souls apart from the life of the world. No work done within its walls was to be directed to an end outside them, even should it give material or spiritual relief to dependants or those in the neighbourhood. The inmates were to be concerned with three activities: *Opus Dei* (liturgical service), *lectio divina* (spiritual reading), and *opus manuum* (manual work). The monks would engage in manual work—domestic activities, farming and crafts, etc.— although not themselves doing all the necessary manual labour, depending on *coloni* to do much of the normal heavy work.

Compared with the statutes of Christian orders, the *Vinaya* shows remarkable differences. The Buddha did not consider it important to provide in monastic life for work, obedience, or worship. And the philosophy of manual labour as an essential part of monastic life, acting as a defence against evil thoughts and the temptations of the flesh, was not a part of the Buddha's thought system, which was concerned with the conquest of mental defilement, not its displacement. While the Benedictine *Rule* and the *Patimokkha* are similar in their ideals of simplicity, community of life, silence and spiritual quest, it is the differences that are dramatic. The Benedictine life entailed the rules of strict obedience to a master abbot, a completely self-sufficient mode of life with minimal contact with the laity, as well as the emphasis on manual work which, apart from its moral effect, would ensure the satisfaction of the material needs of the monks. In contrast, the *Patimokkha* is to a large degree concerned with the regulation of the dealings of monks with the laity on whom they are materially dependent. And it gives little attention to the machinery of discipline enforcement within the *Sangha*.

Placed in its historical context, the Benedictine conception is understandable. The ancient world with its city life, its seats of culture and communication facilities, was rapidly disappearing; in the new world coming into being the estate, village and district were the social units, and society was becoming an aggregate of cells bound to one another by the loosest of ties. St Benedict's monastery was a microcosm of this world, and when later the feudal state emerged in the eleventh century the Benedictine model decayed, and new monastic orders sprang up to meet the complexities of the new society.

To return to the Buddhist precepts. There is a gradation from the 227 precepts which apply to the *bhikkhu*, to the ten, eight and five precepts which apply with subtle distinctions to novices (*samanera*) and householders (*gahapati*).

The five precepts (*pancha sila*) are doctrinal prescriptions that apply to laymen who consider themselves Buddhists. They are abstinence from the destruction of life, from taking what is not given, from fornication (also rendered by some as 'adultery'), from speaking falsely, from consuming spiritous, strong and maddening liquors which are the cause of sloth. Obeyesekere (1968) has commented perceptively on the nature of these precepts. He rightly points out that the precepts are not worded as categorical imperatives or commandments in the Biblical sense, that they lack specificity and precision of formulation, and that because they are impossible to conform to in the fullest sense, they are capable of adaptations and interpretations suited to the local context in which Buddhism exists.

It is readily apparent that there is a spectacular gap between the 227 precepts of the monks, which are formulated positively as a code of conduct, and the five precepts for the householder formulated as exhortations to avoid excess. This once again dramatizes the disjunction between the two modes of life, that whereas the monk is orientated to salvation the layman is orientated to a better rebirth.

Another point needs to be made, however. From an historical (but not doctrinal) point of view it can be said that the five precepts are the fundamentals and the cardinal rules from which many of the more detailed and specific rules of the *Patimokkha* have been elaborated. The precept of sexual restraint is transformed into the state of celibacy (*brahmacharya*) for the *bhikkhu*, minutely elaborated upon. The rule for the layman regarding the proper acceptance or taking of things gives rise in the case of the monk to the rules of gift acceptance from the laity and the proscriptions against avarice, greed and property accumulation. Around prohibition of the destruction of and injury to living creatures are woven the elaborate rules of non-violence. False speech is the essential theme of the rules regulating monastic life and protecting the doctrine. The quantitative increase in rules at some point changes into the qualitatively different life of the *bhikkhu*. Furthermore, these rules are the common basis of the brahmanical codes and the Jaina religion. The brahmanical *pancha sila* differs from the Buddhist only in one respect (if we ignore verbal nuances): it substitutes 'liberality' for the liquor clause (the consumption of liquor being tabooed anyway); and the Jains substitute for the same clause the renunciation or devaluation of interest in worldly things (*aparigraha*).

With the addition of three specific rather than general avoidances, we get the eight precepts. The three additional avoidances may be voluntarily undertaken, by a layman, either permanently or more commonly temporarily on fortnightly *uposatha* days or on the four-a-month 'sabbath' (*poya* in Ceylon, *wanphraa* or *wansil* in Thailand) days. These are avoidance of eating after midday, of witnessing displays of music, song and dance, and of the use of garlands, scents, unguents.

An additional two—the avoidance of the use of seats or couches above a prescribed height and of receiving gold or silver—complete the ten precepts, which again may be voluntarily followed by the layman.

Now these ten precepts which a layman may voluntarily observe are those *obligatorily* avowed by the novice (*samanera*) at his initiation ceremony. They therefore also form a part of the *bhikkhu*'s way of life for his morality is inclusive of the lower states. Correspondingly any pious layman who practises the eight or ten precepts—commonly called *upasaka* (male), *upasika* (female)—is seen as approaching the *bhikkhu*'s or the world renouncer's way of life. But typically in Buddhist countries like Ceylon, Burma and Thailand, this pious layman is an old person who is approaching death and is both socially ready and mentally inclined to remove himself or herself from the entanglements of society.

The novice is distinctly different from the *upasaka*. He is initiated, lives in the monastery, wears robes, and has his head shaved. Typically he is a youth (minimally eight years old) and can later on become a monk. He performs some of the functions of the monk—he can administer the five and eight precepts to a layman[1] and conduct Buddhist rituals and recite a sermon—as the monk does. He is, while in robes, ruled by the ten precepts. Any layman is obliged to pay him the same respect in gesture and language as he does the *bhikkhu*. At the same time, there is a distinct gap between monk and novice: a novice is not strictly a member of the *Sangha*, and is excluded from the deliberations of the monastic assembly concerning matters of discipline and government. His inferiority in the monastery is expressed daily in the fact that he cannot eat in the circle or group consisting of monks; novices eat separately, even if the 'separation' is only a gap in the line of eaters.

---

[1] Sometimes an *upasaka* administers the precepts without the intervention of the monk or novice. 'Administer' simply means that the monk (or *upasaka*) recites each precept first and the layman repeats after him.

The rules of conduct

The gradation of precepts gives us a gradation of statuses: monk, novice, *upasaka*, and ordinary householder. The statuses separate and combine in pairs in many ways. But what these statuses and their inter-relations mean in village religion can only be seen in terms of village ethnography. But before taking that up, as we shall later, we should here seek another level of understanding by comparing the Buddhist statuses on the path or stream of salvation with the brahmanical formulations.

The obvious basis for comparison is the Hindu four stages of life: *brahmacharin* (celibate student), *grahasta* (householder), *vanaprasta* (hermit existence and retirement from secular life), and finally *sannyasin* (world renouncer). A final formulation of the theory in Hinduism is that these statuses represent stages in a life cycle and that each status is *required* and *precedes* the latter. As I have stated before, the *sannyasin* conception is radically opposed to the classical Vedic conception of the natural progression of the other three statuses, but is capable of neat incorporation as the final stage. In actuality, the *sannyasin* stage is not the culmination for the majority of persons, and the true *sannyasin* is likely to reject the world some time before he has actually acquitted the obligations of a householder and head of a family.

The Buddhist statuses present a different configuration. In a sense the novice corresponds to the celibate *brahmacharin*. But from this threshold he can pass on, at the virile age of twenty, to the superior state of *bhikkhu*, the mendicant and goer-forth from home into monastic life, the incomplete but partial analogue of the *sannyasin* (the truer Buddhist counterpart being the hermit monk). The *Sangha* thus is primarily composed of celibates in the prime of adult life.

The Buddhist layman in comparison passes from the state of house-holder to the analogue of the Hindu *vanaprasta* in the role of *upasaka*, and this is in conformity with a life cycle from youth to old age.

The four Buddhist statuses cannot in theory fit into a single life cycle. But in fact in Thailand (as in Burma) the statuses, as stations in life, have been successfully arranged into one cycle, for those who want to follow it. The manipulation is made possible by the classical Buddhist privilege that a man in robes may give them up and return to the lower secular state if he has not found in the doctrine a resting place. As *The Questions of King Milinda* put it: there are ten things that cause a man to neglect the assumption of the yellow robe or tempt him to cast it off: the mother, the father, the wife, children, poor relations who need to be provided for, friends, property, desire for wealth or for worldly honour, and the love of pleasure.

Buddhism and the spirit cults in North-east Thailand

LAY MORALITY FROM A DOCTRINAL POINT OF VIEW

I conclude this chapter with a statement of what can be gleaned from some of the doctrinal texts as regards the recommended conduct for the layman. Let me emphasize that the results of this inquiry cannot be expected to tell us in any complete sense what norms direct the behaviour of contemporary Thai villagers or how villagers relate these norms to classical Buddhist values.

It is clear that, as taught by the teachings of the Buddha, salvation is best attainable by those of the homeless *bhikkhu* state, and that there is a gap between the way of the monk and the life of the laity, who can practise only a lower form of righteousness. The ethic of non-action and pure contemplation is the ideal way of the monk: 'whoever would do good deeds, should not become a monk'.

The ethic of conduct promulgated by early Buddhism for the ordinary householder was not elaborate. I have already discussed the five precepts. Other avoidances and exhortations appear in the texts. Certain trades were expressly forbidden the *upasaka* (lay disciple), namely the butcher's trade, caravan trade, and trade in weapons, poison, alcohol and slaves. The Sigalovada Suttanta, which Buddhagosa rendered as 'The *Vinaya* of the Houseman', is supposed to be Buddha's explicit statement on the whole domestic and social duty of the Buddhist layman. In this homily, Buddha gives Sigala many admonitions on how to avoid six channels of dissipating wealth and how to protect the six quarters: parents as the east, teachers as the south, wife and children as the west, friends and companions as the north, servants and work people as the nadir, religious teachers and *brahmans* as the zenith. Buddha once told another layman that out of his income he should spend one part for his daily needs, invest two parts in his business, and save the fourth part for an emergency.

In the Noble Eightfold Path, or the Middle Path, proposed by the Buddha as leading to the cessation of *dukkha* (suffering), three categories comprise ethical conduct (*sila*)—namely, right speech, right action, and right livelihood—all of which as far as the layman is concerned are defined by the avoidances and admonitions stated earlier. To these we may add exhortations to listen to sermons and temporary asceticism (observance of eight or ten precepts). But one obligation of the pious layman was singled out for emphasis and has come to loom large in religious conduct as defining the concept of *dana* (generosity)—that is the duty of materially supporting the homeless holy seekers. The insistence by the Buddha that the salvation seeker be a homeless wanderer, carrying about him the minimum material needs, made it incumbent on the laity to fill the begging bowls with food. *Dana* came to constitute one of the highest merits available to the lay disciple. The giving of *dana* stems naturally from the story of Buddha himself and his disciples who were invited to meals by the converted layman. ('And Sonadanda the Brahmin satisfied the Blessed One, and the brethren, with his own hand, with sweet food, both hard and soft, until they refused any more'—Sonadanda Sutta (Rhys Davids, Vol. II, 1899, Ch. 4).) In the homily that Buddha preached to Sigala, often taken to be his most comprehensive discourse on the duties of a layman, he is reported to have said: 'In five ways should the clansman minister to recluses and Brahmins as the zenith: by affection in act and speech and mind; by keeping open house to them, by supplying their temporal needs.' In due course support of the religion included building *vihares* and *dagobas*, and making gifts of land and other material goods to the *Sangha*. Such acts took form as the visible expressions of piety, inculcated by the monks themselves in their preachings.

The Pali Canon as such has little to say on the beneficial effects of the practice of *dana* for the layman. We have to turn to the later non-Canonical literature to find such discourse. *The Questions of King Milinda*, which is an early document (Rhys Davids 1963, Part II), began to formulate a doctrine which was later elaborated on in writings for the edification of the laity. For instance, the Forty-Ninth Dilemma poses the question of gifts to the Buddha. On the one hand, the Buddha refused to 'chaunt for wage' ('Gifts chaunted for in sacred hymns/Are gifts I must not take...'), but on the other hand, when preaching the truth, he was in the habit of beginning with the so-called 'preliminary discourse', in which giving took first place and goodness only the second. To this contradiction Nagasena answered that it was the custom of all the Tathagatas to begin with a discourse on alms-giving in order to make the hearts of hearers inclined to the sermon, and then afterwards to urge them to righteousness. 'The supporters of the faith, O king, the lordly givers, have their hearts thus softened, made tender affected. Thereby do they cross over to the further shore of the ocean of transmigration by the aid of the boat of their gifts, by the support of the cause-way of their gifts.'

The Forty-First Dilemma poses the question of why houses should be built for the homeless ones and why this act should be recommended as meritorious. Besides pointing out the advantage of dwelling places to monks, Nagasena pronounced that those who make such donations 'shall be delivered from rebirth, old age and death'.

I have elsewhere (Tambiah 1963) referred to Sinhalese literature extolling the benefits of good deeds to the *Sangha*. I shall here mention one example because it aptly describes the orientations and aspirations of Thai villagers, especially those hopes associated with Maitreya, the coming Buddha. The example is taken from the *Pujavaliya* (The History of Offerings), which was written in the thirteenth century. It gives an account of all the offerings which the Master received as a *bodhisattva*. A most explicit exhortation to an ethic of deeds is contained in the dialogue between Buddha and his chief disciple, Sariputta, given in the *Anagathavansa Desana*. Sariputta beseeches the Buddha to tell him when the next Buddha, Maitreya, will be born and what his nature will be. The Buddha sets out in detail who will and who will not see the holy one: among those who are to be rewarded with *chakravarti* pleasures and sight of Maitreya are those who build monasteries, *vihares*, preaching halls, resting places, plant bo trees, and minister to the needs of the priesthood by donating food, clothes, fans and incense. 'In short if one flower, one lamp or one spoonful of rice is given on behalf of the three *ratnas* (triple gem) and if appropriate *pratana* (wish) is made, that person, O! Sariputta, will see Maitri Buddha and escape from samsara (cycle of rebirths).'

In Thailand, as in Ceylon, the possibility of attaining these earthly ideals is expressed in the lay donor's uttered wish which accompanies the gift; and the monks' 'statement of merit' (*pinvakya* in Sinhalese) recited after acceptance. A Sinhalese *pinvakya* is worth quoting here, for it interjects between now and the final birth many lives of earthly and heavenly splendour, to be climaxed at the very end, in the distant future, by final extinction and the appearance of the saviour Maitreya.

Having first made offering to the Buddha | Now this *dana* offering to the Maha Sangha. | On account of merit thereby acquired | From now till attainment of final birth. | May you not be born in the four hells, but in the six heavens. | Like Chaturmaharajikaya (Sakra's abode), enjoy life there, | Then be born in noble castes in the human world, | Acquire wealth in elephants, horses, cattle and buffaloes, | Attended by thousands of servants live happily, | And when Maitri Buddha is born on earth | See his noble qualities | Serve him in many ways | Listen to his great preaching and wish to become | One of the three *bodhis*, Buddha, Pace Buddha, Arahat | And to attain the great wealth (*sampath*) of *nirvana*, | May you and your dead relatives and friends | All be fortunate; so imagining | With joy of mind this merit should be received.

A question posed by those who take as their point of departure the classical doctrine is whether the Buddha's admonitions to the layman constituted a systematic positive code of conduct for everyday life. Max Weber, for instance, came to the conclusion that the lay morality propounded by Buddhism 'bore the character of an extremely colourless "bourgeois" ethic'. This conclusion was presumably derived from early Buddhism's alleged lack of direct concern with the social order, and the

94

paucity of its precepts and their formulation in terms of rather vague exhortations to avoidance of certain excesses. Hence the content that poured into them can be varied and fluid, depending on the social environment in which Buddhism takes root.

This method of argument can be pursued as well from the standpoint of comparative religion. Thus it can be said that medieval Christianity formulated a methodical lay morality for an organic society (which took a stratified social order for granted) in terms of a status relativism which enabled different persons in the social order to follow different prescribed paths to salvation, and integrated these ethical endeavours with the imperatives of the social order. Mature Hinduism wrought a similar design: paralleling the caste system, which in itself was a religious design, was the idea of different paths to salvation—the way of ritual, the way of *bhakti* (adoration), the way of *yoga* (mental discipline), etc. It is said that Buddhism contains no such complex conception of status relativism linked with the social order, and instead holds a different kind of prospect: each person, whatever his present station in life, can through a succession of future lives rise up and enter the path of salvation. In the end salvation is possible for all, and is not tied to the moral consequences of one single finite life as in the Christian conception. Hinduism by comparison, while firmly grounded in the theory of ethical causation (*karma*) and cycle of rebirths (*samsara*), translated present existence into an ethic of caste-bound morality through the concept of *dharma* (morality). In Buddhism the only firm structuring is the distinction between the monk's superior mode of life and the layman's inferior path; the elaborations concern the former while the latter is an ill-mapped thoroughfare.

A continuation of this mode of analysis—the deriving of deductive inferences from doctrinal tenets—can lead to further propositions. Thus Max Weber has argued that although early Buddhism did evolve some kind of secondary morality for the laity 'it in no way satisfied the specifically religious need for emotional experience of the superworldly and for emotional aid in external and internal distress. Such unsatisfied emotional needs were and are always decisive for the psychological character of all soteriologies of intellectuals.' Hocart, in a different context, argued that Buddhism, being essentially philosophical and rationalistic, provided no consolation for or relief from the mundane distresses and crises of life; and that under such conditions cults, dealing with the powers of darkness, and a corresponding priesthood, dealing with death and decay, must develop. 'If one section (excellent castes) may not concern itself with the inauspicious ritual of death for fear of contaminating the auspicious ritual of life, then some other section must handle death and decay, for

95

these are inexorable facts which must be dealt with' (Hocart 1950, p.19). This deductive logic escalates further to postulate that since the lower ethic fashioned for the laity was not integrated with a salvation goal, lay religion would not later on take the course of innerworldly puritanical asceticism but that of a ritualistic 'idolatrous' religion.[1] In the light of these considerations regarding the nature of pristine Buddhism on the one hand, and the religious needs of the masses on the other, it has been argued that the cult of magic and of saviours will develop.

The foregoing paragraphs indicate well the limiting and restrictive nature—and sometimes the excessive character—of deductions from a certain kind of premise. It is not so much that such deductions are wrong but that they tell us very little about the structure and texture of a people's religious system. From the fact that doctrinal Buddhism did not contain an elaborate ethical code for the layman it is erroneous to postulate that this is a permanent feature of any contemporary people without first investigating their pattern of life in terms of their own formulations. Secondly, to argue that because pristine Buddhism was of a certain sort, certain other religious cults would grow up to fill in the vacuum of its deficiencies is not only to work with a dubious historical hypothesis but indeed to misunderstand the complex nature of religious systems in general. Between the pseudo-historical argument that magical animism develops among the masses (who are 'idolatrous' anyway!) in order to complement the one-sidedness of Buddhism, and the structural logic which postulates that any religious system as a totality is necessarily arranged in terms of oppositions, complementarities, dialectical tensions and hierarchical positions, I prefer the latter, because it is less prejudicial to the discovery and understanding of the ethnographic facts. It is not the above-mentioned Weberian deductions on which I shall rely when later on I unfurl the rich embroidery of Thai religion.

[1] For instance, consider the following quotation from Weber (Gerth and Mills 1946): 'Wherever the promises of the prophet or the redeemer have not sufficiently met the needs of the socially less-favored strata, a secondary salvation religion of the masses has regularly developed beneath the official doctrine' (p. 274). Max Weber's view of the masses was that by themselves they have remained 'engulfed in the massive and archaic growth of magic—unless a prophecy that holds out specific promises has swept them into a religious movement of an ethical character' (p. 277).

7

THE PHASES OF MONKHOOD

The *samanera* and the *bhikkhu* are two religious statuses recognized in
traditional Buddhism and found in all Theravada countries. The *samanera*
(*neen* in North-eastern Thai) is usually translated as 'novice'. The word
itself means 'ascetic'. The classical rule is that to be admitted as novice
the candidate must be at least eight years of age. We have already noted
that a novice is not properly a member of the *Sangha*. Although he can
conduct certain rites he cannot take part in the assembly of monks dealing
with matters of discipline and administration. He is subject to the observance
of ten precepts.

The *bhikkhu* (*phraa* in Thai) alone receives the *upasampada* (ordination).
Bhikkhu means 'mendicant' and is usually rendered in English as 'monk'.
The classical rule is that to become a monk a man must be at least twenty
years of age, and on ordination he undertakes to observe the 227 precepts.
It is also set down in traditional texts that in order to become a novice
or a monk the candidate should have obtained the consent of his parents,
and that he is debarred if he is suffering from certain diseases (including
epilepsy and leprosy) or if he is in debt, or is a slave or a soldier (or
otherwise engaged in the king's service).

The ceremonies by which a novice is admitted and a monk ordained
are also set down in texts and the Theravada countries follow fairly
closely the prescribed procedure. But there are sequences and details of
great anthropological interest that have been incorporated into the rites,
and which I shall describe later as witnessed in Baan Phraan Muan.

The ideal progression in the North-east (and in Central Thailand) was
one through three positions: from *dekwat* (temple boy) to novice to
monk. (In actual practice there have been and are discontinuities which
have increased in recent times.)

The *dekwat* is a young boy who lives either in the *wat* or in the village
with his parents, who ministers to the needs of monks and novices, and
is at the same time taught the rudiments of reading and writing at the
school run by the monks. This is the traditional conception, and, apart
from the fact it was by being a *dekwat* that a village boy could in the past
(when no government-run schools existed) learn to read and write, it is
clear this preliminary training was for some of the boys the first stage in
the ladder of religious statuses.

Thus while today, in the village of Baan Phraan Muan, the institution of *dekwat* is non-existent, it was important in the past. Around the turn of this century the abbot of the local *wat* ran a school for about six or seven boys who lived in the *wat*. They were taught to read and write the Thai script. By about 1930 the government had proclaimed a programme of compulsory primary education. The abbot still ran the school and was paid for it, but the number of students, boys and girls, had swelled to eighty, and it was not necessary any more to be a *dekwat* in order to learn.[1] Soon afterwards secular teachers were appointed, and although until 1966 the school was held in the *wat* premises—in the *sala* (preaching hall)—it had become divorced from the control and participation of the resident monks and novices.

A word also about the religious status of *bhikkhuni* (female mendicant), usually translated as 'nun'. Although ordained nuns were a feature of ancient Buddhist India and appear to have been a feature of Thailand in the past, it is said that the ordination succession has been lost. There are no *bhikkhuni* in the village of Phraan Muan. In other parts of Thailand there are some (old) women who, though not initiated, approximate this vocation, but they are not held in esteem and are peripheral to institutional Buddhism. The salvation quest is very much a male pursuit. The inferiority of women in respect of the Buddhist quest is doctrinally well established. But we shall see that they can receive the fruits of male merit acquisition and are in important ways the 'support' of the religion.

NOVICES AND MONKS

In theory novicehood not only precedes monkhood but is a preparation for it. The religious vocation in Buddhism (as in any of the 'world religions' which have their dogma and doctrine set out in texts) can be followed properly only with the aid of literacy. A novice therefore is supposed to acquire progressively over the years the doctrinal knowledge, to learn the chants and the ritual procedures. Then as a monk he ascends into the higher reaches of Buddhism. While this conventional progression was to some extent true in the past, it is much less evident today. It is therefore necessary to establish the underlying pattern and the contemporary changes.

Novicehood is entered upon in adolescence, usually between the ages

---

[1] The institution of *dekwat* still prevails in many parts of Thailand. Paradoxically, it is on the wane in the villages and persists with greater strength in urban monasteries. The answer to this paradox is that poor or kinless village children attending superior urban schools get free board and lodging in return for relatively light service as page boys for the monks.

of twelve and eighteen. A requirement (which is a regulation of the *Sangha*) today is that a candidate shall have passed the fourth grade in the primary school. In the past it would appear that most novices were initiated in late adolescence—after a gap of some years following the early schooling as *dekwat*. It was usual for a good number of these novices to stay in the *wat* until they were twenty years old and then to become ordained as monks. Thus in terms of numbers novicehood was not in the past (nor is it today) a popular form of religious service, for adolescents became novices primarily in order to learn for a couple of years as a prelude to monkhood of *some duration, if not life-long vocation.* (Quite distinct from this kind of novicehood is the institution of temporary novicehood that is entered upon for a few weeks by grandsons or sons to make merit for a dead grandparent or parent.)

Both traditionally and today, the usual time for becoming a monk is early adulthood (twenty to twenty-one years), and *prior to marriage.* In the village it is unusual for a married man to renounce family life; however, as might be expected, it is not unknown for an old man to become a monk towards the end of his life, especially when he is no longer a family head or has no family.

The formal restrictions to entry as novice or monk are in practice minimal. We have seen that a minimum educational qualification is required of the novice (and therefore of the monk). Formal permission to be initiated is obtained from the *tambon* (commune) abbot. This is really a paper formality and virtually all village candidates for ordination are accepted, provided the local village abbot agrees to recommend. The ordination ritual asks of the candidate whether he is free of certain impediments which are not seriously restrictive.

There are two remarkable divergencies in the village from the doctrinal assertion regarding the salvation quest of the monk as a world-renouncer. First, that both in the past and in the present, ordination to monkhood has been more popular than novicehood; secondly, the period of service as monk has been for the vast majority of cases of short duration, followed by resumption of lay life, marriage, and the founding of a family. A minority continue as professional monks, but are not necessarily committed to life-long service. This feature calls for an anthropological interpretation, since no explanation is provided by the doctrinal texts.

There are elders in the village who have travelled the path from temple boy to novice to monk and then to lay life. The following biographical facts, relating to three elders who are the village's most illustrious citizens, provide good illustration. Phautu Phan ('Grandfather Phan'), who is over seventy years old (1966), is the village's most renowned *mau ya* (physician) as well as *mau khwan* (lay ritual officiant at *khwan* ceremonies), and a leader of the lay congregation at Buddhist rites. From the age of twelve to sixteen years he was a novice, and became thoroughly literate in Tham and Lao dialects. He became a monk at the age of twenty-one and continued for three years of service and study. Achaan Pun is an ex-abbot of the temple and a leader of the congregation. He is sixty-four years old. He went to the temple school as *dekwat* from the age of ten to twelve years; at eighteen he became a novice for two years and then a monk, which he remained for seven years, becoming the abbot in his fourth year. After some time he resumed lay life, and is now a householder. Phau ('father') Champi, aged fifty-nine, is perhaps the most respected elder of the village and the successor of Phautu Phan, who is now too old to be active. Champi started to go to the village school at the time compulsory education was first proclaimed, and studied there for five years (from the age of nine to fourteen); at seventeen he became a novice, and stayed on in the temple to become a monk three years later. He gave up his robes after one year as monk.

The contemporary complication is that since secular schooling, especially secondary schooling, is available, a lesser number of boys become novices because the monastery is not the sole institution of learning nor is its learning competitive with that transmitted by schools preparing for secular occupations. But the institution of novicehood is by no means dead; it is, however, becoming increasingly shorter in point of service, and increasingly approximates the temporary vocation of monkhood which can and does persist without interference because of its brevity. Nonetheless, it is still true to say that novicehood represents apprenticeship to professional monkhood. The minority who function as monks for some length of time or indefinitely tend to have novicehood behind them.

With these preliminaries stated I can now deal with some statistics relating to the annual intake of monks and novices into the village *wat*, and the length of their service. I shall first give the picture for 1961, and then make brief statements for the years 1963–6.

Before the onset of the Lent season[1] in 1961 three young men were ordained as monks in Baan Phraan Muan. Two were twenty-one years old and the third twenty-three; all three left the priesthood at the end of Lent in late November, about four months later. Two other monks who had been ordained previously stayed on after Lent. One was the abbot of the *wat*, who was twenty-two years old and had been ordained in 1959 (after a spell of novicehood in 1954). He gave up his robes in early 1962, when

---

[1] The Buddhist Lent is the three-month rain retreat (*Vassa*).

we were in the field, but returned to monkhood later in the year in November. The fifth monk was ordained in early 1961, having been a novice in 1957; in 1962 he was still in robes, although it was certain he, too, would give them up at any time.

In 1961 three youths were ordained as novices; two were seventeen and one was eighteen—somewhat older than the usual age of ordination to novicehood. In a village those who become novices are likely to stay on in the *wat* in that status for a longer period than most of the young men who are ordained as monks. However, it is the custom that a monk—irrespective of when he was ordained—must complete one entire Lenten season, whereas a young boy may be ordained as a novice for a few weeks only, in order to make merit for a dead relative, usually of the grandparental generation.

All the monks and novices referred to above—except one—were sons of village households; the odd man out was in fact no stranger: his parents had migrated and he was ordained in what was considered the traditional village *wat* of his parents.

The year 1962 was a lean one for the village *wat*. The abbot himself had left the *wat* and no new monks or novices were ordained. But in 1963 there was a relatively large number of ordinations: five monks (three aged twenty and two twenty-one) were ordained. All spent about seven or eight months in the *wat* and resumed lay life in January 1964 during harvesting time. In the same year, seven novices ranging in age from twelve to fourteen years were ordained; their period of stay at the *wat* varied, ranging from four months (two cases), eight months (two cases), and ten months (two cases) to sixteen months (one case).

In 1964 four young men, three of whom were twenty-one years old and the fourth twenty-four years, were ordained; they, too, left the *wat* at the beginning of the following year after eight months of service. Four novices of age twelve to thirteen years also took robes: one left after five months, another after nine months, the third after thirteen months, and the last was still a novice in 1966. During the Lent season of 1966, there were six monks and five novices in the *wat*, of whom five monks and four novices were newly ordained.

The point that emerges from these facts is that annually a group of young men and youths from the village are ordained, and at the conclusion of Lent or soon thereafter the majority resume lay life. At the village level, then, monkhood does not normally imply professionalism or life-long vocation. If ordination to monkhood is in religious terms a rite of initiation, in social terms it is distinctly a rite of passage for young men before they marry and set up their own households.

Buddhism and the spirit cults in North-east Thailand

The turnover in the population of monks in Baan Phraan Muan is dramatic. Usually the abbot of a village *wat* and one or two other monks form a core of professionals or semi-professionals who give continuity by being in robes for some years. Abbot Tongloon, the present abbot, a young man only twenty-two years old, is one of the few professional monks produced by the village. He had his normal village primary schooling from age nine to fourteen; immediately afterwards he became a novice, and remained so until he was twenty. He was then ordained a monk. He has passed three *nagtham* examinations and after his second was given permission by the clerical authorities to teach monks and novices in the village. While the abbot of a village temple may in fact decide to be a life-long priest, others who see a service of more than one Lent usually resume lay life after at most three years. In fact the main continuity in the Baan Phraan Muan *wat* was provided by an elderly monk, born in the village, who had been the local abbot for several years before being promoted abbot of a larger temple in another district. However, he retained his interest in and control over the affairs of *wat* Phraan Muan: he was consulted in financial matters, he conducted the ordination ceremonies or gave his approval to prospective candidates, and he was the chief officiant at major annual collective rites such as *Bun Phraawes*. It is interesting that there were in Phraan Muan two ex-abbots who at the time of fieldwork were elderly household heads.

The fact that, at the village level, true religious professionals are few and monkhood is virtually a rite of passage—not indeed for all young men but for a good number of them—can be established by statistics relating to the religious service performed by a sample of 106 family heads out of a total universe of 182 households. Over half of the family heads had served as monks, about a third as novices, and nearly a fifth as both. This lends substance to my assertion that both monkhood and novicehood must be viewed as rites of passage; this in turn raises the question of how they are integrated with various levels of social structure and how they also reflect underlying social principles.

Why do youths and young men lead a monastic life as a phase of their lives? While of course a novice or a monk makes merit for himself by assuming a religious role, a frequent statement made by both layman and novice/monk is that becoming a monk confers merit on one's parents. It is said in the village, for instance, that a novice in his first year makes merit for his mother, in his second for his father. This is interesting in view of the popular evaluation of women as religiously 'inferior' to men, since only the latter can become monks. A frequent occasion on which a young boy becomes a novice is when a parent or grandparent dies, and the youth is required to make merit for the deceased in order to further the latter's progress after death.

Monkhood is of greater religious merit than novicehood. That a son should show gratitude to his parents by being ordained is part of village ideology and village expression of filial piety. The very 'sponsoring' of an ordination ceremony is considered a meritorious act *par excellence*. This ceremony, then, lends itself to a conspicuous public statement of religious piety. At the village level, and in popular Buddhism generally, merit accrues to everyone who contributes to the holding of a ceremony.

THREE RITUALS: ORDINATION, DE-ROBING, AND HONOURING THE MONK

The rest of this chapter is devoted to the description and analysis of three rituals. The first two dramatize the entry of a man into monkhood, and his departure from it; the third concerns the monk who decides to remain in robes and is periodically honoured by his lay supporters. These rituals use symbols and express themes which we shall meet again and again at different levels and in different contexts of behaviour.

Ordination

I have already stated that the procedure for ordination (*upasampada*) is laid down in the texts and followed in various Buddhist countries, but that the simple classical rite has been elaborated on in different social contexts. Within Thailand itself there are differences of detail. The rite is called *bun buad* in Phraan Muan village. I shall describe briefly the major sequences in the rite of ordination in the village so as to bring out both the merit orientations of the actors and the social implications of what is at first sight a purely religious event.

The rite of admission for a novice does not require a separate description. The usual practice is for novices to be admitted at the same ceremony at which monks are ordained before the Lent season. In the sequence of rites at a monk's ordination, the candidate is first initiated as a novice and then ordained monk by virtue of additional ceremonial sequences. Thus the admission ceremony for a novice is the first part of the ceremony for a monk, and for ceremonial as well as practical reasons a joint initiation rite is feasible. In Phraan Muan village it is the custom to hold village-supported collective rituals in which novices and monks are ordained as a group. A novice or a monk can of course be initiated separately.

I have already, in Chapter 5, elucidated the importance of the rain retreat (*Vassa*) in early Buddhism as an important marker in monastic life. True to the classical time-table, the rain retreat (called *Khaw Phansa* = entering Lent) as practised in the village (and elsewhere in Thailand) is timed to coincide with the height of the monsoon rains. The ordination of monks and novices typically takes place in the preceding few weeks before the start of the Lenten season in July. Since the Lenten season coincides with the monsoon rains we see how conveniently the ordination of young men fits into a particular stage of the paddy cultivation cycle. They are usually ordained during the growing phase of rice, when there is little work to be done in the fields and their labour is not required.

Ordination rites (*bun buad*) take place over two days. The candidate (called *nag*, which is explicitly recognized as referring to *Nag* or *Naga*, the serpent) spends an initial period of 'separation', which lasts seven days, at the *wat*; the ostensible reason for this is so that he can spend the time learning the precepts, the words (in Pali) with which he requests permission to be ordained, and the answers to the questions that will be put to him at the ordination rite at the *wat*.

The day previous to the ordination is called *wan ruam* (or *wan hoam*); the day of ordination is *wan buad*. The word *ruam* means 'bring together' and signifies the preparations of kinsmen and fellow villagers for the following day. They gather at the house of the *nag* to make delicacies, betel packets, cigarettes and candles. The most important feature of preparation is the assembling of the ritual articles of ordination, the eight requisites of the monk (*kryang buad* or *kryang meng*). The articles listed by the local villagers are: a set of robes (two garments), an umbrella, a monk's bowl, a pair of slippers, a lamp, a razor and a spittoon.[1] These articles are bought by the parents. Relatives and friends on this day contribute money-to-the-parents (*ngoen phau*) and other articles for the monk's use, like pillows and cushions. It is said, significantly, that pillows are usually contributed by the girl friends (*phuu saw*) of the *nag*.

On the morning of *wan ruam* the head of the *nag* is shaved at the *wat* by the abbot; the parents and kin of the *nag* do not participate in this sequence. The significance of head-shaving as symbolic renunciation of sexuality is, I think, clear enough (see Leach 1958). Then the *nag* comes home, where he is dressed in *pha mai* (a loin cloth usually red or green in colour) and *pha biang khaw*—a long white cloth worn diagonally over the left shoulder. ('White colour means the Buddhist religion', said an informant. The *nag* shows his transitional status by wearing both a white cloth and a contrasting red or green cloth.)

---

[1] The orthodox enumeration is three robes of different description, a girdle for the loins, the alms bowl, a razor, a needle and a water strainer. These are the symbols of a monk's 'poverty', signifying he should have no other personal possessions.

The phases of monkhood

In the afternoon takes place the most important ritual sequence of *wan ruam*—this is the ceremony of *sukhwan nag* performed at the *sala* by the elders of the village (*phuu thaw*) for all the *nag* who will be ordained on the next day. The 'requisites of the monk' have already been deposited in the *sala* and a conical ceremonial structure (*pha khwan*) prepared. The monks of the *wat* do not participate in this ceremony. It is one of the general class called *sukhwan* rites, the ritual details of which will be analysed in a subsequent chapter. Here I shall focus on what is implied in 'calling the *khwan*'.

The calling of the *khwan* (spirit essence) has a dual purpose. The first is the familiar one of calling the *khwan* of the *nag* to enter his body, which is followed by the sprinkling of perfumed water (*nam haum*) and the binding of the wrists. The elders give the *nag* morale and charge him with confidence before his change of status. Secondly and more relevantly to our present interests, a part of the text recited by the officiant, a lay elder, emphasizes that, in becoming a monk, the *nag* is fulfilling his filial obligations. To him are described the burdens borne by his mother— during her pregnancy, at childbirth, and in bringing him up.

The *khwan* ceremony[1] is followed by the chanting of monks, who now participate for the first time. The monks perform *suad-mongkhon nag* (chanting for the prosperity of the *nag*).[2] Just as the lay elders hold a threshold and blessing ceremony for the *nag*, so do the monks, to enable the *nag's* change from a secular to a sacred status.

Now to describe *wan buad*. The sponsors of the ordination ceremony (usually parents) as well as the villagers take food to the *sala* in early morning to feast the monks. Then a drum is beaten and the villagers congregate to form a procession. The *upacha* (principal officiant at the ordination), the two *achaan suad* (the two teacher monks who will direct and assist each *nag*) and the *nag* themselves are carried in palanquins to the *wat*. The procession circumambulates the *sala* three times in a clockwise direction (*wian sai*); the parents and relatives of each *nag* wash his feet with perfumed water ('to wash away all defects because the "*nag*" is leaving a layman's life'), and then the *nag* are carried into the *bood*.

Then begins the ordination rite proper which is composed of (variant) procedures laid down in Buddhist liturgy accompanied by others of local derivation. (See Kaufman 1960 and Rajadhon 1961 for descriptions of the ceremony in Central Thailand, and Yoe 1896, Ch. 12, in Burma. Also see Paul Levy 1968 who reports variant procedures.) I shall hereafter

---

[1] The *sukhwan* ritual is described in detail in Chapter 13.

[2] The reader is requested to note the occasions when *suad mongkhan* (chant for prosperity) is recited.

describe the ceremony as if only one monk is being ordained, for the same description applies to collective ordination under the same *upacha*.

A *sangha* or chapter of monks will have been called and sits in the *bood*: it consists of the *upacha* (the principal ordainer), two *achaan suad* (literally the teacher-monks who chant at the ceremony, but who also act as the candidate's mentors) and other monks in attendance. A chapter of a minimum of five monks is necessary to validate ordination.

The parents of the candidate stand by the requisites of the monk, with the father holding the robe. The *nag* first approaches his father, does obeisance to him (by prostrating in an attitude of worship), and asks for the robes. The father hands him the robes and leads him by the hand to the *upacha*.

The *nag*, having done obeisance three times to the *upacha*, then asks for permission to be ordained. The *upacha* holds the *nag's* hand and recites the formula of meditation on the perishable nature of the human body. As the villagers put it: 'The *nag* is told that head hair (*kesa*), body hair (*loma*), fingernails (*nakha*), teeth (*danta*); these things are impermanent.' The *upacha* then places the *phabieng* (a yellow sash) on the *nag's* shoulder. The *nag* approaches the two mentors, carrying his robes, and they help him to don them. He requests the ten precepts and the mentors administer them, he repeating after them. Now the *nag* is a novice. This is the end of the first stage of the ceremony called *pabbajja* (to go forth).

Certain subsequent steps (*upasampada*) make him a monk and grant him admission to the *Sangha*. The novice's parents hand over the alms bowl and gifts in cash and kind to the *upacha*, who slings the bowl on the novice's shoulder. The novice again returns to his mentors, who take him aside and one of whom interrogates him as to whether he has the proper qualifications for monkhood. (The questions asked are whether he is a human being, a male, of the right age, has secured the consent of his parents, is free of debt and of certain diseases, and is not a fugitive from justice.) Having satisfied themselves, the mentors report to the assembly and request it to admit the ordinand. The second *achaan* then informs the novice of the more important rules by which he will have to abide (concerning food, garments, residence, the medicine he may use, the crimes that involve expulsion, etc.), and gives a moral discourse on the vocation of the monk.

The mentors begin the chant called *suad nag* which extols the glories of being a monk. The chanting concludes with a full-throated, majestic and jubilant victory blessing (*chayanto*) while the new monk 'pours water' (*yaad nam*) as a sign of transferring merit to his parents and kin; the parents themselves enact the same rite to impart some of the merit they have acquired to their dead parents and other ancestors.

The phases of monkhood

The final sequence is the feasting of monks, kin and villagers by the parents of the newly ordained monk.

The foregoing description brings out the following salient features which surround and penetrate a religious installation. It substantiates village ideology. The sponsoring of and participation in an ordination rite is a channel for acquiring merit; parents as the sponsors are primary recipients; kinsmen and fellow villagers are secondary recipients. Ordination becomes a matter of collective interest to the village in the same way as do mortuary rites, as we shall see later. Moreover, it is clear that ordination is an event in which merit is transferred by the monk who is of a filial generation to his elders, who in fact install him in this office. It is relevant here to note, for example, that when the ordaining monks at the end of initiation chant their blessings, the newly ordained transfers merit to his parents and kin by means of water-pouring. We thus begin to see, in the institution of monkhood, a pattern of reciprocity and exchange of values between the parental and filial generations in the village—a theme which I shall elaborate as we study other aspects of religious behaviour.[1]

At this point it is relevant to comment upon one symbol which will recur later in its multiple facets. We have seen that the candidate for ordination is called *nag* and that villagers explicitly identify this word with the *Nag* (or *Naga*), the water serpent. Why should a man in his transitional status just before ordination be called a *nag*?

The accepted explanation of this usage is the story that a *Naga*, during the time of Buddha, assumed human form and was ordained as a monk. One day he was discovered in his true serpentine form when he was asleep. The Buddha expelled him from the Order, for only a human being can be a monk.[2] But the *Naga* pleaded that if his religious desires could not be fulfilled through monkhood, at least he should be remembered by calling every initiate *nag* before ordination. I shall develop the *Naga* symbolism later. I wish to suggest here that the point of this story is that a human being in entering the status of ascetic monk leaves behind and renounces the attributes of *nag*—virility or sexuality, and similar attributes of secular life; or, to put it differently, *nag* and monk (*phraa*) are opposed states and through ordination a man makes the passage from one status to the other.

[1] I realize, of course, that the details of the ordination ceremony can be interpreted in terms of another frame, namely, legends and historical accounts of early Buddhism such as the First and subsequent Councils. Paul Levy (1968) provocatively links the ordination procedure with the First Buddhist Council, in which Ananda played an important part. This is the province of an Indologist.

[2] This incident is related in the *Mahavagga* (see Rhys Davids and Oldenberg 1881, pp. 217–19). Thus the Thai story is built on classical traditions, though the ending is a subsequent elaboration.

This interpretation throws light on another custom reported for Central Thailand by Rajadhon (1961) and interpreted by him in a rather simple-minded way. The young man who has consented to become a monk is taken in procession on the eve of his ordination so that he can pay his respects to his senior relatives and superiors. On this occasion he carries with him weapons. Rajadhon interprets this as an act of safeguard against enemies who see this as the last chance to avenge an injury, because a monk in robes is inviolate and sacred. It is more illuminating to see the parading of weapons as a ritually heightened expression of the candidate's secular attributes of virility and aggressiveness which he will shed when he becomes a monk and adopts the value of non-violence (*ahimsa*) and celibacy.

Finally, while the ritual as a whole states a reciprocal relation between, on the one hand, parents and kin (and laymen in general) and on the other the monk, it also emphasizes the essential features of a monk's life that distinguish it from a layman's. The public avowal of the precepts and rules of monastic discipline, and the pointed admonition of the *upacha* as to the impermanence of the body, are reinforced by another ritual feature widely encountered in Thailand. When the assembly of monks makes the actual pronouncement of ordination, no pregnant woman should be present. If she is present she will suffer a hard labour. What better statement that the monk's renunciation of lay life is the opposite of sexuality and birth?

De-robing

A noteworthy feature of Buddhist monastic life is the recognition that a monk may give up his robes as freely as he assumed them. The circumstances under which monks may wish to de-robe have been expressly recognized from early times. They are: inability to remain sexually continent; impatience of restraint; a wish to enter upon worldly engagements; the love of parents or friends; or doubts as to the truth of the system propounded by the Buddha (Hardy 1860, p. 46). But lest this privilege be abused by a monk, who while in robes might offend against the rules of discipline and then invoke the privilege to escape sanction, it was decreed that no monk shall give up his robes without express permission being granted by a legally constituted chapter of monks.

Building upon this traditional rule, the village rite of de-robing shows interesting elaborations. We have already seen that the period of religious service is short and that there is a rapid turnover in the religious personnel of the village *wat*.

There is absolutely no odium attached to leaving the *wat* to resume lay life. When a monk or novice feels he wants to leave he must first inform the abbot and then his parents. He also takes flowers and candles to pay his respects to the *upacha* and *achaan suad* who officiated at his ordination. With the abbot's agreement secured, an auspicious date and time are ascertained by the parents by consulting the *maulek* (astrologer). On the appointed day, the monk approaches the abbot and other assembled monks in the *bood* with *khanha* (five pairs of candles and five pairs of flowers) and hands them over. He asks in Pali for permission to leave monkhood; the abbot removes the *sangkati* (robe worn on the shoulder); then the monk changes into lay clothes and approaches the abbot again to receive the five precepts. It is easily seen that these acts are a precise reversal of those enacted in the ordination rite. After de-robing, the ex-monk has to stay in the *wat* for one to three nights (and days), and during this time clean the *khuti* (monk's residence), toilet, and *sala* in order to remove 'all sins committed while he was a monk'.

The ex-monk leaves the *wat* in a direction determined by the astrologer, carrying an umbrella and his suitcase. At the gate of the *wat* he is met and welcomed by a 'virgin' who takes his hand and leads him out. The girl is chosen by the outgoing ex-monk and is usually his girl friend. As one informant put it: 'The girl receives him because they haven't conversed with each other for a long time and therefore she missed him.' It is believed that the virgin will bring him good luck and prosperity. (I will comment later on this incident signifying man's passage from the sacred to the secular world.)

The rite of honouring the monk

A remarkable ritual in North-east Thailand, which is organized and sponsored by the villagers themselves, has for its purpose the honouring of monks by investing them with titles as a mark of appreciation for their piety and services. A monk of long-standing service may earn an array of ranked titles over the years. The ritual highlights not only the prestige and honour that attaches to the vocation of monk but also the symbiotic relationship of the monk and his village congregation.

The holding of these rites is also reported for Laos, and there is some evidence suggesting that the city of Vientianne (Wiangchan), which is an important centre of Buddhism, may have been a focal point for their elaboration and spread.

Informants reported that traditionally in the North-east eight grades of titles were recognized. I give them in ascending order: (1) *Somdet*; (2) *Hua*[1] *Saa*; (3) *Hua Khoo* (*Khruu*) ('teacher'); (4) *Fai*; (5) *Daan*;

---

[1] *Hua* is a prefix meaning 'head', it indicates respect.

(6) *Lug Kaew* ('precious child'); (7) *Yaud Kaew* ('precious top'); (8) *Lak Khan* ('golden post'). Some of these titles have straightforward meanings, given here in parenthesis. A work on Laos (Pathoumxad in Berval 1959) reports six grades recognized there, namely *Somdet, Sa, Khru, Lakkham, Lakkeo* and *Nhotkeo*.

These grades and titles should not be confused with the honorific titles conferred by the King of Thailand on monks occupying high offices in the formal ecclesiastical hierarchy or positions of importance in royal *wat.* (See Appendix to Chapter 5.) This Bangkok system of titles ranges from four sub-grades of *Phra Khru*, to various grades of *Phra Raja Gana*, and finally to *Somdet*, the highest being that given to the Supreme Patriarch (*Somdet Phra Sankarat*). It is curious that the highest (*Somdet*) title in the royal honours is the lowest title in the village. The noteworthy feature of the village *Somdet* ceremony lies not in this curious anomaly, but in the fact that parallel to the system of royal titles there has been a traditional recognition system maintained by village congregations. This has not been reported in historical or contemporary literature on Thailand.

Of the eight grades reported in the North-east, only the first three are of relevance for us.[1] These titles are invested on certain monks by virtue of the village congregations conducting a water-pouring honouring ceremony. When a monk is invested with the *Somdet* title villagers give him a piece of silver whose length covers from 'eye to eye' (*Somdet raub thaa*); with the *Saa* title the silver extends from 'ear to ear' (*Hua Saa raub hoo*); and with the *Khruu* title the length of silver covers the circumference of the head (*Hua Khruu raub gnon*). The sheet of silver is the most important of the gifts given to the monk by the villagers on this occasion. It has inscribed on it the names of the honouring village and the monk honoured. It is reported that sheets of gold accompany higher titles. The details of the ceremony are fascinating and have a far-reaching symbolic significance.

A former abbot of the village of Phraan Muan, who is now a district ecclesiastical head, explained the circumstances leading to the ceremony thus:

When a person has been a monk, in former days for more than five years, nowadays about two years, and has conducted himself well and shows good knowledge, the villagers judge that he is fit to be made *Somdet*. They will then approach the monk with flowers and invite him to undergo the ceremony of water-pouring (*hod song*). The monk is free to decline, but if he agrees the villagers will get together the ritual articles which are the same as those used for an ordinary ordination [i.e., the eight requisites of the monk]. Besides these,

---

[1] The first three titles are the ones most frequently.conferred on village monks.

the most important item they will have to acquire is a piece of silver corresponding to the rank to which the monk is to be promoted.

The villagers then choose an auspicious day. The ceremony is never conducted during the Lent retreat season, but it is timed to take place along with the normal ordination ceremonies just before Lent. The most popular day is the occasion of ordination connected with the rocket festival of *Bunbangfai*, which will be described in Chapter 16.

Thus the *Somdet* ceremony is conducted together with the annual ordination of village youth as monks and novices. The monk who is going to be honoured (referred to as *hod*) is carried on the shoulders of villagers in the same procession as that in which the candidates for ordination are carried. (The procession is referred to as *hae nag hae hod*.) While the postulants undergo the ordination ceremony, the *Somdet*-to-be sits as a spectator. It is only after the *nags* are ordained that the *Somdet* ceremony starts.

First the monk (*hod*) is led out of the *bood* by the chief priest (*upacha*) who conducted the ordination: the latter leads, holding one end of a stick, while the *Somdet* candidate follows holding the other end. The stick is called *mai gaiyasid*, and it is said by villagers to be the sacred wand wielded by Non Thu, the servant of Phra Isuvan (Vishnu) in the *Ramayana* epic. The wand is so powerful that any person at whom it is pointed will die. The *upacha* leads the monk to a special altar built in the temple compound. Buddhists, males only (because monks are forbidden to touch females), lie flat on the ground and *upacha* and *hod* step on them on their way to the altar. There are two interpretations advanced by villagers to explain this walking on human bodies. First, that the villagers trampled on will acquire merit; second, and more importantly, it is believed that the act of trampling drives away illness (*haj rog pay*). It is clear, then, that both the *upacha* and the *hod* are thought of as persons charged with sacred power, and it is noteworthy that the symbolism of the wand derives from Hindu mythology incorporated into Buddhism.

The altar must now be described. The symbolism recorded is that reported by village informants. There is a stone slab on which the postulant will kneel; under the stone are placed seven leaves from the bo tree (under which the Buddha himself sat and found enlightenment). The slab is called the altar (*silaa*) of Buddha. Eight bundles of leafy stalks of a tree called *yaphrae* are also placed under the stone—it is said that Lord Buddha made an altar with the same stalks, which then turned into a stone altar. The most important part of the altar is a long hollow piece of wood (sometimes bamboo) carved in the form of a *Naga*, the water serpent, with a deep groove the length of the spinal column. This

Naga is suspended over the stone slab with the head of the *Naga* right above it. A hole is made in the *Naga's* throat; under this hole is tied a piece of cloth containing the silver described above and a Buddha image.

The postulant is made to kneel on the stone. Three candles are lit and placed on the *Naga's* head. The *upacha* and the other monks chant *suad mongkhon* (chant of blessing). The *upacha* pours water into the *Naga's* groove; it flows through the throat, seeps through the cloth, and falls on the postulant's head. The monks then pour water, followed by all the villagers present, especially the elders both male and female.

After the water-pouring the villagers carry the monk into the *sala* (preaching hall), and there present him with the eight articles of ordination. Each of the robes is chanted over and a sacred mark (*pin thu*) put on it. The monk takes off his wet robes and puts on the new ones. One of the villagers, acting on behalf of them all as the lay sponsor (*chao paab*), holds a gong in front of the monk, who then recites a prescribed *gatha* (verse) called *seeha nathang* (the 'roar of the lion') and hits the gong with his fist in three episodes (first once, then twice, then three times). The louder the noise the better, for the monk thus proclaims his victories.[1] Then the lay sponsor reads what is inscribed on the piece of silver: that the villagers have '*hod song*' the monk of such-and-such a name. The promoted monk, who is now a *Somdet*, chants a blessing to all the assembled villagers.

The symbolism in this drama, and what it signifies in village religious action, can be fully understood only when we have reviewed a variety of rituals. Here let me indicate a few features. Water-pouring is an important ritual act: the theory is that by pouring water people pay respect to their superiors (youth to elders, villagers to monks and the Buddha statue) and honour the celebrants. Another meaning is that it symbolizes the transfer of merit by one who has acquired merit to others. Thus, in addition to the manifest meaning of showing respect, we might recognize the meaning that he who is being honoured is also being cleansed and purified; looked at from this point of view it is the pourer who is in some way transferring vitality.

The most spectacular ritual object in the ceremony is the *Naga*, the water serpent. Villagers say of the role of the *Naga* in the ceremony that 'the *naga* lives in the water; it is cool; the *naga* is also a friend of the

---

[1] The lion symbol is important in classical Buddhist accounts. The Buddha was called the lion of the Sakya clan. More relevant in this context is the description of the First Council at which Ananda, having gone through his ordeal and become an *arahat*, mounts the lion throne of the Buddha (*Simhasana*) with the *Sangha* crowding around him ('like the king of lions among the host of lions') and pronounces the suttas.

Buddha'. We have noted that the water poured ultimately falls on the head of the monk, seeping through the serpent's 'poison bag' which contains the silver sheet and the Buddha statue. In India the poison of the sacred cobra is referred to as its milk, which is a fertility symbol.

The many faces of the *Naga* will occupy us throughout much of this book. In the *Somdet* ritual two aspects are in the forefront. First, as a symbol of rain, fertility and coolness, the water discharged by the *Naga* cleanses and fertilizes the honoured monk. The power that is discharged is not that of fertility in the form of sexuality but rather the transformed force of purity deriving from the silver and the Buddha image. The initial energy comes from the animality of the *Naga*, however, and the adoration of lay householders.

Secondly, the *Naga's* role in the ritual and the villagers' reference to its being a friend of the Buddha invoke a remarkable piece of Buddhist mythology, celebrated frequently in Siamese architecture and sculpture. When Gotama retired to meditate under the shade of the midella tree at the time he attained enlightenment and Supreme Buddhaship, there arose a storm and a wind. Whereupon the snake god Muchalinda entwined himself seven times around the sage's body and spread his seven hoods over his head, thus giving him protection. While the ritual as a whole invokes this incident, there is one important difference: whereas the serpent protected the Buddha from the storm and wind, here it acts as a vehicle for the precipitation of fertilizing and purifying water. The two themes are juxtaposed.

Now these symbolic values of the *Naga* as presented in this ritual appear markedly in contrast to the meaning of *Naga* I developed in the ordination rite (*bun buad*), where the candidate for ordination in his secular status is represented as the virile and aggressive *Naga* who is by virtue of ordination transformed into the non-violent and asexual monk. Nevertheless there is no contradiction but only a difference in emphasis. Expressed are the twin notions that lay life is different from ascetic life, and that it is the source energy of worldly life that has to be transformed into the energy of asceticism.

Viewing the ceremony of honouring in relation to the institution of monkhood itself, it is clear that it is a kind of second ordination. It is significant that it is the villagers who in appreciation of a monk elevate him in this fashion. The theory is that in honouring him, they themselves make merit. For is not a virtuous and pious monk the proper vehicle for the transference of merit and blessings back to the layman?

It is a great honour for a monk to be invited to undergo the *Somdet* ceremony. Most frequently it is the abbot of the village who is thus honoured. All the past abbots of the village of Phraan Muan have been invested with the title; so has the present abbot. A *Somdet* when he gives up his robes and reverts to lay life will be addressed as *jaan (achaan)*, which literally means 'teacher'. In fact, the abbot of Baan Phraan Muan and all ex-abbots are addressed and referred to as *jaan* so-and-so. A monk who has undergone two such ceremonies to become *Saa*, or three ceremonies to become *Khruu*, is addressed and referred to by his title as *Hua Saa* or *Hua Khoo* if he is still in robes and as *jaan saa* or *jaan khruu* when he gives up his robes.

Long after I had written this description of the monk-honouring ceremony as it is performed in the North-east, and its interpretation, I was pleased to come across Paul Levy's (1968, pp. 34–6) summary of an account of the same ceremony performed in Laos. In some details the account differs from mine but more importantly it certainly supplements and reinforces it.

In Laos the induction in the highest rank is marked by a solemn ceremony.[1] At Luangprabang, where it takes place by order of the king, it consists essentially of a solemn shower-bath for the new satthu (Skt. sadhu) or 'saint'. Before the entrance of the sanctuary a bath cabin is erected. Above it is the customary gutter in the form of a naga-makara. Inside, a bronze gong 'symbolises the renown enjoyed by the priest, and a pair of elephant tusks the perfection of the priest's conduct, flawless as the ivory of the tusks'. He will sit on them during his shower. Along the path joining the cabin and the sanctuary a 'dozen little boys stand guard: some hold in their hands screens on which are depicted Brahma, Indra, the four guardians of the universe, and other divinities who travelled to be present at the *abhiseka* of *Sariputra*; the others brandish sacred daggers called *mit kut*, which have flame-shaped blades and are identical with the Javanese kris[2]...which symbolises the knowledge acquired by the venerable one and has the power of destroying vices and warding off evil spirits'. On the path itself 'the faithful, in order to obtain merit, make a carpet with their white sashes...which in this case represent their bodies'. Presently the new *sat'th'u* will walk on them, and in so doing will recall the action of the Buddha who, when he was Sumedha, asked the Buddha *Dipankara* to step on his body.

Before his baptism the priest 'cleans his teeth and has himself shaved'. Then the perfumed water is poured on him, first by his fellow monks and then by the laymen. Three trays of offerings are presented to him. On one are displayed the 'celestial screens' and a *mit kut* dagger; the second bears the customary ritual offerings (trumpets, candles, etc....); and on the third are

[1] According to an account which the author, Mlle S. Karpelès, was kind enough to lend me in manuscript [Levy's footnote, referring to his source].

[2] Laot. *mit*, 'knife, dagger'; Laot. *kut*, 'diamond, precious' by assimilation to the *vajra*; or perhaps Laot. *k'ut*, 'Garuda', by allusion to the handle of the *kris*, generally in the form of a Garuda?

carried the monk's three garments into which he changes, whilst an *acar* (*acarya*) takes off his soaked clothing. The new satthu will then tread the path covered with sashes, but as a 'blind man', letting himself be led to the sanctuary while holding the sash or bamboo-cane held out to him by the abbot. 'In thought he (thus) goes over the eight-fold sacred road in order to follow the same sacred path as his elders.' Relations, friends, believers throw small coins to the children in the courtyard of the pagoda, and they lay their offering before the newly elevated man. There follows the proclamation of his new title and the merit solicited for him.

8

THE MONASTIC ROUTINE
AND ITS REWARDS

In doctrinal Buddhism we are told in great detail about the techniques of meditation and contemplation, by which a monk seeks withdrawal from the world, acquires a hatred for his body, and places himself on the path of salvation. The Maha Satipatthana Sutta (see Rhys Davids 1910, Vol. III, Part II, Ch. 22) is a good example of the practice of four kinds of 'mindfulness'—of body, sensations, thoughts, and mind objects. Or again, the 227 rules of the *Vinaya*, which a monk must in theory observe, are an example of the meticulous technology and morality devised for the professionally religious.

What relevance has all this for village monks? What is the village monk's orientation to his religious office, what is his daily monastic routine, and what activities are particularly emphasized?

The facts that are particularly interesting about the *wat* in Phraan Muan village are not so much those pertaining to the relations between monks as a monastic community, but those which throw light on the pattern of transactions between monks and lay villagers.

The internal structure of the monastic community of the village *wat* of the size of Baan Phraan Muan does not portray complex internal differentiation, hierarchy, and firmly formulated relations between superiors and inferiors and between equals. We have noted before that the local *wat* is in theory a low-level unit in an intricate *tambon*, district, provincial, regional and, finally, national hierarchy, but in fact it enjoys a great deal of autonomy and is run by the village and its monks.

In large monasteries in Thailand, there is at least at the formal level some kind of stratification and role differentiation. The abbot as the head may be assisted by one or two assistants; monks or novices may be divided into residential groups (*gana*), each in the charge of a senior monk. The stratification may take note not only of the distinction between monks and novices but also between 'permanent' and 'temporary' monks or novices, and the former again according to the number of Lents they have served. The relation between monk or novice and his *upacha* (the senior monk who ordained him) may develop into a relation of advantage to the junior; so can the relation between the novice and the senior monk who is assigned to him as his special preceptor and whom he addresses as *luang phii* (respected elder brother).

In the small village *wat* under consideration, such differentiation shows little development; the office of abbot alone is conspicuous, and the distinction between monk and novice, although existent, has no conspicuous significance for everyday monastic life. Although the novices are subject only to the ten precepts, as against the monks' 227, both follow very much the same kind of routine.

The abbot exercises disciplinary authority over monks and novices in his charge. The abbot of the Phraan Muan *wat* gave the following information concerning his disciplinary role. If he was disobeyed, he would report the matter to the *upacha*, the priest who ordained the monk in question. Asked what transgressions he considered serious, he mentioned three—courtship of girls, stealing, and killing animals either intentionally or unintentionally. (The transgressions mentioned are three of the four major *parajika* offences, which are punished by expulsion from monkhood.) Concerning the deportment of monks, he emphasized a matter of decorum: that a monk when he goes into the village must wear his robe in a neat fashion. (We have seen that the *Vinaya* itself lays great emphasis on personal habits and manners.) The abbot's main everyday administrative duties include instructing the other religious personnel to clear the *wat* compound and keep it clean, appointing a monk or novice to give a sermon when one is required, and teaching the *Dhamma* to new entrants during Lent. On the occasion of the annual collective rites, there is, of course, much greater activity and a co-operation with village elders and laymen which will become evident when some of these rites are described.

In the village of Phraan Muan, monks and novices go 'begging' for food only in the morning. This food serves as breakfast. The midday meal[1] is always brought to the *khuti* (monks' residence) by lay donors, when they hear the drum beaten by the novices as a signal. However, on *wan phra* ('sabbath' day), there is no going-forth in search of alms; both breakfast and lunch are brought to the monks by devotees.

The daily routine usually consists of prayers in the early morning followed by cleaning the *khuti* and compound, and going into the village to receive food; after breakfast, the learning of chants, attending to personal matters like washing clothes and bathing, and resting in the slack period before and after lunch; evening prayers at about 6 p.m., and a further studying of chants before going to bed. Odd jobs connected with maintaining the *wat* and its compound may be done as necessity arises.

The novices, on account of their inferior status and juniority in age,

---

[1] This meal has to be eaten before 12 noon.

are likely to be assigned the more menial tasks of cleaning the *khuti*, setting out the meals and washing the alms bowls of monks, and fetching water for the abbot to bathe. There are texts which say that before the recitation of the *Patimokkha* (now applied to the four *wan phra* each month) it is the duty of the novice to sweep the preaching hall, light lamps and candles, spread mats and carpets and fill the water pots. While such duties are primarily those of novices, in practice in the village the abbot, monks and novices may without obvious status distinction and privilege jointly clean the *wat* buildings and compound.

In ordinary times, then, the life of a monk or novice is not arduous. The chief deprivations are no food after midday and chastity. They have a lot of time on their hands. If there is any religious preoccupation, it is not so much with practising salvation techniques as with learning Pali chants which are necessary on various ritual occasions. The knowledge of chants has implications for subsequent lay life—which explains in part why they are so assiduously chanted and memorized.

This rhythm of life changes somewhat during the Lent season, when there is an intensification of religious preoccupation on the part of both layman and monk. The abbot himself teaches the monks and novices in the mornings and afternoons, and prepares those who will stay in robes for longer than one Lent for religious examinations. Every evening a sermon is preached to a village congregation, each monk taking his turn. There are additional observances—mainly concerning freedom of movement[1]—which have to be kept by monks in conformity with the classical regulations pertaining to the rain retreat.

The liturgical training of monks and novices can be taken up under three headings: training to read, memorize and recite chants; training to recite sermons which are used in various rituals; and formal instruction for passing religious examinations held by the ecclesiastical authorities. The first two are more crucial for the public performance of a monk's role in the village and will be considered first.

Before doing this, however, it is necessary to say a few words about languages and scripts in North-east Thailand. (See Tambiah 1968*a* for a detailed treatment of these and other issues pertaining to traditional literacy in the village.) The Lao language of the North-east and the Thai language of the Central Plain (or Bangkok Thai) can be said to be different dialects. Although they belong to the same language family,

---

[1] During Lent a monk's physical movements are carefully regulated. He is not allowed to spend a single night away from his monastery, except when grave need, such as serious illness of parents, necessitates absence. Even so he is permitted to stay away not more than seven days and nights; if he stays longer he is considered to have broken Lent. (See Chapter 5.)

Thai is not completely intelligible to a Lao-speaker and *vice versa*. However, in recent times, considerable blurring has occurred primarily as a result of the educational policy of the Thai government, which has decreed that Central Thai should be the national medium of instruction in furtherance of its policy of assimilating all minority and regional groups to a common national culture and system of administration. Although in the North-east today most adult males (but not necessarily the females, especially the elderly) and children are bilingual, the Lao–Thai linguistic distinction remains valid; the language of conversation and of traditional non-Buddhist ritual and literature is Lao.

Further complications set in when we examine the scripts traditional to the North-east and to Laos. The history and exact nature of the scripts of Thailand and Laos (and the neighbouring countries of Burma and Cambodia) is a complex matter not yet fully unravelled by scholars. However, as far as the traditional literature of North-east Thailand is concerned, the following three points are relevant for our purposes:

1. the sacred or ritual literature was written in the Tham or Lao Tham script;

2. at the same time there was a secular Lao script connected primarily with the state and administrative matters; it was also the alphabet of poetic and romantic literature;

3. since the political incorporation of the North-east by Siam in the nineteenth century, the Thai script has also been introduced.

The basic differentiation is between the sacred Tham on the one hand and the secular Lao and Thai scripts on the other. It would appear that secular Lao writing is in fact an extension of the Thai script. This writing is said to have been 'invented' by King Ramkamhaeng in A.D. 1283 and represents a cursive form of the epigraphic writing of Cambodia (Khmer). This Sukhodaya writing was transmitted with few alterations to Laos and to the Siamese kingdom of the Central Plain (Ayudhya).

But in contrast, the sacred Tham writing of the North-east and Laos is a branch of Shan writing rather than Sukhodaya writing. According to Finot, there are at the present time three local varieties of Shan writing—Tham used throughout Laos, Lur confined to the northern extremity of Laos, and Yuon of Chiengmai (North Thailand). The word Tham derives from the Pali word *Dhamma*, which means Buddhist doctrine and the corpus of sacred texts. As its name indicates, the Tham script is used solely for religious writing. As a type of writing it is a mixed form, influenced by Mon writing rather than by the Khmer form.[1] In the North-east

---

[1] Corresponding to the Tham script of the North-east and Laos is the Korm script (Khmer) of Central Thailand, which was traditionally the script in which Siamese

today all religious writings are referred to as *nansy Tham* (i.e. *Dhamma* books), but this label is interpreted loosely.

The literature used in the village temple is *nansy Tham*.[1] It includes not only chants and Buddhist texts but also *nitarn*, stories of a purely regional origin which are recited as sermons by monks and therefore included in the category of *nansy Tham*. A good portion of the texts of ceremonies performed by laymen (e.g. *khwan* rites) and texts relating to medicine are also written in Tham. However, judging from texts which I collected in Phraan Muan village, the literature can sometimes be written in a mixture of sacred Tham and secular Lao scripts. The key would be the type of person at the village level who did the actual copying: a Buddhist monk would in the past have tended to employ Tham while a lay copyist would have been more flexible.

In the village of Phraan Muan there is also another type of literature, folk opera (*mau lum*) and 'wise sayings' (*phaya*), which is usually written in the secular script. Traditional literature in the village thus appears to have been written in a range of scripts; at the one end is Tham for sacred and ritual literature, which is by far the major category; in the middle are mixed forms; and at the other end is the secular Lao type. Traditionally, the village temple was the place where both scripts, but more especially the Tham script, were learned. The implications of the *wat* and of religious office for the acquisition and use of literacy is an important issue that will be taken up at the end of this chapter.

CONTENT AND MODE OF LEARNING OF NOVICES AND MONKS

We are now in a position to examine the content and mode of learning among the novices and monks. This account deals with the situation fifty years ago, as described by elders, as well as with that prevailing today. The two time periods can be dealt with together, because teaching and learning techniques and the content of learning have remained largely

Buddhist literature was written. Thus a monk in Central Thailand has to learn the sacred Korm script in order to have access to scriptural writings. This situation is changing today with the increasing use of Thai script for printing sacred literature. It is also relevant to note that traditionally in Siamese court circles the Khmer language, civilization and kingship provided the model for Thai court culture. Words of Thai–Lao origin were considered less polite than words of Khmer origin, and the language of the aristocracy had its euphemisms and hierarchical nuances (Graham 1912, p. 568). Such phenomena are of course common to many aristocracies and hierarchical societies.

The Khmer script and language, which belongs to the larger family of Cham–Khmer languages, achieved its maturity between the ninth and twelfth centuries, when the Khmer civilization rose to its peak.

[1] I am indebted to Mr Stuart Simmonds for identifying the script in which these texts are written.

the same. Whatever changes there are relate to script rather than content. Fifty years ago the village school was run on a voluntary basis by the abbot. The candidates for novicehood had their primary schooling and learned to read and write Thai as temple boys. Today boys theoretically can become novices only after completing grade 4 (i.e. passing the examination) in the government primary school; even if they do not conform with this ruling they will normally have had four or five years of schooling and learned the rudiments of reading and writing Thai.

In the past the education of the novices was in three areas: first, learning to read *nansy Tham* and to write the Tham script; second, memorizing a collection of chants (*suad*); and third, practising the art of rendering sermons (*teed*).

Study of nansy Tham

Novices had to learn to both read and write the Tham script. Instruction took place after breakfast. First of all, the abbot wrote the alphabet on paper and read out the letters. When the novices had learned the letters, they practised reading; each student in the class held the palm-leaf book in his hands and read aloud, while the teacher, standing behind him, checked his reading. After reading had been mastered, writing was practised on paper. In importance, writing was secondary to reading. Each month, or once in every two months, the abbot tested his pupils; physical punishment with a stick was administered if mistakes were made.

Today (1966) certain changes have taken place in the learning of *nansy Tham*. Teaching monks and novices to read *nansy Tham* takes place primarily during Lent when the school is active, but learning to read it is no longer compulsory. Those who want to learn are taught by the abbot, and the technique of learning is precisely the same as it was fifty years ago. The voluntary learning of *nansy Tham* is a major change, and most novices (and monks) can no longer read the Tham texts. However, those who propose to spend more than a year in the temple will have to learn to read sermons, most of which are still in the Tham script, though increasingly it is being displaced by the Thai script. What is not acquired today is the ability to write *nansy Tham* because, with the advent of the printing press, the copying of manuscripts is no longer necessary.

Memorizing chants

In many religions, especially the 'higher literate' religions, a feature of the priest or religious virtuoso, be he Buddhist monk or Brahmin priest or Islamic *mallam*, is his remarkable command of chants and texts which he has memorized. Since the training of village religious specialists consists primarily in memorizing texts (without a corresponding accent on the understanding of them), I shall discuss briefly the method of learning chants.

In the past (as well as today), it was on memorizing chants that a novice or a newly ordained monk was likely to spend most of his time. Every religious occasion in the temple, or a major rite of passage like death, or a rite of house-blessing, requires chanting by monks. Village monks and novices are expected to memorize a certain body of chants (*suad mon*) that are recited on these occasions. In addition, they must commit to memory chants which are used in the daily worship of the Buddha (*tham watr*), and other texts such as the *Patimokkha*, which they recite fortnightly. This second category relates to the monastic régime and concerns monks alone.

Below, I give a list of the major chants which novices were, and are, expected to learn during their normal two-year period of study. They can be divided into the two categories noted above: *suad mon* and *tham watr*. If the reader notes the occasions at which the *suad mon* chants are rendered, he will get an idea of the ritual role of the monks in relation to the layman. Monks are concerned with the transfer of merit to laymen at collective temple festivals, at rites of passage, and at merit-making household rites such as house-warming and house-blessing. Together with blessing go protection and the removal of danger; these effects are achieved by the *paritta* chants. Contrary to the ideas of some observers, village Buddhism is not solely concerned with the other world as opposed to this world.

Chants frequently memorized and recited by novices ('neen')
and monks ('phraa')

The language of the chants is Pali, written in the past in Tham script and today increasingly in Thai. The following are the collections of chants that a monk or novice is required to memorize, and which comprise the repertoire adequate for everyday purposes.

1. *Tham watr*: this is a collection of chants recited by monks in the temple in their morning and evening worship of Lord Buddha. This worship is part of the monk's religious discipline and régime, quite apart from his parish role *vis-à-vis* the laity.

2. *Suad mon*: these are chants recited by monks at collective merit-making rites at the temple (*gnan bun*) in which the laity participate, or at the houses of laymen or other locations outside the temple (e.g. cemetery) where ceremonial is held. The chants are divided into two groups: *avamangala* and *mangala*. *Avamangala* refers to inauspicious occasions or occasions which, being charged with danger, have to be 'desacralized',

and *mangala* to occasions which are auspicious or at which 'sacralization' or 'charging' with blessing takes place. For example:

(*a*) *Suad kusala* is an *avamangala* chant, which is recited in a funeral house *immediately* after a person dies;

(*b*) *Suad mongkhon* are an important and frequently recited collection of *paritta* verses which give protection from misfortune as well as positive blessing.

The *suad mongkhon* are also referred to as *suad mon yen* and *suad mon chaw* (evening and morning chants). At any merit-making festival at the temple, for example *Bunkathin* (collective village offerings to monks at the end of Lent), or at home, or after the completion of cremation, monks will first recite at night and then on the following morning chant the blessing, during which laymen fill their bowls with food and give them gifts. The sequence is 'protection' followed by 'blessing' and 'gift-giving'. In the case of post-cremation sacralization, monks chant for three consecutive nights in the funeral house and are feasted on the fourth morning.

The following are an example of the collection of *paritta* that comprise *suad mon yen* (evening chants):

(i)   either *namo pad* or *sum putte*;

(ii)   *mangala sutta* (*asevana*), usually in abbreviated form;

(iii) *ratana sutta*, usually in abbreviated form;

(iv) *karaniya metra sutta* (*suad karanee*), either in full or in abbreviated form;

(v)   *vipassi* (*atanatiya sutta*).

The concluding *suad mon chaw* (morning chant), which transfers blessings to the laity, is usually referred to as *suad pahung*; the best known is the victory blessing *chayamangala katha*. The morning chant (*suad pahung*) is also chanted by monks at the *wat* on *wan sil* (Buddhist sabbath) during the presentation of food to the monks (*sai bart/tak bart*).

The technique of learning chants is as follows. The *tham watr* are not memorized from printed texts. Since they are chanted by monks daily in the early morning and at night, a newcomer repeats what he hears and memorizes them fairly quickly. But essentially the *suad mon* chants and the *Patimokkha* confessional are learnt by the pupils not only collectively in school but also privately, with the aid of printed texts.

The abbot gives each student the task of learning a set of chants. After about five days, at a common class, each student is asked to recite in turn. The task in question is not merely a matter of learning words but of chanting them according to certain tunes. Early morning before school, or after school in the afternoon, novices and monks practise chants individually in their cubicles (*khuti*).

Buddhism and the spirit cults in North-east Thailand

The fact that Buddhism is aesthetically a musical religion, and that the memorizing of words is closely linked to musical rhythms, gives us a clue to the technique and the way in which novices and monks are in fact capable of memorizing an impressive amount of words in their correct order.

There are essentially three musical rhythms employed in chanting. The Magadha form breaks up the chant into phrases. The Samyoka style, on the other hand, is somewhat staccato; stops are made irrespective of meaning in those places where words are joined by certain consonants like *k, c, t, p, d*. Both these styles are employed in the chanting of *mangala* (auspicious) chants. A third style is Sarabhanna, which employs a higher pitch of voice and also slows down the speed of chanting, again breaking the chant into phrases; the Sanghaha is a similar mode of 'lengthened' chanting. Sarabhanna chanting is employed on *avamangala* (inauspicious) occasions, such as immediately after death, when its slow and mournful grandeur suits the occasion.

The verbal structure of the verses (*gatha, sutta*) has discernible implications for facilitating memorization. The chants use the method of repetitions in stylized form. As Rhys Davids wrote:

Two methods were adopted in India to aid this power of memory. One adopted chiefly by the grammarians, was to clothe the rules to be remembered in very short enigmatical phrases (called *suttas* or threads), which taxed the memory but little, while they required elaborate commentaries to render them intelligible. The other, the method adopted in the Buddhist writings (both Sutta and Vinaya), was, firstly, the use of stock phrases, of which the commencement once given, the remainder followed as a matter of course and secondly, the habit of repeating whole sentences, or even paragraphs, which in our modern books would be understood or inferred, instead of being expressed (1881, p. xxiii).

It is clear, then, that the Buddhist *gathas* (like the Vedic prayers) initially belonged to the oral tradition and were designed in a particular form to facilitate transmission. Committing them to writing came later.

In village religion the Buddhist chants present a problem for interpretation. The language of the chants is Pali. Traditionally, they were written in Tham script; today they are available in printed books in the Thai alphabet, which is one reason the study of Tham is declining. Yet whether written in Tham or Thai alphabet, the Pali language itself is alien to most village novices and monks; some who stay in robes for a length of time may actually learn Pali, but this is infrequent. In effect, most village novices and monks do not understand the chants, or at best understand them imperfectly. The lay congregation, all the women and most of the men, are in even greater ignorance about the actual content of chants. However, many of them can recognize particular chants (especially those recited frequently), and often know which chant is appropriate for which occasion; some men who were previously novices have a somewhat better idea of the content.

If this is the actual situation, there are two questions we may ask. To what extent does the knowledge of chants which are in Pali (and to a lesser extent, the ability to read *nansy Tham*) constitute an esoteric and exclusive body of knowledge confined to the clergy? Secondly, if Pali chants are essential at rituals performed by monks and novices and if at the same time they are largely unintelligible to the laity, what, then, is communicated in the rites? The first I shall answer in this chapter; the second in a subsequent chapter.

Sermons ('teed')

Sermons are also chanted and therefore require practice. The quality of recitation itself, apart from the words, is a matter of great aesthetic appreciation on the part of the congregation.

In the village, sermons are not free creations of the novice (or monk) who gives them. They are standardized and there is an appropriate one for each particular occasion or set of occasions, written down in palm-leaf manuscripts. In the past the writing was inscribed by human hand; today, one frequently sees palm-leaf documents on which the words are printed. The latter applies to documents in the Thai script, which are increasingly supplementing the older Tham texts.

Types and content of sermons. 1. One kind are those which enumerate or 'tell' the advantages of making merit (*baug anisonk*), which in fact means giving gifts to the monks and the village temple. Typical occasions when merit-making is extolled are:

Bun prasaad pueng: making merit for a dead person after the cremation rites are over by carrying a palanquin of gifts to the monks and also feasting them;

Bun kathin: giving of gifts by the village to the monks after they have completed Lent seclusion (during the rains), and emerge again into the world. It is after this ceremony that the temporary monks resume lay life.

2. Another set of sermons are rather specialized and are reserved for the celebration of the opening of newly constructed (or repaired) *khuti* (monks' living quarters), *sala* (preaching hall), *wihaan* or *bood* (sacred place of worship). These buildings are always constructed by laymen; it is a classical requirement that monks cannot construct these buildings for their use.

3. The third category of sermons deserves special attention. They are called *teed nitarn* (sermons which relate stories), and these sermons not only have implications for the villagers' understanding of the morality and ethics of Buddhism but also represent the focus of genuine audience participation and a channel of cultural transmission beyond the narrowly religious. Traditionally, the *teed nitarn* constitute a major component of *nansy Tham* (sacred palm-leaf books). *Teed nitarn* can be differentiated as follows: (*a*) *Pathom Sompote*. These are stories (*nitarn*) concerning the life of the Buddha, especially his birth, the renouncing of his kingly life, achievement of *nirvana*, and also the episodes of his previous lives embodied as *Chadok* (*Jataka*) stories. These stories are a common substance of sermons, and are widely known throughout Thailand, but each region has its own version or adaptation. The sermons mentioned here are thus north-eastern creations. (*b*) *Lam Phrawesandaun*. This is a story of the same category as (*a*) above but deserves special mention because it is a work of many chapters, based on the great and moving story of Buddha's penultimate life, as related in the *Wessaundon Chadok* (*Vessantara Jataka*). It is the major sermon listened to (the reading takes a full day) on the occasion of *Bun Phraawes*, which is the village's largest religious and secular festival held after harvest. The north-eastern version of this story has its counterpart in the *Maha Chad* ('Great Story') known in Central Thailand. (*c*) Stories which are primarily local and regional myths and folk tales, and which are not found elsewhere. These are particularly appreciated by the listeners, for whom their moral significance is secondary to their dramatic value as stories. The best known stories are, to give examples, *Pha Daeng Nang Ai*, *Tao Sowat*, *Tao Phii Noi*, *Tao Chan Samut*, *Tao Ten Don*, and *Tao Nokrajog*. The first named of these stories will concern us in a later chapter.

All the categories of sermons (1–3) are given on the occasion of the major collective calendrical temple festivals or are read by monks to laymen during the Lent season. For example, *Lam Phrawesandaun* (3(*b*)) is read on the last day of the three-day *Bun Phraawes*. Category types 1 and 3 sermons are preached at *Org Phansa* (the conclusion of Lent and the 'coming out' of the monks) and *Bun Khaw Chi* (making merit for the dead with puffed rice); some of them also comprise minor sermons during *Bun Phraawes*.

I have already stated that the Pali chants have little meaning content for the layman; the chanting of them on certain occasions is regarded as efficacious in a 'magical' sense. By contrast, the various sermons read and explained in the north-eastern language are better understood by the listeners. It is interesting to note that, on merit-making occasions, it is the villagers who choose the sermon they would like to hear, and it was reported by the abbot that for the major festivals the villagers invariably choose a sermon of category 3.

Whereas stories of the life of the Buddha are universal in Thailand and are heard in variant forms by all Buddhist congregations, we see that the propagation and transmission of tales which have originated in, or at least are confined to, the North-east (and perhaps Laos) help to maintain regional cultural identity *vis-à-vis* other cultural regions of Thailand.[1] The temple, of course, is not the only channel of transmission —folk opera (*mau lum*) transmits the same stories through a different medium; furthermore, literate villagers may themselves possess copies of *nitarn* and read them at funeral wakes to entertain the mourners and guests.

In recent times, as may be expected, the sermons of categories 1 and 2, which are common to Thai Buddhism in general, have tended to become standardized by virtue of their being written or printed in the Thai alphabet. Increasingly, the stories (*nitarn*) of category 3, including the north-eastern tales and myths ($3(c)$), are also being printed in the Thai alphabet while linguistically retaining the local dialectal form.

The education of monks

From the point of view of learning and literacy, village monks are of two kinds: those (a minority) who have been novices and are then ordained as monks, intending to stay for some time in the temple, and those (the majority) who are ordained temporarily for one Lent season.

For the first type the period of monkhood is a continuation of their liturgical and philosophical learning. A novice in the course of his second year of service would normally prepare for the *nagtham* examinations (*nagtham* means one who is versed in the precepts and doctrines of the religion) held by the district ecclesiastical authorities. Preparation for *nagtham* is intensified, and in many village temples engaged in only during Lent when the clerical school functions systematically.

The *nagtham* syllabus may be said to consist of four parts. Pupils are required (i) to show competence in writing essays in the Thai language, and to study (ii) the life of the Buddha (as embodied in stories of his life), (iii) the essentials of the Buddhist doctrine (*Dhamma*), and (iv) the 227 rules of the *Vinaya*, which are the rules of conduct that apply to monks; included in this is the study of the *Navakowad*, which is the admonition given to a new monk (*bhikkhu*) about the rules of the *Vinaya*.

[1] It is very probable that the Central Plain and the North have their own tales and myths which are culturally transmitted through the temple. Examples for the Central Plain are *Ramakien (Ramayana)* epic, *Unarud, Nang U Thay, Mahasot, Worawongs, Wetyasunyin*, etc. (Graham 1912, pp. 569–70).

Buddhism and the spirit cults in North-east Thailand

The *nagtham* examinations range from grade 3 (lowest) to grade 1. In the lowest grade the study of the above syllabus is begun at an elementary level, and in the next two grades more advanced study is made. Most village monks from Baan Phraan Muan do not get beyond grades 3 and 2; the abbots nowadays may pass grade 1 in the course of time, but this was not necessarily so for abbots in the past. In 1962, for instance, only the abbot and one novice had passed the second grade; four of five monks had passed the lowest grade 3, and the fifth none; two of the three novices had failed the lowest grade. In subsequent years the abbot passed the highest grade 1 and is now officially entitled to run a school in the Lent season.

The three *nagtham* grades do not include the study of Pali, the language of the chants and Buddhist doctrinal texts. Pali studies are conducted separately and the relevant examinations are called *prayog*, which consist of seven grades (3-9). In theory a monk may embark on Pali studies concurrently with *nagtham* studies or after concluding them. In practice Pali studies are not easy to engage in because, even if the monk or novice is motivated to learn, he faces the difficulty of finding a competent monk to teach him. Few village monks are versed in Pali and therefore this specialized learning is rare. It is for these reasons that I argue that the majority of village monks or novices are largely ignorant of Pali (or at most have a shaky knowledge) and therefore of the content of Pali chants and Pali doctrinal texts. While the latter are accessible in translation in local script, the chants cannot be reduced into the words of the local language, for then they would lose their sacredness and their efficacy.

A monk whose service is a continuation of novicehood enlarges his repertoire of chants and takes up for special study the *Navakowad* (the 227 *Vinaya* precepts) and the *Patimokkha* confession.

What does a monk study who serves only for one Lent? He is expected to acquire the following competence: he is trained in *tham watr* (morning and evening worship of the Buddha), and in giving the five and eight precepts of the laity (*haj sin dai*); he tries to memorize the *suad mongkhon* chants; and he is taught the *Vinaya* rules. It is not an exaggeration to say that temporary monks primarily take back to lay life a limited repertoire of Pali chants which they will never use again. But while in robes they will have participated in many temple and household rites where the chants will have been recited. The life of the novice who later becomes a monk and spends some years in the temple can be, as we have seen, quite different.

The monastic routine and its rewards

THE SATISFACTIONS OF MONKHOOD

What satisfaction do monks get from their religious role? The abbot enumerated the following benefits. The villagers, he said, pay greater respect to continuing monks, than to those who have left monkhood, because they keep the precepts and observe the rules of the *Sangha*. Since there are so many *wat* in the country, monks have a place to stay wherever they go. Being a monk gives time for study and acquiring more knowledge than a layman. He also said that villagers work much harder than monks; unlike monks, who lead a sheltered life, villagers have to work in the fields in sun and rain.

Only one of the benefits enumerated, the second, requires amplification. Monks do in fact travel widely except during Lent and find ready shelter and hospitality in other *wat*. In this respect they enjoy a much greater advantage than laymen, whose contacts in the outer world are much more restricted. This incentive to physical mobility—aided by the leisure at a monk's command—has further advantageous implications for the scholar–monk, who moves not only geographically but upwards educationally through the network of country-wide monastic institutions. I shall deal with him later and indicate the manner in which it is true to say that this mobility in both senses signifies a transformation of the concept of 'homeless wanderer' of pristine Buddhism.

FROM MONK TO LAYMAN: THE USES OF LITERACY

The monastic experience, especially if it has been of sufficient duration to have allowed the acquisition of literacy (the ability to read in the sacred Tham and secular Lao scripts and to copy extant texts, rather than to compose creatively), can be used to great advantage when lay life is resumed. This I would claim is one of the most important rewards of monkhood, which, although not necessarily formulated by the actors, is nevertheless a significant implication of sociological analysis.

The acquisition of literacy, which gives access to ritual texts, is *via* the village temple. In earlier times attendance at the temple school was an essential first step on the ladder: the progression was from *dekwat* (temple boy) to *nen* (novice) to *phra* (monk). What becomes of the ex-monk who becomes a householder? His service in the *wat*—especially if it has been long enough for him to have learned Buddhist chants and ritual procedures and to have acquired literacy (as defined above)—will enable him to become, if he so wishes, a ritual expert and a religious leader in the village. Let us begin the analysis by taking a general view of the specialist statuses in the village that require literacy. Below, I have enumerated the village specialists and for purposes of convenience divided them into ritual and secular kinds. It is the ritual specialists that concern us here (incidentally, I also introduce the variety of ritual specialists and their cults, which will concern us in later chapters), for the village headman, who keeps records, and the schoolteacher, dispensing primary education, are associated with the 'new' literacy and are the products of recent administrative measures (since the 1930s) of the central and provincial governments. The *mau lum* (see B2), though traditional and though they went to temple schools for primary education, did not in the past necessarily improve their literacy through service as monks and novices nor did they require mastery of the sacred Tham script for the practice of their art (see Tambiah 1968a).

SPECIALISTS IN PHRAAN MUAN VILLAGE

(A) Ritual specialists for whom literacy is essential

1. *Phraa (monk)*: Number in village temple during Lent 1966 = abbot + 5 monks + 4 novices. Traditionally novices and monks who had been in robes for some years could read fluently Tham, secular Lao and Thai scripts. Competence in writing, however, was variable, again depending on length of service. The learned monks, especially the abbots (*chao wat*), tend to be proficient writers, today in Lao and Thai scripts, in the past in Tham as well.

2. *Achaan wat* (ex-abbot or ex-monk and lay leader of Buddhist congregation): Number in 1965 = 3. Each was an ex-monk whose literacy was good as far as reading of Tham, Lao and Thai scripts went. Usually could write in Lao and Thai scripts, but ability was variable and not essential. Strictly speaking, the title is conferred only on ex-abbots.

3. *Mau khwan/paahm* (lay officiant at *khwan* (spiritual essence) rites): Number in 1966 = 2 + 1 occasional practitioner. *Khwan* rites are typically threshold rites and rites of passage, performed especially at birth, marriage, ordination and pregnancy. (They also extend into rice cultivation, and rites of affliction.) The officiant was invariably an ex-monk. Reading ability of Tham and Lao scripts essential; usually could write Lao and Thai scripts, but not necessarily Tham.

4. *Mau ya* (physician): Number in 1966 = 1. Attainments similar to *mau khwan* (3). Ability to read medical and ritual texts in Tham and Lao scripts essential. Indigenous medicine includes ritual frills and techniques of ritual healing as supplement to herbal and other medicines to cure organic illnesses.

5. *Mau du* (astrologer): Number in 1966 = 3, possibly more. Usually has some qualifications as 3 and 4 above. Should be able to read charts and make simple calculations.

(B) Secular specialists for whom literacy is required

1. *Puyaiban* (headman): Number in 1966 = 1. Tradionally literacy not required, although in theory required. Primary role is mediating between village and district administration. Today, usually versed in Lao and Thai scripts, though, since records kept are minimal, writing competence is not advanced. Has usually been a monk, and may be a village elder with the prestige and qualifications of *mau khwan*.

2. *Mau lum* (folk opera entertainer): Number in 1966 = 2. Entertainers are both male and female. Reading and copying ability in Lao and, today, Thai scripts required, but not Tham script; special emphasis on memorization of words. Elementary schooling is essential but not service as monk/novice.

3. *Khruu* (schoolteacher): Number in 1966 = 4. As a professional specialist he is quite recent (since the 1930s) and has replaced the teaching monk. He has to teach Thai in the Thai script in village school. Perfectly fluent—both in reading and writing—in Lao and Thai scripts, but not in Tham sacred script which gives access to traditional regional Buddhist and other ritual texts. Teachers are not interested in the forms of literacy of the *paahm/mau khwan* type. Since Buddhist texts are today being increasingly printed in Thai script, they are versed in Buddhism.

(C) Ritual specialists for whom literacy is not required

1. *Mau song* (diviner): Number in 1966 = 3 or 4. The diviner's art consists of manipulating ritual objects (e.g. looking through an egg or into a mirror) and interpreting signs. His techniques do not require writing and calculating on paper. He need not have been a monk and reading ability is not required; is usually semi-literate as far as reading is concerned.

2. *Cham* and *tiam* (intermediary and medium, respectively, of village and temple guardian spirits = *Tapubaan* and *Chao Phau Tongkyang*). Number in 1966 = 1 + 1; a village can have only one of each kind. Only memorization of a few words of address to the guardian spirits is required. Reading ability in any script not essential; same as *mau song*, 1 above. Usually these personnel have never been novices or monks in the Buddhist temple.

3. *Mau tham* (exorcizer of malevolent spirits): Number in 1966 = 2. Memorizes charms and spells, some of which are portions of Buddhist *pali* chants, other magical formulae without explicit meaning. Literacy

Buddhism and the spirit cults in North-east Thailand

not required; invariably has never been a novice or monk, and usually has very poor reading and writing competence in any script. However, exceptions can be found—there are none in Phraan Muan village—of persons who possess, read and use magical texts; these persons, significantly, have learned to read esoteric texts and to practise their arts from certain 'extraordinary' monks or lay teachers (*guru*).

4. *Mau lum phii fa* (medium of sky spirit). Number in 1966 = 1. Usually female. Memorizes words and chants, but accuracy not important. Reading ability not required. Excluded from monkhood by virtue of sex. Village medium is illiterate.

(D) Secular specialists for whom literacy is not required

Craftsmen and experts in manual skills (e.g. carpenter, blacksmith, cloth-weaver).

In respect of the ritual statuses, the basic distinction I want to bring out here is that some of them require and are associated with literacy and others not. The village monk, the *acharn wat* (the lay leader of the Buddhist congregation), the *mau khwan* or *paahm* (the officiant at *khwan* rites), the *mau ya* (the physician), and the *mau du* (the astrologer) can read texts in Tham, Lao and Thai alphabets with varying degrees of competence. In fact, apart from the monk's, the other roles are lay, and it is possible for the same man to practise all of them, or some of them, concurrently. All these specialist roles are interlocked in a manner which, in general terms, can be stated as follows. Except in the case of a few persons, monkhood is of temporary duration. Some of the ex-monks who have reached the required level of literacy can and do become lay ritual experts whose art is dependent on the reading and consultation of ritual texts. Buddhism and Buddhist rites are allied to those practised by the *mau khwan* (and to the art of the physician) because they are rites of auspicious 'charging' and do not traffic with malevolent spirits (*phii*). The monk does not practise *khwan* rites; but he is not opposed to them and can himself be the client or patient.

In contrast, all such ritual specialists as *mau song* (diviner), *cham, tiam* (intermediary and medium of village guardian spirits), *mau tham* (exorcizer), and *mau lum phii fa* (medium of the sky spirit) are distinguished as dealing with spirits (*phii*), with whom both doctrinally and in practice monks have no truck and to whom Buddhism is 'opposed'. Reading (and, much less, writing) ability in any script is not required of these practitioners; their art consists of manipulating objects and memorizing divining codes, or spells or forms of invocation and thanksgiving; mediumship especially, inasmuch as it stands for possession by a spirit, is furthest removed from the monk or ritual expert, who is associated with learning and with texts.

In light of this, it is understandable that in the village the ritual specialists who are literate have higher prestige than those who are not literate— partly because Buddhism and its allied rituals are ethically superior and opposed to the spirit cults; partly because the former's art is associated with specially valued learning and literacy *per se*. This herarchical distinction is not merely a matter of prestige; it directly impinges upon leadership. The most important village elders (*phuu thaw*—or *thawkae*—both words mean 'old persons' and 'mediators'/'witnesses') are those who are *achaan wat, mau khwan* or *paahm*, and *mau ya*. Together with the abbot, they comprise the membership of the village temple committee which organizes Buddhist festivities and manages the finances of the temple. They are also the officiants at marriages and other rites of passage (except death, which is the province of the monk), the settlers of disputes, and the witnesses to marriage and divorce transactions.

No specialist in the cult of the spirits (*phii*) is a village elder or leader in this sense. He may be individually respected but he is not a leader in the community. This is as much as evaluation of the lesser respect due his cult as of his lower level of personal achievement in both a technical and a moral sense.

Three kinds of ex-monk literate specialists are particularly important in Phraan Muan village: the *achaan wat* (lay leader of Buddhist congregation), *mau khwan* or *paahm* (officiant at *khwan* rites), and *mau ya* (physician). The purist can legitimately criticize my inclusion of medicine under ritual specialisms. My reasons for doing so are: the literacy in question was learned in the temple; one man can combine all three specialisms; the folk science of medicine has ritual frills; and often, in village Thailand, monks practise medicine and may later function as lay *mau ya* or while in robes teach medicine to lay students.

Achaan wat: the role of the *achaan* is to invite (*aratana*) the monks on behalf of the congregation to give precepts, or to chant, or to make a sermon, and to receive food and other gifts presented by laymen. Every merit-making occasion which monks attend requires the chanting of invitations in the Pali language.

The following chants of invitation are some of the most frequent that an *achaan* recites:

aratana sil: to invite monks to give the five or eight precepts;

aratana tawai sankatarn: to invite monks to accept food;

aratana pahung: to invite monks to chant before alms are given to them, followed by breakfast;

aratana theed: invitation of a monk or monks to give a sermon. In the festival of *Bun Phraawes*, there is a special invitation requesting monks to read *Lam Phrawesandaun*;

aratana Uppakrut: invitation to Phraa Uppakrut (a mythical being who lives in the swamp) to accompany villagers to the temple before the *Bun Phraawes* proceedings start.

In Phraan Muan there were three persons who enacted this role and their paths of literacy conformed to a standard pattern: preliminary education as a child *dekwat* in the school run by the monks; then, in adolescence service as novice during which skills in reading and copying the sacred Tham and secular Lao languages were acquired, and finally a period of service as monk in which ritual skills were perfected. In Chapter 13, two of these ritual experts will engage our attention in detail.

Mau Ya and Mau Khwan/Paahm: the physician's art is not within the scope of this book; the village's most successful physician, Phau Tu Phan, was in fact also an *achaan wat* and a *mau khwan*. He learned the arts of medicine and the conduct of *sukhwan* rites, after he had given up his robes, from his mother's brother and a kinsman of his grand-parental generation respectively, but his previous acquisition of literacy in the *wat* was an essential qualification.

The *khwan* rites and its officiants will be treated in a subsequent chapter. Here it is sufficient to note that the most popular *mau khwan* in the village in 1961 was Phau Champi, who had been a novice and a monk, was an *achaan wat*, a pupil of and successor to Phau Tu Phan (a distant kinsman), a member of the '*wat* committee', and the village's most respected and pious leader. His ritual expertise was acquired after service in the *wat*, where he gained literacy.

The recruitment to these positions may be summed up as follows: the practice of medicine and *khwan* and associated rites requires literacy of the type acquired in the temple; yet a person who has been a novice and monk does not automatically become a medical or ritual expert. Traditionally these arts have to be learned from an existing practitioner, who is likely to nominate and train a kinsman to succeed him; the apprentice usually waits until his teacher is ready to give up before he himself practises on his own. This appears to be the professional etiquette within the village.

Thus this interlocking relationship of teacher and chosen disciple means that recruitment for the learning of the arts of *mau khwan* and *mau ya* is not completely open nor a simple commercial transaction. The eligibility and suitability of the candidate are assessed by the teacher, and the prescribed qualities of character are intrinsic to the role of ritual elder.

The monastic routine and its rewards

Throughout Thailand each *wat* and its monastic community communicates for certain purposes with the outside world of lay parishioners, and *vice versa*, through an organization called the *wat* committee, which is composed usually of the abbot and a few secular lay leaders. The members of the committee (excepting the abbot) act as the lay trustees of temple affairs. Thus while the monastic membership and the village households are two distinct communities, they are formally linked through the *wat* committee for the facilitation and regulation of their reciprocal communication.

Wat Phraan Muan, like all other *wat* in Thailand, had a committee; it consisted in 1961 of the abbot and three elders, all of whom had served their time as monks and were in fact leaders of prestige. (One was Phau Champi; other ritual leaders described earlier had in former years been active members of the committee.) There is no popular election of a *wat* committee; the present members were appointed by the previous abbot. Their duties are to organize village labour and finance for holding collective calendrical rites, to see that the *wat* is provided with the necessary equipment, and to act as treasurers for money collected in the merit-making ceremonies. The role of these lay elders in village affairs must not be minimized. It is they, in fact, who structure and channel the collective participation of the village as a religious congregation. Ritual leadership is the only conspicuous leadership in the village, and it is always available to an ex-monk of exceptional qualities and mature age.

TRADITIONAL LITERACY: SOME QUANTITATIVE ASPECTS

I shall now extend this discussion of the traditional literacy of novices, monks and lay ritual experts (all ex-monks) by commenting on the number of people who travelled on the traditional path of literacy and emerged literate. In modern educational jargon, I am considering the problem of 'educational wastage' from the point of view of literacy, not in terms of other benefits.

In the figures given earlier on the number who became novices and monks, I have indicated that although more than half of the male family heads had seen some kind of religious service in the temple, only about a fifth of the total number had been both novices and monks, and therefore could be assumed to have had the time and training for mastering the art of reading *nansy Tham* and documents in the secular Lao–Thai scripts. But even this minority could not be assumed to have retained their ability to read when they resumed lay life. There are many elderly persons in the village today who, although they had studied *nansy Tham* in their youth, have virtually lost their literacy.

In 1966 a very rough count was made of the number of laymen who were versed in the traditional Tham and Lao scripts. Seven elders were mentioned by villagers as having this capacity. Of these, only three were lay ritual leaders and medical practitioners of the type we have discussed: *achaan wat, mau khwan,* and *mau ya.* The other four, although able to read the occasional literature that might come to hand, were not using their literacy in a manner that had any visible impact on the village.

This leads us back to other facts already cited. A novice or monk does not automatically acquire lay ritual and medical skills; after a lapse of years, he may learn from a practitioner who is willing to have him as his successor. Interest and effort on the part of the recruit (individual achievement factors) as well as the right kinship connections (ascribed criteria) come into play.

In the village, then, monkhood and novicehood as such are not restricted; they are virtually open to any male, and it is not beyond the means of most villagers to have their sons ordained. In fact, in Baan Phraan Muan ordination is a collective rite to which the entire village contributes financially. However, certain individual or idiosyncratic factors primarily determine which of the many young men will serve long enough in the temple to attain literacy and religious knowledge. Once lay life is resumed, individual factors of interest and personal effort as well as restrictive criteria (i.e. finding a teacher who will pass on knowledge to a chosen or approved successor) play their part in determining the total number of men who in their middle age will become ritual experts, highly appreciated in the village.

What are the implications for traditional ritual and medicine of the fact that in recent years there have been hardly any young men in the village who can read the traditional manuscripts, both because of the government's educational policy of teaching children only in the Thai language and because the novices and monks of today need not, and in the main do not, master the Tham script?

Village elders are very much aware of this as a problem, for the number of *mau khwan* and *mau ya* in the region is dwindling, but not, as yet, the public demand for their services. The *khwan* rites are still widely practised. Most villagers are treated by their own village physicians rather than by government doctors. Nevertheless, the loss of traditional literacy will seriously affect the emergence of traditional specialists in the future. Already, the death of elderly specialists is causing a visible shortage.

The monastic routine and its rewards

In the last section I shall look beyond the narrow universe of village Buddhism and discuss briefly two features of extra-village literacy in order, on the one hand, to remind the reader of the confines of my discussion of village literacy and, on the other, to indicate the complex educational network that encompasses an isolated village. Clearly, in Thailand, networks of monastic educational institutions exist on a regional level, with urban and historic rural centres being focal points. In turn, these networks converge upon Bangkok, the national capital. Apart from famous monastic schools Bangkok has two universities for monks, which teach subjects ordinarily taught in secular universities.

Village youths, especially novices who are promising and keen, may leave their village temples and go to district monastic centres. From there they may be sent to historic provincial centres of learning, and even finally find their way to Bangkok. This path of literacy is made possible by certain features peculiar to monkhood. First, a young novice or monk always has assigned to him an older monk as preceptor (called by the younger man *luang phii*, that is, 'respected elder brother') who teaches, sponsors and supports him. This relationship between *upacha* (preceptor) and pupil monk can be an important one for mobility within the Order. Secondly, the abbot of a village temple has contacts with other abbots and with his district head, so that he can find a place for a keen student in a monastic centre which gives superior education. Further, the status of novice or monk is a 'detached' one and in theory any such religious person can be mobile, going from temple to temple, provided he can find a place through the active collaboration of his preceptor and sponsor. Placement in other communities through kinship, as is done in the secular world, is more circumscribed than the mobility that is possible for a monk. Here is indeed a transformation of the concept of 'homeless wanderer' of pristine Buddhism.

That such networks are used and that village youths of promise have climbed the ladder of literacy is attested by certain writers (e.g. Klausner 1964). In another essay (Tambiah 1968a) I have recounted the educational career of an extraordinary monk who was born in a north-eastern village, not in Baan Phraan Muan but in the province of Mahasarakam, and who has reached the apex of monastic learning in Thailand, being currently engaged in Sanskrit studies in the University of Cambridge. The account describes in detail many of the points I can merely mention here: the network and levels of monastic centres of learning, the institution of preceptor–pupil relationship, the number of novice/monk pupils in these centres, and finally the kind of instruction in Pali studies given at the centres.

Now it is clear that, compared with the story in that account, the village of Baan Phraan Muan is undistinguished and has not systematically nurtured gifted young men who have then entered the network of higher learning. But I must hasten to add that Baan Phraan Muan, in fact, falls into the lowest and largest category of villages in the hierarchy of traditional learning in North-east Thailand; its situation is shared by many others.

In estimating in a crude way the efficacy of monastic educational networks and the proportion of novices and monks who go beyond the elementary *nagtham* studies to Pali studies, it is relevant to note the following facts. There is no systematic recruitment of novices or monks from villages into higher centres of learning. The point is rather that a gifted student, adequately sponsored, can find his way into the upper reaches. The system does not work in the manner of contemporary national educational systems which channel students from primary schools to secondary schools to universities. Another way of saying the same thing is that the vast majority of village novices and monks do not aspire to become learned in Pali studies. This is due not only to the custom of temporary religious service. Even those who stay in robes for some length of time do not in the main aspire to become Pali scholar-monks.

There are many reasons for this. The role of the monk in a village is primarily a ritual one; we have already seen that in order to perform his parish and monastic role he needs only to acquire a certain amount of literacy in the sacred Tham and secular languages and to memorize a body of oft-used chants. Pali studies are not essential for this purpose. Furthermore, a monk who becomes engaged in Pali doctrinal studies is in all probability also one who becomes increasingly committed to following that kind of doctrinal Buddhism which, if taken seriously, results in progressive detachment from the world and involves practising meditation and self-control and entering into mystical realms which promise *nirvana*. In other words, he tends to become a world-renouncer, and only a few are capable of engaging in this higher pursuit.

From the point of view of literacy, a most relevant consideration is that which stands in contrast to the situation of the Islamic *mallam*. In Islam Arabic studies are a necessary vehicle for mastery of legal, judicial and other codes which have a direct secular significance. The learned man is an interpreter of law and a judge and counsellor of men in everyday affairs. The Pali doctrinal texts of Buddhism have no implication for the laws and customs of everyday life of the laity. For a village monk, we have seen, his pay-off is primarily ritual eldership in the village, for which he requires only a kind of literacy that is acquired at the village level.

It is for these reasons that few monks take their *nagtham* studies seriously or enter upon the more complex Pali studies. Some do learn Pali, for it confers prestige and entitles them to conduct village religious schools. Thus, centres of learning feed their pupils back into the villages. But such monks rarely go beyond the first few grades of Pali studies. It is not a matter of importance to the village congregation that they should have in their midst a Pali scholar—it is enough that someone is available in the neighbourhood to perform the required rituals.

However, a professional monk may wish to climb the religious hierarchy; he may aspire to become abbot of his village temple and then become a district head (*chaokana amphur*). Such a monk must have a certain amount of intellectual training and service in other temples. While the village of Phraan Muan has never produced a scholar-monk, it has produced one monk in recent times who has climbed the clerical hierarchy. He is Phra Khru Anurak Punnaket, forty-eight years of age, and at present the ecclesiastical head of Pen District. He is the son of Phau ('father') Puay, an ordinary and undistinguished farmer in Phraan Muan village. Phra Anurak spent about fifteen years in a temple at the provincial capital of Udorn and several years in Bangkok, then returned as abbot to his native village from where he received his promotion. He has some knowledge of Pali but would not consider himself a scholar. His local influence is great because of his position, his varied experience, and his wide network of contacts, both ecclesiastical and secular.

THE BUDDHIST AND HINDU STAGES OF LIFE

A question raised in Chapter 6 concerning the relation between the Hindu four stages of life and the Buddhist life cycle statuses can be answered now.

The Hindu formulation is that of a progression from celibate student, to householder, to withdrawal from secular responsibilities, to homeless wanderer and world renouncer. These stages were theoretically possible to any person.

In contrast, the Buddhist conception appeared to state two distinct paired progressions. For the seeker of salvation, a progression from novice-disciple to monk (a radical world renunciation at the threshold of adult life); and for the layman a leisurely journey from simple householder to piety and withdrawal from worldly preoccupations in old age.

But in actual fact, in the Thai village described, we see that for the majority of male laymen another more comprehensive life cycle has been worked out which exploits the classical option that a monk may give up his robes without dishonour. A village boy, who in the past started as a temple boy (*dekwat*), becomes novice as an adolescent, then a celibate monk at the dawn of adulthood. After this religious service and education, he resumes lay life to marry and set up a household and to materially support the monks in the *wat*. In the course of lay life, those who had undergone a sufficiently long period of religious education could become ritual experts and lay leaders of the congregation, sponsor the ordination of village sons, and intensify their religious piety towards the end of their lives and in the face of death.

Only a minority of village youth adhere to the narrower path of passing from novicehood into a lifelong state of monkhood, renouncing marriage, the founding of a family, and active participation in the affairs of this world. But even these permanent monks lead a community life in monasteries, which must depend on the laity for daily material support, and are honoured by the laity and are called upon by them to transfer merit by virtue of their own excellence acquired as renouncers of the layman's way of life.

The logic of the village scheme whereby renunciation and withdrawal is practised by most males in late youth and early adulthood, followed by the full life of a householder and culminating in, again, religious piety—in other words the successive stages outlined above—can best be understood not as a derivation from classical tradition but as a transformation of classical possibilities[1] which finds its basis in village social structure: the expectations and obligations between parents and sons and between generations, the notions of collective merit-making and merit transfer, and the orientation that merit-accumulation is not so much a private quest but a public action which not only states but reinforces and increases one's social status and prestige, which are in turn themselves indices of ethical well-being.

[1] This transformation is not, of course, unique to Thailand; roughly similar patterns are found in Burma, Laos and Cambodia.

9

THE IDEOLOGY OF MERIT

THE LAYMAN AND THE MONK

We have already noted that the *wat* as an architectural complex is set apart from the village, and that at the same time it is the centre of village life. In the same way the distinction between monk and layman is fundamental, though the monk is the focus of merit-making and religious ceremonial on the part of the layman. The fact that it is the young men of the village who are monks, and it is their elders who are benefactors, does not stand in the way of the relationship between layman and monk taking on a particular asymmetrical and symbiotic pattern.

The monks and novices live apart—the villagers visit them rather than they the villagers. A monk keeps his visits to the village settlement to a minimum; he does not socialize with villagers and he enters a home primarily to conduct rites. When village women bring the morning and midday meals to the monks there is very little verbal exchange. Although a monk's home is usually in the village his visits there are also minimal; a novice has greater freedom of contact with his family. While a monk is separated from family and kin, the latter can and do visit him in the *wat*. A monk is free to visit other *wat* and he often does so; nor is he barred from going to a town where he may visit a bigger *wat* and transact personal business. His freedom of movement is curtailed only during Lent.

A layman of whatever age or either sex must show formal respect to a monk. The fact that a monk's head is shaven and that he wears a saffron robe automatically induces the asymmetrical etiquette. The rules of contact with laymen are particularly stringent in the case of women— not old women, contact with whom gives no cause for public suspicion, but younger women, especially unmarried girls.

The concepts of formality, respect and distance are expressed in the language of conversation between monk and layman. In fact, the linguistic categories show a combination of two criteria of status differences. In general, generational and relative-age distinctions are vital in village behaviour, and kinship terms express these distinctions. Monkhood is a specially venerated status, and it commands respect irrespective of the age of the incumbent. In the case of a young monk *vis-à-vis* an elderly layman, the two criteria are in contradiction and the language devised expressed both nuances in a fused fashion.

Thus a man or woman who is an actual parent or of the parental generation of the monk calls the latter *hua luug* (head child); *hua* is a term of respect, because the head is the most sacred part of a man's body. An older layman of grandparental or *phuu thaaw* status calls a monk *hua laan*, the latter word meaning grandchild. A layman younger than a monk calls him *hua* plus the appropriate kinship term. Thus a younger male or female of the same generation, whether married or not, addresses him as *hua aaj* (respected elder brother), and persons of the generation below him address him in terms of the appropriate kinship term (e.g. *hua naa* = respected mother's younger brother). In general, all villagers refer to a monk as *mom* and a novice as *juaa*, both of which are terms of respect. (Aristocrats outside the royal family have the prefix *mom* in their titles.) These same terms are used as address terms towards him by a monk's older 'siblings', real and extended (of the same generation), thereby not compromising their higher relative age position in the kinship reckoning.

A monk in turn calls his parents and all persons of his parental generation *phau org* ('father of leaving' the secular life) or *mae org* ('mother of leaving' the secular life). Alternatively, he may call elders who are not his parents by the appropriate kinship term (e.g. *phau lung* = father's or mother's elder brother) and use *phau org* or *mae org* as a suffix (e.g. *phau lung phau org*). The words *phau/mae org* refer to the concept of sponsorship in ordination; parents, primarily, and all elders of the village have made possible his ordination. The use of the words in respect of all elderly persons is tantamount to saying that the monk is the son of all the elders of the village. A monk addresses persons younger than himself by personal name and small children as *soo chaaw*.

The linguistic evidence I have cited eloquently tells us how a monk, venerated on account of his sacred status which implies removal from village society, is nevertheless very much a part and parcel of the village social universe categorized in terms of kinship statuses and the rights and obligations that ensue from it. This latter point has not been sufficiently documented and appreciated in previous ethnography. The respect accorded to a monk and given expression in language is, of course, not unique to monkhood but is an essential aspect of the Thai status system documented in historical works: the use of different classifiers for nouns, of a differentiated set of pronouns and verbs nicely graduated in terms of the relative statuses of speaker and the person addressed (second person) or referred to (third person). De la Loubère himself was sensitive to this Oriental linguistic elaboration in the late seventeenth century. Thus, whereas *khon* is the classifier for ordinary people, and *tua* for animals, *ong* is the classifier for royal or revered personages, Buddha images, and monks. The general pronouns in Central Thai for a revered third person of royal or religious status is *phraa-ong*, for a respected third person *than*, for a familiar person *kee*, an outsider *khaw*, and for an inferior person, child or thing *man* (see Noss 1964). Similar differentiation occurs in verbs; whereas the word for 'to eat' commonly used by ordinary laymen amongst themselves is *kin* or *taan*, it is *chan* when used in respect of a monk or other revered person.

A monk does not follow lay occupations—there is a strict taboo on their practice. In theory he must also not directly handle money, but there are in practice some neat circumventions of this rule, as, for example, when money is included in a package which contains other, directly acceptable items. When a monk goes to a market, however, a layman or *dekwat* accompanies him and handles money on his behalf, a provision allowed for in the *Vinaya* rules.

The symbiotic nature of the relationship between monks and novices on the one hand and laymen on the other is exemplified in a two-way reciprocity. The requirements of the monks and the local *wat*, including daily food, are supplied entirely by the laity. The monks in return perform certain ritual roles of great concern to the laity. (Hereafter when I speak of monks, I include novices.) It is this set of double transactions that is central to merit-making and merit-taking, in which monk and layman, the elders *phuu thaw*, and the junior generation *lung laan* stand in opposed and complementary relationships.

I shall first examine the layman's services to the monks and distinguish which aspects of interaction are elaborations of doctrinally stated or recommended rules, and which are peculiarly village and non-doctrinal developments. I shall then devote ensuing chapters to the analysis of Buddhist ritual and focus on the monks' services to laymen.

MERIT-MAKING ('THAMBUN')

Traditionally a basic obligation of the Buddhist layman has been that he should materially support the wandering monks. Although today the monks live in village monasteries, the begging bowl is still an important symbol. In Baan Phraan Muan no food is ever cooked in the *wat*; it is regularly provided by villagers. Thus feeding the monks is the most common religious merit-making act in which a villager engages. There is a noticeable sex distinction concerning this activity. Men never offer food to the monks on their daily rounds, nor do they bring food to the monks' quarters for their midday meal. On ordinary days at 11 o'clock when the drum is beaten, old women (grandmothers) and young girls will bring food to the *wat*, set it out for the monks, watch them eat, and then carry the utensils back, having received the monks' blessings. Strict decorum is preserved during this daily meeting with the female sex. A monk does not express gratitude or pleasure at receiving food, because he must show aloofness, and because it is he who confers merit by receiving it. Technically, a monk 'should not look into the face of the woman who is giving the food', and this is observed both when a monk goes begging and when he is served.

We have the situation, then, that women—old grandmothers past child-bearing and young unmarried girls—readily approach and minister to the monks' daily needs.[1] The latter can do so without danger because the monk has suppressed his male sexuality and is *asexual*. His relations with them are formal; but when he gives up his robes, it is one of these same girls that he will marry or have sexual dealings with.

Just as old women readily approach monks, so do elderly men, though their contact on the whole is limited (except for those who serve on the *wat* committee). But in comparison with young girls, young men of the village tend to avoid the monks (who are of their own generation and age-group). Young men keep away from the monks during *wanphraa* (Buddhist Sabbath) and make their appearance only at collective calendrical rites and festivals. In general it may be supposed that young virile men find it uncongenial to approach their peers who have temporarily renounced the world and whose religious preoccupation, in theory at least, is with salvation rather than with blessed life here and now.

Daily merit-making, then, is a function of women rather than men, but the latter also gain merit as heads and members of households. On the whole, the more conspicuous practising Buddhists are women rather than men. Or to put it differently, except for a few elderly male leaders, it is women who have more contact and traffic with the monks.

The frequency of food offerings to monks was measured for a sample of 106 village families. Only 13% said they had never offered food in 1961–2 and these were in all likelihood newly formed families whose parental families would have acted on their behalf. While only about 17% of the families offered food daily, another 42% offered on some days each week. There is another small segment which made merit only on *wanphraa*, while the remainder offered food only during the Lent

---

[1] Whenever there are collective ceremonies at the *wat*, young unmarried girls are assigned the duty of carrying water from the pond to the monks' quarters for the use of monks when they are feasted.

season, when religious action was intensified. There are certain times when individual households will intensify their food offerings for a short period; examples are at times of illness or impending childbirth.

These facts establish that giving food to the monks is an important and frequently indulged-in category of merit-making. A good way of estimating the religious orientation of villagers is to compare the pattern of food-giving with attendance at the *wat* for purposes of religious instruction and edification.

Now *wanphraa*, the Buddhist Sabbath, occurs four times a lunar month, and can be utilized not only for offering food to the monks, saying private prayers, and receiving the five precepts and the blessings of the monks but, more importantly, for engaging in religious action that is not typical of everyday life. Sermons may be delivered by monks in the mornings and/or evenings, and pious persons can practise the eight precepts for a day, thereby observing a temporary asceticism and devoting time to meditation. However, in Baan Phraan Muan *wanphraa*, outside of Lent, is not characterized by such religious action. There is no sermon delivered, and people do not observe the eight precepts. A few more people than usual do bring food for the monks.

In comparison with behaviour on the usual *wanphraa*, religious orientations during the Lent season show a different pattern, especially among some of the older people. Since there are more monks and novices in the *wat* than usual, more food has to be provided. And on *wanphraa* during Lent some elderly people—more women than men—receive the eight precepts and spend the whole day in the *wat*. Before breakfast and in the evening, sermons (*theed*) may be preached for them.

The same sample of 106 households were asked about their attendance at the *wat* on religious occasions in 1961–2. Fewer than ten people in the sample had observed the eight precepts at one time or another. Such persons achieve the kind of piety associated with the concepts of *upasok* (male) and *upasika*[1] (female)—religious virtuosi in the Weberian sense. About eight men and thirteen women in the sample reported regular visits to the *wat* on *wanphraa* outside of Lent, and similar numbers reported irregular visits. Thus it is clear that the ordinary villager's religious orientation is by and large not committed to more than the ordinary five precepts. The practice of meditation and other religious techniques for achieving 'salvation' is of very limited incidence. The old and not the young show piety, and amongst them women are more frequent 'churchgoers' than men.

The sample results showed that 60% of the male family heads and

---

[1] *Upasaka* and *upasika* in Pali.

48% of their spouses went to the *wat* only on the occasion of the major calendrical collective rites. This is to say that the majority of villagers participate as a large congregation only when major merit-making rites are held. On these occasions it is the making of merit through giving that is the villagers' primary concern; sermons and chants are recited by the monks, however, and I will deal with this aspect of religious communication later. Here I want to establish the pattern of gift-giving behaviour. The frequency of gift-giving at calendrical rites is as follows: about 70% of the families reported four gifts a year per family. These gifts include not only the usual cooked food but also other items which require a cash outlay; only 13% reported that they had no occasion to give any gifts.

Wanphraa and the calendrical rites do not exhaust the occasion of attendance at the *wat* or gift-giving to monks. Large numbers usually attend the ordination ceremonies of monks and novices just before the beginning of Lent; mortuary rites always conclude with merit-making at the *wat*. There are other occasions (merit-making rites at the house (*thambunhuean*), and for dead ancestors at the burial-place) at which monks officiate and receive gifts. At marriages monks usually have no role, but gifts may be sent them. On ceremonial occasions monks are given gifts of money and of manufactured articles. As may be expected, it is manufactured goods bought in the urban market that appear as valued items, appropriately given to monks as special acts of merit-making on ceremonial occasions. They are more expensive than the articles a villager can produce or grow locally, and are hence considered more merit-making.

RANKING OF MERIT-MAKING ACTS

We have now arrived at a point where we can make a rough estimate of the villagers' orientation to and evaluation of various kinds of religious action subsumed under the concept of *thambun* or merit-making.

A sample (seventy-nine) of family heads were requested to rank eight types of religious acts which were presented in a random order. Table 4 presents the rank distributions. While, of course, there was no complete agreement among villagers, it is remarkable that the distribution showed a noticeable pattern and that the majority of respondents were by and large agreed on the hierarchical position of each category of action in relation to the rest.

The final hierarchy can be reduced to six positions:

1. completely financing the building of a *wat*—this is the act *par excellence* that brings most merit;

TABLE 4. *Ranking of religious acts by seventy-nine family heads*

Categories of religious acts	Number of persons assigning to each rank								Final rank
	Highest rank 1	2	3	4	5	6	7	Lowest rank 8	
Financing entire building of a *wat*	67	5	6	1	—	—	—	—	1
Becoming a monk oneself	6	36	29	5	1	2	—	—⎫	2
Having a son become a monk	5	34	32	7	1	—	—	—⎭	
Contributing money to the repair of a *wat*	—	4	—	31	35	6	1	2⎫	3
Making gifts at a *kathin** ceremony	—	—	3	29	29	6	5	7⎭	
Giving food daily to monks	1	2	7	5	2	30	14	18	4
Observing every *wanphraa* at the *wat*	—	—	—	1	10	27	22	19	5
Strict observance of the five precepts	—	—	—	—	1	9	36	33	6

* Traditional presentation of robes and other gifts at the end of Lent.

2. either becoming a monk oneself or having a son become a monk;

3. contributing money to the repair of a *wat* or making *kathin* (post-Lent ceremony) gifts;

4. giving food daily to the monks;

5. observing every *wanphraa*;

6. strictly observing the five precepts.

There are several implications in this pattern of evaluation. The most conspicuous act of merit-making by a layman—building a *wat*—is open only to the rich; it represents an outstanding act of financial charity. However, an ordinary layman can either become a monk or have a son become one, and this also rates high. Thus a lowly villager is not excluded from making great merit—although in actual life sponsoring an ordination ceremony requires a financial outlay, and a family should be in a position to dispense with a son's labour so that he can temporarily withdraw from the world. Despite these limitations, having a son ordained is a realistic possibility for most village households.[1]

[1] No villager in Baan Phraan Muan has had the wealth to build a temple single-handed. But spectacular acts of merit-making are known in Thailand. I refer the reader to Nash (1965, pp. 115–40) for a penetrating analysis of the sociology of conspicuous charity in a Burmese village as an indication of a man's ethical *cum* worldly status and as a vehicle for its increment. The analysis is equally applicable to Thailand and to Ceylon (see Tambiah 1963, pp. 97–107, 112–25).

Ranking next are gift-giving or money contributions of an order that again implies a drain on household resources. Many villagers make such donations, although the wealthier among them make conspicuously larger presentations.

Giving food daily to the monks is possible for almost every village household—for it involves only the setting apart of a portion of the family's cooked food. Since it is a daily act and relatively inexpensive, and because almost all indulge in it, it has a low position with no scarcity value.

A remarkable aspect is that the specifically 'Buddhistic way of life' is ranked lowest. Observing *wanphraa* at the *wat* and strict observance of the precepts—both of which connote individual ethical or moralistic conduct—seem not to be valued highly.

On the whole then we must conclude that merit-making through gift-giving is more valued than merit-making through the observance of Buddhistic precepts and the pursuit of Buddhistic ethical aims. But here certain nuances have to be introduced in order to get the picture right.

Strict observance of the five precepts (especially that exhorting avoidance of killing) and meditation on the philosophical assertions of the *Dhamma* have little positive interest for the villager, either because lay life is not possible without breaking some of the prohibitions or because one must renounce lay life altogether to pursue such aims. He therefore rates these pursuits, in so far as they have relevance for his life, low on the merit-making scale; this is not because he devalues them but because they are not normally open to him. Moreover, these pursuits, the core of Buddhistic striving, are thought to have pertinence primarily for the monk and secondarily for the aged approaching death. The way of the monk is different from that of the householder, and the monks' way of life is accorded the more meritorious status.

This structuring of the divergent but reciprocal orientations of monk and layman rests on two paradoxes. As Obeyesekere (1968, p. 38) has put it, 'the self-denials of the extreme ascetic may serve as models for the good life of the ordinary man', not so much models to be imitated, for lay life makes that impossible, but because as Durkheim (1926, p. 316) perceived, 'It is necessary that an elite put the end too high, if the crowd is not to put it too low'.

But this very proposition itself rests on another paradox: it is because the ordinary man labours in this world and takes on himself the burdens of polluting activities that the religious specialist can be freed to pursue purity freed from the world's contaminations. The monks do not kill but must be provided with meat; they do not cook rice or make curries, for this, too, is taking life, but rice and curries are lovingly cooked for

1a Image of the Buddha seated on and being shielded by the seven-headed royal *Naga* (snake), Muchalinda (see Chapters 7 and 10)

1b Mortuary rites: on the third day after cremation, the bones are collected in a pot, and the monks are here seen chanting and transferring merit to the deceased before the pot is buried (see Chapter 11)

2 The *Bun Kathin* procession at the end of Lent. In front are men sweeping the ground, and a man carrying the Buddha image, followed by monks and laymen carrying money trees, gifts and flags (see Chapter 10)

them; they do not weave cloth but cloth is woven and dyed for them; they cannot build monasteries but these are built for them by lay bene-factors. Seculars receive and pay out money on their behalf because a monk cannot touch it without breaking a monastic rule. In the past land was endowed to major *wat*, and lay trustees supervised and serfs cultivated so that the monks might be maintained and could be free of the danger of destroying life by digging the earth. Monks cannot replace themselves because they are sworn to celibacy, but laymen must marry and dedicate their sons to ascetic life.

These exemptions from pollution and the snares of the world so that purity can be actively pursued are, after all, a major premise as well of the Indian caste system. The Brahmin in order to be pure and to reach upwards for greater purity requires the washerman, the barber, the farmer and many other labourers to shield him, to provide for him, and to remove his impurities. And, if we extend the argument, does not any aristocracy—whether it be Roman patricians or the English gentlemen—gain its right to creative 'leisure', in the way Plato meant it, only because there are slaves and servants to 'work'?

If the villagers thus free the monks for higher pursuits, then their labourings—even though polluting—are positively virtuous, too, and merit is their reward.

BUILDING A 'BOOD': A LONG-TERM ECONOMIC PLAN

The economy of Baan Phraan Muan is such that no man is rich enough to engage in the conspicuous merit-making act of building a *wat* or any of its component structures. Sponsoring the ordination of a son or relative or holding mortuary rites and various merit-making rites in the home, at which a group of monks are feasted and given gifts, is possible by an individual or a household but usually necessitates wide-scale rendering of mutual aid and financial donations by kinsmen, neighbours and friends.

I shall now describe a collective attempt by the village community to plan, gather resources, and build a *bood* for the village. The description reveals two features which are worth emphasizing in the context of the doctrines of 'loose structure' and 'economic inefficiency', which some writers attribute to the kind of society I am describing: one, the voluntarily accepted and implemented obligations on the part of villagers, which shows the propensity to co-operative effort; and two, the sense of long-term economic planning and rational systematic marshalling of the economic resources of the village in order to achieve something it regards as worthwhile.

Buddhism and the spirit cults in North-east Thailand

The village *wat* lacks a proper *bood*, which is the hallmark of a well-established *wat* that can ordain its own monks. Some years ago the village *wat* was moved to the present location, which was the site of a previous *wat* that lay in ruins, and was, no doubt, 'ancient' as evidenced by the statues dug up. The remains of a *bood* and the presence of *sima* stones (which signified that the ground was consecrated for all time) were sufficient precedent and stimulus for the villagers to aspire to build an imposing new *bood* which would give prestige to them and their village.

The *wat* committee consisting of the abbot and three elders met together in late 1965 with the headman, discussed the project and the necessary steps to be taken, and agreed to call a village meeting at the headman's house. The traditional bamboo device (*khau rau*) was sounded at night to call the villagers and some hundred of them, mostly males, assembled ('women', it was said, 'do not attend meetings'). Those assembled agreed to accept the following recommendations of the *wat* committee:

1. every household was to contribute 500 bricks. Instead of making the bricks themselves, villagers were asked to contribute the cash value of 80 *baht* per household so that well-made bricks could be purchased. This was a compulsory obligation;

2. a plea was made for two kinds of voluntary contribution: (*a*) donations of paddy to the amount of 3 *muen* (about 36 kilograms) per household were solicited (*pae khaw pleng*); (*b*) adults and youth, both male and female, were requested to contribute free labour (*khau laeng*).

The district abbot of Amphur Pen—a previous abbot of Phraan Muan village and still its patron and counsellor—went to Bangkok to secure a building plan from the Department of Religious Affairs. Building operations were commenced in February 1966 after the completion of harvest when the granaries were stocked and the villagers were free of agricultural work.

A set of contractors of Annamese origin undertook to build the foundations for a fee of 4,000 *baht*. After digging for the foundations and installing the bases for pillars, they pulled out, demanding a fee of 1,500 *baht* for the work done. This incident is typical of diasters that plague village-based monumental projects undertaken with insufficient money and business knowledge. Subsequently, another group of Thai contractors, from the town of Udorn, were employed to complete the foundations for 3,000 *baht* and to build the pillars for 1,500 *baht*.

The collection of sufficient money for buying building materials and for paying the builders has been a difficult task. By August 1966, village households had freely contributed over 300 *muen* of paddy, which was transported from the village by young women to the market and sold for

3,216 *baht* (US $120). Of the 149 households, 79 had made the cash 'brick' payments. Money collected at previous festivals, constituting the bank balance of the *wat*, was also committed to the project.

By August 1966, the initial operations were successfully completed at the cost of 20,000 *baht* for building materials, 1,500 *baht* to the Annamese contractors, and 4,500 *baht* to the second group of builders. The result of meeting these commitments was a debt of 3,700 *baht* which the *wat* committee owed to fellow villagers, who loaned money to them on interest in order to meet the bills.

It should be noted that the contracting workmen, about three in number, provide only the expert services of mason and carpenter. The unskilled manual work of transporting the building materials from the town, helping the artisan-craftsmen by carrying sand and water to the building site, digging the ground, etc., is provided free by village men and women, especially those of the junior *luug-laan* generation. Meetings are called at which they receive work instructions.

Thus, some seven months after the building was commenced, there stands the incomplete shell of the *bood* with firm foundations and sturdy pillars. Villagers estimate that it would take them 10–15 years and (for them) an astronomical sum of money to complete the edifice with floor, walls, roof, ornamentation, statues and furniture. Barring the calamities of international politics, they will, if left in peace, accomplish their long-term economic plan with the sweat of their brow and the denial of luxuries for their personal comfort and enjoyment. The building itself will be a substantive representation of their co-operative effort and sacrifice. Have not deliverance from old age and death, and more sumptuous treasures of the world, been promised them for such acts of charity? And has it not always been the case that it is on the labour of the masses that the edifice of a spiritual *Sangha* can arise to pursue higher things, even if the donors are not humble peasants but magnificent kings?

10

THE CYCLE OF COLLECTIVE 'WAT' RITES
AND THE AGRICULTURAL CALENDAR

In Baan Phraan Muan, as in every Thai village, a cycle of collective calendrical rites is held at the *wat* and conducted by the monks. The rites I shall refer to here are representative of all the villages of the region around Phraan Muan. These are collective in the sense that the entire village participates in the annually recurring rites. Characteristically, they are merit-making occasions and the names of the rites have the prefix *bun* (e.g. *Bun Kathin*).

What I want to demonstrate now is that the cycle of Buddhist temple rites is closely interwoven with the cycle of village economic activities, especially the cycle of rice cultivation, which forms the basis of the local economy. Secondly, I shall indicate briefly how each cosmic rite, occurring at a specific time of the year, weaves in particular social themes and integrates them into the Buddhist religious system, and conversely how such religious institutions as monkhood and ancestor beliefs fit into the rhythm of social life.

While it would be false to postulate that Buddhism gets its primary meanings from the agricultural preoccupations of the villagers, it would be surprising if Buddhism had no linkage with the agricultural cycle. Table 5 gives the pattern of *wat* rites in relation to the rice cycle. The dating of *wat* ceremonies is in terms of the lunar calendar, and in the villages of the Phraan Muan region the first lunar month falls in December. The traditional Thai New Year is *Songkran*, which falls in April.

Buddhist events such as *Wisaka*, Lent and *Makha Bucha* are fixed by long religious tradition, in which the local villagers played no part; however, it is significant that early Buddhism converted the season of rains into Lent. The villagers are completely free to time their post-harvest merit-making rites (such as *Bun Phraawes*) to suit local circumstances, and their timing may vary from village to village and from year to year.

Starting with *Songkran*, the major emphasis of each calendrical rite and its linkage with the rice cycle appears to be as follows.

(*a*) *Songkran* falls at the end of the dry season when rains are imminent. There is thus a dual orientation in this transition period—the end of the old year and the beginning of the new, the end of the scorching dry

The cycle of collective 'wat' rites

TABLE 5. *Calendar of 'wat' ceremonies and the agricultural cycle*

Name of ceremony	Western calendar	Phase of agricultural cycle
Songkran (traditional New Year)	13–15 April	DRY SEASON Approximate end of dry season and expectation of rains Change in seasons
Wisaka Bucha (day of birth, enlightenment and death of Buddha)	May	RAIN Rains and wet season begin Time for ploughing fields
Khaw Phansa (entering Lent)	July	GROWING RICE Transplanting completed Growing period of rice Season of rain (*Vassa*)
Bun Khaw Saak (making merit for spirits of the dead with puffed rice)	September	Rice at critical stage when grains begin to form Height of growth season
Org Phansa (leaving Lent)	October	Grains have formed and are maturing; end of rains
Bun Kathin (*kathin* presentation)	Between full moons of October and November	END OF RAINS
Makha Bucha (All Saints Day)	February	HARVESTING
Bun Phraawes (merit-making for *Phraawes*)	February, March	Harvest celebrations

season and the beginning of the rains—and the ritual activities reflect both themes.

The three days which comprise *Songkran* are categorized thus: the first day is the end of the old year (*Songkran*); the second day is the intervening day (*Wan Naw*), and the third day is the beginning of the new year (*Thalerngsok*). On each day the villagers present food to the monks in the morning.

On the afternoon of the first day the Buddha statue and the monks are bathed by villagers to wash away their sins and to pay respect. In the evening monks chant *suad mongkhon*; the principal ritual objects are stones in a basket, which are strewn afterwards in the house compounds to drive away all defects.

Buddhism and the spirit cults in North-east Thailand

On *Wan Naw* the dead are allowed to visit the living. This is a day for commemoration of dead ancestors and the transfer of merit to them. The monks are invited by villagers to perform ceremonies in the village cemetery (*tham bangsakul ha putai*). On this day, also, young people take perfumed water to bathe their elders in order to wash away their sins; they ask forgiveness of their elders and get their blessings. It is believed, too, that if merit is made on this day it counts as much merit, and if de-merit is committed it counts as much sinfulness. Thus monks and villagers, especially young folk, bring sand to the *wat* to build pagodas and later decorate them. In the evening the villagers sit by the pagodas and the monks chant the victory blessing (*chayanto*).

The first day of the New Year is not characterized by any special rites, except that merry-making reaches its climax. Throughout the *Songkran* period young people of both sexes engage in water sports, throwing water on each other in a spirit of high fun and horseplay.

Thus the *Songkran* shows a multiplicity of themes and interests. The past year's sins are washed away by bathing the Buddha statue, the monks and elders; at the same time there is a deeper meaning to this in that these same venerable objects are being purified and rejuvenated by the young for the coming year. The dead are allowed to visit the living and they, too, are laden with merit before being sent back to the spirit world. The young folk indulge in straightforward fertility rituals, and rains are invoked.

(*b*) Next come the rains in May, and this is a period of hard work spent in preparing the fields, ploughing and transplanting, and therefore inappropriate for elaborate rites. But in fact an event of great Buddhist importance falls at this time—*Bun Wisaka*, the day on which the Buddha was born, attained enlightenment and died. In Baan Phraan Muan this occasion is unimportant; the rites are observed because they belong to the Buddhist calendar (popularized on a national scale) rather than because they have special significance for village life. The only ritual activities are the feeding of monks in the morning and a procession at night with lighted candles and joss-sticks which circles the *bood* three times in a clockwise direction.

(*c*) Then in July, still at the height of the rains (and when the amount of rainfall will crucially determine future yield), the monks go into retreat (*Khaw Phansa*). *Phansa* (or *Vassa*) is the rainy season of three months, usually referred to as the Buddhist Lent.

The weeks preceding *Phansa* in late May and June are when the young men of the village are ordained as monks; we have seen that monkhood for these men usually consists of religious service for the period of one

Lent only. The Lenten period coincides with a particular phase of the agricultural calendar. This is the time when the transplanted or sown rice is growing. The period of growth is one requiring little work and is devoted by the elderly villagers to intensifying piety, especially by going to worship at the *wat*, listening to sermons, and sometimes observing the eight precepts. Commonly in Thailand it is considered improper to stage marriage ceremonies during Lent, thereby emphasizing it as a period of piety and asceticism.

The main ritual sequences on *Khaw Phansa* day are the following: in the morning the villagers make merit by feeding the monks and novices at the *sala*. This is followed by the *khwan* ceremony at which the lay elders (*phuu thaw*) recall the *khwan* (spirit essence) of the monks and bind their wrists with cord, so that the *khwan* will be united with their bodies before they go into retreat.

After this is the presentation of bathing cloths to the monks (*pha abnam fon* = cloth for bathing in the rain), which they must use to bathe when the *Vassa* starts. The monks give the *anumodana* blessing, preach a sermon on the merit acquired by laymen in giving this cloth to the monks, and are again feasted by the village. At night there is a candlelight procession round the *bood*, and finally the monks and novices chant *suad mongkhon*— which is a threshold ceremony giving protection and blessings on the eve of entering Lent.

Are we to see any significance in the fact that the monks go into retreat when the rains are falling, the young rice plants are growing, and sustained rainfall is hoped for? It is said it was the Buddha who prescribed this retreat for monks in order that they should not, during their travels in the rainy season, crush or destroy vegetable life and small creatures. As the institution operates today, it may seem that the monks' retreat and intensified religious preoccupation is directly connected with the successful growth of paddy and the precipitation of plentiful rain.[1] That this interpretation is not entirely fanciful can be seen from two other, independent bits of evidence. The first is that the villagers conduct a rain-making ceremony at around the same time, which is addressed

---

[1] It is interesting to note that Wells (1960) cites two mythological incidents which have a bearing on the theme under discussion. In the first, drought resulted from the fact that a monk had to sleep in the open air for want of shelter: rains came when a shelter was made for him (p. 90). The second tale relates that the Buddha attracted rain by wearing a bathing robe and standing near a pool, thereby ending a great drought and famine (p. 95). The exposure of the Buddha image in order to cause rain is the basis of *Songkran* rites in Northern Thailand. Geiger (1960) relates that the Tooth Relic was used as a rain charm in medieval Ceylon (p. 215). The close correspondence of these rain-making rituals with those connected with Upagotha (Uppakrut), to be discussed later, should not escape the reader.

to the local village guardian deities. And the villagers see to it that on the day before this ceremony is held a couple of novices are ordained, so that the merit accruing can be transferred to these deities. The actual rain-making ceremony (*Bunbangfai*) excludes the participation of monks; thus it is all the more remarkable that ordination is linked with it. The second piece of substantiating evidence comes from the *Bun Phraawes* rites, especially the rites associated with Phra Uppakrut, the swamp spirit which also symbolizes rain. The rites will be described later in this chapter.

(*d*) In terms of the agricultural cycle, we next come to September, the tenth lunar month, when the growing rice is at a critical stage and is running to ear. At this period is staged *Bun Khaw Saak*, which means merit with puffed rice. This ceremony is addressed to dead relatives and ancestors. The main rite, after the monks are fed and a sermon preached on the special merit to be made on this day, is that of the villagers, acting as one collective assembly—but each household acting individually—putting out packages of puffed rice, cooked rice and vegetables on the ground near the *bood*, and, while the monks chant, transferring merit to their dead relatives by pouring water on the ground (*yaadnam*).

I have already referred to *Songkran* (which falls in the fifth lunar month and is the end of the old year and the beginning of the new) as an occasion when the dead visit the living. *Bun Khaw Saak*, which falls in the tenth lunar month and is the mid-year of the old calendar, is again a transitional period, and the villagers say that the dead are allowed to visit the earth for seven days.

A point of ritual importance is the significance of puffed rice as opposed to raw rice. Puffed rice in its various preparations is specifically offered to dead relatives and supernatural beings. Thus *khaw saak* (puffed rice mixed with sugar) is offered to the dead on *Bun Khaw Saak* or *Bun Sib Peng*; *khaw tog taeg* (puffed rice without sugar) is strewn on the path during a funeral procession as an offering to dangerous spirits, and to show that 'death is like puffed rice which cannot be planted to grow again'. Roughly at the time *Bun Khaw Saak* takes place at the *wat*, villagers also place puffed rice with sugar in the paddy fields so that the guardian spirit of the field (*chao naa*) and dead parents 'will see that the fields are being cultivated and therefore will guard the crop'.

In contrast, raw rice grains (*khaw saan*) are used as a ritual item in marriage rites. When the marriage payment is taken by the groom's side to the bride's house, the money is mixed with rice grains and put on a tray (*khan ngoen*). I do not wish to insist on the puffed rice/raw rice distinction as vital in ritual, but the anthropologist has grounds for concluding that, since puffed rice is appropriate food for spirits as opposed to human beings, it is intimately connected with the notion of death and raw rice with life and fertility.

From the standpoint of this present study, what is of relevance is that, at the critical time when the rice grains are forming in the fields, the dead are propitiated with 'dead rice' and merit transferred to them with the assistance of monks, so that the rite is categorized as a collective *bun* ceremony. The living view the caring for the dead owners of the fields as necessary to ensure good crops; 'dead rice' is exchanged for newly 'living' rice.

(*e*) By October the rains end and this marks the end of the Buddhist Lent (*Org Phansa*). The end of the rains signals the emergence of the monks from their seclusion. From now on *wat* festivities begin to take on an air of conspicuous merit-making.

The day on which the monks leave their retreat is marked by *Org Phansa* rites. In the early morning the monks chant in the *bood* to announce the end of Lent; villagers gather together at the *wat* to feast the monks and to present them with robes, which are a collective gift. The villagers themselves then eat a communal meal. After the meal young males and children gather in the *wat* compound to witness the setting-off of a large balloon filled with hot air. Following this there is a day-long sermon, with the life of Prince Sowat being read chapter by chapter, punctuated by firing of crackers and the throwing of puffed rice at the Buddha statue. While old men and women listen to the sermon, the young people concern themselves with firing crackers.

The monks are feasted again before noon, the sermon is resumed, and the rites are rounded off at night with a candlelight (*wian thian*) procession three times around the *bood* and *sala*.

(*f*) But the grand village merit-making ceremony which celebrates the emergence of the monks and the completion of rains is *Bun Kathin*. That is the occasion when the monks and novices are presented with robes and gifts; thereafter, the monks are free to resume lay life.

The *kathin* (*kathina*) presentation is an old Buddhist tradition in both Ceylon and Thailand (see Geiger 1960 and Wells 1960) and is perhaps closely linked with the beginnings of monastic life (see Chapter 5). It is a universal rule in Thailand that a particular *wat* can receive only one *kathin* gift; the custom is that a village *wat* usually receives its *kathin* gift from donors in another village. If this is not forthcoming, people of the local village will make the presentation. This is what happened in our village in 1961. Every household contributed cash as well as gave presents in kind.

As in all major merit-making rites, the activities are spread over two (or even three) days. On the first day of the 1961 Baan Phraan Muan celebration after the feeding of the monks, decorations were put up, and the gifts to the monks were assembled in the *sala*. All afternoon, individuals brought gifts of coconuts and other small items, and these were placed on the *hau kathin*, a decorated wooden palanquin. Monks from other *wat* in the *tambon* arrived to participate. In the evening all the monks chanted *suad mongkhon*: about twenty old men and fifteen old women were present. That night a miniature fair was held in the *wat* grounds—a film was shown, a professional *ramwong* (popular dance) orchestra ran an open-air dance with hostesses provided, and an open-air *maulam* (folk opera) was performed.

The *kathin* presentation took place on the following morning. The *hau kathin* was brought down from the *sala* and the procession of villagers formed. I propose now to give some details about the ritual objects in the procession, the nature of the procession, and the final presentation of gifts to the monks so that the reader can appreciate the many facets of a major merit-making ceremony in the village.

The *hau kathin* is the most conspicuous item in the procession. It is a wooden palanquin highly decorated with intricately cut banana stems and paper. Villagers said it represented a palace (*prasaat rajawang*),[1] and in it were placed the *kathin* gifts, chief among them a set of robes, to be used later in the rites. The symbolism explicitly formulated by the villagers is instructive. The palace represented the hopes of all participants that in their next life they would be able to live in such an abode. (This is an expression of a prosperous rebirth envisaged on the *chakravartin* and not the *nirvana* model.) From the four corners of the roof were hung pin-cushions with needles stuck into them: this expressed the wish that in their next birth the devotees would be blessed with keenness of mind. The roof ends of the palanquin used the *Naga* (serpent) motif (which is the usual motif on the roof of every Thai *bood* and *viharn*). This symbolized, villagers said, Buddha's conquest of craving; also, at the time of Buddha's enlightenment, a *Naga* protected him from the intrusions of the world.

Flags are another category of items in the procession. Those used had pictures of a mermaid, mermonkey (said to be the son of Hanuman the monkey, of *Ramayana* fame) and the Goddess of the Earth, Nang Thoranee. Informants said these were the symbols of victory in the Mara Yuddha; when Mara attacked the Buddha with his demon hordes, Nang Thoranee wrung her hair to produce a flood, and the creatures of the water, such as

---

[1] The *prasaat* (Skt = *prasada*) is a 'palace'; it typically has projecting flame-like points which are the terminals of the roof or are ornaments of the eaves. The latter are heads of hooded snakes (*Naga*). This ornamentation is also to be seen in the roofs of ancient Cambodian temples. The symbolism of this temple architecture will concern us later.

crocodiles and mermonkeys, attacked and dispersed the army (see p. 52). The other articles carried in the procession were sugar-cane branches, money trees, and ordinary flags and standards.

Four men swept the ground with brooms in front of the procession. The procession was led by a man (an ex-monk and currently a part-time barber) who held the image of the Buddha over his head. (I interpret this as the 'return of the Buddha' to the world after the rains.)[1] Next followed four monks who held a yellow cord attached to the *hau kathin*: the bearers of money trees, all males, were behind the monks, and they were followed by the *hau kathin* carried by male elders (see Plate 2).

The second half of the procession was gay. A band of musicians playing long drums and flutes led a large body of males and females, both youth and adult, all dancing to the music, the children enjoying themselves the most. The rear was brought up by a merit-making group consisting of customs officials temporarily stationed in a settlement near the village. They carried their own money tree.

The procession circumambulated three times, first around both the *bood* and *sala*, and then twice around the *sala*, before it entered the latter. Before the presentation began, a long yellow thread was tied round the *sala*, thus enclosing the people within. The meaning of this was explained to us as signifying that all who were inside the *sala* were within the boundary of *kathin* merit-making and thereby acquired merit.

After the requesting of the five precepts by a lay elder came the ritual of presenting the robes. In order to allocate the village gift of robes to a particular monk, a set procedure is followed: one monk asks the others who amongst them is fit to receive the gift; another answers that it shall be the abbot, and this is assented to by all the monks. After one elder had presented the robes and the congregation had been blessed in return, another presented the money trees (*ton ngoen*) to the monks. (See next section for the symbolism of money trees.) The elders counted the money on the trees and noted down the amount. The *kathin* ceremony then concluded with the monks and novices chanting a blessing appropriate after receiving gifts.

[1] This cryptic statement requires an explanation. In Central Thailand I have witnessed rites of *Org Phansa* the meaning of which is clear: the coming down of the Buddha from the world of *devas*, where he had gone in the rainy season to preach to his mother, is dramatically enacted at a massive *saibart* (filling of monks' bowls) ceremony. Wells (1960) says that it is traditional in certain temples to bring an image down from a hill or to lower an image from the top of the *cetiya*. The text usually recited is reported as the Devorohana Sutta ('coming down from the *deva* world'). In Baan Phraan Muan this symbolism appears to be incorporated in the *Kathin* ceremony. Yoe (1896, Ch. xxxii) describes for Burma the elaborate Tawadehntha Feast staged in November, dramatizing Buddha's ascent to the heavens to preach to his mother. See Chapter 4, p. 61 of my text for a description of this event.

The *kathin* gifts altogether consisted of money (140 *baht*), robes for the monks, coconuts, and other small gifts for the monks' use.

(*g*) From the end of November until the end of January the village is busy again with agricultural work. Harvesting is the peak working season of the year, and there are no collective *wat* rites.

In February, when the harvest has been gathered in and the agricultural cycle has been concluded, comes the climactic village ritual, *Bun Phraawes*. (It is significant that this festival is preceded by *Makha Bucha*, the Buddhist All Saints' Day, which is more or less ignored by the villagers except for the usual candlelight procession.)

Bun Phraawes is the grandest merit-making complex of rites in the village. It weaves in multiple themes—the celebration of harvest; the dedication of nature and man to a higher ethical purpose and thereby the securing of peace, prosperity and health; the inviting of Uppakrut and the *thewada* as well as human beings to listen to the recitation of Buddha's magnificent and supremely moving life as *Vessantara*. This festival is the subject of detailed analysis in the next section.

Reviewing this account of the cycle of collective *wat* rites and their linkage with the agricultural calendar, what appears to emerge is a pattern of alternation between 'ascetic' Buddhism and 'festive' Buddhism, the former prominent during the period of rains (monks in retreat, the elderly full of salvation thoughts) and the latter prominent from the end of rains (monks emerging, the old presenting gifts, and the young participating in fairs and collective merit-making). During the period of rains the Buddha himself is in retreat and is inaccessible; after the rains in the *Org Phansa* and *Kathin* he, too, has returned to the world. Then there is a period of ritual quiescence during harvest; until once again Buddha is actively present (as are Uppakrut and *thewada*) during the *Bun Phraawes* rites, when his deeds in this world are recounted. Finally, the old year ends and the new year begins with the bathing, rejuvenation and reinstatement of the Buddha images, the monks and the elders, by the living, the community and the younger generation respectively.

'BUN PHRAAWES'

Bun Phraawes is the grandest merit-making ceremony in the village. The name of the festival derives from the story of *Phraa Wes or Wesaundon* (*Vessantara*), which relates the story of the Buddha in his last birth before the one in which he attained Buddhahood. For all Buddhists this is pre-eminent for its moral implications of selfless giving and its deeply moving drama that leads from tragedy to final vindication and triumph. In Thailand

160

The cycle of collective 'wat' rites

it is often referred to as the *Mahachad* (great *Jataka*) and is written for the purpose of being read in merit-making rites in the form of 1,000 verses (*Gatha Pun*) divided into thirteen chapters. Villagers count *Bun Phraawes* as *bun-fang-teed* or merit from listening to a sermon. Listening to the recitation of this long text is believed to confer great merit and the fulfilment of a devotee's wishes.[1]

But *Bun Phraawes* is not merely an annual religious ritual. It is the village's major festival, appropriately occurring after harvest, and combines merit-making with secular interests. In terms of the agricultural cycle it reflects two themes—thanksgiving and looking forward to the next cycle. Occurring as it does in the middle of the dry season, it looks forward to the onset of rains. The particular interest this festival has for our study of village Buddhism is that it embraces a number of themes and interests which are given theological integration under the auspices of Buddhism.

Structurally, the *Bun Phraawes* rites divide into three sequences. First comes the invitation to Uppakrut to attend the festival; he is associated with protecting the village and ensuring the rains. In this sense the first phase is man's communion with natural forces. The next phase, the inviting and propitiation of the divine angels (*thewada*), is man's communion with the upper spirit world. Uppakrut mediates with nature,

---

[1] The *Vessantara* story does not require a detailed telling here. Students of Buddhism know it only too well; others who may not will be edified by reading the literary texts even if they are not Asianists. For the indisposed I quote a summary from Alabaster (1871, pp. 184–5) with some additional details at the end:

According to legend, Wetsandon (the last human existence of Gotama Buddha previous to that in which he attained the Buddhahood) was the son of Sanda, a king of Central India. His great delight was the performance of works of abnegation and charity. He was blessed with a very loving wife and two children, and, among other treasures, owned a white elephant, which had a wonderful power of causing rain to fall.

In a neighbouring country, drought led to famine; but on some Brahmins coming to ask for his rain-causing elephant, he gave it with delight for the benefit of the sufferers.

This act caused much dissatisfaction among his father's subjects, to appease which he was ordered into banishment. Before leaving, he gave in charity seven hundred slaves, seven hundred elephants, horses, chariots, buffaloes, and treasures of all kinds. His affectionate wife accompanied him, taking her children.

On his journey he first gave away his chariot, and then his horses, to Brahmins.

His next alms caused him some pain; for he gave his two children to be slaves to a Brahmin. Finally, he gave his wife to a Brahmin who came and asked for her; but the Brahmin was, indeed, the angel Indra, who, to prevent her being really given away, disguised himself as a Brahmin; and having had her presented to him, left her with the Prince, saying, 'I leave her with you; but as you have given her to me, you cannot give her to any other.'

Indra informed Vessantara that all the dewas and brahmas had rejoiced in the gifts he had offered, assured him that he would most certainly attain the Buddhaship, and that in seven days he would receive back his children and the kingdom, including the white elephant he had given away. These things came to pass (see Hardy 1880, for complete story).

the *thewada* with the divine. The ideologically central part, enacted in the third phase, is merit-making by recitation of and listening to the great story (and other subsidiary sermons). Every night of the festival the village fair is held in the *wat* precincts.

I shall give a brief ethnographic description of these sequences and analyse their implications.

Preparations

Preparations go on during the two days preceding the first major ritual sequence. Stages are built for *maulam* (folk opera) and *ramwong* (popular dancing); a pavilion to store paddy contributions is constructed; four posts are planted to enclose the *sala*, with large flags attached to them at the top and baskets fixed at the bottom; the *sala* is decorated with painted cloths and *kryang hoi kryang phan* (100 things, 1,000 things), special decorations connected with this festival. Special ritual articles connected with Uppakrut, *thewada* and *Phraawes* have to be made locally or purchased.

A striking pattern of the preparations is the differential male–female roles. Old women roll cigarettes, make betel-nut packets, candles, etc. This is a role that in fact old women perform in every religious or social ceremony in the village. The men—both old and young—decorate and construct pavilions (or, in other contexts, coffins or other ritual furniture), the old doing the lighter and the young the heavier work. Young girls and young married women are the cooks. It is they primarily who, supervised by older women, bring food for the monks on ceremonial occasions.

In the afternoon of the second day the Buddha image is brought down from the monks' quarters and installed in the pavilion. Monks sit in the pavilion with begging bowls, waiting for villagers to bring them gifts of paddy. Paddy contributions are the main gift made by villagers at this festival.

The invitation to Phraa Uppakrut

In the late afternoon is staged the first main ritual of the series—the invitation to Phraa Uppakrut, who lives in a perennial pond or swamp (*byng*). Villagers said that before preaching the story of *Phraawes* it was the custom to invite Phraa Uppakrut to the *wat*. Since the meaning of Phraa Uppakrut poses problems, I propose to deal with it in some depth in the final section of this chapter.

The set of ritual articles important in this rite is called *kryang* (things) *Phraa Uppakrut*. They are: monk's bowl, a set of monk's yellow robes, umbrella, a pair of monk's sandals, two small images of the Buddha, *karuphan* (made of various kinds of flowers), puffed rice, two banana-leaf trays containing locally made cigarettes, and a kettle. All these articles were placed on a cushion which rested in the centre of a wooden sedan chair. The procession actually started from the *wat* compound and was led by three monks, who were followed by elderly leaders (*phuu thaw*) carrying the sedan chair. Then followed a large body of villagers—men, women and children. Guns were carried, and music was provided by a bamboo flute and drums. Conspicuous were the flags with pictures of Nang Thoranee (goddess of the earth), a mermaid, a crocodile, etc.; these were, as noted earlier, used in the *Bun Kathin* rites, to represent Buddha's victorious battle with Mara. The procession, after passing through the hamlet, headed for a pond in the paddy fields. The ponds selected must have water all the year round.

After the usual preliminaries in any Buddhist ceremony—lighting of candles, offering of candles and flowers to the Buddha, and requesting of the five precepts—Uppakrut was invited. An elder placed the two small Buddha images on the cover of the monk's bowl. Another held a dish of flowers and a candle in his hand (as an offering to Phraa Uppakrut), while the former chanted the invitation to Uppakrut to come and be guardian of the ceremony. As he chanted, he threw some puffed rice on to the sedan chair, again as an offering to Uppakrut. Next the guns were fired several times, the drums were loudly beaten, and all the people shouted '*chaiyo*'. (It was said that the guns were fired to frighten off *Praya Mara*, and '*chaiyo*' was shouted in order to proclaim victory.) After this the monks chanted '*chaiyanto*', the victory blessing—this was to bless all those who had joined the procession. The kettle was then taken by an elder to the pond and filled with water, and placed on the sedan. The Buddha images were put in the bowl, and the sedan chair lifted. The procession returned by a different route, entered the *wat* by a different gate, and circumambulated the *sala* three times in the usual clockwise direction. The sedan chair was carried into the *sala*, and the articles (*kryang*) were put on a shelf in the corner. All the flags were placed near the pulpit. The kettle of water was put on a high shelf. (Informants said that when the entire *gnan bun* (merit ceremony) was over, the water would be ceremonially thrown away: '*Uppakrut lives in the water; that is why the water is brought.*')

Later in the evening, the monks chanted *suad mongkhon* and sprinkled holy water on the congregation, which consisted only of old men and women.

The events of the next two days form one continuous series, but I shall in the following subsections separate out two major ritual sequences: the *thewada* ceremony and the recitation of *Mahachad*.

Buddhism and the spirit cults in North-east Thailand

In the afternoon of the day following the invitation to Uppakrut, a sermon concerning Pramalai (Malaya Sutta), was preached by the monks. Since listening to such sacred texts is considered a highly merit-making act, a large congregation consisting of men, women and children of all ages were present. The gist of the sermon is as follows: Pramalai was a monk who went to hell (*narog*) to preach to all sinners. His visit and his preaching helped to alleviate their sins. Then he ascended to the heavens (*sawan*)—with sixteen levels—to preach to those who had made merit. He then came to the world of human beings (*log*) and told them what he had seen in heaven and hell.[1] This sermon in a sense appropriately reflects the three major sequences of the *Bun Phraawes* festivities—the inviting of Phraa Uppakrut who lives in the swamp, and of the *thewada* who are heavenly beings, followed by the great sermon addressed to human and supernatural devotees.

The homage to 'thewada' ('Bucha Thewada')

On the morning of the third day, at 2.30 a.m., when the village fair was in full swing, a ceremony was staged in which respects were paid to the *thewada* (divine angels). It was village dogma that before the *Phraawes* story could be recited (or as a matter of fact any merit ceremony begun), *thewada* must be invited to come and be witnesses to the act. What is of significance here is that in no other ritual are the *thewada* propitiated in

---

[1] Wells (1960, pp. 234–6) gives a translation of a sermon composed by Bangkok scholar (*parien*)-monks and called 'The Fruit of the Thousand Gatha'. The following excerpt conveys some sense of the belief in the merit acquired through the reading and listening to the *Vessantara* story; it also shows how appeal is made to the Malaya Sutta, especially the prophecy of the coming Buddha, Maitreya, to legitimate the belief.

> When it is not possible to read the story of Vessantara in detail or to listen to it being read in one day, then we have the reading of the Gatha Phan in order to hear the full thirteen chapters in such a period of time. The hearing of the Vessantara Jataka with its thousand verses is a means of achieving all of one's wishes and is attended with great fruit of merit.
>
> This is shown in the story found in the Malaya Sutta which says that Phra Malaya the heavenly thera received a lotus from a poor man and then went to the Tavatimsa Heaven in order to worship before the Culamani Cetiya. This is the sacred place of worship of all the male and female devatas in Tavatimsa. Phra Malaya met Phra Sri Ariya Maitreya the great Bodhisattva and conversed with him. Finally Ariya Maitreya said, 'O Lord, when you return to the world of men tell the people of Jambudvipa (India) that I say to them that whoever wishes to meet me when I become an enlightened Buddha, let that person refrain from the five great sins, that of killing his mother especially, and let him perform acts of merit of all kinds, especially keeping the precepts, engaging in meditation, and hearing the preaching of the Maha Vessantara Jataka which contains a thousand verses. Let him worship with gifts of rice, flowers of all kinds, and candles and incense sticks a thousand of each kind. In one day let him finish the thirteen chapters. Then he will meet me when I become an enlightened Lord Buddha in the future. When he dies he will be born in a heaven and dine in plenty on heavenly food. When the time comes for me to be born in the world to become an enlightened Buddha, such persons will be born in the world of men also...

a special rite and made the sole recipients of offerings. It was said that if the *thewada* were invited and worshipped they in turn would make the villagers 'live well and in health' (*ju dee mee haeng*), that rain would fall as usual and much rainfall might be expected (*fon fah cha dee*).

A procession consisting primarily of old men and women (except the drummers, who were young men) formed at the *sala* with candles and flowers in their hands, and bowls containing balls of glutinous rice (which in theory should number 1,000 to represent the number of *gatha* of the *Phraawes* story). It is in fact called the 'procession of 1,000 lumps of rice'. No monks took part in the procession. It went round the *sala* three times in a clockwise direction, and whenever it passed one of the four posts with a flag at the top and basket at the bottom, rice balls, candles and flowers were dropped into the baskets. These posts were called *han* (*ran*) *bucha*, and were said to be *khong* (things) *thewada*. The offerings, informants said, were intended for both *thewada* and *Phraawes*, but they were unable to say why the processions and offerings had to be carried out in this particular fashion.

The *han bucha* can perhaps be related to Buddhist symbolism unknown to the villagers. They appear to resemble the 'trees that gratify the desires of men' (*Kalpavriksha*). These trees have no likeness to any tree at all, but are hollow wicker baskets on the ends of long poles. In popular Buddhism they are said to represent the four trees that will blossom at the four corners of the city in which the next Buddha, Maitreya, will be born. They will then produce all kinds of delicious fruits in fabulous quantities (see Young 1907, p. 243). The money trees that appear in merit-making rites may also be seen as associated with this symbolism.

Recitation of Mahachad

When the circumambulation was over the participants in the procession entered the *sala*, placed the bowls of glutinous rice near the pulpit and took their seats. The ritual articles associated with merit-making for *Bun Phraawes* as such are: *miangmak* (betel-nut packets), locally made cigarettes (*gawk ya*), small flags, candles, joss-sticks; each of these items must be 1,000 in number. Other items are: *sanaam*, four pans filled with water containing fish and turtle, and these represent the four ponds in the forest in which Phraawes lived in banishment; a bee hive (in memory of the monkey's offering to Buddha); bunches of coconuts and bananas.

The main sequences in the recitation of the story were as follows: after presenting flowers and candles to the Buddhist trinity, and the request for the five precepts, two elders in turn invited the *thewada* to come and listen to the great story (*fang tham lam Mahachad*). 'Chaiyo' (victory) was shouted three times.

The next sequence was the sermon called *Teed Sangkaad*, delivered by a monk. Its delivery has to be requested by a village leader of the congregation. This invitation, called *aratana Sangkaad* (which I summarize as recited in the village), is a recounting of the Buddha's renunciation of the kingly life and his wife and son, his departure on his best horse, Maa Keo, one of the seven treasures of the Emperor (Chakravartin), the death of this horse through sorrow, the Buddha's cutting off of his hair and its reception in a golden vessel by God Indra, who took it to his heaven and deposited it at the Phra Choolamani monument.

The theme of the monk's sermon which followed was the well-known Mara Yuddha (see Chapter 3); the features given prominence were the tricks resorted to by Mara in order to defile Buddha's state of enlightenment. Mara sent his three daughters to excite Buddha's sexual passions. He rejected them, and the girls 'finally became old women'. Informants said that this sermon was an essential prelude to the *Mahachad* recitation. Monks took turns in reciting the long text of the *Mahachad*, and the recitation, which started early in the morning, did not conclude till 8 p.m. First a Pali verse was recited; then the audience threw puffed rice at the Buddha image; then the monks told the story in Thai. People came and went and the attention to the sermon was not intense (see Plate 3).

At the conclusion of the recitation, villagers brought money trees (*ton ngoen*) and presented them to the monks and *wat*. People came in procession in groups. Finally a monk made lustral water (*nam gatha phan* = water of 1,000 verses) and sprinkled it on all those present. Villagers took home some of the sacred water to sprinkle on their buffaloes in order to drive away illness. Thus were concluded the *Bun Phraawes* ritual and festivities.

There is a belief associated with the *Mahachad* recitation that it must be completed in a day; if not, unfortunate accidents and misfortune will occur. This is why, we were told, the *thewada* ceremony had to be staged in the early hours of the morning, so that the recitation could be started very early and concluded in the evening.

The themes of the monks' preaching of the *Dhamma* were renunciation of the kingly life and family, selfless giving in the *Mahachad*, rejection of sexuality and passion in the encounter with Mara's daughters, and the after-death phenomena of heaven and hell. It could be said that the last phase of the *Bun Phraawes*, the sermonizing and recitation of texts, recounts the great episodes of the Buddha's life: renunciation of secular glory and comfort, the ardours of the search for the truth, and final achievement of detachment and salvation. At the same time the paradox is that these words of renunciation and selflessness (as well as the other ritual sequences) are viewed by the participants as endowing them with merit, and ensuring a 'good and healthy life' and plentiful rain. Mara, the enemy of Buddha and man, is held at bay, and the lustral water of the thousand verses (*nam gatha phan*) confers health on man and buffalo. Thus a problem is posed as to the mechanics of the Buddhist ritual—how the use of sacred words which deal with the virtues of renunciation transfer to the participants the seemingly opposite benefits of life affirmation.

The activities of the fair

I have thus far concentrated on the Buddhist rituals. I must now describe the fair briefly in order to give a rounded picture, for *Bun Phraawes* combines with merit-making robust fun and sheer entertainment. The annual temple fair is the chief recreational event in village life and characteristically Buddhism shows its robustness by combining it with conspicuous merit-making.

The fair ran for three days and two nights, the nights being the time of peak activity. Shops—mostly selling food and drink—were set up in the *wat* compound. The chief attractions were *ramwong* (popular dancing), conducted by a professional orchestra and dance hostesses from a nearby village; *maulam* (folk opera), also performed by a visiting professional troupe; and movies.

The monks, true to their rules of priesthood, avoided the *maulam* and *ramwong*, but did not avoid interest in the movies. They were, however, mainly involved in ritual merit-making activities in the pavilion with the Buddha statue. There, the two main activities were: *takbart sawan*—laymen put money in the monks' bowls and in turn were sprinkled with holy water; and *pidtong phraa*—laymen bought pieces of gold leaf and daubed them on the Buddha statue. (An additional money-making device was *khai dogmai*, in which laymen bought flowers in order to present them to Buddha.)

Persons of all ages and both sexes attended the fair. Most old persons, male and female, first engaged in merit-making by contributing money, then looked at the movies for a while, and then gravitated towards the folk opera. Adults watched the movies and *ramwong* and also found the *maulam* of absorbing interest; the young men were primarily interested in the movies and *ramwong*, while young girls of the village found the movies and *maulam* their chief attraction. Children were the most consistent audience at the movies. No local village girl took part in the dancing. The fair was an occasion for flirting between the sexes. Some ritual sequences of *Bun Phraawes*, which ran parallel with the fair, were largely ignored by the young people.

A few words about the scale of participation. *Bun Phraawes* in all the villages around Baan Phraan Muan is staged with a fair. It therefore attracts devotees and pleasure-seekers from a number of adjoining villages. People from at least seven or eight *tambon* (communes) were present at the Phraan Muan proceedings: they made merit, contributed money and had fun. Particular hamlets or groups of villagers from elsewhere often acted as a merit-making group, each contributing a gift of paddy or a money tree. Twenty-six monks from other *wat* took part in the *Bun Phraawes* proceedings. It is usual to send out invitations to other *wat*, and for the latter to send representatives. The following distribution shows the range of inter-*wat* co-operation—15 monks came from 15 *wat* in the same *tambon* in which Baan Phraan Muan is located; 6 monks came from 6 *wat* in the adjoining *tambon* of Mumon; the remaining 5 monks came either from the same district (Amphur Muang) or from the adjoining districts of Pen and Pue. The vendors of food and drinks also came from a widespread area. Of a total of 40–5 vendors only 5 were from the local village; 4 came from the town of Udorn and the rest from at least 8 adjoining *tambon*.

These facts, I think, establish the nature of festive Buddhism as a supra-local religion. It is true that it is local people who primarily patronize a village *wat*; but merit-making is a society-wide ethic and such prominent merit-making occasions as a *gnan wat* attract many others who see participation in them as a chance of acquiring greater merit than usual. Just as outsiders attend grand merit-making rites at Baan Phraan Muan, so do residents of the latter participate in the *wat* festivals of other villages. By contrast, the cult of the village guardian spirit (*Tapubaan*) is of an essentially local character, being bound up with a settlement (*baan*) and its land and people. All the villages around Phraan Muan propitiate the same village guardians; the cult is widespread but no outside villager needs to propitiate the guardian of another village. But traditionally the villages in the region combined to propitiate a common swamp spirit which expressed a regional identity and interest. (The guardian spirit cults will be described in a later chapter.)

INTERPRETATION: WHO IS UPPAKRUT?

In this final section I examine the symbolism of Uppakrut in terms both of the limited context of village behaviour and of the links between locally observed symbols and those of the grand Buddhist (and Hindu) historical traditions.

The cycle of collective 'wat' rites

Who is Phraa Uppakrut? What is his role in these *Bun Phraawes* festivities? This is indeed an intriguing question and I do not know whether I can provide an answer. I will report in detail the points of view expressed by village informants. First some references found in the literature: according to Harry Shorto (personal communication), the Upagupta legend and cult has a fairly long history. Upagupta was the subject of a local Indian cult centred in Mathura. There are literary Canonical texts which refer to him (e.g. Asvaghosa's *Sutralamkara* (extant in Chinese); *Divyavadana*, and *Lokapannatti*). I have not been able to consult these Indian texts but Shorto says the striking point expressed in them is that Upagupta converted Mara, Buddha's enemy, to Buddhism and is called *alaksonako Buddo* (probably 'the crypto Buddha'). However, Duroiselle (1904) gives a translation of the legend found in a Burmese Pali version of the *Lokapannatti* which makes the same assertions and is similar to the Thai legend reported by Wells. Wells (1960, p. 113) states, in regard to the *Loi Kratong* festival (festival of lights) in Thailand, that one of the popular explanations advanced for it is that 'King Asoka once decided to build 84,000 cetiyas but Mara threatened to destroy them. The king appealed to the Lord of the Nagas, Phraa Upagota, to help him by capturing Mara. This the Naga Lord did, and since then the people have shown their gratitude to the Naga by this river festival.' The *Loi Kratong* festival is not celebrated in Baan Phraan Muan; but Upagota (Uppakrut) appears in the *Bun Phraawes* festivities.

The villagers were by no means agreed as to who Uppakrut was, and it is precisely because he represents several ideas that he is especially interesting.

1. Two elderly informants, one of whom was very learned in ritual matters, gave roughly the same version. Phraa Uppakrut was a novice who lived in the water of the swamp (in a subterranean town). He was the son of Buddha and his mother was a mermaid. It is said that once the Buddha forced his semen (*beng nam asuchi* = forced out impure water) into the water and a mermaid swallowed it, became pregnant and gave birth to Uppakrut. He was subsequently ordained as a novice (or monk) and lives in the water, for he is a mermaid's son.

One of the elders who advanced this story said on further questioning that Phraa Uppakrut has great supernatural power (*rit ah-noo-phab*), more power and authority than monks who have attained the highest level of religious merit (*phraa arahan*) (*arahat*). Whenever a big ceremony is undertaken, he must be invited to ward off dangers caused by Praya Marn, a giant (Mara the demon king, Buddha's enemy and signifying death). He finally explained Uppakrut's power to subjugate Mara in this way:

'When we make merit, we invite Phraa Uppakrut to come so that he will prevent fighting and killing and damage by fire.' Uppakrut is not invited for any other village ceremony or collective *wat* rites.

It is important to note that all informants, whatever original story of Uppakrut they give, are consistently agreed that Uppakrut is the enemy of Mara and is invited to the *Bun Phraawes* in order to safeguard the proceedings, to prevent participants from fighting or killing one another, and to bless them in order that they may live long and in good health (*ju dee mee haeng*). His absence will enable Mara to sow disaster.

2. The second version collected from laymen said that Uppakrut is a *Naga* or serpent spirit. This *Naga* lives in the water; at the same time, water is Uppakrut. He is invited to guard the proceedings; if he is not, then murder, storm and lightning will occur through the acts of Mara.

3. As might be expected, the monkish version is different. A monk of *wat* Phraan Muan said: about 236 years after the death of Lord Buddha, King Asoka called together a meeting of 1,000 monks in order to eliminate doctrinal differences. It was the third meeting of this sort since Lord Buddha's death. The monks assembled but someone was sorely needed to preside. There was in the gathering a novice, ordained while the Buddha was alive, and greatly respected, but he declined to be the head. Instead he went and invited Phraa Uppakrut to preside; he was in the water meditating.

While Uppakrut was on his way to the meeting he was met by King Pasenathikosol, who, seeing that he was a thin man, decided to test his strength. An elephant was let loose to attack Uppakrut but he vanquished it; he then successfully presided over the meeting, eliminating controversies in respect of the *Dhamma* and contributing to the success of Buddhism.[1]

The following structural elements can be discerned in the three stories.

In the first story Buddha (human being with spiritual power) is opposed to a creature of the water (nature), and from their union springs a *novice* who resides in the water, thus combining both elements. Tentatively, we

---

[1] I was pleasantly surprised after this legend was recorded in the village to find that some of its details hark back to a classical Buddhist historical legend. This passage in Eliot (1954, Vol. I, pp. 270–1), describing the Third Buddhist Council held in India in the reign of King Asoka, has its source in the Sinhalese chronicle, *Mahavamsa* (Ch. 5).

It is said to have been held two hundred and thirty-six years after the death of the Buddha and to have been necessitated by the fact that the favour shown the Sangha induced heretics to become members of it without abandoning their errors. This occasioned disturbances and the king was advised to summon a sage called Tissa Moggliputta (or *Upagupta*) then living in retirement and to place the affairs of the church in his hands. He did so. Tissa then composed the *Kathavatthu* and presided over a council of one thousand arahats which established the true doctrine and fixed present Pali Canon. (See also Thomas 1951, pp. 31–2.)

may postulate that this story represents the taming of the spirit of the natural element (water) and its conversion into a Buddhist agent (*novice*).

In the second story human beings and their solidarity (society) are opposed to their mortal adversary Mara, embodiment of passion, death and malevolence (chaos). The *Naga* as nature's powerful agent allies himself with humans to protect them.

In the third story, the latter half poses the opposition between religious or spiritual power (thin ascetic) and royal power (symbolized in the elephant, symbol of royalty). Uppakrut as monk is superior to temporal power, and also defends Buddhism by reconciling theological differences in the *Sangha*.

Now to go back to the ethnography. The rite of the 'invitation' of Uppakrut at the swamp consists of words chanted by a village elder combined with the act of manipulating ritual objects. I shall just deal with the words.

The invitation begins with the Buddhist Pali verse repeated three times: '*Namo tassa bhagavato arahato samma sambuddhassa.*'

There is then a shift to the local Lao language and I give a free translation into English of the words said:

We, bearing a bowl of puffed rice, and flowers, joss-sticks and candles, come to invite Phraa Uppakrut, Mahathero,[1] who is clever, has magical power and is like Prom (Brahma). We all come to invite Phraa Uppakrut, Mahathero, who resides in the city under the great ocean. He, whom we love, creates beneficial things in ethical ways. We therefore assume the position of worship before Phraa Mahathero and supplicate him to subdue the Mara-kings[2] (namely Tuddha Limaan, Tai Limaan, Paya Talimaan and Pohti Limaan), who come to harm us.

We all come to invite the Sun (Phraa Atit), the Moon (Phraa Chan), Mars (Phraa Angkaan) to protect us from danger. We also invite Mercury (Phraa Poot), Jupiter (Phraa Preuhat-sa-bau-dee), Venus (Phraa Sook), Saturn (Phraa Sow), Rahu,[3] Phraa Lamana.[4] Six of you, please come from the east, south-east, south, south-west, west, north-west, north, north-east, to subdue the Mara-kings. We invite you all to attend and listen to the sermon to be recited at the *wat* in our village. We too are invited to attend.

The words thus begin with a Pali formula used in all rituals in which monks participate. They make it crystal clear that Uppakrut is an opponent and subduer of Mara, the archetype enemy of the Buddha. We also

---

[1] Literally 'great elder', a title given to distinguished monks. Note, however, that in the legend Uppakrut is a novice.
[2] Mara-kings are 'demon' kings.
[3] Rahu is the monster who is believed to cause eclipses by swallowing the moon and sun.
[4] Refers to the auspicious time fixed by astrologers for beginning an activity or project or ceremony.

note that, together with Uppakrut, the denizen of the water, are invoked the cosmological and planetary entities to lend their power to the great battle and also to participate in the worship at the *wat*, where the supreme deeds of the Buddha as a world renouncer will be recounted. The monks come into the picture only after the invitation is completed by lay elders, to chant in ringing tones the victory blessing.

If we now examine the rite *in toto*, concentration on the non-verbal acts and manipulation of objects, we are able to perceive a slightly different emphasis in the proceedings.

We have seen that some of the ritual articles carried were conspicuous symbols of monkhood—the begging bowl, sandals and robes. What was interpreted as 'invitation' by the villagers seems to me the taming and conversion of the *Naga* or spirit of the water to Buddhism. Note that the Buddha images were shown to Uppakrut, that he was then coaxed with puffed rice to come on to the sedan. Finally the kettle of water is carried to the *sala*. Cries of victory and the monks' victory blessing express the success of the encounter. Thus the ritual successfully recruits the power of the *Naga* to protect human society and Buddhism, and it enacts the two phases: submission (invitation) and then protection.

There is, however, another dimension of meaning. Uppakrut lives in the never-drying pond. As mermaid's son, or as *Naga*, he represents water. In the villagers' statements continual references are made to rain, long life, good health and absence of conflict. The preoccupation with rain is real and this agricultural interest is reflected, I think, in the *Bun Phraawes* rites.

Good grounds for my linking Uppakrut with rain appear in the ethnographic facts pertaining strictly to the village as a contextual field. The villagers of Baan Phraan Muan have a cult of the village guardian spirit (*Tapubaan*); he is the 'owner' of the village and acts as a communal guardian and disciplinarian: he has a counterpart who is the guardian of the *wat* (*Chao Phau Pha Khaw*); both are on the one hand distinguished and on the other fused in a common shrine. Uppakrut then takes over their roles at *Bun Phraawes*; he is incorporated into Buddhism, while the two guardians in their non-Buddhist aspect remain intact. Buddhism cannot entirely secure their submission or, to put it differently, the submission of natural forces in the service of man and religion. The village and *wat* guardians are again, as an entity, differentiated from the owner and spirit of the swamp, who is propitiated for rain at the same time as the former are propitiated separately for village security and prosperity. Uppakrut in *Bun Phraawes* takes on the aspect of rain spirit and thus is brought under the aegis of Buddhism; but the swamp spirit also preserves his separate identity and autonomy. Thus I see in the Uppakrut rite the universalizing aspects of Buddhism, its attempt to bring nature under man's metaphysical control; but its comprehensiveness must remain partial, for man's control over nature is always incomplete.

Now to turn to a level of ritual symbolism which poses problems for the anthropologist if he tries to shift from his immediate ethnographic context and the conscious thought processes of his subjects to the realm of historical traditions and mythology on the grand civilizational scale.

Villagers identify Uppakrut with the *Naga*, with water and rain, with protection against the machinations of Mara as an antisocial agent. The villagers are also familiar with fragments or 'distorted' versions or re-interpretations of mythology several centuries old. While not imputing these cognitive associations to the villagers, I want briefly to indicate the wider implications of the *Naga* symbolism.

To begin at the village level and then to move away: as indicated in Chapter 7 before, the Thai word for a man in his transitional status just before ordination as a monk is *nag* (*Naga*), and in that chapter I interpreted the symbolism implied. I also described the ceremony for honouring a monk, in which the *nag* in the form of a wooden serpent appears as a conspicuous ritual object, namely the vehicle for bathing the monk with water, and uniting in its person the dual themes of animal sexuality and potency transformed into the energies of asceticism and of faithful benevolent service to the Buddhist faith.

A brief consideration of the *Naga* in Hindu and Buddhist literature helps to illuminate the symbolism of Uppakrut in our village ceremony. In Hindu symbolism, the *Naga* and the *Garuda*, the serpent and the eagle, are opposed as eternal enemies, and this opposition is finally resolved in the attributes of Vishnu. The spiritual antagonism between them is symbolized in terms of natural elements: the serpent represents the earthly waters, it is a subterranean creature, it is the eternal life force; the eagle is the sun principle, it is free from the bondage of matter and represents the higher spiritual principle of the infinity of heaven (Zimmer 1946, Ch. 3). In Buddhism the *Naga* has an important role as pious devotee and as representing animality. It is said that all the creatures of nature, together with the gods, rejoiced upon the birth of the Buddha and guarded his progress towards enlightenment. A telling illustration referred to earlier[1] is the story of the cobra Muchalinda who protectively enveloped the Buddha seven times and spread out his hood as an umbrella over his blessed head to protect him from a storm as he sat, absorbed in his bliss,

[1] See Plate 1a. The story is old and is reported for instance in the *Mahavagga* (see Rhys Davids and Oldenburg 1881, pp. 80–1).

173

under the *bodhi* (bo) tree. An important function of the *Nagas* is that of door guardian, in their proper attitude of pious devotion. Geiger writes that the *Nagas* 'are always adherents and worshippers of the Buddha. The Bodhi tree, when it was brought to Ceylon, was protected by them, and they wished to get it for themselves... In their possession were the sacred relics of the Master which afterwards were deposited in the great Thupa at Anuradhapura' (1960, p. 166).

Alabaster (1871), who deals with Thai sources, not only refers to the Muchalinda legend, which is frequently depicted in Thai temples, but also adds that 'In the "Life of Buddha" we read of the Naga King Kala, who wakes only when a new Buddha is about to illumine the earth, and who, having arisen from his subterranean abode, honours the Buddha with innumerable songs of praise and then returns to sleep' (pp. 300–1).

The serpent also is the symbolic vehicle representing Buddha's conquest over life. (The *Naga* symbol as representing Buddha's conquest over craving is known to the villagers.) As Zimmer (1946, p. 68) comments:

In this legend and in the images of the Muchalinda-Buddha a perfect reconcili-ation of antagonistic principles is represented. The serpent, symbolizing the life force that motivates birth and rebirth, and the saviour, conqueror of the blind will for life, severer of the bonds of birth, pointer of the path to the imperishable. Transcendent, here together in harmonious union, they open to the eye a vista beyond all the dualities of thought.

I may add that the *Naga* was the symbol of Konagamana, a Buddha who preceded the historical Gotama Buddha.

To return to the village temples of Thailand: while the *bood* and *sala* in Baan Phraan Muan are singularly meagre in architectural elaboration and decoration, a vast number of them, in both villages and towns, have balustrades in the form of long *Nagas* (i.e. the temple rests on the serpent), and gable ends in the form of *Nagas* with their heads as eaves, or alterna-tively with *hang hong* or 'swan's tail' (actually tail of *hamsa*, the gander or wild goose). The *hamsa* in Hindu symbolism represents the twofold nature of all beings—it is at ease in both the upper celestial and the lower earthly spheres and not bound to either, a perfect symbol for expressing the Hindu ideas of *maya* and *atman* and the Buddhistic idea of salvation through conquest of our human condition.

The better known duality in Hindu and Buddhist (especially Mahayana) mythology and sculpture (and art in general) is the opposition between the *Garuda* (the mythical sky bird) and the *Naga* (water-serpent), enemies but also reconciled and united in God Vishnu who rides on the *Garuda* (his vehicle or *vahana*) and also rests on the *Naga* (*sesha*) of the ocean.

It is unnecessary to document the importance of these symbols in Southeast Asian art: Khmer architecture, for instance, never tired of the drama between the *Garuda* and the *Naga* and represented it in various ways (e.g. see Lawrence Briggs 1951).

It has been argued by some writers (see Waddell 1912/13) that the fierce brahmanical sun bird was transformed by Buddhism to the golden peacock and the milder golden goose of the Asokan pillars, and of the Burmese and Thai temples. Nevertheless, the *Garuda* persists as an important symbol in these Buddhist countries, perhaps most importantly in Cambodia, which went through various religious phases.

In some astrological charts currently used in Phraan Muan village the *krut* (*Garuda*) is opposed to *nag*. Perhaps it is not accidental that popular tradition transformed the name Upagotha to Uppakrut, thereby making the serpent of the water share the name of the mythical sky bird and reconciling both in the service of Buddhism.

The problem of interpreting the symbolic significance and role of Uppakrut has taken us on a long and devious journey. There are complex levels of communication between village tradition and the grand tradition, a complexity at least showing, rather than a *separateness* between them, a *mutual reinforcement* and *illumination*. The anthropological perspective as it focuses on contemporary village behaviour and traditions demonstrates more than this: the *contextualization* of literary and artistic themes and forms of a grand past may be in a humbler form, but importantly not as a dead past but as a living reality; one also sees the elaboration and expansion of meaning of these themes as they are closely woven into the texture of contemporary social life and interests. In this way the anthropological present gives flesh to the historical past while at the same time the past persists in the present.

Uppakrut, his legends and rites, are known in Burma, Thailand's neighbour. In the appendix to this chapter I review the Burmese data and interpret them, and show that the features demonstrated for the Thai case are reflected in Burma as well.

The symbolism of the *Naga* in Thai religion is not exhausted yet; we shall encounter the *Naga* again in a later chapter, not as a servant of Buddhism but as an agent in its own right. It is only after seeing these more general contrasts that we may better grasp the many facets and the internal structure of the religious kaleidoscope.

APPENDIX TO CHAPTER 10

UPAGOTHA FROM BURMESE SOURCES

Upagotha appears in Burmese legend and ritual, and it is therefore intriguing to examine the Burmese data in order to find out whether, and to what degree, the structural conclusions derived from Thai data are confirmed in them.

Maung King gives a legend which is quite obviously a more elaborate version of one of those related in our Thai village. According to this legend, Maccadevi (The Fish Princess) was found in the stomach of a fish and she preserved its odour, which got stronger as she grew older. She was therefore placed on a raft and left to drift with the current of the river. The *rsi* Upa prayed to her to receive him on the raft so that he could cross from one bank of the river to the other. Upagupta (Upagotha) was born to Maccadevi as the result of this encounter with the *rsi* (Duroiselle 1904). (One is immediately reminded of the legend of the birth of Vyasa, the son of the *rsi* Paracara and the boatwoman Satyavati in the *Mahabharata* 1, 63.)

The encounter between Upagupta and Mara appears to be the most frequently known legend in the Buddhist literature; for example the *Jinatthapakasani*, the Burmese history of the life of the Buddha, gives a story of the encounter. The oldest Burmese source is the Pali text *Lokapannatti*, which is discussed by Duroiselle (1904): in this version Upagupta struggles against Mara to protect the acts of piety of Asoka, which are disturbed by Mara, and converts him to Buddhism (a story that is close to the Thai version cited by Wells and to the monkish version recited to me in the Thai village). The *Lokapannatti* legend is long, has many colourful incidents, and deserves an intricate analysis in its own right. Incidentally, our protagonist in this text is called Kisanaga Upagutta: the appearance of *Naga* in his name is important and lends weight to my interpretation.

Let me now allude to some other Burmese sources. Shway Yoe (1896) describes Shin Oopagoh as a universally honoured payah-nge, a lesser divinity, who lives down at the bottom of the river in a brazen spire where he zealously keeps the sacred days. In pictures he is represented as sitting under his brazen roof, or on the stump of a tree, eating out of an alms-bowl which he carries in his arms. Sometimes he is depicted gazing sideways up to the skies, where he seeks a place not polluted by corpses.

Grant Brown (1908, 1921) confirms this legend. Shin Upagok, one of Buddha's disciples, born after the Buddha's death, lives in a many-roofed pavilion surrounded by water, and anyone wishing to invoke his aid had to send him a message in a golden bowl, which floated to its destination.

Both authors refer to a story that explains why Upagotha is compelled to remain naked in the water: it is a punishment for having, while a boy in a previous existence, run off with the clothes of another boy with whom he was bathing, so that his companion, being modest, had to remain in water up to his waist till Upagotha relented and returned the clothes. It is perhaps plausible to comment that his nakedness is consistent with his character as the god of water; also that while his companion was only temporarily half-naked (half-immersed), Upagotha is fully and permanently immersed.

Local Burmese legend and ritual clearly associate Upagok with Buddhism, as seen from these additional facts. Yoe reports that Upagok is condemned to remain in his watery abode until the arrival of Aramadehya (Maitreya), the next Buddha, when he will be set free; upon entering the Khenga[1] (*Sangha*) he will become a *yahanda* (someone who has entered the path of salvation) and attain Nehbau[1] (*nirvana*). One notes that just as the Thai imagine him to be a novice, so do the Burmese represent him as a disciple not fully ordained, that is, he is not fully incorporated into the Buddhist quest. He is, however, destined to be a future Buddha. Furthermore, it would appear that statues of Upagotha (fully clothed) are found in Burmese pagodas; they are represented as doing homage to the Buddha images.

I have already reported in the text Shorto's information that Upagotha has a literary history in Indian Canonical lore which states that he converted Mara to Buddhism and is called *alaksanako Buddho* ('the crypto-Buddha'). The feature of Upagok holding an alms-bowl in his hands and the recommendation to a supplicant that he should float a bowl to him on the water reminds me of the following Buddha legend. After the night of the last watch before his final effort to reach salvation, the maiden Suchada brought him savoury rice in a golden bowl. Having finished his meal, the Buddha floated the bowl upstream, and having travelled 80 cubits, the bowl sank into the realms of Kala, the *Naga* King, and it clashed loudly against the bowls which had been similarly set afloat by former Buddhas and placed itself beneath them. The *Naga*, hearing the noise, awoke, made offerings and sang songs of praise. I interpret this marvellous legend as Buddha's final leap from animality into liberation: the bowl, the symbol of mendicancy, is left to the safekeeping of the *Naga*, and the Buddha goes forward to his final meditation under the bo tree, which brings him to *nirvana*.

The Burmese legends thus appear to convey two features about Upagotha

[1] Modern transliterations would be *Thin-ga* and *Neikpan* respectively.

which are also stated in the Thai legends: that he is a creature of the water who brings rain, and that at the same time he is a benevolent Buddhist agent who is the enemy of Mara. These features, I would claim, are also the properties of the *Naga*: animality tamed and made subservient to the Buddhist cause.

There remains a puzzle to solve about the rituals associated with Upagotha that are practised primarily in Lower Burma. It concerns the timing of the ritual, sometimes coming before and sometimes after the rains.

Grant Brown relates one type of rain-making ritual: when there is a break in the rains which endangers the crops, or when the monsoon is late in coming, the Burmese resort to rain-producing rituals, one of which is to take the Upagotha image from the pagoda and put it out in the broiling sun. The logic of this is, it appears to me, that Upagotha as a water creature is 'opposed' to the sun (he is pictured as looking up at the sun), and through this confrontation of the two rain is produced by the union of opposites and falls from the sky.

A second type of ceremony, however, is the more usual and elaborate. Shway Yoe describes it as happening at the end of Lent (i.e. at the end of the rains); Shorto (personal communication) witnessed the same rites at the end of harvest and the beginning of the agricultural close season. This is the well-known festival of setting adrift little oil lamps fastened to floats of bamboo or plantain stem—called in Thailand *Loi Kratong* and in Burma *Yay-hpoung hmyaw thee*. In Burma, at about the same time, houseboats or rafts with partitions constructed on them and sometimes containing images of Upagotha are launched, heaped with gifts and offerings. People who come upon them make further offerings and send them on their way.

The question here is why, if Upagotha is a rain god, are these rafts launched after the rains?

The answer, I venture, is that as a rain god he can appear in two different kinds of ritual, *before* and *after* the rains. When rainfall is scarce he is induced to make rain by being taken out of his watery abode and exposed to the sun. On the other hand, at the end of the normal agricultural season, when rains have fallen, or more extremely, when there is too much rain, it is appropriate that thanks offerings are made to him and he is sent on his way back to his watery element. We are told that 'in order to stop the rain and restore good weather it is sufficient to take a statue of Upagupta and plunge its head in the water while setting out some offerings in his honour' (Duroiselle 1904).

In the Thai village of Phraan Muan the invitation to Upagotha takes place at the post-harvest festival and his role there has been explained in the text.

11

DEATH, MORTUARY RITES, AND
THE PATH TO REBIRTH

The 'death orientation' of philosophical Buddhism is only too well known, and requires no elaboration here. In its presentation of the human predicament, the painful *a priori* meaninglessness of human life, and the preoccupation with death and its conquest, philosophical Buddhism shares much with contemporary existentialism. In village Buddhism, too, there is great ritual emphasis placed on death. Death is in fact the most important rite of passage. It is significant that mortuary rites are officiated by monks and are conceived of by all participants as Buddhist ritual.

In terms of the themes examined in this study, our major interests in mortuary rites are two. First, death causes a change in man's status, and his fate after death is defined in terms of *bun/baab* and *kam* (*karma*), and rebirth. Village mortuary rites not only state the change in status but are also concerned to secure for the dead a good status by merit-making and transfer of merit. Participation in mortuary rites is itself defined as merit-making for the living. Death brings into action the village social structure, especially the relationships and obligations *vis-à-vis* different generations. These in particular include the ritual obligations of the junior generation of *luug-laan* to the senior generation of *phuu thaw*. The second focus of interest is the role of the monk in mortuary rites. Monks in their ritual roles have often been described as mediators between death and rebirth. How in fact do they mediate, how do they derive the power for effecting this dangerous transition, and how does this role link up with monkhood as a village institution?

Villagers distinguish between normal death and abnormal death. The latter is sudden 'unnatural' death (*tai hoeng*), brought about by childbirth, accidents, homicide, and sudden virulent disease. The form of death is believed to have vital significance for the fate of the soul (*winjan*), and special precautions are taken in the case of sudden death. My method of exposition is to describe first in some detail the sequences in the mortuary rites pertaining to normal death, and subsequently to state briefly how abnormal death is handled. I follow the convention of stating within parentheses the meaning attached to ritual acts by the actors. I describe an actual case study in order to provide context for the proceedings.

179

Buddhism and the spirit cults in North-east Thailand

Doy (dressing and laying out of the corpse)

Soon after death the corpse was cleaned and dressed in new clothes by the immediate relatives living in or visiting the house of the deceased. One of the ritual acts was the 'bathing of the corpse', which consisted of pouring water on the deceased's hands. This rite is usually performed by the kinsmen present, especially the *luug-laan* (children and grand children). (We are already familiar with the ritual act of bathing and pouring water in *Songkran* rites; as in those rites, here, too, it is said that the living pay their respects to and ask forgiveness of the deceased. Also it is said that the corpse is cleansed for the passage of its *winjan* to heaven.) The hands and feet of the corpse were tied together with thread, and the body was laid out face up on a mat and pillow in a sleeping attitude.

A coin (one *baht*) was put in the deceased's mouth, which was then closed with beeswax. (This is to enable him 'to buy his way up to heaven' and purchase a house and land there.) A pair of flowers and a pair of candles ('everything is done in pairs') and a 2-*baht* note were placed in the hands, tied together in the *waj* (worshipping) position. (The money serves the same purpose as the coin in the mouth; 'the candles and flowers will be used by the deceased to worship Buddha'.)

The corpse was laid out with the head pointing west. (This means that he has already gone to the new world. 'Normally when we are alive we point our heads to the east when we sleep. The dead are pointed in the opposite direction.' West is the direction of death.)

The visible orifices—the eyes and the mouth—were closed by means of wax. ('This is to prevent the living members of the family from losing interest in life. For they know that finally they too will die in the same way.')

At the head of the corpse were placed a number of ritual articles. (Informants said that all the things the deceased used when alive were put near the coffin so that they might not forget to take them to the cemetery. When these objects are placed at his head, the living say: 'The articles that you used, we give them to you to take away' (*khong cao kei chai, kha hai pai*).) The objects were: (1) the mattress and blanket he used when alive (these will be taken to the cemetery and burned with the corpse); (2) a basket containing a dish of rice and another of fish and chilli ('for the *winjan* to eat'); (3) a vessel containing water ('for the *winjan* to drink'); (4) some clothes (for the deceased to wear in heaven); (5) a knife (to be given to the monks for use in the temple); and (6) a red cloth (which is later to be used to cover the coffin—*pha pok heep*).

3 *Bun Phraawes* festival: the great story of Wesandaun is recited from the decorated pulpit; the painted cloth draped at the back depicts the story (see Chapters 10 and 12)

4*a* *Sukhwan* ceremony being performed for two pregnant women, who are wearing head rings of cotton and are sitting to the right of the officiant (*paahm*) who is reciting with hand held in the attitude of worship and with the palm-leaf text in front of him. In the centre is the decorated *phakhwan* and food offerings, lustral water, etc. (see Chapter 13)

4*b* Women worshipping on the Buddhist Sabbath at the *wat*

Death rites, and the path to rebirth

At the head and feet a string was tied to posts just above the corpse, and on this string was draped a white cloth called the *pha hak hua*. (It was compared by the abbot to the five precepts—'the mourners wish the dead body to be pure as the white cloth'.) The anthropologist, however, notes other symbolic meanings. The white cloth above the corpse is later also used to cover the coffin and is finally given to a monk as the *bansakula* cloth. White signifies death; it is also ideally the proper colour for a layman to wear to the temple. The red cloth (which is also used later to cover the coffin) is brought home directly after the cremation, and is later purified by the monks. It thus represents normal secular life and its continuation.

The place where the corpse is laid out has symbolic significance in relation to the values attached to different parts of the house (see Chapter 2). It lies in the centre of the *huean yaai* (the 'large house' which is the sleeping room), bridging or straddling the 'invisible' barrier between the parents' room (*hong peueng*), which is the eastern half, and the room of the married daughter and son-in-law (*hong suam*), which is the western half. Death obliterates the taboos that surround the *huean yaai* in ordinary life; normally closed to distant kin and outsiders, the most sacred part of the house is thrown open to all mourners. Furthermore, the position of the corpse—head to the west lying in the son-in-law's quarter, and feet to the east lying in the parents' quarter—is a reversal of the normal auspicious directions, and especially in the case of parents is a 'denigration' of the dead body.

The death had been reported to relatives and the headman, the latter of whom in turn is said to have instructed villagers to help the bereaved household. (This highlights the norm that death requires the participation of the community.) People of the village, kin and non-kin, assembled to 'make the coffin' and help conduct the mortuary rites. A large gathering of all ages was present, and many household heads contributed money gifts ranging from 1 to 5 *baht*. These amounts were meticulously noted down.

Old women of the mother category (*mae*) prepared cigarettes and betel-nut packets; the young women—both married and unmarried—cooked food; and the men of all ages constructed the coffin and decorated it. When the coffin was ready it was carried into the house and the corpse, with the mat and clothes, was put into it. Four paper flags were stuck in its corners, and all the paper money contributed by the mourners was stuck on bamboo sticks, which were then planted in its sides.

Some of the men, mostly young, were entrusted with the task of cutting firewood in the forest and making a pyre at the place of cremation there. Once they had gone into the forest they would not be allowed to return home until the cremation was over. (If they did, they would carry disease to their relatives.)

In the mid-morning monks and novices arrived to chant and were presented with food. It was after lunch that a long spell of chanting took place, two sets of chants being recited. The first was *suad kusala*, which said that whatever merit and demerit the deceased had acquired, might the merit increase and the demerit disappear. The next was the *suad jod muk*, recited by two monks. (We were told by the abbot that it 'tells the *winjan* of the deceased the way to heaven'. A second interpretation of this particular *suad* was given by a layman, and this is the fullest interpretation we recorded. He said that at death the four elements, *tat winjan* (soul), and *khan ha* (body and mind) become scattered. The recitation of the *suad* by two monks has the purpose of calling together these elements and reconstituting them;[1] at the same time the way to heaven is indicated. All the chants were in a general sense meant to give merit (*haj bun*) to the dead.)

Funeral procession

The coffin, as is always required, was carried out with the feet of the deceased leading and pointing west. (Villagers said that the coffin also is carried to the cemetery pointing 'west', once again emphasizing the direction of death.) As it was being taken out of the house, jars of water in the house and the house ladder were turned upside down. Then the jars were filled with water again and the ladder replaced in its original position. The anthropologist notes these as ritual reversals. (Villagers said it is done so that the *winjan* will not find its way back to the house. A Buddhist twist was also given—that these acts meant that human beings are subject to the cycle of existence.)

The coffin-bearers were three sons of the deceased and a son-in-law (*luug kei*). Before they actually lifted the coffin, flowers and candles were distributed to them—a ritual act common in all situations when 'specialist' services are requested. (But the flowers have additional significance in this context. The coffin-bearers are exposed to the danger that the dead man's *phii* may take hold of them or harm them. On arrival at the cemetery, therefore, they will use the flowers and candles to pay respect to the deceased and acquire for themselves the power and strength of *Phraa Buddha* and *Dhamma* to counter the possible malevolence of the *phii*.)

The funeral procession was led by monks. A long cord (*dai chung phii*) was fastened at the foot of the coffin, and the monks held it at the other

---

[1] This probably refers to the *skandhas* or five 'heaps' of which a human being is constituted—body, feelings, perception, impulses and emotions, and consciousness.

end. (The monks are said to lead the way (*hon tang*) to heaven.) If a young kinsman of the deceased, usually a grandson or son, has been specially ordained to make merit for him, he would lead the procession. The monks were followed by the coffin, then by the males, and finally the females. Persons of all ages attended the cremation.

On the way puffed rice was thrown on the ground. ('Once a person dies he will never be reborn as the same person. The puffed rice similarly cannot be grown again.' A second meaning attached to this act is as follows: 'Puffed rice is thrown so that *phii* will come and welcome the dead man. If it is not offered to them, they will enter the coffin, which will become heavy for the bearers; puffed rice is thrown to lure the *phii* to the cemetery so that they do not prowl around the village.')

When the procession reached the cemetery, it was met by other monks. It is worth noting that it is customary, at a grand rite of passage, to invite monks from other village temples to officiate together with the local monks. Monks from five nearby villages were specifically invited. Altogether there were twenty-two monks and novices conducting the cremation rites.

The cemetery is situated away from the village, in the proximity of the *wat* and to its west—a clear expression of the fact that death is the business of the monks and of the distinction that the place of death is separated from the stage of life.

Cremation

The funeral pyre had already been built by the young men despatched in the morning. The construction consisted of two posts planted in the earth, with firewood piled laterally between them.[1] The coffin was conducted three times around the pyre in a *counter-clockwise* direction. It was then placed near the pyre with the dead man's head pointing west. (The circumambulation was explained by informants in two ways: (1) old laymen said that it represented encirclement by death and birth (*wian taj wian koed*), or the cycle of death and rebirth. (2) a monk explained that each circumambulation signified in sequence: (*a*) *roop-pa-pob*—body state—that is, 'let the dead man be reborn as a human body', (*b*) *kamma-pob*—'let the dead man be reborn and have wife and children' (actually the strict meaning of the Pali concept is the 'state of sensual existence'),

[1] The funeral pyres that I saw in the village were not elaborate, but the structure does symbolize a *prasaat* (palace) or rather, in this context, a funeral monument (*chedi*). Tall elaborate pyres are seen in the cremations of wealthy persons in Thailand. Sweet-smelling woods are used and as De la Loubère remarked: 'But the greatest honor of the funeral consists in erecting the pile, not in eagerly heaping up wood, but in a great scaffold, on which they do put earth and then wood' (1693, p. 123).

and (c) *juan-ra-pob*—state of walking—that is, 'let the deceased travel a good path in his next life'.[1] The anthropologist notes that the counter-clockwise circumambulation is a reversal of the clockwise circling of the *wat* in collective Buddhist rites. If the latter 'binds' the sacred and also signifies 'ascent', the former 'unbinds' or scatters the body to its destiny after death.)

The people assembled at the cemetery collected dry sticks and placed them on the pyre. ('It brings merit to help burn the corpse.')

The white cloth covering the coffin was taken off and two men, standing on either side of the coffin pyre, threw it to each other three times. This is the *bansakula* cloth already referred to.[2] (Villagers interpreted the throwing of this cloth three times in much the same way as they interpreted the circumambulation.)

After the monks rendered a set of chants, they were presented with gifts of packets containing tobacco, betel and money, and they chanted a blessing in acceptance of the gifts.

The next sequence was the pouring of water on the corpse. Two monks in succession poured coconut juice on the corpse's face ('Water of the young coconut is as pure as the Five Precepts.') Relatives of the deceased and villagers poured scented water on the corpse. (While pouring, one usually says 'I come to wash your face, may you ascend to heaven.' As one informant put it, 'The face is washed because after death he goes to the other world. Water is poured to cleanse and make the corpse beautiful. People usually say, while pouring: "When being reborn, don't bring any disease with you. Don't starve, be rich in the next birth."' He also explained that monks cleanse the corpse first because they 'keep the precepts and practise morality'.)

The cord which had previously been attached to the foot of the coffin when the monks led it to the cemetery was now fastened to its head. Two monks held the cord and recited a brief chant. (This is called the *suad-anit-cha*, which says that all bodies are impermanent; ageing, struggle and death are inevitable processes.) Three other groups of monks repeated this sequence. A log had been placed between the coffin and the monks, and none of the monks stepped over this barrier. (No interpretation of this was forthcoming. The anthropologist is tempted to say that monks stand at the threshold of death, but do not actually enter that realm.) This

---

[1] The concepts are, of course, derivations from the three orders of existence—*kama loka*, *rupa loka* and *arupa loka*—in the Buddhist cosmology (see Chapter 3). It is interesting to note the transformation in village thought of these classical concepts.

[2] The Pali word *pamsukula* means rags found in dust heaps and *pamsukulin* is a *bhikkhu* who wears garments made of such rags patched together. A group of ascetic monks existed in medieval Ceylon called *pamsukulins*, the name being a symbol of utmost poverty (see Geiger 1960, p. 202).

concluded the ritual role of most of the monks, who then returned to the *wat*. Before leaving they were individually presented with gift packets (*bang-maag*) which also contained money.

The ritual was now approaching the actual cremation. The four paper flags were removed from the coffin and planted on the pyre. The abbot moved to the head of the coffin and held one end of the white cloth placed on its top. He rendered a brief chant and then took the cloth. The clothes, mattress and blanket of the deceased were placed near the pyre, the coffin was lifted on to the pyre, and the remaining monks and the villagers lit the firewood. While the corpse burned, the monks chanted. ('This is to tell the way to heaven.')

The people left the cemetery after the pyre was ignited. It is the custom that when they return to the village from the cemetery, they must first go into the *wat* compound and only then to the funeral house (home of the deceased), where they are feasted. The *wat* immunizes the dangers of death.

That evening a ceremony took place in the funeral house which I should like to emphasize. Beginning on this evening, the monks came to the house for three nights in order to chant *suad paritta mongkhon* 'for protection and for blessing'. Certain objects were put in a fishing net: these were the clothes of the deceased left in the house and the tools used for cutting wood for the pyre. A thread was attached to the Buddha image, then it was held by the abbot; next it was wound round a bowl of water, then it was held by the other monks, after which the end was attached to the net. In a subsequent section I shall deal with these protection ceremonies and the making of lustral water. It is obvious that the monks were purifying the objects mentioned or, to put it differently, were themselves 'absorbing' and neutralizing their impurity. As one informant put it, 'the thread is tied to those objects, and sacred words in Pali pass through it to drive away disease and the dead man's *winjan*'.

The chanting was followed by the wake 'to make the family members happy (*gnan hyan dee*)'. Many people, both old and young, stayed on in the funeral house until very late, the old conversing and the young playing games. This was an occasion for young people of both sexes to have fun together. On the following two nights as well people visited the funeral house, both to listen to the monks' chanting and to make the bereaved family happy.

Buddhism and the spirit cults in North-east Thailand

On the third day after the cremation the second part of the mortuary rites took place—the collection of bones and merit-making for the deceased. On the previous day a large number of people congregated in the bereaved household to 'make the *prasaat peueng*'.

Making the 'prasaat peueng'

The *prasaat peueng* is a palanquin-type structure, which is said to represent a palace. It may be noted it is similar to the *prasaat rajawang* made for the *Bun Kathin* rites (see Chapter 10, p. 158).[1] (The village interpretation is that it is made so that the dead man can live in it in heaven.) Various gifts are placed inside and are presented to the monks on the following day, in order to make merit for the dead man.

The assemblage of people for making the *prasaat* was far in excess of those actually needed. Large quantities of food were cooked on this day, both to feed the participants and, more importantly, to feed the monks on the following day at a grand merit-making ceremony.

Collection of bones

Early next morning a party of villagers who had assembled at the funeral house left for the cemetery. The party was met at the cremation site by seven monks invited to officiate. The funeral pyre was found to be still smouldering after three days. Water was sprinkled on it by a brother of the deceased's wife, an ex-abbot, in order to put out the live coals. Then the collection of the bones began. A monk initiated this activity by first picking up a bone and putting it in a pot. Then all the others followed. While collecting the bones, they raked the ashes in order to find the coin that had been placed in the corpse's mouth. ('This coin, after the burning of the corpse, is used to counter *phii* (spirits). Before using it for this purpose certain magical spells have to be recited (*sek-katha*).' It is used as a medallion.)

The bones were all collected in the pot, in the bottom of which a hole had been bored by the ex-abbot. Then the young people present (*luug-laan* of the deceased) washed the bones by pouring scented water into the pot. (This ritual act is described as the *laan* asking the forgiveness of grandparents (*laan somma pu, somma ya*), and is reserved for the *luug-laan*.)

---

[1] The *prasaat* type architecture is usually a building with tiered roofs typical of religious buildings and royal palaces, and is strictly regulated by sumptuary laws. Conical structures appear in various rituals in the village; what is not allowed or possible in real life makes its appearance in ritual situations which invoke successfully the grand religious and royal styles.

Two male elders (one being the ex-abbot) then thoroughly washed the bones. After this, 'siblings' of the deceased made a human figure from the ashes. They first made it with the head pointing to the west, then reversed it. (The west is the direction of death; when the 'body' is pointed to the east it means rebirth and the emergence of a living human being.) While this was taking place a classificatory brother of the deceased dug among the ashes to uproot the ends of the two posts of the funeral pyre construction. ('If the remains of the posts in the ground are not pulled out, the *winjan* of the dead will hover around near the place of cremation.')

The deceased's son then covered the mouth of the pot with a piece of white cloth, and secured it with a thread, one end of which, about two feet long, was left dangling. A lighted candle was placed on the rim of the pot's mouth and the pot placed on the chest of the figure made with the ashes. 'The candle lights the way. The pot is placed on the chest because the heart is there.')

The monks then approached the figure, stood near its head, and chanted three different *suad*. During one of them, the deceased's classificatory brother poured water on the ground to transfer merit to the deceased (*yaadnam*). The monks also chanted *suad acirang*. (According to the abbot this chant refers to the impermanence of human life, which is compared to firewood which decays with time.) During this chant the monks held the thread attached to the pot (see Plate 1*b*).

Then a son of the deceased made a hole in the cloth covering the mouth of the pot with a knife ('to let the *winjan* escape'). A hole was dug in the ashes, the pot was put in it by another son of the deceased and covered with ashes while his brother held the thread. All the males present then collected branches from the surrounding forest and used them to cover the place where the pot was buried.[1]

This concluded the bone-collection ceremony. In this second phase of the mortuary rites the *winjan* has been purified and despatched to heaven and subsequent rebirth.

The presentation of the 'prasaat peueng' to the monks

While the bone-collection ceremony was drawing to a close, the next ritual sequence had already been started in the village. A son-in-law and a classificatory son-in-law of the deceased had carried the *prasaat*

---

[1] In Phraan Muan village it is not customary to take any portion of the ashes and keep it in a shrine in the house, as may happen in some parts of Thailand (e.g. Central Thailand); nor is it common to build a funeral monument (*chedi*) in the *wat* grounds and deposit the ashes at its base, in imitation of the pagodas which contain the relics of the Buddha, or holy men (*arahat*) or royal personages. Such acts in imitation of the 'royal style' are found in urban areas.

peueng from the funeral house to the monks' living quarters and placed it on the wide verandah.

Some people had already assembled there, among whom the majority were women. This pattern is understandable, because the first part of the proceedings is giving food to the monks. The women had brought baskets of food with them, not only that cooked on the previous day but more which they had cooked in their own houses. For this is an occasion for merit-making for any villager who chooses; thus twenty of the fifty-two adults present were non-kin by village recognition.

While food was being offered to the monks, another food-offering was taking place in the compound near the *bood*. This was the *chakkhaw* or offering of rice to the deceased's *winjan*. Eight persons performed this rite, seven of whom were close kin of the deceased: two sons, a daughter, two sisters, a classificatory brother and a classificatory sister (mother's brother's daughter). They placed *kratong* (banana leaf-containers) with food near the *bood* and lighted a candle; an elderly relative—the classificatory brother—then planted a bamboo pole with a flag attached on the western side of the *bood*, thereby signifying that food was being offered to the deceased. This same elder then poured water on the ground (*yaadnam*): the *winjan* of the dead was told to receive the gifts in the *prasaat peueng*, and Nang Thoranee (the earth goddess) was requested to convey *bun* and the gifts to him.

The next sequence was the presentation of the *prasaat peueng* to the monks. The gifts placed inside it were: a monk's robe, a pillow and mat, two pieces of cloth, a pair of pants, an aluminium pot, a torchlight, an exercise book and pencil, candles and matches, and a kind of sweet delicacy made of rice (*khaw tom*).

The deceased's son and a brother of the deceased's wife (the ex-abbot) carried the *prasaat* and placed it near the monks. A candle was lit and put on the *prasaat*, marking it as the gift to be given. The ex-abbot tied a cord to it and handed the other end to the monks; he then said a Pali stanza offering them the gifts.

The final phase of the merit-making for the dead was the preaching of a sermon by a monk. A brief summary of the sermon, given us by the abbot, is as follows: 'Once there is birth, there will follow ageing, pain and death. Animals, houses, motor cars are no exception to this rule. The performance of cremation rites brings merit to those conducting them; merit accrues to the sponsors of the rites.'

The sermon concluded the mortuary rites.

Death rites, and the path to rebirth

KINSHIP PARTICIPATION IN MORTUARY RITES

Death is not solely a concern of the kin of the bereaved family; neighbours and fellow villagers are obliged to participate. No concepts of pollution apply to close kin or participants; rather, participation is regarded as merit-making. The scale of social participation at three crucial moments in the mortuary rites may be judged from these figures. On the day of coffin-making, on the day of making the *prasaat peueng*, and finally at the merit-making for the dead—the number of adults present was 62, 78 and 52 respectively, and of these the number of kin (*yad*) was 32, 23 and 30.

The concepts of kinship in Baan Phraan Muan must now be defined: both cognatic and affinal kinsmen are classed as *yad*, and a classificatory terminology of the generation type is consistently applied to them (see Chapter 2). Our data on participation in various rites show that when in fact large numbers of kin on both sides were present in the village there was a wide spread, up to second cousin range, on both ego's and his wife's side.

The concept *yad phii naung* in fact embraces all kinds of kin on all sides. And in this village, where generation and relative age are important criteria of social classification, the terms for parents, siblings, children and grandchildren are applied widely (although the kinship terminology contains more specific terms).

Within this wide range of community and kin participation, it is the close kin of the deceased and his or her spouse who play the crucial roles —notably children of both sexes, sisters and brothers and their spouses, and wife's siblings. But from the point of view of social ideology, the kinship categorization (from the standpoint of the deceased) is in terms of the *phii-naung* (siblings of same generation), playing the role of ritual leadership, and the *luug-laan* (children and grandchildren in the classificatory sense), playing the vital ritual and manual roles connected with paying respects to the deceased. All the manual tasks—making and carrying the coffin, cutting wood for the pyre, cooking food, cleansing the corpse—are devoted to enabling the elders of the parental generation to go safely to the other world, and to the making and transferring of merit on their behalf.

ABNORMAL DEATH

Villagers view abnormal death with great fear, because the *winjan* may become a malevolent *phii* called *phii tai hoeng*. These spirits are said to hover on earth because of their attachment to worldly interests, having been plucked from life before completing a normal life cycle. The corpses are denied cremation because of the fear 'that disease may affect the *luug* and *laan* (children and grandchildren or other living descendants) who may die like their predecessors'.

The corpse is buried quickly after death; this is done even if death takes place at night. Monks are not called upon to chant beforehand or to officiate at the burial. The corpse is not put in a coffin; its feet and hands are tied and it is simply covered with a bamboo mat and buried. The burial is devoid of ritual.

It is only after the body has been hastily disposed of, so that the earth may contain its dangerous powers, that the monks are invited to conduct rites, to invest the deceased with merit and grant protection to the living. They are invited to chant in the deceased's house for three nights; they are not given food on the succeeding mornings but are given gifts.

The corpse may be left in the earth for a period extending from three months to two years, at the end of which its dangerous powers have been immunized and it is ready for the normal mortuary rites. The bones are dug up and cremated; they are then cleansed and put in a pot, and buried in the manner described earlier. The monks officiate. Finally a *prasaat peueng* ceremony is held to transfer merit to the dead. Thus sudden death is also treated with ritual of the double obsequies pattern, the first phase being the burial and the second the normal mortuary rites performed as one continuous sequence.

ANCESTORS AND BUDDHISM

Transfer of merit by the living to the dead does not stop with mortuary rites but goes on long after death. Parents and elders become ancestral spirits and are generally talked of as a category; there is no firm genealogical structuring or individual remembrance of persons beyond the parental generation.

Transfer of merit to the dead takes place on many occasions with the aid of monks and under the rubric of Buddhist ritual. In the majority of cases, the ashes of parents lie buried in the cemetery, where monks are invited to chant in order to transfer merit. We have seen in the previous account of calendrical *wat* rites that at the rituals of *Songkran, Bun Khaw Saak* (merit-making with puffed rice) and *Org Phansa* (end of Lent), merit is transferred to the dead and offerings are made to them collectively. In the course of every *wat* ceremony, *yaadnam*, the pouring of water to transfer merit to the dead, is performed; the living, having given gifts to the monks, transfer some part of the merit while the monks chant their blessings. In the course of some rites the monks themselves pour water from one vessel to another, and transfer merit to the living, the dead, and all non-human living creatures.

While it can be said that villagers commemorate the dead, it cannot be said that they practise 'ancestor worship' in the sense of a systematized cult of propitiation of the dead and a formalized relationship by which the dead interact with the living. The possibility of occasional punitive acts by the 'normally' dead is a far cry from a developed theory of morality of benevolence/punitiveness by which the dead live in the present and sanction the social order. Rather the accent is that the living should succour the dead and remember them when merit is made. Or a man on whom fortune has smiled may celebrate his status by honouring his parents long dead. De la Loubère made an observation about the great which is also true in a lower key of the villager: 'It sometimes also happens that a Person of Great Quality causes the body of his Father to be digged up again, maybe a long time dead, to make him a pompous funeral; if when he died, they made him not such a one, as was worthy of the present Elevation of the Son' (1693, p. 124). During the course of my field work, the headman of the village honoured his father and mother in this manner.

SOME IMPLICATIONS OF MORTUARY RITES ASSOCIATED WITH NORMAL DEATH

The mortuary rites show a pattern of double obsequies which can be analysed in Hertz's terms (Hertz 1960). The intervals between death, cremation, and collection of bones are brief in this north-eastern village[1] (in Bangkok and other urban centres it is much longer, and is graduated in relation to the social status of the deceased). The ideas that soon after death the *winjan* is a *phii* with dangerous powers, that the corpse attracts malevolent spirits, and that in a general sense death can be dangerous for the living are present in a clear form. The collection of bones after cremation, their cleansing and burial, followed by merit-making for the deceased, are generally concerned with separating the *winjan* from this world, despatching it to the next (and then rebirth), and at the same time with converting the *winjan* from the status of *pret* to *ancestor*.

The outstanding theme is the objective of leading the dead man's *winjan* to heaven and making possible a better rebirth. Monks and laymen do all they can to achieve this. We have seen that while the ritual manifests

---

[1] In the case described cremation took place the day following the death, and the collection of bones on the third day after cremation.

anxiety about the potential malevolence of the *winjan*, and ensures against any such possibility, it also shows a marked optimism, as in the *prasaat peueng* presentation, that with the help of the living the *winjan* will in fact go to heaven. A conspicuous feature is the direct participation of monks and the direct incorporation of Buddhist ideas and mythology in the rites. In no other rite of passage—excepting ordination for monkhood —is Buddhism so directly concerned with a human event. The monks not only act as mediators between death and rebirth, but also absorb and neutralize the dangers and pollution of death. Their religious status makes them immune to these dangers.

From the point of view of interpreting ritual, we have seen that the actors may give multiple or diverse meanings to the same ritual act. The monks' version, pitched in Buddhist terms, may be slightly different from that of laymen, who in turn may show differences among themselves. However, in the case of mortuary rites, interpretations seem to converge around some basic ideas associated with death and its aftermath. Where death is concerned the actors on the whole appear to have conscious ideas about the meaning of their acts which the anthropologist also often finds adequate. Such a close correspondence was lacking when we dealt with the cycle of *wat* rituals.

From a comparative point of view, it is striking that there is a common idiom in the mortuary ceremonies of the Buddhists of Thailand, Burma and Ceylon. Thailand and Burma show a remarkable similarity in the sequences and verbalizations of the actors; Ceylon, however, while distinctly portraying the Buddhist orientation to death, has more elaborate notions of death pollution, stemming from the caste system.

In the case of Burma, sources such as Shway Yoe (1896) and Manning Nash (1965) report some details which in essentials compare with the description I have given: for example, the dressing of the corpse and the placing of the coin in the mouth as 'ferry-money to pay for the passage of the mystic river', the conspicuous and indispensable participation of the monks, who preach the essential truths of the inevitability of death and the impermanence of the body and whose 'presence...[is] invaluable in keeping away evil spirits' (Yoe); the monks' role in the funeral procession, and their purification of the house afterwards; and the feasting as an act of merit-making. Contemporary villagers in Nondwin in the Mandalay region, as described by Nash, bury their dead; Shway Yoe, however, reports that traditionally in Burma, and in the non-British territories of his time, it was customary (except among the very poor), especially in the case of the aged, to cremate and to conduct double obsequies (bone collection and burial of bones after cremation) analogous to the sequence practised in Baan Phraan Muan today. Both Nash and Yoe report the different ceremonials related to natural/unnatural deaths.

It is clear that two themes are emphasized in the Burmese mortuary rites. First, the 'soul of the dead', malevolent and sensuously attached to this world, must be safely conducted to the next form of existence.

It is not sorrow for a life ended, a consciousness cut off, but rather to guide the nucleus of kan to its proper destination, to help a soul over the blank spots between existences, to ensure speedy transfer, and to keep the chain of being intact, without anomalies, like wandering souls or lost spirits that may trouble the village and even bring it calamity. (Nash 1965, p. 154.)

The second theme is that available kin, friends and villagers should collectively engage in the rites, and in helping to transport the dead themselves earn merit as well as transfer merit to the dead.

These features and the contextual setting of death in Thailand and Burma raise a comparative issue in respect of the Hindu notions of death, as portrayed for instance by the Coorgs (Srinivas 1952), Malwa villagers (Mayer 1960), Havik Brahmins (Harper 1964), and Kallar (Dumont 1957) or as reported in other general literature (Stevenson 1954). In the Hindu case various categories of kin are obliged to undergo obligatory mourning interdictions; secondly, formalized notions of death pollution attach differentially to these categories of persons and are expressed in behaviour such as social isolation, systematic purification baths, inability to enter the temple, to cook food, etc., during the specified period of mourning.

No such customs attach to death in Phraan Muan village. Although death is inauspicious and the person (and spirit) of the dead man is dangerous and malevolent, still no pollution from the dead man attaches to his kin, nor for that matter are such notions linguistically present. Correspondingly, no formalized mourning behaviour is imposed on the kin.

Let me elaborate this point. While there is no doubt that death itself is an inauspicious event and that the corpse has malevolent properties, it is not because of the dead flesh and bones but because the spirit (*winjan*) of the dead hovers dangerously. This spirit may attack the closely related living kinsmen because of its previous attachment to kin, property, and house. This feared malevolence—which from another point of view states that the attachments of the dead must be severed—is expressed in various acts and beliefs: as in Burma so in Thailand, anyone who dies outside the community or village cannot be brought into the village and his previous home in the form of a corpse; ritual reversals like inverting the ladder and upturning the pots, the requirement that the funeral procession not enter or go through the village but skirt it, the funeral wake to keep the spirits at bay, and the chanting of the monks to purify the house—all these highlight the idea that death and the corpse are dangerous.

But in contrast to Hinduism in India, no pollution as such attaches to the kin, or to the mourners. On the contrary, we have seen that a strong ideological orientation, which gives impetus to community-wide solicitude in the death rites of a member household, is the idea that it is an act of merit to participate. A son or grandson is positively enjoined to become a temporary novice or monk so that the merit accruing may be transferred to the deceased. An aspect of behaviour which throws light on how villagers face death is the conspicuous absence of mourning, whether in the form of felt or ritualized wailing or other behaviour connoting loss. The point at issue is not that the bereaved do not shed tears but that the rites do not emphasize or accent lamentation. It is interesting that Nash reports for his Burmese village that only women and girls are permitted to wail, and then only in a controlled manner without the tearing of hair, gnashing of teeth, and extravagant display of grief seen in Mexico, Guatemala, and (I may add) Ceylon and India. That this represents a cultivated and recommended Buddhist attitude to death is lent credibility by the observation of Evans-Wentz in *The Tibetan Book of the Dead*: 'it was stipulated that at the time of reading the *Bardo Thodol* to the corpse no relatives should weep or make mournful wailings near the dead nor in any other way disturb the process of separating the spirit from its earthly counterpart, but rather the family is enjoined to perform virtuous deeds of merit' (Evans-Wentz 1960, p. 195).

One cannot help but remark on the similarity of conception between the verbally elaborated and conceptualized passage from death to rebirth (or liberation for extraordinary individuals) represented in the *Tibetan Book* and the village mortuary rites which effect the transition through ritual acts.

12

LIBERATION THROUGH HEARING: THE SACRED WORDS OF THE MONKS

The problem I am concerned with here is the role of the sacred words in Buddhist ritual. In my essay 'The Magical Power of Words' (Tambiah 1968c), having pointed out that the orthodox anthropological approach devalued the role of words in ritual, I took as my point of departure the position that most rituals consist of the word and the deed, and tried to probe the basis for the widespread belief in the power of sacred words.

The major concern of this chapter (and also some of the subsequent ones) was introduced in that essay and will be examined in greater depth here: viz., Buddhist monks in Baan Phraan Muan (and elsewhere in Thailand) conduct rituals which combine words and action, with the primary accent on the words. The sacred words are chanted aloud and for long stretches of time. They are meant to be heard but paradoxically they are not understood by the majority of the congregation (nor by some of the monks themselves), because the sacred language is the dead Pali language. Yet the view of all participants is emphatic that through listening to the chants the congregation gains merit, blessings and protection. Of course, formalized Buddhist ritual consists not only of Pali chants but also, though less frequently, of sermons in which, if the doctrine is expounded, the commentary and elaboration of Pali verses is in the local tongue. In these sermons, then, the congregation appears to receive intelligible moral instruction. While agreeing that in the case of sermons the normal communication function of language (i.e. speaker and addressee share the sense of what is being said) is not by and large violated, I would yet point out what is known to all observers, that audience interest and concentration on what is being said is partial, if not minimal. There is much going to and fro, of sleeping and turning off, and of murmuring. Sheer attendance and hearing without necessarily understanding is efficacious and brings its reward. Similarly, let me make a counter-statement about the non-intelligibility of Pali chants to the audience which does not materially change my formulation. Many villagers can recognize chants, know which are appropriate for which occasion, and understand some of the key words. Women's knowledge is much less than men's, because a number of men have been monks or novices in the past, but this is countered by the quick obsolescence of liturgical learning that has no direct relevance in lay life. Thus all considered, it is not a distortion to say that more important than the understanding is the hearing, in the proper context and setting, of chants and sermons delivered by the appropriate persons.

There are celebrated Buddhist moralistic tales which proclaim the virtue of listening without understanding. One example, contained in Buddhagohosa's *Wisudhi-margga*, is this story:

When Gotama was preaching by the side of a pond near the city of Champa, his sermon was heard by a frog, which praised the sweetness of his voice and exercised faith in him. Immediately afterwards, a man who was watching calves, drove a stake into the ground, and inadvertently pierced the head of the frog so that it died; but it was born in the Tawutisa dewa-loka and had a mansion of gold twelve yojanas in size. (Hardy 1880, p. 392; see also verse 129 of the Sinhalese text *Lovadasangarava*.)

The moral is that if animals after so short, but ardent, a hearing of the *bana* can enter heaven, a human being could do likewise or better.

An additional illustration is the story of the bats that is interwoven with the great *Vessantara* story in the text called *Anisansa Gatha Phan* ('The Fruit of Merit of the Thousand Verses') which is read as a sermon in Central Thailand. The congregation is exhorted to fix their hearts upon hearing the reading, even if the Pali *gathas* are read without explanation, for benefit arises from this hearing as was experienced by the 500 bats which listened to the rehearsing by monks of the *Abidharma* in Pali, and in becoming absorbed by the sound, released their hold on the walls of the cave and fell to their death. The bats were reborn as deities in heaven, dined upon heavenly food, and were surrounded by female *apsara* attendants. (Wells 1939, pp. 235–6.)

Bearing this in mind, let us now approach the problem of the efficacy of hearing from another direction. It is highly suggestive that *The Tibetan Book of the Dead*, the *Bardo Thodol*, signifies 'Liberation by hearing on the after-death plane'. This imaginative ritual, verily a forest of symbols, consists of the recitation of the *Bardo* to the dead man's soul for forty-nine days or more in order to give it the knowledge and power to control consciously the processes of death and regeneration. The words describe in colourful visual images the whole cycle of *sangsaric* (phenomenal) existence intervening between death and rebirth. The *Bardo*, however, differs from the ritual of Baan Phraan Muan in that it provides the means for liberation through the hearing of words which the dead man's soul is in theory expected to understand and act upon as a conscious agent. It puts the accent on the hearer as a subject and active agent (though, in fact, the ritual as actually performed probably treats the dead man as the passive beneficiary of the reading).

The Buddhist religion places a striking emphasis on the words said by the Buddha in dialogue, as admonition and as sermon. This emphasis on instruction and dialogue is perhaps a feature which it shared in early times with other wandering sects in contradistinction to the ritualism of brahmanical religion. In a more general sense, most reforming movements portray a similar opposition to the existing established and formalized religion: the Reformation is a case in point. 'To Luther, the inspired voice, the voice that means it, the voice that communicates in person, became a new kind of a sacrament, the partner and even the rival of the mystical presence of the Eucharist' (Erikson 1958, p. 198).

But the established Buddhism of today is markedly different from the pristine Buddhism. While the Buddha preached in the local tongue—Pali—to increase understanding among the faithful and in reaction to the exclusive monopoly by the *brahmans* of the Sanskritic Vedas and other sacred texts, Pali in time became the enshrined language of Theravada Buddhism and was not understood by the laity at large. It is strictly held today that in religious ceremonies the sacred words recited should be in the language of the authorized sacred texts. Thus it has come about that in all the so-called world religions—Buddhism, Hinduism, Islam, Occidental Catholicism—there is a disjunction between the religious language (Pali, Sanskrit, Arabic, and Latin respectively) and the profane language of the congregation. This process is not unique to these religions only, for successful reforming movements which begin in some native tongue also in the course of time come to adhere firmly to their authorized texts, the words of which are treated as enshrined and authoritative. Thus it could be said that texts tend to acquire authority because they are ancient, but it is the authority that matters rather than the antiquity (Tambiah 1968c).

The sacred words, then, acquire their power and efficacy not so much because they are in a sacred language which is different from the language of ordinary use, but because of a threefold character represented in most if not all religious systems.

First, there is an original authority—be it God, or prophet, or first ancestors—who is the source of the sacred words, the doctrine, myth and message.

Secondly, this doctrine itself becomes a heritage and a sacred object in its own right, transmitted over time in orderly succession. Writing, by giving physical existence to the words and by endowing them with a relatively unalterable standardization, increases the authority of the doctrine (but is not necessarily the source of that sanctity). The sacred words are thus believed to create effects in their own right, provided they are recited under the right circumstances and by the appropriate persons.

Thirdly the words are effective because there are religious experts who recite them (and perform other ritual acts) and who have a pedigree of links with predecessors (leading back to the first source). The predecessors have transmitted the ritual art to successors, who have demonstrated their proper qualifications and have undergone the necessary training appropriate to the religious status.

Perhaps in no other religion are these three interrelated propositions more pointedly and explicitly affirmed than in Buddhism, when the congregation at the beginning of every rite at which monks officiate recites the 'three refuges' three times in succession.

'I take refuge in the Lord Buddha.'

'I take refuge in the *Dhamma*.'

'I take refuge in the *Sangha*.'

What the three 'refuges' or 'gems' of Buddhism state is that the Buddha, the all-enlightened one, was the source of the sacred words; the *Dhamma*, the doctrines preached by the Buddha and inscribed in the texts, are themselves holy objects in their own right, which when recited or indeed even when simply used as ritual objects can transmit virtue and dispel evil; and the *Sangha*, the monastic order whose ordained members practise good conduct, is the appropriate agent for a recital of the sacred words and performance of the accompanying ritual acts of transfer.

These preliminary statements provide the general framework for tackling the specific problem posed earlier: the role of the sacred words used in Buddhist ritual, which places great emphasis on the chants; the mechanics by which the sacred words are combined with the grammar of the non-verbal acts that accompany them; the logic of the transfer of grace by the monk to the layman, and why the monk is believed to have access to this power and the potency to transfer it. One fascinating problem in the technology of the ritual is the paradox that the actual words recited deal with the great acts of renunciation of the world by the Buddha, but the grace transferred by virtue of their recitation is an affirmation of this world. When we have examined these problems we shall have largely answered the question of the nature of the reciprocal relationship between monk and layman, between doing merit and receiving merit.

Liberation through hearing

Before dealing with the sacred words recited by monks in Phraan Muan village, it is necessary to elucidate the concept of *paritta*, for this is the name (*paarit* in Thai) given to the chants rendered by monks in most rituals.

The word *paritta* means protection. Tradition has it that the *paritta* originated in Ceylon and were brought to Thailand. Geiger (1960) refers to the institutionalized *paritta* ceremonies in Ceylon in early times (see also Rhys Davids 1963). The Sinhalese term is *pirit*. But, in fact, *paritta* have a longer tradition and their character is better understood by referring back to India.

The *paritta* of Southern or Theravada Buddhism have their counterparts in the *mantra* of brahmanical Hinduism and the *dharani* of Mahayana Tantric Buddhism. *Mantra* are secret sacrificial formulae of Brahmanism, frequently referred to as 'spells'. Hinduism and Buddhism, especially in their Tantric forms, developed the notions of *mantra* and *dharani* to extents unknown in Theravada Buddhism.

The efficacy of *mantra* lies in the fact that they are or can become the 'object' they represent. This presupposes that the mystical sounds or phonemes of which the *mantra* are composed are signs or representations of the deities in the cosmic pantheon, as well as of the subtle organs of the practitioner; they are also supports for concentration which thereby enable the practitioner to homologize his body with the pantheon. The *mantra* is simultaneously the symbolized cosmic reality (as a pantheon) and human body, as well as the symbolizing sign or vehicle for uniting them. Once again we are confronted with the threefold character of sounds and words, in this case as representing the external cosmos and its agents, the internal person of the devotee, and a mediating or uniting force.

The *dharani*[1] is the Northern Buddhist analogue conceived in the same way.

It consists of short talismanic formulas of words or verses sometimes in the shape of a sutra or discourse, usually ascribed to Buddha, and credited with 'holding' irresistible magical power which is exerted each time the formula is repeated or remembered or (in the written form) worn as an amulet. It is addressed to particular spirits or deities of the cosmos whom it propitiates or coerces... (Waddell 1912/13, pp. 157-8.)

In both Tantric Hinduism and Buddhism the character and efficacy attributed to *mantra* and *dharani* were apparently transformed into greater mystical potency than was present in the pristine notion, which Theravada

---

[1] *Dharani* literally means 'the holder or vessel (of charmed power)'. In Pali *dharana* means 'holding or supporting'. The Sanskrit root is *dri* (to hold).

Buddhism appears to have adhered to to a greater degree. For instance, while in the Rig Veda *mantra* are hymns of praise or grateful prayer to the gods for warding off demons, in the later Arthava Veda (dating back to about 600 B.C.) they had become incantations of stereotyped formulas which force the unwilling or unfriendly gods and spirits by their magical power.

Similarly, in Tantric Mahayana Buddhism the simpler *sutra*[1] forms developed into esoteric types to the degree that their recitation was believed to encompass and materialize worldly desires, to achieve miracles and, even more important, to aid spiritual advancement, and by a short-cut so to say, lead to the attainment of Bodhisattvaship or *nirvana* itself. Thus one section of the Mahayanists elevated the collection of the *paritta* called the *Parittan Pitaka* to the position of *Mantra-yana*, a means of quick conveyance to *nirvana* or to the more popular Amitabha's Western Paradise.

The Pali word *paritta* (Sanskrit: *Paritra*)—rather than *dharani*—is the epithet well known and widely used in Theravada Buddhism, and means 'protection or defence'. In their original meaning and in their present use the *paritta* consist of certain *gatha* (verses) or portions of *sutra* (discourses of the Buddha) which are used for defined purposes; these may be described by such words as 'protection and blessing' or a 'form of exorcism and purification'. Though the use Southern Buddhism makes of them is nowhere as potent or ambitious as that of Tantric Buddhism, yet there is in them sufficient ambiguity and seeming contradiction of the philosophical assertions of doctrinal Buddhism to warrant a subtle analysis.

A classical acknowledgment of the use of *paritta* in early Buddhism and the rationale for their use is contained in *The Questions of King Milinda* (Rhys Davids 1963). The dilemma posed by King Milinda was that, while the Buddha had declared that no man could escape death's snare, he had also promulgated the *pirit* service (i.e. recitation of *paritta*) in order to give protection to humans. Nagasena's dialectical skill wore thin on this issue: he said that no ceremony (or artificial means) can prolong the life of one whose allotted span of existence has come to an end, but those who have a period yet to run can profit by the 'medicine of *pirit*', thereby invoking the analogy of a disease that can be cured by medicine. He stated, however, the proviso that *pirit* may fail to give protection in the face of *karma*, of sin and of unbelief; while it is a protection against the malevolent acts of others, it loses its power against sinful acts done by the sufferer himself.

[1] The Pali counterpart for the Sanskrit term *sutra* is *sutta*. I shall use both interchangeably.

Liberation through hearing

This early Buddhist document merely affirms the potency of *paritta* and sheds little light on the mechanics and semantics of the ceremony. The *paritta* express a paradoxical element in the communication between monk and layman which has to be unravelled by other means. On the one hand, they are requested by the laity and chanted by the monks to confer good fortune and protection from misfortune. On the other hand, they contain *gathas* from scriptural texts and moralistic tales, or are adaptations from them, and these textual sources reveal the remarkable paradox that the actual words said by the Buddha are not exorcistic but by and large ethical and moralistic, while in the 'historical' circumstances of their enunciation they did yield practical effects against mortal dangers. Thus a *paritta* is a *gatha* (verse) or a (portion of a) *sutra* (discourse) recited for its potency effect.

Most, if not all, of the *paritta* in use can be related to Canonical literature such as the Buddha's discourses (*sutra*), Jataka stories, etc. *The Questions of King Milinda* (Rhys Davids 1963, Part I, pp. 213 ff.), for instance, refers to the following as being elements in the *Pirit* service—Ratana Sutta, *Khandha Paritta, Mora Paritta, Dhagagga Paritta, Atanatiya Paritta* and *Angulimala Paritta*.[1] Most of these are in use today and are a pointer to the continuity of established traditions. In the course of time *paritta* collections were made and elaborated in the Buddhist countries: examples for Thailand are the Seven Tamnan, the Twelve Tamnan, the Royal Book of Chants (*Suad Manta Chabab Luang*).[2] Introductory verses summarizing an entire *sutra* were composed; eventually, in some instances these summaries alone were recited to save time. I do not propose to consider the history and content of the Thai collections (see Wells 1960 and Satira-Koses (1960) for details) and shall limit myself to those *paritta* in frequent use in Phraan Muan village, using them as a vehicle for making general statements about the technology of this ritual.

In Chapter 8 I listed the names of the chants to which novices and monks devote much time in memorizing, for these are indispensable for the conduct of rites. Of them, the chants categorized as *mangala* (Thai: *suad mongkhon*), used on auspicious occasions, are the ones in question here. They are *paritta* which give protection from misfortune as well as positive blessing. The *mangala* chants in the list are divided into 'evening' and 'morning' chants, recited in these two phases at a ceremony, and

---

[1] Rhys Davids (1963, Vol. I, p. xxix) states that the text of *The Questions of King Milinda* gives Pali references to some of these *paritta*: Sutta Nipata II for Ratana Sutta, *Jataka* nos. 159, 491 for *Mora Paritta*, *Jataka Book* for *Dhagagga Paritta*, Digha Nikaya for *Atanatiya Paritta*. See also Rhys Davids, Vol. IV, Part III, 1957, p. 185.

[2] Tradition also has it that in A.D. 357 some Sinhalese monks in Ceylon, led by Revatta, compiled a collection called the *Bhanavara*.

Buddhism and the spirit cults in North-east Thailand

I shall take a number of them and comment on the alleged historical context in which the Buddha delivered them and on their verbal content. Appendix 1 to this chapter gives one version of the full verbal content of some of these *paritta* as currently recited in Thailand.

Mangala sutra (sutta)

This *sutra* was preached by the Buddha at Jetavana in answer to a question asked by a *deva* as to which are the auspicious things (*mangalani*) in the world. The *sutra* describes thirty-seven auspicious things including such as the avoidance of fools, association with the wise, honouring those worthy of honour, etc. In the Sutra Nipata it is recorded that at the preaching of this *sutra* countless *devas* were present and countless beings realized the truth (Malalasekera 1960, Vol. II, p. 410).

It may be remarked that there is nothing 'exorcistic' about this *paritta*: it gives admonitions in the form of auspicious acts, and it incorporates the gods as part of the larger Buddhist community.

Ratana sutra (sutta)

The alleged historical circumstances of this *sutra* called 'The Jewel Discourse' are a part of contemporary popular village lore. It was preached at the city of Vesali under remarkable circumstances. The city was devastated by pestilence, drought and famine, and its citizens begged of the Buddha to rid it of its calamities. The Buddha consented to visit the city and as soon as he commenced the journey rain began to fall. According to one version, the Buddha first taught the *sutra* to his disciple, Ananda, and asked him to circumambulate the city and recite it while sprinkling water from the Buddha's bowl. When he did so the spirits fled from the city and the people recovered from their calamities. Afterwards the Buddha preached the *sutra* to a large assembly composed not only of the citizens of Vesali but also of the *devas* of two *deva* worlds with Sakka (Indra) at their head. (The full story is reported in Nanamoli 1960; also see Malalasekera 1960, Vol. II, pp. 709–10; Hardy 1880, pp. 243–4.)

The Ratana sutra is one of the most famous and often-used *paritta* because of its dramatic warding off of evil and misfortune. But what do the words recited actually say? Out of its total seventeen verses the first two contain a request to the *devas* to receive the homage and offerings of men and protect them in their danger; then follow twelve verses extolling the virtues of the Buddha, the *Dhamma*, and the *Sangha*; it ends with three verses spoken by Sakka on behalf of the gods, expressing adoration of the Buddhist Trinity. The words, then, affirm the twofold character of gods—their benevolence and acceptance of propitiation by humans, and their adoration and subordination to the Buddhist Trinity; the most important implication is that blessings are *transferred* to the laity by virtue of the attainments of the Trinity. The great potency attributed to the words, the imperative dispersal of misfortune, is not actually contained in the words.

Karaniya metra sutra (sutta)

It is said that this *sutra* on loving kindness was preached by the Buddha to 500 monks who engaged in meditation in a forest region in the Himalayas, and were harassed by the tree deities who were forced to evacuate their tree mansions by the monks' presence, and who were also alarmed by their courage and goodness. The Buddha preached that the monks should practise goodwill and compassion towards the deities (Nanamoli 1960, Ch. IX). In Thailand today, this *paritta* is supposed to keep demons from displaying their horrible characteristics because of its potency.

Once again we are faced with the intriguing paradox that while anti-demon power is attributed to the *paritta*, the words of the *sutra*, as such, say that one should practise non-violent *metta*, that is, one should be diligent and upright, gentle, and should not, out of anger or resentment, wish misery on another. A person should cherish boundless goodwill towards others (see text in Appendix 1; also Nanamoli 1960, Ch. IX; Malalasekera 1960, Vol. II, p. 657).

Atanatiya sutra (sutta)

This is usually the last in the set of evening chants. It is also a potent *paritta* that wards off evil spirits, and is particularly valued to combat illness. The mythological origins of the *sutra* are especially interesting inasmuch as it was taught by the king of the demons, Vessavana, to the Buddha.

The Atanatiya Suttanta (Rhys Davids, Vol. IV, Part III, 1957) relates this story: the four great guardians (*lokapala*) of the four quarters visited the Buddha with their hosts, and Vessavana, the leader of the *Yakkha* hosts, told the Buddha that the Exalted One's 'code of abstaining from the taking of life, inchastity, lying and intemperance' was distasteful and not congenial to the *Yakkha* and aroused their antagonism, but that in order to protect the Buddha's disciples who dwelt in the remote forests where also the *Yakkha* dwelt, Vessavana would volunteer to teach the *Atanatiya paritta* to the Buddha. 'The Exalted One by his silence gave consent.' (p. 189.)

The actual words of the *sutra* first give a list of the seven Buddhas, beginning with Vipassi, who preceded Gotama; these 'splendid seers' and 'perfected saints' give glory to Gotama. Then comes a long and colourful description of the guardians of the four quarters and their brilliant hosts, who all affirm 'The Buddha do we worship, Gotama'.

Vessavana assures the Buddha that this is the ward rune whereby both brethren and sisters of the Order, and laymen and laywomen, may dwell at ease, protected from the molestations of the *Yakkha, Gandharva, Kumbhanda* and *Naga* hosts. Should any of these latter, however, molest, the threatened person should appeal to the great superior gods, chiefs, and commanders of these demons. The names of the gods are then listed.

It may have occurred to the reader that the *Karaniya metra sutra* and the Atanatiya sutra are closely related in structure. In the former the gods harass the pious monks whose goodness they are *jealous* of because it *competes* with their own. The Buddha's words of compassionate restraint constitute the victorious goodness by which the gods are reconciled. In the latter *sutra*, the *Yakkhas* are *opposed* to the Buddhist morality which violates the demonic code of conduct, but the *Yakkha* king voluntarily accedes to the superiority of Buddhist virtue while retaining for his *Yakkha* hosts their own given nature. We may note that the words of the formula state the pantheon, with the Buddhas placed superior to the gods, and by implication both are then ranged against the inferior *Yakkhas*, who can be overpowered (but not converted).

In Appendix 1, I reproduce a translation of a text of the Atanatiya sutra as currently recited in Thailand. It deals mainly with the attainments of the Buddhas, affirms that both devatas and men make obeisance to the Buddhas, and transfers blessings to the congregation.

Jayamangala gatha (suad chaya mongkhon)

This chant is the most important of the 'morning chants'—succeeding the 'evening chants'—and is a victory blessing *par excellence* usually followed by the sprinkling of lustral water. It recounts the eight victories of the Buddha, and after the proclaiming of each victory the blessing is transferred thus: 'May triumphant good fortune come to you with the power of the Lord Buddha's blessed triumph.' The victories are those over Mara, Alavaka the demon, the fierce elephant Nalagiri, the robber Angulimala, the evil accusation of Cincamanarika who pretended that she was made pregnant by the Buddha, the contending wise man Saccaakarnigaranath, the *Naga* king Nandopanananda, and the Brahman Baka. (See text in Appendix 1.) The blessing recapitulates the dramatic victories of the Buddha in his last life over evil demon spirits, evil humans, and antagonistic forms of nature, in short his domination of *kama loka*, the sensuous world.

Liberation through hearing

I have thus far reviewed the most important and most frequently chanted *paritta* in Phraan Muan village. They are considered to be appropriate for a wide range of ritual occasions. There are many others which are chanted less frequently because they are relevant to more specific occasions; since they are of considerable interest for Buddhist mythology and symbolism I consider some of them in Appendix 2 at the end of this chapter.

Two points can be inferred from the *paritta* already considered and from those examined in Appendix 2. In a large number of them are embedded the Buddhist cosmology and pantheon, as well as the dynamics that relate the two consistently in terms of the beneficial co-operation of gods with men. But note that the principles of co-operation and antagonism hinge on the ethical and moral superiority of the Buddha's conduct, his virtue, loving kindness, and abstinence from self-aggrandizement. This is the core proclamation and it is the *potency* of this kind of victorious superiority and heroic action on the part of the Buddha and his disciples that provides the basis for protection from evil for those human beings who affirm the faith and to whom are transferred blessings. The technique is a *metaphorical* transfer of grace through words.

Essentially the *paritta* profess the doctrine of amity; they are meant to suffuse the hostile beast or man or spirit with benign, fraternal emotion —with *metta*. As Rhys Davids noted, the *paritta* render homage to this wonderful vista of faith, wherein even the most malignant spirits and beasts were looked upon, not as hopelessly and eternally damned, but as erring unfortunates upon their age-long upward way, and capable of being doctored and softened by the power of love. (See my comments on *Khanda Paritta* in Appendix 2.)

The next level of analysis is to tackle the problem of how the sacred words are integrated by the monks with their ritual acts and manipulation of objects. First we should briefly review the ritual occasions on which *paritta* are chanted in the village.

In the description of the cycle of collective merit-making rites at the *wat* (Chapter 10), we noted that at different points in the rites *suad mongkhon* was recited: in *Bun Phraawes* at the conclusion of the invitation to Uppakrut and before the ceremony proper (recitation of *Mahachad*) started; before the monks and villagers entered Lent and again before they left Lent. The usual formula is that every *ngan bun* (merit-making rite) begins with *suad mongkhon*. It is clear in this context that the recitation of *suad mongkhon* is a threshold ceremony, both for purification and protection, in the passage from the secular to the sacred and *vice versa*.

Another occasion on which it is recited—at a particular phase of mortuary rites—has also been briefly described (Chapter 11). Between the two major phases—cremation and collection of bones—which are related to the change in status of the *winjan* soul, the monks chant *suad mongkhon* for three consecutive nights at the house of the bereaved, and purify the possessions of the deceased and sprinkle lustral water on the living. Here the recitation is explicitly concerned with driving away the malevolence of death and detaching from the world the spirit of the deceased. The villagers also, however, consider this sequence as merit-making for the dead, and the monks in fact are feasted and given gifts on the fourth day.

A third major occasion at which *suad mongkhon* is recited is a household rite—*kynhuenmai* (entering a new house) or *thambunhuen* (merit-making at the house). In the case of the first occasion, the ceremony is again a threshold rite, but monks and villagers are explicit that its purpose is to protect the new house and drive away the spirits of the land on which the house was built and the spirit of the trees used for constructing the house.

To describe briefly the ritual technology of house-blessing. It is divided into two phases: *suad mon yen* (evening chant) and *suad mon chaw* (morning chant). In the evening phase, monks chant *suad mongkhon* and make lustral water. A cord is tied around the house; it begins at a window, around which it is wound and knotted; it is then attached to the Buddha image, and the next length is held by the abbot; then it is wound around a bowl of water and the final length is held by the other monks. The technique is clearly one of 'charging' or sacralizing the house or, negatively, of driving away or keeping at bay evil forces. The power of the sacred words travels through the cord and charges the water and the house. The water is consecrated as follows: at a certain point in the chanting the abbot picks up a lighted candle standing on the bowl, drops some wax into the water, and then at the concluding words of the chant, completely immerses it. The next morning the monks return. They are given breakfast, which act is rewarded with the *anumodana* blessing; they now chant *suad chaya mongkhon*, the victory blessing, and finally sprinkle lustral water.

The *thambunhuen* rites are conducted on the same lines. In any single year they comprise the most frequent category of all the rites—of passage and household—at which monks officiate.

Finally, there is one other class of rites at which *suad mongkhon* is recited, and here the effect sought is the curing of illness and the granting of long life (*thaw ayu*). Typically, when a man of great age is sick, a long-life ceremony is performed. In such a ceremony *suad partita mongkhon* is

chanted to drive away disease, *suad kusalayasaming* is chanted 'so that
the virtues will be retained by the patient and the vices dispelled', and
suad acirang, when rendered, so as to cause 'life in the patient to increase'.
The ritual technique is that of sacralization involving cord, which is later
cut and used to bind the wrist of the patient, and the sprinkling of lustral
water. The ceremony of *suad thaw ayu* is really a last-rites ceremony
when a man is near death, and can be interpreted again as a threshold
rite. Monks are in fact also called upon to chant in other, similar situations
—when a man's astrological properties are defective (*chata kaad*) or if
illness is caused by an imbalance in the four basic constituent elements
of his body (earth, water, fire, and air). But this kind of curative role of
monks is marginal and infrequent, and there are elderly lay practitioners
with their specialist ritual who monopolize this role; these latter will be
considered in subsequent chapters.

In village ideology these *paritta* recitations are merit-making rites which
secure specific results of blessing, good fortune, and the driving away of
malevolent spirits and misfortune. One major point stands out. The
monks are antagonistic to malevolent spirits (*phii*); but they do not
directly deal with them so as to propitiate, placate, or exorcize. The
technique is one of positive charging through the use of sacred words,
combined with 'realistic' use of cord and lustral water.

It would therefore be revealing to examine more closely the critical
acts in the transfer of blessing. The reader will have noticed the great
amount of redundancy in the ritual: each of the *paritta* formulae concludes
with a verbal transfer of blessing, but these repetitions are climaxed by
further acts of heightened transfer. Through these repetitions, which are
additive and cumulative, the message of transfer is unambiguously relayed.
Critical acts of heightened transfer are, by way of example, the making
of sacred water (which is later sprinkled on the congregation in conjunction
with the victory blessing) and the receiving-with-satisfaction blessing
(*anumodana gatha*) recited by the monks after they receive food and gifts.

At a climactic point in the chanting the candle is extinguished by
immersing it in the water in the alms-bowl. The chant recited during the
extinguishing of the candles affirms, as do many other chants, the three
refuges and the happiness that comes through submitting to them, the
conquest over desire by the *arahats* and the Ariya men of religion, and the
happiness that comes from this affirmation of the conquest. The actual
immersion of the candle is done at the concluding line of the chant, which
says that these wise men who have destroyed the seeds of existence and
whose desires do not increase 'go out like this lamp'. This draws the
analogy between extinguishing suffering and extinguishing the candle.

But note the paradox, which illustrates an important aspect of the use of sacred chants in Buddhist ritual. The lustral water has been 'charged' with words expressing ideas concerning *nirvana*-type extinction of life and the conquest of worldly desires; but this water when sprinkled on the laity gives blessings, good fortune, and long life.

The *anumodana gatha* (receiving-with-satisfaction blessing), recited when monks receive food and gifts in formal manner, very explicitly makes the same transference. The gist of the blessing is: as a result of the power of the Buddha, the *Dhamma* and the *Sangha*, may blessings accrue and may the gods protect those present. The blessings include long life, fair complexion, strength and happiness. Wells (1960) cites in detail the chants used in Buddhist rites in Thailand. An *anumodana gatha* he cites is representative of the nature of the blessing (p. 122):

May all evils vanish, may all diseases disappear, may danger not come to you. May you have happiness and old age. May all evils vanish, all diseases disappear, may danger not come to you. May you have happiness and old age. May the four *dharmas*, namely old age, health, happiness and strength, come to those who bow to and prostrate themselves before the eternally Great One.

It is when such blessing is being given to the living that they in turn transfer some of it to their dead, to the gods, and to all living beings through *yaadnam* (water-pouring).

I have so far concentrated on the role of chants and the accompanying ritual technology in order to unravel the semantics of the rites under consideration. The question remains whether the employment of sacred words in sermons, as distinguished from that in chants, constitutes a different channel or medium and is therefore not capable of incorporation in one overall solution.

In Chapter 8 I enumerated the kinds of sermon delivered in Phraan Muan village; these sermons are rendered not at all rites but at the major collective merit-making ceremonies at the *wat* and on *wanphraa* (Sabbath days), especially during Lent. Sermons typically come as the last sequence in the proceedings after the offering of food and gifts and the chanting and the transferring of merit. If we exclude the local and regional myths and folk tales from consideration here (see Tambiah 1968a), we see that most sermons are based on the *Dhamma* texts and, most frequently, the *Jataka* (Thai: *Chadok*) stories. Pali stanzas and *Jataka* stories are recited, then expounded and commented upon in the local language. Sometimes printed sermons in Thai, based on the same materials, may be used.

On the face of it the sermons appear to be a use of words different from that employed in chants. While the chants are exclusively in Pali, which is not understood by the majority of the congregation, the sermons are expounded and commented upon in the local language. While comprehension of the chants is not essential for the efficacy of the ritual, the sermons would appear to aim at instruction and inculcation of moral truths. The *Jataka* tales have their own distinct structure—an introduction setting out the 'historical' circumstances of the narration by the Buddha, the story itself, and the final summation in which the narrator sums up the fruits of action in terms of the fates of the actors and identifies the principal actors in their present lives. It could be said that, whereas the chants transfer blessings and grace, the sermons teach the beneficial results of engaging in heroic meritorious action.

Other features, however, bring together the chants and the sermons under one, more general rubric. I have already referred to the belief in the merit-conferring virtue of listening to sermons, even if they are not understood. (Actual audience behaviour tends to confirm the lack of emphasis on intense listening.) Furthermore, the sermon itself is a stylized melodic recitation in the manner of chanting and is in some ways a similar sound sequence in the proceedings. The cord for the transfer of merit is used in both sermons and chants alike.[1]

[1] In this context it is worth introducing an issue which has not been satisfactorily commented upon by observers. The orthodox practice is that a monk should on certain occasions, for example while administering the precepts, or at the beginning of reciting chants or rendering a sermon from a preaching chair, or giving a formal blessing of thanks, hold his fan with his right hand in front of his face. In the case of a monk reading a formal sermon (*bana*) from a pulpit, he is completely hidden from view, the monk being seated and the sides of the pulpit facing the congregation screening him. The stated Thai view is that the monk shields himself from being distracted by the congregation, especially by the sight of women. A more revealing interpretation is possible by applying communication theory. It can be said that the intervening screen or fan cuts off or formalizes the distinction between monk and layman. Moreover, since it is the monk who is vocalizing and the audience listening, from the point of view of the monk what is important is the concentration on the act of reading and de-emphasis on the feedback from the audience, whereas for the audience the meaning is that the event (of hearing) is more important than the person (the vocalizer) enacting it. This symbolic gesture reflects and reinforces the nature of the relation between the monk and layman which we have probed with other data. On the one hand, the importance of hearing the sacred words is emphasized; on the other hand, the gesture emphasizes the firm distinction between monk and layman when they confront each other, the ambiguity that what is relevant to the monk is different from what is relevant to the layman, and that by bringing them together certain reciprocal but dissimilar exchanges take place.

In a different context, the same symbolic gesture takes on a different meaning depending on the social status of speaker and hearer. It is often observed that a Thai (or Ceylonese) inferior shields his mouth with his hand when talking to a superior. Here the inferior is assuming a submissive role, and apart from ideas of shielding the listener from polluting breath, he is also stating that his request is not worthy of the attention of the superior person. (The meaning here is the opposite of that embodied in the monk's act of holding the fan in front of his face. The monk is superior as the speaker.) When a Sinhalese *kapurala* ties a piece of cloth over his mouth (like a surgeon taking precautions against infecting the patient) when he approaches a god, he is symbolically avoiding polluting the god.

Buddhism and the spirit cults in North-east Thailand

The major sermons relate the supreme exploits of the Buddha—the selfless giving on a scale portrayed in the *Phraawes* story (which no human being can approximate), his defeat of Mara, his conquest of desire and achievement of *nirvana*—all of which, if viewed literally, emphasize the other-worldly and salvation orientations of Buddhism. There is no doubt that these doctrines are at one level expounded for the edification of villagers, who are exhorted to observe precepts, control their emotions and desires, and cultivate equanimity.

But there is also another mechanism of transference which elucidates the attitude of the majority of villagers to the sacred words and texts and their transmitters, the monks. The mechanism is the same in both chants and sermons. The wisdom of the Buddha, by which he triumphed over the powers of darkness and found his release in *nirvana*, is found in the *Dhamma*, which is a repository of power because it contains the wisdom that conquers *karma*. And the recitation of these texts and chants which represent ethical conquests and triumphs, results in merit, blessings and protection for the listeners. Moreover, it is the monk alone who can appropriately recite the texts, for he is in theory dedicated to following the path of wisdom and can transmit their virtues to the layman. There is a logic in making holy water by 'charging' it with words that extinguish desire and by immersing in it a lighted candle symbolic of total extinction. The water then, by transformation, enhances and affirms life in this world full of suffering. There is a logic in the monks' eulogizing the heroic deed of charity and world renunciation by the Buddhas and the *arahat*, and the congregation viewing these deeds as conferring on them strength to lead a blessed life free of misfortune; for the great deeds of renunciation transform and lend an accentuated if vicarious meaning to the smaller acts of giving and self-deprivation performed by man rooted in the world.

Monk and layman stand in a particular relation. The monk, by virtue of his asceticism and way of life, is partially aggregated to the world of death and final release. The layman is not, and is emphatically in this world. Through proper ritual procedures the monk as mediator and specialist can transfer Buddha's conquest of the dangers inherent in human existence, transmuting it into prosperity and mental states free of pain and charged with merit. But at the same time ethical effort and right intention are required from the layman; the most conspicuous manifestation of this is making merit by materially supporting the monks and temples.

All this brings out a duality in Buddhist ritual and religious action that I have tried to cope with. Let me state three dualities or paradoxes which derive from the trinity—Buddha, *Dhamma*, *Sangha*—itself. The Buddha has achieved *nirvana* and does not live; the Buddha or, better still, a material representation of him—his image or relics—has spiritual potency. The *Dhamma*, as sacred texts, relate primarily to the conquest of life, desire, and the seeking of release and salvation by attaining *nirvana*; the sacred texts have the power to confer the blessings of a good life on ordinary mortals. The *Sangha* and its monks represent human beings who have renounced life and are seeking salvation through the practice of an austere religious technology; the monks are as well human mediators who have access to mystical powers, deriving from sources which represent negation of life, but which are pre-eminently of a life-intensifying character when transferred to the laity. Supernatural power of a certain sort is located in the other world of the dead, and it can be reached only through the practice of asceticism and through asexual mediators.

In my view it would be a distortion of the facts to see in Buddhism therefore merely an emphasis on the 'other world' and to treat the monk's role as opposed to 'this world'. To interpret Buddhist orientations in this Thai village as being focused entirely on death–rebirth preoccupations is to give a stilted interpretation of the ordinary villager's relationship to the Scriptures, the Buddha, and monks.

There is every possibility that in more 'sophisticated' circles, both in Ceylon and in Thailand, there is a tension between the actual doctrinal position taken by monks and the lay orientation (which in turn may show divergent views as between the religious virtuosi and the untutored peasant). There are monks (not in Baan Phraan Muan) who realize that it is not their province to confer merit and blessings on the layman, and that the chants have no property of mystical power in themselves. The laity, on the other hand, often exerts a pressure towards using the monks and the *Dhamma* for just such purposes. From a theological point of view this represents a tension. From a sociological point of view our interest lies in the duality of orientation and the attempt of both laymen and monks to use their religion to state and solve existential problems.

To summarize the major propositions arrived at in respect of the semantics of the rites conducted by monks, which are composed of words interconnected with acts to constitute a single totality:

(*a*) The ritual *per se* is a *metaphorical* transfer through words of the virtues of the deeds of the Buddha (and his supreme followers) combined with a *metonymical* transfer through acts (the use of sacred cord, lustral water, etc.). While the words evoke the great deeds of the past and bring them into the present, the manual acts lend an operational or technical reality to the mechanics of transfer. It is this device that transforms the victories of world renunciation by the saints into victories of life affirmation by ordinary humans. Thus are the glories of an ideal past united with the prosaic present to transfigure it.

(*b*) While this is the logic on which the Pali chants and the accompanying acts are constructed, its semantic basis is not consciously understood by the actors either monk or congregation. The latter, particularly, in the main do not and perhaps need not understand the Pali words.

(*c*) The sermons, although appearing to constitute a different communication channel in that the ordinary language is used in their exposition, nevertheless share a basic similarity with the chants in that hearing without necessarily understanding is by itself efficacious.

(*d*) The basis for the belief of congregation and monks in the mystical power of the sacred words, which play the major role in Buddhist ritual, is three-dimensional and is explicitly and regularly affirmed in all rites: the Buddha, as Renouncer and Compassionate Teacher, was the source of the words, the *Dhamma* is the embodiment of those words transmitted untarnished; and the *Sangha* and its monks are the appropriate human transmitters of the words. The Buddha is immanent in the consecrated image and relic chambers, the words are objectified in the book, and the monk in human form. This trinity of ideas is not peculiar to Buddhism, as similar ideas are expressed in other religions. The semantics of the ritual system here described are of wider scope and generality as well.

(*e*) Ultimately, the reciprocities in Buddhist ritual transactions rest on a sociological and religious relationship between monk and layman, the former as a specialist and intermediary committed to the ascetic ideal and the latter as gift-giver within the Buddhist fold but committed to this world. In the Thai context this reciprocity gains additional meaning through the monks being village sons (most of whom have temporarily renounced their virility and the secular mode of life) and the householders and providers being the village fathers and mothers and elders.

Having argued thus far that the logic of the ritual transactions stems from a number of distinctions and complementarities between monk and layman, let me conclude by bringing into focus a new dimension of meaning which shows that the layman rooted in this world and engaging in gift giving is in one sense behaving in a manner that parallels the behaviour of the ascetic monk. It is easy to see that the ascetic monk in renouncing this world, its pleasures and its obligations, has freely given himself up to the cause of deliverance. Furthermore, the vehicle of this deliverance is the practice of discipline upon his mind and body, that is, positive action in order to negate his personal life. This free surrender and giving away is also an aspect of the layman's gift giving. The recommended mode and attitude of *dana* (generosity) is stated thus in the Payasi Suttanta (Rhys Davids, Vol. III, Part II, 1910): 'Give ye your gifts with thoroughness, with your own hands, with due thought, and give not as if ye were discarding somewhat.'

There is a discrepancy, or rather a difference in emphasis, between the ethic of gift giving in Buddhism and the sociology of gift giving. Normally, as Mauss pointed out, a personal claim is bound up with every gift. The ethical aspect of giving, of the freely given gift, is that the gift represents the giver, that the giver is giving something that belongs to himself, that indeed he is giving himself up. A gift becomes a true surrender, a sacrifice, if the giver forgoes the implied intention of receiving something in return. As Jung put it, 'All absolute giving, a giving which is a total loss from the start, is a self-sacrifice' (Laszlo 1958). This indeed would be the doctrinal recommendation, nor is it lacking in village attitudes. Gifts to the monks never return in material equivalent form. The idiom of such transfer is that of 'free gift', in which case the donor's altruistic intention has ethical value. In so far as this attitude is represented in the intention of the layman, then it is quite plausible to argue that from his own inferior level of world-rootedness he is 'surrendering' himself through the medium of giving up his worldly possessions, which are a part of him. The receiver is the monk. The truly ascetic, world-renouncing monk accepts the gifts without any obligation to return, for he is not responsible to the world; he is in the world, yet not of the world. Such non-recognition of reciprocal obligation on the part of the taker would complement the idea of 'free gift' on the part of the giver.

But we know that behind this theoretical double negation of reciprocity stands firmly the affirmation of reciprocity. The layman, by giving material gifts, expects to accumulate merit in the form of ethical energy; the monk in turn in accepting these gifts confers merit on the donor. This conceptualization of giving and receiving likewise appears in Hindu practice, where the *brahman* receives gifts, thereby enabling the giver to indulge in meritorious action. The *brahman* makes return wholly by religious services. The theory of *danadharma*, the law of gift, has been elaborated in Hindu literature, and Mauss (1954) explicitly referred to it in expounding his theory of reciprocity. His references were taken mainly from the *Mahabharata*, which is chronologically post-Buddhist. It is not relevant here to engage in historical problems of dating, but I do want to indicate that Indian ideas expressed in the texts are helpful in understanding a Thai villager's merit-making activities:

The thing given brings return in this life and in the other. It may automatically bring the donor an equivalent return—it is not lost to him, but reproductive;

or else the donor finds the thing itself again, but with increase. Food given away means that food will return to the donor in this world; it also means food for him in the other world and in his series of reincarnations. Water, wells and springs given away are insurance against thirst; the clothes, the sunshades, the gold, the sandals for protection against the burning earth, return to you in this life and the other. (Mauss 1954, pp. 54–5.)

APPENDIX 1 TO CHAPTER 12

SOME 'PARITTA' FREQUENTLY RECITED IN THAILAND

The following are English translations of some *paritta* frequently recited in Thailand today. The source for examples 1–4 is a book called *The Pali Chanting Scripture with Thai and English Translation Donated on the Occasion of the Birthday (72) of Mrs. Chaemvijasorn (Phin Niyomhetu) May 17, 1963*. (Such books, primarily dealing with religious topics, are customarily printed and distributed to guests by families of means on such occasions as birthdays, marriage anniversaries and cremations.) The source for example 5 is Wells (1960, pp. 234–6). The translations are imperfect but except for minor corrections I have not tampered with the wording in the sources.

1. *Mangala sutta*

Thus have I (Ananta) heard: once Lord Buddha was staying at Jetavana Temple built by a very rich man named Anathapindika at Savatthi. A *deva* approached Him at midnight and after paying due respect to Him inquired:

'Many *devas* and men disagree about the nature of bliss. Please explain.'

These great blessings were well-preached by Lord Buddha:

Not to associate with the unwise, to associate with the wise, to respect those worthy of respect. Each of this is a great bliss.

To reside at a favourable place where the good and virtuous live, to benefit from past merits, to have strong will-power to do good. Each of this is a great bliss.

To be learned and well instructed in science and arts, to be well disciplined, to speak only true and pleasant words. Each of this is a great bliss.

To honour, support and attend on parents, to look after wife and children, to engage in undisputed undertakings. Each of this is a great bliss.

To practise charity and righteous living, to help relations, to engage in undertakings of a righteous nature. Each of this is a great bliss.

To avoid evil, to be free from intoxicating things, to be always mindful. Each of this is a great bliss.

To honour those worthy of respect, to be humble, to be contented, to be grateful, to listen to the doctrine at suitable times. Each of this is a great bliss.

To be patient and obedient, to be able to see the holy ones, to engage in religious discussions at suitable times. Each of this is a great bliss.

To be self-controlled, to live a chaste life, to realize the Four Noble Truths. Each of this is a great bliss.

To be well-balanced in the presence of the eight manifestations of worldly changes, not to feel sorrowful, to be faultless, to be calm in everything. Each of this is a great bliss.

Those who practise the above mentioned ways of bliss are never defeated and will always be clear of danger. This is a great bliss.

2. *Karaniya metta sutta*

He who is wise in his dealings with beings should follow (in the footprint of) the Noble One who has attained the tranquil state of Nibbana. Let him be brave, truthful, fair in his dealings, obedient, gentle and humble.

Let him be contented, satisfied with whatever is obtained. Let him have few cares. Let him be unburdened and have his senses calmed. Let him not be haughty nor cling to families.

He should not commit even the slightest mean act that can be blamed by the wise; he should extend his compassion to all beings, thinking 'May all beings be happy, free from suffering and enjoy their happiness.'

May all living beings attain happiness, whether they show fear or are fearless: whether they are tall or big or middle sized or short or thin or fat.

Visible or invisible, staying far or near; already born or seeking birth, may all beings enjoy their happiness.

Let not anyone deceive others nor look down upon others in any way. Let not anyone cherish ill-will towards others because of anger or resentment.

Just as a mother guards her only son at the risk of her own life, so one should extend his unlimited loving-kindness to all beings.

Let him extend loving-kindness towards all beings: above, below and between, in such a manner that his loving-kindness will be unobstructed, be without hatred and without enmity.

Standing, walking, sitting, lying, as long as he is awake, he should be mindful of the practice of unlimited loving-kindness, which is regarded by the wise as 'the divine state of the mind' in Buddhism.

He who has disengaged from wrong views, is endowed with morality, is perfect in right views, and has removed the craving for sensual pleasure, will never lie again in the mother's womb (i.e. be born again).

3. *Jayamangala gatha*

The Buddha, through his ten Perfections, beginning with charity, has conquered Mara the Evil One who, having created a thousand hands all armed, came riding on his war elephant Girimekhala, together with his army. By this power, may you be endowed with conquests and blessings.

The Buddha, through his peaceful training of self-restraint, has conquered the impatient, aggressive and terrible demon Alavaka who, being superior to all other demons, fought against Him throughout the night. By this power, may you be endowed with conquests and blessings.

The Buddha, through the sprinkling of the water of loving-kindness, has conquered the noble elephant Nalagiri who, completely bewildered, was as dreadful as a jungle-fire, a disc missile or a bolt of lightning. By this power, may you be endowed with conquests and blessings.

The Buddha, through the exercise of his psychic power, has conquered the formidable robber Angulimala who, brandishing a sword, had covered a distance of three Yojana in pursuit of Him. By this power, may you be endowed with conquests and blessings.

The Buddha, through self-possession and modesty in the midst of the audience, conquered the insult of the woman named Cinca who feigned pregnancy by attaching a piece of wood to her abdomen. By this power, may you be endowed with conquests and blessings.

The Buddha, brilliant with the light of wisdom, conquered the bewildered, unscrupulous Niggantha called Saccaka who, being self-absorbed by the flag of falsehood, was befooled by his own words. By this power, may you be endowed with conquests and blessings.

The Buddha, through his instruction of psychic power to his mighty son (The Elder Moggallana), had the powerful serpent-king Nandopananda, the misbeliever, tamed (by the Elder). By this power, may you be endowed with conquests and blessings.

The Buddha, through administering his elixir of Insight, conquered a Brahma (god) called Baka who, misled by his own transcendental and super-normal psychic powers, had his hands tightly bound by the snakes of his own misconceived ideals. By this power, may you be endowed with conquests and blessings.

A wise and industrious reciting or recollecting every day of these eight themes of the Buddha's conquests, shall overcome dangers and obstacles and attain the highest bliss of Emancipation.

4. *Khandha paritta*

You should practise loving-kindness toward these four kinds of snakes namely: 'Virupakkha', 'Erapatha', 'Chabbya-putta', and 'Kanhagota-maka'.

You should practise loving-kindness toward beings who have no legs, beings who have two legs, beings who have four legs, and beings who have many legs.

You should hope that no harm befalls you from beings who have no legs, from beings who have two legs, from beings who have four legs, and from beings who have many legs.

You should wish that all beings be free from suffering and be happy.

The virtues of the Buddha, the Doctrine, the Order are immeasurable and unlimited.

The virtues of other beings can be measured and are limited. All beings cannot be harmed if they always remember the Buddha, the Doctrine, and the Order and practise loving-kindness to all.

5. *Atanatiya paritta*

My obeisance is made to the Lord Buddha whose name is Vipassi, the all-seeing, the glorious.

My obeisance is made to the Lord Buddha whose name is Sikhi, who gives help to all creatures.

My obeisance is made to the Lord Buddha whose name is Vessabhu, who is purified from lust, who practises asceticism.

My obeisance is made to the Lord Buddha who has the name Kakusandha, who put down Mara and the attendants of Mara.

My obeisance is made to the Lord Buddha whose name is Konagamana, whose misdeeds have floated away, who has acquired the ascetic virtues.

My obeisance is made to the Lord Buddha whose name is Kassapa, who has escaped from all lust.

My obeisance is made to the Lord Buddha, whose name is Angirasa, who was the son of the glorious Sakya Lord.

The Buddha Lords proclaimed this Dharma as the means of alleviating all suffering. All the Buddhas who have extinguished lust in the world have seen clearly the Dharma according to the truth. Those Buddhas were without wickedness, were great in virtue and were without anxiety.

Devatas and men make obeisance to the Lord Buddha who was Gotama Gotara, the benefactor and helper of devatas and men, who was filled with wisdom and right conduct, was great in virtue and was without anxiety.

We all worship the Lord Buddha Gotama Gotara, who attained wisdom and knowledge of right conduct. All the Buddhas, whether these or others —more than a hundred kotis in number (10,000,000)—all these Buddhas are equal, and no one is equal to them in power. All these Buddhas are filled with strength and with courage. All these Buddhas, possessing enlightenment, attained a place of leadership. All these Buddhas were brave, fearless, their greatness was known to the four groups, they set in motion the Brahma-wheel as no one else has ever done in this world.

All these Buddhas possessed the eighteen Buddhadharmas and were leaders who led creatures out of suffering. They possessed the thirty-two characteristics and the eighty characteristics and had radiance which extended six feet on each side of them. They all were munis.

All these Buddhas were omniscient, without lust—having conquered desire, they possessed great glory and great power, great wisdom, great strength, great mercy. They were sages who brought happiness to all creatures. They were islands, refuges that protected against evil and places of retreat for all creatures. They were examples, kinsmen, joyful ones, objects of reflection, and seekers of benefits for creatures of this world and in the *deva* world.

All these Buddhas were in advance of men. I humbly worship the feet of all these Buddhas with bowed head. I humbly worship all these Buddhas who were glorious beings, who were Tathagatas in word and heart, in lying, in standing, in walking—at all times.

All the Buddhas who attained peace, may they care for you at all times. Those whom the Buddha Lords have cared for attained peace also, they escaped from all danger, they escaped from all disease, they escaped from all anxiety and from all recurring ills (evil karma), their suffering was extinguished. May you be free from all ills, may all disease be destroyed, may no dangers come to you. May you have happiness and old age. May the four *dharmas*, namely old age, health, happiness and strength come to those who worship before the one worthy of reverence. We bow before that one who is eternally good.

APPENDIX 2 TO CHAPTER 12

MORE EXAMPLES OF POTENT 'PARITTA' CHANTS
(NOT DISCUSSED IN CHAPTER 12)

The *paritta* examined here are illustrations of those popularly considered potent for warding off evil happenings of a dramatic character, such as eclipses of the sun and moon, snake bites and other harm by wild creatures, difficulties of childbirth, etc. They invite us, however, to consider the problem that their avowed potency paradoxically derives from the mild non-violent ethical merit of the Buddha and his disciples.

1. *Mora paritta*

This *paritta* and certain *Jataka* stories from which it is derived are the basis for the elaboration of important symbols like the peacock and *Garuda* (mythical sunbird), which stand opposed to the *Naga* and snakes in general; these symbols link up with the planets, the sun and moon and Rahu, in the cosmology.

To fully understand the implications we must refer to three *Jatakas*— the *Mora Jataka*, *Ghatasana Jataka*, and the *Pandara Jataka*.

Mora Jataka: this story was told by the Buddha to a backsliding monk who was upset by the sight of a woman magnificently attired. The *bodhisattva* was once born as a golden peacock, 'fair and lovely, with beautiful red lines under his wings', and lived on a golden hill in Dandaka. He used to recite a spell in honour of the sun and another in praise of the Buddhas and was thus protected from harm. A queen of Benares saw in a dream a golden peacock preaching, and longed for this to come true. But all attempts to catch the peacock failed and the queen died without obtaining her wish. Six successive kings failed to snare the peacock until in the reign of the seventh a hunter snared the peacock with a peahen which he used as a lure. The peacock, snared because 'leaving his charm unsaid, he came towards her' who woke desire in his breast, was, however, able to prove to the king that he was not immortal and that the eating of his flesh would not confer on him the immortality he desired. Before he departed he discoursed on the theme of *nirvana* which alone is everlasting. (Cowell 1895, Vol. II, no. 159.)

Ghatasana Jataka: once the *bodhisattva* was king of the birds and lived with his subjects in a giant tree, whose branches spread over a lake. The *Naga*-king of the lake, Canda, enraged by the dropping of the birds' dung into the water, caused smoke to rise and flames to dart up from the water to the tree, and the *bodhisatva*, perceiving the danger, flew away with his flock. (Cowell, *ibid.* no. 133).

The story was told to a monk whose hut in the forest was burnt by fire and who delayed finding another shelter, which interfered with his engaging in meditation. 'And if beasts were so discerning, how could you fall short of them in wisdom.' (Cowell, *ibid.* no. 133.)

Pandara Jataka: a shipwrecked, wandering, naked and destitute man called Karambiya was mistaken for an ascetic by people who built him a hermitage. Among his devotees were a *Garuda*-king and a *Naga*-king called Pandara. At the instigation of the *Garuda* the fake ascetic wheedled out of the *Naga* the secret of how the *Nagas* prevented themselves from being carried off by *Garudas*, namely the swallowing of large stones which made them heavy. By seizing the *Naga* by his tail the *Garuda* was able to carry off the *Naga*, who was then forced to disgorge the stone. The *Naga*, lamented his foolishness in divulging his secret and on begging for mercy, was released by his captor, who set him free with the warning: 'His secret no man should disclose, but guard like a treasure trove.' Thereafter they lived in harmony as friends. The snake took his revenge on the fake ascetic by uttering a reproof which resulted in the head of the ascetic being split into seven pieces. (The Buddha identified himself as the *Garuda* and Sariputta as the *Naga*, and Devadatta as Karambiya.) (See Cowell 1905, Vol. v, no. 518.)

The *Mora paritta*, the great 'peacock' spell, combines all these (and other) themes—it comprises words addressed by the peacock, first to the sun to preserve himself safe in his feeding ground, then to the Buddhas who have passed away to protect him from harm; and other words to preserve himself from evil.

The *paritta* is said to protect humans against snakes, dangerous humans, animals and birds. Its best known use is against snake bite, on the basis of all the elaborations by which the peacock preys on snakes.

2. *Khanda paritta*

The potency of this *paritta* is to make the poison of deadly creatures, especially snakes, innocuous. In general it wards off all danger from creatures. The Canonical basis for the *paritta* is the reference to the Buddha issuing in the *Anguttara Nikaya* and the *Cullavagga* a charm against snake bite and recommending its use by monks.

The antidote recommended is, however, quite in line with what we have noted before: it is not an exorcistic spell but an asseveration of love for snakes and an affirmation of Buddhist *metta*, and is charmingly described in the *Khandhavatta Jataka* (Cowell 1895, Vol. ii, no. 203). The *bodhisatva*, it is said, was once born as a *brahman* in Kasi and later became an ascetic. On its being reported to him that many ascetics died of snake bite, he gathered them together and having admonished them 'If you showed goodwill to the four royal races of snakes, no serpents would bite you', taught them how, by cultivating love for the four royal races of snakes, they could prevent themselves from ever being bitten by them (or any other creature). 'Creatures all beneath the sun,/two feet, four feet, more, or none—/How I love you, every one!' (*Ibid.* p. 101.)

3. *Candima paritta*

The moon in Buddhist cosmology is inhabited by a *deva* called Candima or Canda. The Candima Sutta in *Samyutta Nikaya* records the incident of the Buddha's request to Rahu (the evil planet which swallows the moon and causes eclipses) to free its victim. The narrative says the moon (Canda) was seized by the *asura* Rahu, and the victim, remembering the Buddha at that moment, appealed thus: 'O conquering Buddha, I adore thee! Thou art perfectly free from evil; I am in distress; be thou my refuge!' Then Buddha spoke this stanza to the *asura* Rahu on behalf of the god Canda: 'Rahu! Canda has taken refuge in the holy Tatagatha. Release Canda. Buddha compassionates the world.' Upon hearing this, Rahu released Canda and fled to the chief of the *asuras*; trembling with fright when questioned why he had released Canda, Rahu replied: 'My head would have been split into seven pieces; I should have had no comfort in my life; I have been spoken to by the Buddha...otherwise I would not have released Canda.' (Hardy 1880, pp. 47–8.)

4. *Suriya paritta*

A narrative similar to the above is related about the Sun and Rahu, and the *paritta* affords protection of the sun from eclipse.

5. *Angulimala paritta*

This one is believed to ease the pains of childbirth and more generally, like the other *paritta*, to ward off all dangers. Its 'historical' antecedents are intriguing, for it is associated with the famous story of the Buddha's encounter with the killer of men, Angulimala.

The following is a summary of the story: a son was born, under the ominous 'thieves' constellation', to the wife of the *brahman* chaplain of the King of Kosala. While a student, the boy Angulimala aroused the jealousy of his fellow students, who falsely accused him of improprieties with the teacher's wife; the teacher in revenge asked as his fee for further instruction the slaughter of a thousand men and a finger from each victim as evidence of death. Angulimala murdered 999 victims, thereby causing great fear and depopulation, and on the eve of apprehension by the king was in mortal danger of murdering his own mother, who had set out to warn him, as his thousandth victim. The Buddha forestalled this crime by appearing before Angulimala, who then pursued the Buddha for twelve miles without being able to overtake him. The Buddha subsequently converted him and ordained him as a monk, and secured a reprieve from the king.

221

Buddhism and the spirit cults in North-east Thailand

One day when returning from his own natal village after an unsuccessful round of begging there, Angulimala saw a woman in severe labour pains and, being helpless and full of piety, reported the event to the Buddha, who said to him: 'Go to the place and say "I have never knowingly put any creature to death since I was born; by the virtue of this observance may you be free from pain".' On remonstrating that this was untrue of his own life, Angulimala was told by the Buddha that since becoming a monk he was indeed reborn and that his new life was virtuous. Angulimala did as he was directed and the mother gave birth with as much ease as water falls from a vessel. (See Malalasekera 1960, Vol. i, pp. 22–3; Hardy 1880, pp. 257–61.)

This story embodies several points regarding the theory of *paritta* in particular, and Buddhist teaching in general. The formula of the *paritta* emphasizes that it is the merit of the virtuous *arahat* that withstands worldly misfortune, and that the benefit of this merit is transferred to the layman. The Buddha's own act of conversion of Angulimala through compassion constitutes again the same message proclaimed in the other *paritta* discussed. Furthermore, it is appropriate that the former killer of men should now preside over their births.

From the point of view of Buddhist doctrine, Angulimala's conversion and becoming an *arahat* wiped out his former misdeeds, that is, a beneficent *karma* can arise and destroy an evil *karma*. But Angulimala, though destined not to be reborn, had to suffer the punishment of demerit in his last life. He was stoned and hit by people in his goings to procure alms.

13

'SUKHWAN' RITES: THE ELDERS SUMMON
THE SPIRIT ESSENCE

If we turn the kaleidoscope now, after reviewing the types of rituals in which monks officiate, we confront another class of rites which are referred to as 'calling the *khwan*' (*sukhwan*). What I propose to show in describing and analysing these rites is how they are complementary and linked to Buddhist ritual, and how the participants in these rites stand in a relationship of reciprocity that is a reversed image of that between monk and layman, youth and elder, as signified in the village institution of monkhood.

Apart from this theme, I also pursue further the communication aspect of ritual. The *sukhwan* rites are in a sense prophylactic and therapeutic; they are consciously intended to achieve certain effects in the celebrants. Hence I shall examine how these rites are structured and what kind of message they seek to convey to the celebrants, and in what relation they stand to the rites which monks perform. This exercise in investigating the intended effect of ritual as a communication device will reach its conclusion only in a subsequent chapter, when the *sukhwan* rites are contrasted with another class of healing rituals addressed to malevolent spirits.

In the discussion of primary concepts (Chapter 4), I dealt with a pair of complementary and opposed concepts relating to spiritual essences, *khwan* and *winjan*. Both essences animate human life, but while *khwan* is conceptually identified with life and its vicissitudes, *winjan* is related to death and the fate of the soul. At certain crises the *khwan* leaves the body, and its temporary absence is the cause of affliction or misfortune. Hence it must be recalled to restore morale. *Winjan* rites are mortuary rites, which have been described in Chapter 11; in them both monks and junior generations play important roles in effecting the passage of the soul of deceased elders. *Khwan* rites are performed by elders for their youthful successors, and in them we see the complementary ritual services that match the services of monks.

Villagers say that a human being has thirty-two *khwan* corresponding to various parts of the body, of which the head is foremost. No villager can actually name the thirty-two *khwan*, or rather the body parts in which they reside. Collectively they comprise a unity, *khwan*, which is thought to be a kind of spirit essence.

The essence of the *khwan* rite is the calling of the *khwan* (*sukhwan*), and binding it to the body of the celebrant by tying a piece of thead to his or her wrist. The symbolism is that of aggregation.

The binding of the *khwan* is believed to have certain effects which are the focus of much verbal elaboration on the part of the villagers. An expression often used is '*haj ju dii mii raeng*', which means 'confer good living and strength'. Other expressions are:

> *haj sod haj sai*   (give luck)
> *mii chok mii chai*   (have luck)
> *haj ram haj ruai*   (give wealth)
> *haj kam haj koon*   (give prosperity).

These are all expressions of good fortune and prosperity, naturally associated with the mental state of happiness. The mystical effects of *khwan* ceremonies may be compared with those of Buddhist religious action subsumed by the central concept of *bun* (merit). In *khwan* rites good fortune is conferred by means of restoring to the patient or recipient his spiritual essence. The *khwan* escapes and is recalled. This does not involve the kind of ethical action on the part of the recipient required in the case of merit acquisition, but is accomplished by virtue of the elders' ritual action and transfer of mystical power vested in them.

KINDS OF 'SUKHWAN' RITES AND OCCASIONS OF PERFORMANCE

The significance of the rites will be readily apparent when we examine the occasions on which they are performed. The occasions are numerous and there is a profusion in the names given to the ceremonies. I shall therefore group and classify the ceremonies to indicate certain uniformities and distinctions.

1. *Rite of passage*: (*a*) marriage (*sukhwan phua mia mai*). The rite is a major component of marriage proceedings and is performed to give the couple a prosperous life together. During the rite the couple are instructed about proper behaviour towards each other and towards relatives; the couple pay their respects to elders, who in turn bind their wrists. (*b*) ordination (*sukhwan nag*). One important sequence in the ordination into monkhood is this ceremony, in which the *khwan* of the *nag* is called and bound. A noteworthy part of the ceremony is that the officiant tells the *nag* about his obligations to his parents, especially the mother, who have brought him up, and to his kin who have contributed gifts and furnished the eight requisites of a monk.

The elders summon the spirit essence

2. *Pregnancy*: the state of pregnancy is a focus for *sukhwan* rites. Between the third and seventh months, two rites may be performed for the mother. One rite, which is held for every mother before every childbirth, is the *sukhwan maemarn*, the calling of the *khwan* of the mother and of the child in her stomach. The second rite, obligatory for the first childbirth only, is more elaborate and is called *taengkae maemarn* (to loosen or untie the pregnant mother). This rite is addressed to supernaturals pictured as 'old mothers' (*than* or alternatively *mae gao mae laang*) who allow children to be born as humans.

The stated purpose of the pregnancy rites is to give the mother strength and an easy delivery. A pregnant woman's *khwan* is prone to leave her and roam because she is frightened of and anxious about the pain and difficulties of childbirth.

3. *Threshold ceremonies before starting an enterprise*: these ceremonies are essentially similar to rites of passage. However, there is no change of status as such, but merely the entering of a new phase of activity which requires protection, blessing and morale charging. Examples are: *sukhwan phraa*, performed at the temple for monks by lay elders before the monks go into retreat during the Lent season (*khaw phansa*); and *sukhwan thammada*, 'ordinary' ceremony, performed before a man goes on a trip or before a youth goes into military service.

4. *Ceremonies of reintegration*: such occasions are when a man returns to the village after a long or extended trip (the rite is performed 'because his *khwan* may have stayed behind'), or when he returns after serving a prison sentence or completing his national service. Another is when a person recovers from an illness. All such occasions thus connote reintegration or reacceptance into village society. The patient who was in an abnormal status, removed from day-to-day life, returns to normal life. In the case of the man who returns from jail, the villagers consciously recognize the need to accept him publicly and reintegrate him into village life.[1] What I call here ceremonies of reintegration are referred to as *sukhwan thammada* (as 3 above). This means that for the villagers there is a similarity between the threshold rites held before starting an enterprise and rites of reintegration: what they have in common is that both relate to periods of transition—the former to periods preparatory to separation from the community or the course of normal life, and the latter

---

[1] I saw a ceremony held for two youths on their return from prison, after serving sentence for being embroiled in a brawl at a temple fair. The ceremony was public and was attended by a large number of the elders. The youths were not condemned or in any way ostracized; rather, the ethos of the village was such that they were greeted, accepted and reintegrated. This is an object lesson in rehabilitation and an impressive demonstration of the community ethos.

to periods preparatory to reuniting with the community or resuming normal life.

5. *Rites for those suffering from prolonged illness*: these are rites wherein the celebrant for whose benefit the ceremony is being performed has been suffering from a prolonged illness. The patient has already been subject to various kinds of treatment and has not recovered, and the *khwan* ceremony is performed to charge him with morale and to give him hope and 'long life'. It is important to note here that the *khwan* rite is performed not so much to cure the patient as to reconstitute the morale of a dying or very sick person.

The following are examples:

(*a*) In the case of sickness in children: *kae kamlerd* or *gae mae gao mae laang*—to dispel sickness caused by 'former spiritual mothers' (*mae gao mae laang*); *baeng khaw baeng kai*—to recall the *khwan* of a child under ten years of age who is suffering from a prolonged illness owing to the fleeing of its *khwan* (in this ceremony rice balls and boiled eggs are cut into halves).

(*b*) In the case of sickness in adults: *sutra khwan luang*, a *khwan* ceremony for the continuation of life performed for an adult who has been suffering from a serious and prolonged illness. It is performed while the patient is asleep. A similar ceremony is *taeng kae promchati*, in which the heavenly creators of human beings (Thaen) are propitiated to prolong life. Closely related to the latter are misfortunes caused by such planetary agents as Rahu, for which *Gae* (dispelling) *Rahu* is performed, and *Bucha Tua Sawoei*, a ceremony performed for the animal of the year in which one was born.

6. Comprising a final category are rites for dispelling bad luck betokened by inauspicious happenings, that is, when objects considered unlucky impinge on human beings by 'moving out of place'. Ceremonies called *sia krau* or *gae ubad* have to be performed when unusual inauspicious events take place—such as lightning striking a tree in the house compound or the house itself, a vulture alighting on the house roof, a toad entering the house, or a domestic buffalo lying down in the mud under the wash place (*hong naam*). Readers familiar with Mary Douglas' ideas (Douglas 1966) will recognize these situations of certain objects or creatures being out of place as signifying dirt or pollution or bad luck, for example an inauspicious animal like the toad moving from outside into the house, which represents 'sacred' space; or a 'sacred' animal like the buffalo moving from a clean into a dirty place.

This list covers a wide spectrum of situations, which can be classified in different ways. We should keep in mind that villagers refer to all the rites listed above as *sukhwan*, and that the technique of the ritual—the calling of the *khwan* and the binding of the wrist with cord—is always the same. Usually when villagers talk about *sukhwan* rites they have in mind situations 1–4 in my list: that is, assumption of new status, pregnancy, initiation of an enterprise, and reintegration into normal village life of persons temporarily removed from village society. It is in relation to these situations, then, that I propose to probe further concerning the purposes and structure of the rite and what it does.

The *khwan*, it is said by villagers, stays with the body when a person is in good health, has strength, and is leading a good life. But it is prone to leave the body when the 'state of mind is not good' (*caj bau dii*). These words are significant; the flight of the *khwan* is attributed to the state of the mind. But, as noted in Chapter 4 (p. 58), 'The causes and consequences of the *khwan's* departure are formulated in a circular manner...' It is said that 'when the mind is stirred or agitated, the *khwan* leaves'. And when the *khwan* flees the body, this will *result* in sickness; correspondingly, the ceremony must be held to *forestall* the flight. Conversely, sickness of the body can *lead to* agitation of the mind and the *khwan's* flight; correspondingly, the *khwan* must be *called back* to the body of the ill person. In either event, through this circular formulation, the crisis is agitation leading to flight of the *khwan*. Therefore the *khwan* must be 'bound' to the body, that is, secured or restored. The *sukhwan* thus addresses itself to agitations of the mind which are either prelude to or result of sickness.

We can now take up the role of the ceremony in pregnancy. When a woman is pregnant, it is said, she is frightened about the pains and difficulties of childbirth or that she may die. The *khwan* may in these circumstances leave her. Ideally the ceremony should be performed in good time, before it leaves; if it does leave and she becomes ill, the *khwan* is called back to the body, so that the woman will be restored to good health and have an easy delivery.

In marriage, the ritual is performed in order that the couple may have a prosperous life together and in order to prevent marital quarrels and divorce. Before ordination, the *nag* may be anxious about the rigorous monastic life ahead of him, or he may be thinking about the girl he loves. When a young man returns from a long trip, his parents fear that his *khwan* may have stayed behind or strayed on the way.

It would appear, when we examine village theory and the occasions at which *sukhwan* is performed, that there are two features to the rite which relate to timing and to influencing the mental state of the celebrant. Many of the situations embody both features, others emphasize one more than the other. In rites of passage (marriage and ordination) the transition to a new status is a point of great elaboration; threshold ceremonies prior to initiating an enterprise also emphasize a new phase. A second emphasis is the reassuring of the mind, the charging or restoration of morale and health, which finds its greatest elaboration in dangerous physical states like pregnancy or in sickness. But of course just as pregnancy anticipates motherhood and is a transition period, so are an ordinand or the couple to be married considered as being 'agitated' and needing a morale-booster. Thus village theory sees an underlying uniformity in the situations.

Now these statements of uniformity about *sukhwan* and the occasions on which it is performed set the problem I wish to probe in the rest of this chapter. Because it is said that the *khwan* flees owing to the agitations of the mind, the ritual must in some way address itself to making an impact on the minds of the celebrants. And because the ritual is so clearly recognized by the villagers as conferring a happy state of mind, prosperity and good health, a challenge is posed to unveil the mechanism by which the intended effect is transmitted. If *sukhwan* rites are in some sense prophylactic or therapeutic, what is the method used?

Using the rite of passage (marriage and ordination), and the pregnancy ceremony as two foci of crystallization of ideas within the wider *sukhwan* class, I shall proceed with a detailed analysis in order to unravel their structure and meaning as ritual forms. The experience gathered in earlier chapters in analysing rites performed by monks now enables me to state a formalized scheme which will be utilized not only here but in later appropriate contexts as well.

1. Analysis should first specify the *occasion* or the context of the ritual. (This has already been done for the rites in question.) The occasion itself will specify what kind of message is going to be transmitted to the celebrant and why the celebrant is assumed to be receptive or prepared to receive the message.

The *khwan* ceremony at marriage or ordination is only *one*—albeit crucial—sequence in a greatly elaborated set of ceremonies which bring together large numbers of people, and which are considered auspicious (*mongkhon/mangala*) and therefore joyous. The celebrants—the marrying couple or the ordinand (*nag*)—are presumed to be ready to receive a particular kind of message which characterizes for them the role commitments of their new status. This assumption is made by those who participate in the ritual, and they consider the holding of the ceremony as both a ritual and a social imperative.

For the pregnant woman, the ritual is by contrast an independent ceremony performed to restore something (morale and health), and to

228

remedy a negative situation. It is presumed in holding the ceremony that the patient, being unwell and unhappy, wants to be reassured and healed or reintegrated. The ceremony is a cultural remedy and it, too, is considered to be an imperative when the appropriate situation occurs or is believed to be likely to occur.

2. Thus what I call the *'occasion'* or the context of the rite can also be seen as portraying the community's definition of the celebrant's situation, the effect or transition he is expected to experience. There is thus a specification of the *receiver* of the message. Note that I avoid imputing to the celebrant or patient this state of mind, which is defined socially. Analysis of the ritual as prophylactic or therapeutic, as undertaken here, does not postulate or much less prove the supposition that what is culturally defined for the celebrant is subjectively experienced by him, although if the ritual is to be actually effective—that is, to achieve what it intends—a correspondence may be necessary. I can only suggest the possible effectiveness of the cultural technique as a teaching or indoctrinating device in the appropriate social context.

3. The third level of analysis is to decode the message that is being transmitted by the ritual, and the framework for this has been developed in the preceding chapter. We saw there that the message is contained in a configuration of events which are composed of two types of ritual acts: (*a*) physical acts and manipulation of objects; (*b*) the recitation of words or texts. In all *sukhwan* ceremonies, as in the Buddhist rites, that part of the ritual which consists of manipulating objects symbolically tends to be uniform with only minor variations. The differences in the message transmitted to suit one kind of *sukhwan* rite rather than another are to be discovered in the words recited. Thus again, as in the case of Buddhist rites, we must pay attention to the words here too, for they are considered by the villagers to be the most essential part of the rite. The recitation of words is in fact the main part of the ceremony, and the only uniformity in the content of the individual rites is the common formula for 'calling the *khwan*'.

But there is one feature that distinguishes *sukhwan* ritual from the ritual of Buddhist monks: its words are in the local Lao language of ordinary use and are understood by officiant, celebrant, and audience. This is a different use of words from that of the Pali chants of monks and will be commented upon further.

4. The effectiveness of the ceremony also depends on a fourth factor, namely the status and characteristics of the *sender* of the message (the officiant) and the *supporting cast* of witnesses and mediators whose presence is considered necessary. Why are the occupants of certain statuses the

right persons to perform and help at *sukhwan* ceremonies? And why are they considered the appropriate persons whose acts will achieve effects in the persons who are the receivers?

This scheme for analysing the *sukhwan* ritual may be summarized as specifying the following levels of analysis and then fusing them—the occasion, the sender, the receiver, the supporting cast, and the message (the latter being a combination of the language of object symbols and physical acts, and the language of words).

I shall now describe and analyse two rites of passage and a rite of affliction, concentrating first on the ritual as a sequence of acts, next on the text recited at the rites, and finally on the special properties of the supporting cast. Since the officiant in all *sukhwan* rites is a village elder and since his social position and ritual role are critical, I shall deal with him separately in a subsequent section.

'Sukhwan' ritual at marriage: case illustration 1

The *sukhwan* ceremony at formal marriage is only one phase in the proceedings. The following is an account of a rite which was performed in the morning.

The *phakhwan* of the marriage ceremony is a conspicuous ritual item, under other names, in all *khwan* ceremonies. It is a tiered conical structure built on a tray, and on it are placed a boiled egg, bananas, flowers and a lump of rice. The participants sit around it. The *phakhwan* is an offering to the *khwan*. When the officiant invites the *khwan* of the celebrants to come, they first come to the *phakhwan* because they are attracted to it. The rule for marriage ceremonies is that elderly married women who are still living with their husbands should make the *phakhwan*; widows and divorced or separated women should not be assigned this task. There is a taboo on the performance of *sukhwan* for the bride and groom together if a parent (or the parents) of either of them is dead, for if it is done under these circumstances the pair will not live or stay together long. If a parent is dead, separate *khwan* ceremonies must be done for the bride and groom. Villagers cannot say why this taboo exists. As in the case of other *khwan* ceremonies, this particular one was performed in order to make the bride and groom 'rich, live well, healthy and happy'. The observer can reasonably infer that the *khwan* ceremony avoids the participation of widows and divorcees because it is meant to affirm the stability of marriage. Similarly, marriage is 'opposed' to death and this notion is marked by a separate performance for the couples when a parent is dead. After the bridewealth had been ceremonially presented, the ceremony was conducted in the presence of the assembled guests in the sleeping room (*haung yaai*) of the bride's parents' house, in that section used by parents and located in the eastern quarter (see Chapter 2). The officiant was a ritual elder called *pupaahm* or *paahm* (which is derived from the Indian word *brahman*). He sat on one side of the *phakhwan*; the groom and bride sat close together on the other side, the former on her right. Sitting in a circle between the *paahm* and the groom were three men, between the *paahm* and the bride four women. (The numbers were said not to be significant. It is not necessary that these men and women be married; they are friends of the couple and include both married and unmarried young adults.)

A cord was attached to the *phakhwan* and passed through the hands of the women, next of the groom and the bride, then of the men, and its end was held by the *paahm*. The cord is called *fai monkhon* (thread of good fortune). The officiant then placed a bamboo ring, with pieces of cotton wool attached, on the head of the groom; an elder's wife did the same for the bride. (The villagers interpreted this act as marking the pair as the beneficiaries of the rite.)

A candle was lit, after which the officiant chanted the invitation to the *thewada* or divine angels. (The *thewada* are always invited to come and witness the marriage rite: they are told that on such and such a day the marriage is being held for so-and-so. They are requested to help call the *khwan* of the bride and groom so that they will come, 'join as a pair', and enter the bodies of the couple.) Then followed a long chant which is the actual 'calling of the *khwan*', and which I shall discuss presently.

Next the officiant gave advice and moral instruction to the couple. Thus, for instance, the groom was told that he should not show interest in divorced or separated women but must be true to his bride. The bride was told that she was a daughter-in-law and must love her husband and her husband's parents. The officiant then made sacred water (*fai naam lao*) by pouring liquor and/or perfume into a bowl of water, and sprinkled the couple with it. (From this point on, the young people in the audience intermittently joked and pushed the bride and groom so that their bodies touched.)

The *paahm* picked up the lump of rice, a banana, and the egg from the *phakhwan*, put them in the groom's hand, and then tied his wrist with a piece of white thread (*fai mongkhon*). The procedure was repeated for the bride. (This may be said to represent the transference of the *khwan* from the *phakhwan* to the couple, followed by the binding of the *khwan* to the body.) The elders, men and women, and the young people followed in tying bits of thread to the wrists of the couple. The elders at this point gave the couple gifts of money. This sequence is referred to as *puk-khan*.

What has been described is the *sukhwan* ceremony proper. It is followed by a sequence called *somma phuu thaw* (which is enacted without the *sukhwan* when the latter is not appropriate, that is, when parent or parents of bride or groom are dead). The words *somma phuu thaw* are critical for understanding village social and kinship relationships and obligations, especially the place of elders in the village community. *Somma* means 'forgiveness', *phuu thaw* means 'old person'. These *phuu thaw* are also, in the context of marriage proceedings, called *thaw gae* (old old persons), which term is understood in the sense of intermediaries or witnesses. Traditionally *somma phuu thaw*, 'asking the forgiveness of elders', is an essential part of the marriage ceremony. 'Forgiveness' in fact means two reciprocal things: the couple pay their respects to elders, the elders confer their blessings on the union.

The '*somma phuu thaw*' on this occasion took the following form (a standardized pattern). Two cushions were placed end to end and a bowl containing flowers and candles was placed on top of them. The couple sat on one side of the cushions and the officiant on the other. (Male and female friends may or may not sit next to the couple.) The officiating elder (the same person as the officiant of the *sukhwan* rite) first touched the bowl—this he explained as 'accepting the flowers and candles given as the gift of the groom and bride to the elders'. He then gave them lengthy advice (a longer version of the advisory sequence in the *sukhwan* described above). For instance, since in the case of this marriage the couple were expected to live uxorilocally (for a while at least), the groom was told how to behave as a good son-in-law of the household—that he must respect his new 'parents' and work hard. The wife was given an even longer instruction. She was told: Do not argue with your husband, prepare food for your husband to eat when he returns from work, look after the house and keep it clean, get on well with the husband's relatives, do not commit adultery, save money from your husband's earnings, etc.

Following this, an elderly married woman led the bride and groom to their sleeping quarters (the western quarter of the sleeping room), where the bed had been prepared for them. They then returned and candles and flowers from the bowl were distributed to all the *phuu thaw*. (This is a 'gift' to them from the couple and 'marks' them as witnesses.) With the wedding rites thus concluded, a feast was given to all those present.

Now for some comments on the ritual symbolism. That in the *sukhwan* ceremony is pretty obvious and requires no lengthy elucidation. The ceremonial structure, *phakhwan*, or its equivalent, is to be found in most village rituals; it reminds one of the *prasaat* (palace) in Buddhist rites, the conical pagoda, and the seven-tiered umbrella of royalty. The name of the structure, however, changes with the rite and this is conceptually important. In this case the *phakhwan* stands as the object that will attract the *khwan*; it is the place where the *khwan* will alight; in other words, it becomes the externalized and objectified *khwan* itself. Items of food—boiled egg, lump of rice, bananas, etc.—are placed in the *phakhwan*; the *khwan* is attracted by them and enters them, and when the officiant transfers the *khwan* to the bodies of the celebrants it is these items of food that are first handed over to the couple. In every ritual in the village, food items are used symbolically as offerings, as the objects that attract supernaturals, and as a medium for the transfer of sacredness. In this *khwan* rite we may note that the food objects and other offerings are called *kryang bucha*, that is, objects for making worship, the word *bucha* being derived from the Indian word *puja*. The offerings in this case distinguished by the fact that they lack meat and are primarily, except for the egg, vegetarian, and that they are offered to *pure benevolent sacred* agents. (The logic of these category distinctions can only be expounded later when we have examined other rites, especially those addressed to *phii* (spirits).)

The white cord is the object through which 'charging' or 'sacralization' takes place, and it is also used to bind the wrist (*puk-khan*). Through this act the *khwan* is tied to the body. The ritual role of the cord is similar to that in certain Buddhist rites examined earlier in Chapter 12. The role of the lustral water as a cleansing agent before the *khwan* is received by the celebrant is also readily evident.

The *officiant* is signified by his wearing on his arm a package containing cooked rice, banana, and coins; this package also constitutes the nominal payment for his services. The signification of the celebrants requires a gloss: a bamboo ring with pieces of cotton wool is placed on the head. The white colour of the cotton symbolically connotes purity in this context. The head is crowned because it is the head that is considered the pre-eminent residence of the *khwan*. The mode of signifying the recipient differs in different *sukhwan* rites, and I shall elucidate the logic of this in the rites to follow. An additional object is the candle, which is always lighted before the ceremony starts. In the wedding ritual a single candle signifies both celebrants, and is not a focus of elaboration as in the other two situations that will be examined.

Finally, the pushing of the bride and groom so that their bodies touch, and their being led to the bridal chamber, are clear enough in their implications for a couple being married and about to initiate sexual union.

Now to comment on the supporting cast in the ceremony. It is elderly married women who are neither widowed nor divorced or separated who make the *phakhwan*. The women thus stand for established stable marriage.

Young friends of both sexes, married and unmarried, sit on either side of the groom and bride, themselves holding the cord. Youths are selected to transmit good wishes and to give moral support to the couple. It is a married elderly woman who leads the couple to the chamber, and it is elders who take precedence in the binding of the wrists of the couple and in turn receive respects and gifts from the couple—all of which signifies that it is the elders who are establishing the marriage and who are appropriate for transferring blessings. The *somma phuu thaw* sequences underline these features. Youth takes a secondary place in these sequences, and in fact throughout the entire marriage proceedings.

'*Sukhwan nag*' ritual: case illustration 2

The calling of the *khwan* of the ordinand for monkhood is, like the *sukhwan* at marriage, one sequence in the ordination ceremonies (*bun buad*) which cover two days. In Chapter 7 I have described the sequences: the first day is the day of 'bringing together' (*wan ruam*) the ritual articles, especially the eight requisites of the monk (*kryang meng*), and the preparation of food for feasting; and on the second day is staged the ordination in the temple.

It is in the afternoon of the first day that the *sukhwan* ceremony is held. In the morning the *nag* will have been shorn of his hair at the temple, brought to the home of his parents, and dressed in a loin cloth of red or green colour (*pha mai*) and a long white shawl (*pha biang khaw*) worn diagonally on the shoulders. The red or green colours of the cloth are auspicious life-affirming colours, while the white shawl 'represents Buddhist religion'—a vivid symbolization of the combination of characteristics in a man in the transition from secular virile youth to ascetic sexless monk.

The main sequence of ritual acts at *sukhwan nag* parallels that described for marriage: here I shall make special note of the features which are different so as to indicate the distinct features of ordination as such, thereby permitting us to decode the special features of the message transmitted.

Let me briefly repeat some of the facts already stated. Ordination in the village of Phraan Muan is invariably a collective ceremony at which a group of boys becoming monks before Lent are ordained together. The entire village participates; the boys not only are sons of particular families (the heads of which are the chief lay sponsors) but are also village youth whose ordination is sponsored by the entire village.

The *sukhwan* rite is appropriately held in the preaching hall of the temple. In addition to the ceremonial structure called *phakhwan*, a central object in the ritual is the *kryang meng*, the eight requisites of the monk (robes, umbrella, begging bowl, slippers, razor, etc.), which are the contribution of parents, relatives and fellow villagers (all collectively called the elders (*phuu thaw*)). These articles are the objective symbols of the monk's mode of life.

The ordinands sit on one side of the *phakhwan* and the *kryang meng*, which are in the centre, and the officiant (*paahm*) sits on the other. The cord attached to the *phakhwan* passes through the hands of the ordinands, terminating with the officiant. This is similar to the marriage rite except that no youths sit on either side of the *nag* holding the cord—for clearly, their presence would be inappropriate in a situation which anticipates the renouncing of lay life.

But a more remarkable difference from the rite at marriage is the method of signifying or marking the celebrants. Candles play a significant role here, and they are of two kinds: *thian wian hua* (candles of the length of the circumference of the head) and *thian kha khing* (candles of the length from shoulder to waist). Each candidate's head and body are measured and candles made with wicks of the appropriate length. The 'head' candles are attached to the *phakhwan* and lit during the ceremony; the 'body' candles are attached to the *kryang meng*. The symbolism here as decoded by the anthropologist is the dichotomy of head and body, or spirit and body. The 'head' candles signify that the candidates' spirit essences (the chief manifestation of which resides in the head)[1] should return and be attached to their heads; but the 'body' candles signify that their bodies become attached to the monk's articles and are dedicated to the service of monkhood as symbolized by these articles.

The sequence of recitation, sprinkling with lustral water, transference and binding of the *khwan* is the same as that described for marriage. The role of the supporting cast of witnesses and mediators (*thaw gae*) is the same: parents, elderly relatives, and elderly villagers play the significant roles as sponsors. While of course youth are present at the proceedings, ordination (even more than marriage) is more emphatically a concern of the elders.

This is a convenient place to digress in order to make a general statement about the symbolism of lighted candles in *sukhwan* ritual. The lighting of candles in front of the statue of the Buddha is a common mode of worship and paying respects: we could say that in a sense the lighted candle (or fire) 'animates' the Buddha, and initiates the arrival of sacred time, the period of the ritual. In *sukhwan* the *thian wian hua* or head candle is usual: its lighting starts the ceremony, and the candle, in addition to representing the celebrant, also informs of the purpose of the ritual,

---

[1] For the Thai the head is the most sacred part of the body, and of the thirty-two *khwan* that reside in a person, the *khwan* of the head is the foremost.

which is that the *khwan* (which resides in the head) should return to the body. Sometimes an additional candle is used which also transmits a message that is special to the particular ceremony being performed. In ordination the *thian kha khing* states the subservience of the body to the ascetic régime of monkhood. In another *sukhwan* ritual, say a long life ceremony, the second candle is called *thian ayu*, candle of age, which expresses the hope of long life.

'Sukhwan maemarn' ritual (pregnancy): case illustration 3

The details of the pregnancy ritual are the same as for the rituals already described: in the centre is a *phakhwan*; the officiant is the *paahm*; the text is read, lustral water sprinkled on the celebrant, and the cord of good fortune tied (*fai mongkhon*) by the *paahm* and the witnesses. The ceremony is completed with a feast for the guests, who themselves usually make small money contributions. The ritual, however, is an entity by itself rather than a sequence in a larger ceremony, and is usually held early in the morning around 8.00 a.m. on an auspicious day. The pregnant woman is marked with a head ring made of thread, and a candle of the head (*thian wian hua*) is lit to begin the ceremony; the symbolism of these is the same as in the other rituals described (see Plate 4*a*).

The main differences between the pregnancy ritual and the *sukhwan* at marriage and ordination is in the content of the text read and the status of the supporting cast or 'witnesses' who are present in the ceremony. Both features symbolize something special about the occasion of the rite and the position of the celebrant.

Let me illustrate the second point by referring to an actual *sukhwan maemarn* that I witnessed. The ceremony was intended primarily for a young woman called Jandaeng, who was experiencing her first pregnancy. Her father and mother sponsored the ceremony for her—Jandaeng and her husband were, like most young couples, living uxorilocally. Another pregnant woman—Jandaeng's mother's younger sister (who had had other children)—also took part in the ceremony. She and her husband contributed a small portion of the expenses.

Both women's husbands were present at the ceremony; the only other males present were Jandaeng's father and the officiant himself. The ceremony was, apart from the males mentioned, essentially an affair of elderly women. If we take Jandaeng as the point of reference, there were two women of grandparental generation (Fa Mo Yo Br Wi and Mo Fa Yo Br Wi) and five of mother's generation (Mo, Mo Ol Si, a distant affinal relative, and two elderly neighbours) present as *thaw gae* (mediators/witnesses/old persons). Two women, in this case the two neighbours, who were said to be women of respect (*nabthy*), held the cord which passed from the *phakhwan* to the celebrant. Two unmarried girls were also present at the ceremony, but their role as helpers was entirely subsidiary.

Now, this pattern of participation of witnesses, essentially limited to elderly women and husbands of the pregnant women, differs from the supporting casts at marriage and ordination. This is obviously related to the fact that this ceremony was being held to 'cure the mind of a pregnant woman' (*pua caj maemarn*). How the ritual defines the celebrant's state of mind and what kind of therapy it attempts will become clearer when we scrutinize the text that is recited.

The content of the texts read in each of the three ceremonies will be discussed in turn. The texts themselves are printed as an appendix to this chapter. All *sukhwan* recitations begin with a standard invitation or invocation which immediately places the ritual under the umbrella of the divine angels (*thewada*) and the Buddha. The opening sentences constitute the invitation to *thewada*, a sequence called *sagkhe*, who are invited to attend the ritual and make it auspicious. They are to act as witnesses to the proceedings, in the same way as do the mortal elders. Immediately after this are recited the Pali words used by all Buddhists in worship, meaning: 'We worship the Blessed One, Arahat, Supreme Lord Buddha.' We note the point (for subsequent comment) that the Buddha here follows the *thewada*; it is the latter who are the benevolent mediators and the conferrers of blessings. On the one hand, the ritual is more a concern of lesser deities than of the inaccessible Buddha; yet it is clear, on the other hand, that the ritual is performed by persons who identify themselves as Buddhists.

THE 'SUKHWAN' TEXTS AND THE SACRED WORDS

Text of 'sukhwan' for marriage

The text pictures the marriage as a 'royal occasion', a magnificent mythological event in which deities and nobility are present and great wealth is displayed. Those familiar with Indian ceremonial will recognize this tradition of viewing marriage as an auspicious and grand event. The text is peppered with Pali words meaning 'auspicious', 'power', 'excellence', 'splendour' and 'success'.

The sequence of the text may be summarized as follows: the *phakhwan*, the tiered structure made of fragrant flowers to which the *khwan* of the couple will come, is described as made by royal persons; and around it are heaped in abundance gifts not only of food but also of necklaces and rings. The occasion for the ritual—marriage—is mentioned. Hindu brahmanical ideas are perhaps evident in the reference to the founders of *gotra* (lineage) and the virtue of giving a daughter in marriage (which is reminiscent of the concept of *kanya dana*—'gift of a virgin'). A significant point in the recitation is that the elders of parental and grandparental generations are assembled to marry the couple, who are supported by their young friends. (This describes faithfully the actual assembly of persons at a village marriage.)

The attention then focuses on the couple, who are described as beautiful persons: the *khwan* of beauty is called upon to sit with them and royal persons are said to admire them. The *khwan* of the legs and shins (the lower extremity of the body) of the couple is called first.

The words which follow state that the marriage is divinely sanctioned and that the marriage procession was led by the mythical *Garuda* with *Naga* at the rear. The legitimation by divine agents of the marriage reinforces the previous declaration that the marriage has been sanctioned by parents and elders.

Now the words focus even more specifically on the individual persons of the bridegroom and the bride. The bridegroom was sent by God Indra to live with the bride; he is handsome and fabulously wealthy. The bride is described as waiting for him in a bed-chamber sumptuously decorated with silk and lace. The *khwan* of the bride and groom should forsake old lovers and come together to be married. The *khwan* that are recalled at this stage are those of the eyes, eyebrows and other parts of the face, and the breast, that is, the upper extremity of the body.

The next idea suggested by the words is that of sexual intercourse, a blissful union, and material plenty (a barn full of grain and gifts from well-wishers). Then follows the instruction given to the groom as a son-in-law, emphasizing the proper behaviour towards his parents-in-law. The wife in turn is instructed to behave properly as a daughter-in-law, and she is given a discourse about her relationship to her parents and her siblings—attitudes of love and respect, and acts of sharing of food are recommended. Her duties to her husband also are elaborated: she should not roam at night, she should be constant, and assiduous in her domestic duties. The couple are exhorted to make merit at the temple on the Sabbath. The text ends with the traditional blessing that the couple may love each other, live long, enjoy good complexion (which echoes the Indian colour preoccupation), and have happiness and power.

Text of the 'sukhwan nag' ceremony

This text, collected in the field, is shorter than the one used in marriage ritual; the brevity corresponds to the fact that whereas in marriage the ritual is built around *sukhwan,* in ordination the calling of the *khwan* rite is one sequence in a series which culminates in the ordination ceremony in the temple. Furthermore, the cultural definition of what the ordination is is expressed in a number of sequences other than *sukhwan.* Nevertheless, the *sukhwan* is a rite of formal instruction in which words explicitly express certain ideas about kinship and community obligations.

The text begins with the statement that village elders and nobility are assembled to conduct the ceremony for the *nag,* who is about to be separated from his parents in order to receive the three Buddhist gems; it is clearly indicated that the experience awaiting the monk is of a special sort.

Then begins the most important message to be transmitted to the ordinand. As monk he will make merit and transfer it to his parents, and the justification for this obligation is enacted by recreating the life experience of the ordinand, beginning with his existence in his mother's womb. The ordinand is informed in minute detail of the trials faced by his mother when she was pregnant, how she fed and bathed him as a child, sheltered and embraced him, and put him to sleep. This evocation of childhood dependency on the mother is interesting, in that a woman, who according to Buddhism has inferior chances of salvation, can rely on her son to transfer to her some of his merit. The period of adolescence, when a youth becomes a novice, is briefly referred to and the recitation then focuses on the immediate situation: that when the *nag* was ready to be ordained, he went and informed his relatives, who have now got ready for him the eight articles which will enable him to become a monk.

Next the *khwan* of the *nag* is called: this calling is characterized by emphasizing that his *khwan* has been enticed away by the animals of the forest and other pleasures that are found in the mountains, caves and ponds. Finally, the hoped-for 'pay off' for the youth who gets ordained is mentioned: that he may be a prosperous and powerful person with servants and a retinue, blessed with fame and victory over Mara (death). The image evoked is that of a feudal lord or royal personage.

Text of the 'sukhwan maemarn' ceremony

Keeping in mind that this text is recited for a pregnant woman, who it is said is anxious about childbirth and for whom the ceremony will ensure easy childbirth, let us look at the sequence of ideas and their content.

The *sukhwan maemarn* text begins in a manner that we are by this time familiar with: the day chosen for the ceremony is declared to be an auspicious one, and this theme of auspiciousness is given grandiose elaboration. The gods and astrologers and monks and thirty village elders have declared the day to be auspicious; the day is appropriate for the enthronement of a king; for the birds to build their nests; for divorced and separated women to go up the mountain; for the Buddha to shave his head; etc.

The text then calls the *khwan*. The *khwan* of the legs, eyes, and flesh, that is, the entire body, are requested to return. The distinctiveness of this text, however, lies in the fact that the *khwan* of the pregnant woman is asked not to stay and linger with a young man of the city in heaven, not to aspire to enjoy heavenly pleasures, but to return to her earthly husband who is described as slender and handsome and as shedding tears and waiting for her. (We note that these words echo some of the words in the marriage ritual: there the husband, who is described as being handsome, is asked to join the wife who is awaiting him in the bed-chamber; here, however, it is he who is anxiously awaiting her. Thus these words attempt to focus the pregnant woman's attention on her husband, who is described as desirable and as desiring her.)

The text next focuses on the immediate ritual situation. It describes the *phakhwan* and the food set out, and mentions that elders, children, young unmarried or divorced or separated women, and the midwife await the return of the *khwan*. (This mention of all kinds of females once again differs from the other texts described: pregnancy and childbirth are presented as desired by all *females*, apart from its interest for the elders; children are appropriately assimilated to this interest of females.)

The words shift now to describing the situation before and after childbirth and appear to be addressed to the baby that is to be born. In other words, the pregnant woman is given a precise account of her present condition, an anticipatory picture of childbirth successfully accomplished, and the details of the care of the baby. Let us follow the successive images presented because they contain the core message from the point of view of the stated intention of the ceremony.

First is mentioned the physical discomfort and labour pains of the mother who carries the unborn child. Then the birth of the baby and the cutting of its umbilical cord, as well as the manner of birth of a female child (flat on its back) and a male baby (flat on its face) are referred to. After the baby is recognized as a 'human', the mother's solicitude for it and the manner in which it is cared for (feedings, bathing, sleeping, etc.) are described. The village belief that a male child is more difficult to bring up than a female child is mentioned, and also the cultural preference for a male child, who it is hoped will become a wealthy and powerful man, riding in a procession seated on an elephant.

The text shifts its focus again to make a long, compelling calling of the *khwan*. If the *khwan* is in the jungle, or by the pond or river, or up the mountain or in a cave, it is asked to return, it is urged not to follow the tracks of wild animals. If it is engaged in cultivation in the upland (forest) fields, or if it is keeping a tryst with a lover in the jungle, it is recalled. It is enticed to come and enter the house, where women await it, where the baby in the cradle awaits it, where elderly relatives of the parental generation, both paternal and maternal, await it.

THE 'SUKHWAN' AS A RITUAL TECHNIQUE

I will now sum up the logic of the structure of the *sukhwan* ritual and the effect it is meant to transmit.

Village theory is that persons in particular situations experience mental turmoil or disturbance, which is represented as the flight of the *khwan*, a spiritual essence. We noted that the ceremony is held not so much to cure a disease—organic or mental ('madness')—but to charge or restore morale, especially at rites of passage or situations of transition. The ceremony is a cultural imperative, which implies that society attributes to the celebrant the state of mind in question; essentially the ritual is devised to say something to the celebrant and to create in his mind certain effects.

The general form of the ceremony, whatever the occasion at which it is performed, is the same: the calling of the *khwan* and the physical transference of it. But each of the three situations we examined has its particular features as regards the kinds of persons present at the rite in a supporting role. In marriage, the elders, both male and female, are the sponsors, gift givers, receivers of respect from the couple, and the chief binders of *khwan*; at the same time, young persons sit with the couple and hold the cord and charge them with vitality. In ordination the elders once again figure importantly, but the special feature of initiation into ascetic monkhood in theory excludes any layman (except the officiant) from holding the cord; but it is possible, I think, for elders also to do so. At the rite of pregnancy, only elderly women hold the cord and act as witnesses; the husband's presence is recommended.

These patterns of participation of supporting witnesses of specified status link meaningfully with the messages transmitted by the sacred words, the recitation of which comprises the major part of the ritual. In marriage certain cultural norms are transmitted: the elders together with the gods, it is said, are assembled to legitimate the union; the couple is subjectively influenced to accept each other as desirable sexual partners; and finally, kinship norms are inculcated in detail. In ordination, the ordinand is told that filial obligation is the justification for his having to

241

undergo an ascetic regimen; he is also informed of the 'pay off' that awaits him as a maker and transferrer of merit. The situation of the pregnant woman is somewhat different—she is after all in an uncomfortable physical condition and moreover faces an objective danger. Childbirth is, in the village in question, a dangerous occasion and the mortality of mother and child a real danger. The ritual therefore is more therapeutic in construction, more concerned with moulding the mind. The method we observed was directed to making the pregnant woman consciously focus upon and become aware of her present condition with all its discomforts, to binding her to her husband and the reality of married life, to making her imaginatively experience childbirth, and to formulating for her the care of the baby as a desirable and desired end. The image created of a successful childbirth and the support derived from elderly women, who have been successful mothers themselves, are effectively conceived modes of assurance and of restoring morale.

Thus the sacred words have an ambit of significance—defining status and role requirements, binding a person to his role or status (internalization of norms), using of word pictures to revive past experience, formulating present experience and anticipating the future, painting the ritual situation as a grand mythological event in which the actors become gods themselves—apart from that of the technology of the ritual as such, which takes the standard form of invoking the errant *khwan* and transferring it to the body. But even here, certain objects like candles transmit subtle messages which reinforce the messages transmitted through words.

We are now in a better position to understand why the words recited in *sukhwan* ritual have necessarily to be in a language that can be understood by the participants. In so far as the ritual is instrumentally constructed to act as a prophylactic or therapy, the contents of the verbal message have to be understood for achieving the specified effect, which is of course buttressed by the other message contents and the role of elders. By contrast, the semantics of the rituals conducted by monks are more complex and the effects sought non-specific. On one side are the lay worshippers, who by ethical intention and the act of giving gifts express a kind of renunciation; on the other side, the monks by virtue of their ascetic qualities and acts are the proper vehicles for transferring grace. The ritual words and acts are interconnected through metaphorical and metonymical devices, and while the understanding of their immediate meaning is not necessary for the laity, they do believe in the efficacy of the transfer of grace through the power of the sacred words, because of their three-dimensional links with Buddha, the *Dhamma* and the *Sangha*.

The elders summon the spirit essence

I conclude with a question, one which I hope is not merely rhetorical. What does the *khwan*, a metaphysical concept of spirit essence, 'objectify' as a spirit substance?

I have already contrasted the *khwan* with *winjan*, and rites of life intensification (*sukhwan*) with mortuary (*winjan*) rites. There is another contrast to be made.

The *sukhwan*, as noted earlier, is a prophylactic *cum* therapeutic ritual. The *khwan*, we have seen, leaves the body in certain situations; its flight from a person connotes a particular mental state, an agitation of the mind. The *khwan* must be recalled and aggregated to the body in order to make the person whole. We can translate this as follows. A part of me, my spirit essence, becomes alienated from me and disperses into the outside world; it is as if my mind is elsewhere. It is significant that, in the texts cited, the spirit essence is thought of as having gone to that part of the external world which is the very opposite of society and human habitation (village)—the forest, cave, mountain, river—lured there by animals of the forest. How insistently the ritual calls the *khwan* from these places! In other words, the escape of the spirit essence from an individual is suggestive of the escape of a person from his village and community members and into the forest and its non-human inhabitants. Typically, we note that the *sukhwan* is an imperative at certain rites of passage (ordination and marriage), at situations of reintegration into the village or social group, or at moments of actual or potential departure from them. These are contexts wherein the interests of the village, or elders, or family require the individual to bring his attention to bear on the situation at hand and to conform to norms, assume a new status, or return to a previous status. From the society's point of view in these situations there is the danger that the individual may actually withdraw from its requirements or be unhappy about, or unequal to, fulfilling them. When the elders call the *khwan* and restore it to the body, it is they who are charging the celebrant with the vital social force of morale, and they thus enable the celebrant to accept and bind himself to what is expected of him.

This interpretation of what the *khwan* signifies will have greater credibility if the exact reverse of the relations represented here are to be found in a different therapeutic situation. The reverse is that situation where a person is disturbed or ill because an alien external agent has penetrated or entered him (rather than some part of him escaping into the outside world). The agent or force from the outside world, by penetrating the individual, creates a kind of alienation from society represented

243

by withdrawal and conduct that is not normal in society. The individual is out of contact with society, he is inwardly directed and preoccupied. In such a hypothetical situation, the therapy must consist of expelling or extracting the foreign agent and re-establishing contact with society. Such a class of rituals indeed exists in the village and will be examined in Chapter 18.

APPENDIX TO CHAPTER 13

'SUKHWAN' TEXTS

'Sukhwan nag' text

This is an English translation of a ritual text which is recited by the *paahm* or *mau khwan* at the ceremony of calling the *khwan* [spirit essence] of the candidate [*nag*] before his ordination as Buddhist novice or monk.

The text begins with the '*namo*', which is a Pali prayer in praise of the Buddha commonly used in Buddhist worship. The Pali words, repeated three times, are '*Namo tassa Bhagavato Arahato Sammasambudahassa*' meaning 'We worship the Blessed One, Arahat, Supreme Lord Buddha'. The words of the rest of the text are in the ordinary North-east Lao language and are freely translated here.

This is an auspicious day and year. All of us consisting of elders and *thao phaya*[1] have come together to perform *sukhwan* ceremony for the *nag*, who is going to be separated from his parents in order to receive the Buddhist triple gems [Buddha, *Dhamma* (doctrine) and *Sangha* (order of monks)]. You [the *nag*] will see happiness, doubt, self emptied of soul, disease, death and the transformation into spirit [*phii*] and of not returning to life. You have faith, your relatives have faith, merit is made and transferred. Parents have brought you up since you were a child, since you were in your mother's womb. Whatever the trials faced by your mother, she showed perseverance and patience before childbirth. Then you were born. Your mother had to feed you with chewed rice three times a day and bathed you three or four times a day. Your mother was industrious. When it rained or thunder broke, she embraced you and held you close to her breast and put you to sleep. She placed a pillow next to you to make you warm.

When you grow up you become a novice and study the Buddhist precepts. When you are of the right age to be ordained, you go and inform your relations. They get ready your mat and pillow, upper and lower robes, your monk's bowl, bag, walking stick, fan and needle. [These are

[1] Nobility, noble persons.

the requisites of a monk.] All these are put together with your other possessions such as knife and cushion. The pile of gifts looks beautiful, and it is gathered together so that the one to be ordained may be free from suffering, live happily and long, for at least a hundred years. May your life extend to 5,000 years and be blessed with good fortune.

Today is said to be an auspicious day. We are gathered together to conduct the *Khwan Chao Nag*[1] ceremony. Come *khwan*, don't go to the forest in search of pleasure. Don't go to look at the gibbon for your pleasure. Don't look for wildfowl and be enticed by its pleasing call. Don't go in search of the wild bull; don't be led astray by looking at a herd of elephants in the forest; don't be led away by looking into caves for pleasure in the mountains. Don't lose yourself by looking at the wild monkey, sparrow, tiger, lion, rhinoceros and elephant. Don't tarry in the cave or at the pond looking at the beautiful fish and the scented lotus. Bring all these *khwan* and enter your body and reside with us. If ordained may you become the head of the *wat*; when you are a layman may you be a master with servants. May you have honour and fame which will spread to near and far places three times a day. May you have a retinue to accompany you when you make a trip. May you be blessed with power and victory over cruel Mara [the demon enemy of Buddha]. May Mara prostrate himself at your feet, and may all your enemies come and worship you with offerings every day, every hour in the manner of my prayer.

'Sukhwan' text recited at a wedding ceremony

Namo tassa Bhagavato Arahato Sammasambudahassa (three times). *Sri, sri, siddhi praporn*.[2] Flowers exude fragrant odour. Khun Kuan Chao and Khun Nang Chao[3] have made the *phakhwan* [tiered structure made of flowers for the *khwan*]. The *phakhwan* is surrounded by all who are present. There are provided in abundance cotton strings, rings, beads, necklaces, and food; also bowls of areca nut for chewing. Also flowers, liquor, bananas, boiled rice, *Bai Sri*,[4] and eggs. The mighty ones (blessed with ten powers) came down from the sky, wielding bows and arrows. Their names are: *Khun Sri* [auspicious], *Khun Pandh* [bind together], *Somsri* [beautiful], *Sri Sawan* [heaven]. All of them are very beautiful to behold.

Om siddhi chaya praporn. This is leap year, B.E. 2,505, the year of the Tiger. The season of the year is winter. I'll wed Mr —— and Miss —— in accordance with custom. The bowls of flowers are now being lifted to

---

[1] Ceremony for the ordinand.
[2] *Sri* = auspicious; *praporn* = best; *siddhi* = success.
[3] These references are obscure, and probably say that the *phakhwan* has been made by a noble couple.
[4] This is the central ceremonial structure, also called *phakhwan*.

the level of the eyebrows. The *saa* [forgiving] bowls are being presented to *chao gotra* [founders of the lineage]. The first-born daughter, the middle ones, and the youngest one are of high price. The elders are here to wed the couple according to their wish. It is of great merit to let a daughter get married. Among those who are present here are grandfathers, grand-mothers, parents, old people, and young people who on your [couple's] right and left sides are assisting the *mau khwan*.[1] Going round and round (clockwise and also counter-clockwise) is a vessel of liquor. The older people are sitting on the upper floor.

Now I should like to call upon the *khwan* of the beautiful bride to sit beside the bridegroom, and the *khwan* of the bridegroom to sit beside the bride. Now the *khwan* have arrived. They wear *khoom foom* [a kind of flower] above the ears. The blooming flower, above the eyes, is *kud kao* [a kind of fragrant flower].

On this auspicious day your *khwan* should return. *Khwan* of the shins should return to the shins. *Khwan* of the legs should return to the legs. All the *khwan* should return today.

On the far left is *Chaya*. He shows courage when he is among other people. Everybody displayed signs of happiness while they were in the procession. The procession was led by *Garuda*[2] and followed by *Naga*[3] [*Garuda* was the head and *Naga* the tail of the procession]. The iron posts of the palanquin are being guarded by *Phii Luang* [guardian spirit of city], as described fully in the *Dhamma*. *Thaen* [Creator deity] has destined you two to become husband and wife and to live a married life.

Now, I'll call upon *khwan bakaen* [young man, i.e. groom] to return to the groom. The groom, being slim and slender, is just right for the bride. Indra[4] in the heaven has sent him to live with his wife. May he live 100 years. May he have many sons and daughters, but not as many as 100,000. He already owns elephants, horses, and golden saddles. Phraya Dham, the brave, who has power, has arranged for you to become a husband. When the sun is going down, your *khwan* will return immediately. The bride has already made a bedroom for you. She is waiting for you. In the bedroom there are *pha kasa* [a kind of cloth], silk, lace, etc. Let the *khwan* of the bride return, and also the *khwan* of the groom that is wander-ing far away, please come back today. *Khwan* that is still following former

---

[1] The officiant.

[2] The mythical sky bird (see Chapter 10).

[3] The serpent (see Chapter 10).

[4] This is Indra, who in Buddhist Thailand is known as king of the *Tavatinsa* heaven, the second of the six heavens. In cosmology there are six lower heavens. *Tavatinsa* means heaven of thirty-two *devas*. Indra is dark in colour. It is said that, as a human being, he was king and had a retinue of thirty-one assistants. Because they made great merit, Indra became king of this heaven after his death and his retinue became *devas*.

lovers should also come back today. *Khwan*, please come and be adorned with flowers and cosmetics. They have already got these things ready for you. All the friends of the groom [*baw*] and of the bride [*nang*] are looking forward to seeing you. Rumour has it that you are of great merit. Please come and eat your breakfast placed in the *phakhwan*. Please come and feed the couple with egg-rice according to old custom. The fortune teller has already stated that today is a good day. So I'll wed this couple, who will continue to preserve the family tree and inherit the family wealth. When it is the 7th or 8th day of the lunar month they should observe precepts. When it is the 14th or 15th day of the lunar month they should always give food to the monks.

Decha chaya,[1] *khwan* of the eyebrows, should return to the eyebrows, *khwan* of the eyes should return to the eyes today. *Khwan* of the cheek, *khwan* of the chin, *khwan* of the waist, *khwan* of the breast should also return at once. Please come and sit down around the *phakhwan*.

Today is a very auspicious day. Today is the beginning. They say the old will be young again, the old people with white hair will become as young as children; servants and the poor will be owners of wealth; during sleep one will get 10,000 *baht*; when awakened one will get 100,000 *baht*; Phraa Chao will be given a good ring.

The groom's legs will be on top of the bride's legs; the barn will be filled up with rice. All these will take place today. I'll perform *sukhwan* for you for three days. May the husband's legs rub against the legs of his wife. May the couple be happy and live joyous days and nights. May they be humble towards each other.

As a son-in-law you should be broad-minded. Please do not complain. If you want to drive away the chickens from the house you should say 'So'. If you want to drive away the dogs, you should say 'Se'. If you want to drive away the cattle you should say 'Hue, Hue!' Please do not disobey your relatives. Watch what you say. Don't be too critical of others. Love your wife. As a daughter-in-law, you should love your husband. Don't talk behind his back. Make merit. Listen to sermons. During the dark moon nights please do not roam away from home. That low house belongs to your *ah* [uncle or aunt].[2] The tall one belongs to *phau* [father]. The one connected with that corridor belongs to *lung*[3] [uncle] and *pa*[3] [aunt]. The one with a wooden floor, a baked clay roof, *Naga*'s head, jars, and a horse[4] statue with beads will belong to you. Both of you should

---

[1] Pali words meaning splendour, power.

[2] *Ah* = father's younger sister or younger brother.

[3] *Lung* = elder brother of father or mother or spouse of *pa*; *pa* = elder sister of father or mother or spouse of *lung*.

[4] The horse is one of the seven treasures of the Chakravartin (world conqueror).

try to improve yourselves. You should make merit every *wan phraa*. When you have meat, please give some to your aunt. When you have fish, please give some to your grandmother. They love you very much. May you have a very good son. Please listen to what your grandfather, grandmother, father, and mother say to you. Be kind to your relatives. Your left eye should not look to seek another man; your right eye should not look for your old lover. You should cook in the morning and in the evening. Don't get up late. You should make *mag* and *ploo* [betel nut] for your husband, in the morning and in the evening. When you are married you should do away with your former thoughts. Serve liquor in the small jar to your servants. Serve liquor in the big jar to your superiors. That would be good for you. You will have blessing from Phraa Indra. When it is night-time you should be in bed and not anywhere else. Today it is good for the two of you to share a pillow. Love each other and show good-will to each other. *Chaya—chaya mangalang.* May you live long and enjoy good complexion, happiness, and power.

'Sukhwan' text recited for a pregnant woman
Si si pra porn [auspicious blessing].

The air is filled with the fragrance of flower pollen. *Khwan* [spirit essences] will be summoned to come together. This is an auspicious time and day of the year, laden with good luck. Thirty *phau-mae-thao* [respected old persons of parental generation] say that the time and day are auspicious. The astrologers [*mau hone, mau yam, mau huhah*] say the time and day are good. Phraa Narai[1] has said in thirty words that the time and day are good.

A servant who wishes to consult his master should do so today. It is said that the accession to the throne of Phraa Khun Myang[2] should be done today. It is an auspicious day for the *grankaew*[3] bird to build its nest. It is a good day to train the white gourd plant to climb the bamboo frame. It is said that a divorced or widowed woman who wishes to climb to the top of the mountain should start today. Thao Songchai[4] lulls his younger siblings to sleep saying that today is a good day. Monks beat the victory gong and proclaim that today is a good day. Phraa Mettaai[5] will have his head shaven today, which is a good day. Kings of one hundred countries are crowned on this day. Today is a full moon day, a good day. Please come, *khwan*. Let the *khwan* of the shin return to the shin,

---

1 Phraa Narai is the Thai version of the Hindu high god, Vishnu.
2 The ruler of a kingdom.
3 Probably parrot (*noggaew*).
4 *Songchai* means 'bearing victory', hence victorious person.
5 Maitreya, the Buddha to come; the headshaving refers to the act of becoming a monk.

The elders summon the spirit essence

khwan of the eyes return to the eyes, and *khwan* of the flesh come and stay in its place. Don't run away, hurry to our house. Come and eat *khaw tom* [rice gruel] mixed with sesame oil; come and eat fish. Don't go and stay with a young man in Myang Thaen.[1] Don't go and stay in the garden and rice field belonging to others. *Khwan* of the head, young *khwan*, the dearest to your husband, return to your house today, at this moment. Come and look at your slender and most handsome husband. At this moment your husband might be shedding tears waiting for you who was born from an elephant's tusk[2] as Nang Sida[3] was. Don't go away and stay in Phya Thaen's castle in heaven—that beautiful castle will never be given to you. Return, *khwan*, don't stay beside the carpet and pillow in the castle; you will never have that pillow beside you because you do not have enough merit. You shall never be the owner of the royal elephant.[4]

Return, *khwan*, and wear flowers behind your ear. Thirty old persons [*phau-mae-thao*] are gathered here to celebrate your coming. Ninety *brahmans* are awaiting to celebrate you. This, here, is a large tray made of sandalwood, and this bowl is made of *maikeo* wood. All these things have been got ready for you—there are food and fruit that are the delight of young children. There is also rice for you. Children, young unmarried women, divorced and separated women have come to see you. The person who will handle the placenta and cut the umbilical cord is present here.

Your mother carries you for months when she is with child. During that time she has to climb down the ladder and climb up to the house; she complains that she has labour pains. Brothers and sisters have assembled to watch and guard with care. When your mother carries you, she takes medicines; she is weary of heart when she sits, walks or lies down, until the baby is born.

A female baby is born lying flat on its back; a male baby is born lying flat on its face. After the umbilical cord is cut, siblings and relatives will wrap the baby with cloth. The *nog khaw* bird[5] sings 'coo coo', and if it is her baby let her come and take it away today; otherwise from today, the baby is mine.[6] Your [baby's] mother shows solicitude towards you—she picks you up with her hands and places you in a cradle. Your mother feeds, bathes you, and then puts you to sleep in the cradle. Her two hands rock the cradle all day long. She leaves the cradle to drink hot water, and

---

[1] City in heaven.   [2] The tusk refers to fair complexion, the white of ivory.
[3] This is Sita, wife of Rama, the hero of the Indian epic *Ramayana*.
[4] That is, you will never be the consort (queen) of the King.
[5] Turtle dove, dove.
[6] If the baby is a non-human spirit child it should be claimed today. There is a belief that a new-born baby is a spirit child and becomes human in about three days.

the heat burns her mouth.[1] Your mother ties thread to your wrists; the binding of your left wrist makes you grow big as your uncle [mother's brother], as tall as the sky, and to have a rank equal to that of others.

If you [mother] have a female baby, may you be happy. If you have a male baby, may you bring him up with care. If your son receives an elephant, may it be a large one. Let him sit in the middle of the elephant's back, and have others follow him in procession. Let him possess 1,000 *baht* weight of silver and 100 *baht* weight of gold. If he has servants, let him own 100. If he goes anywhere, let people respect him.

Come, *khwan*, if you have gone away to stay in the jungle with birds, come back today, now, at this time.

Come, *khwan*, if you have hidden yourself in the jungle, come back today.

Come, *khwan*, if you are staying in the big pond, return today, now, at this time.

Come, *khwan*, if you have gone to grow *taro* in the forest, return today.

Come, *khwan*, if you have gone away to play at a riverside quay with steps leading down, return today, at this moment.

Come, *khwan*, if it rains don't go any farther; if it thunders don't go away too far. After the rains, don't go and drink water near the rhinoceros' track; when the sun shines don't go in search of water along the buffalo's track. In the late morning don't drink water near the elephant's track. My little slender one, come home to live in the house with a wooden floor and a roof made of long grass.

Khwan, if you are engaged in upland cultivation, return today at this moment.

Khwan, if you are conversing with your lover in the jungle, come back today, at this moment.

Khwan, if you have gone hunting deer in the jungle, return today.

Khwan, if you have left the body because of a scorpion's sting, return today.

Khwan, if you are away from your home, come back today.

Come, *khwan*, come and reside in the house in which there is a three-cornered pillow that is suited to you. Beautiful girls await you around the *phakhwan*, and divorced and separated women have assembled to open the *bajsi*.[2] I invite Thao Kamfan,[3] who holds firm the pillar of the house, and Thao Kamfua,[3] who guards the house, to come and celebrate your return.

---

[1] Mothers after childbirth are given heat treatment—they sleep near a fire (*ju fai*) and take hot food. This is supposed to cleanse the blood.

[2] A ceremonial structure made of flowers and leaves in which offerings to the *khwan* are placed.　　　　[3] Probably guardian spirits.

The elders summon the spirit essence

Come, *khwan*, I invite at this moment the little baby sitting in the rattan chair to help celebrate your return. Come, *khwan*, I invite *phuu thaw* [elders], *phau gae* [elders], both father and mother, *lung* [parents' elder male siblings], *pa* [parents' elder female siblings], *nah* [father's younger siblings] and *ah* [mother's younger siblings] to celebrate your coming.

Chayate chaya mangalang.

14

THE CO-EXISTENCE OF THE 'BRAHMAN'
AND THE BUDDHIST MONK

The term for the *sukhwan* officiant, *paahm*, etymologically derives from *brahman*; alternatively he is called *maukhwan* (expert in *khwan* rites). It is the first term that acts as a cue beckoning us to investigate further.

The *brahman* and the *bhikkhu* were in their country of origin, India, unaccommodating antagonists; the *brahman* did in time virtually eliminate the Buddhist monk while incorporating in his religion some of the ethical achievements of Buddhism. The questions that therefore spring to mind are: How is it that the *brahman* and the *bhikkhu* can co-exist peacefully in Thai society? What different circumstances experienced by the *brahman* and *bhikkhu* in further India have made possible this co-existence? Finally, what is the connection between the classical *brahman* priest and the contemporary village *paahm* or *maukhwan*?

These are largely historical questions whose answers require us to map the route travelled by the *brahman* and the *bhikkhu* from India, and to note the successive transformations in their roles. The matter can hardly be adequately treated in this book, but a few observations will be made to give perspective to the problem that will ultimately interest us—the complementarity of the roles of the *paahm* and the monk in contemporary village religion.

In previous chapters we have, to some extent, discussed the path travelled by Pali Buddhism from India to Ceylon and thence to Siam, but we have had no occasion to discuss the *brahman* priest, who in fact travelled along a different route: from India to Cambodia (Angkor) and thence to Siam (especially to the kingdom of Ayudhya). The presence of the *brahman* in these parts is intimately related to the political constitution of the 'Indianized states of Southeast Asia', to borrow an expression from Coedès.

The Khmer (Angkor) civilization in its later stages shifted from Hinduism to Buddhism, but its conception of kingship always remained as an adaptation of Hindu ideas, and most of its court and royal rituals were performed by *brahman* priests, who had originally come from India. In Burma, too, the rituals of kinship were conducted by *brahman* priests, while Buddhism was the pervasive national religion. Thailand, in its

Ayudhya period, heavily influenced by Angkor, similarly depended on a *brahman* priesthood to conduct the royal rituals of installation and coronation, first ploughing, the swing ceremony, top-knot cutting, etc. (see Wales 1965).

The existence of brahmanical court rituals in Buddhist polities calls up some fascinating questions, especially of comparison with institutional patterns in India. One important difference is that these South-east Asian kingdoms did not transplant to their soil a caste system at the same time that they borrowed many cultural items. And it would appear that their under-lying social scheme was also different, for on their soil the *'brahman'* and the *'kshatriya'* (secular ruler) combined in a new relation, different from that in India. Dumézil postulated a tripartite division of Indian society in which the first function was the role of the priest, which combined magico-religious power and moral authority (*mitra* and *varuna*); the second function was that of the warrior, who gave physical protection to society; the third function belonged to the cultivator, whose role was to maintain physical well-being. The superiority of the priest to the secular ruler was fundamental to Dumézil's interpretation of classical Indian society and mythology. Dumont, building upon the Dumézil foundation, indicated that the Dharmasastras postulate three human ends—*dharma, artha* and *kama* (duty, profit and pleasure). All are lawful activities but they are graded in a hierarchy so that an inferior activity may be pursued only so long as a superior one does not intervene. *Dharma*, conformity to the world order, is more important than *artha* (power and wealth), which in turn is above *kama*, immediate enjoyment. In terms of the social order, *dharma* corresponds to the *brahman* priest, *artha* or temporal power to the king or Kshatriya, and *kama* to the rest of society's ranks.

It is my thesis, which I cannot substantiate here but hope to establish elsewhere, that in further India the relation between priest and king that prevailed in India was *reversed*, and that this transformed relation between a divinized king and the *brahman* priest can best be seen in the royal cult of Devaraja in Cambodia. The same relation, or perhaps an even greater elaboration of it, was the hallmark of the Buddhist polities of Burma and Siam where the king, the focal entity in the society, united in his person both Indra and *bodhisattva*, god and Buddha-to-be. Thus in Siam, for instance, the king was divinized by a small number of *brahmans*, who were employed as court ritualists but who did not represent the superior values of *dharma* (morality) in relation to *artha* (force and power) of the king. Kingship appropriated both these values, and also became the protector of Buddhism as the state religion.

The court *brahmans* of Thailand played an elaborate role in the mid-nineteenth century (Bowring 1857, pp. 308–9) and continued to do so well into the twentieth. More recently their ritual functions have been severely curtailed, but the *brahmans* still exist. Though originally brought to Thailand from Cambodia and India, they married Thai women and in time all the *brahmans* became thoroughly Siamese. The *mantras* they use today are apparently in corrupted Sanskrit and Tamil. Although in important respects quite unlike the Indian pure caste *brahman*, the Thai court *brahman* prominently distinguishes himself from the Buddhist monk by wearing the sacred thread and white ceremonial dress, his hair long, and propitiating solely the deities Siva, Vishnu and Ganesh.

Quaritch Wales reports that apart from their presence in Bangkok the court *brahmans* or their descendants are to be found in South Thailand (e.g. in towns like Nakorn Sri Thammarat and Pattalung where *brahman* temples exist). Apparently in times past there were *brahman* temples in the ancient capitals and in the main provincial centres. Thus the village *paahm* of today is very likely a development from this historical situation, and he performs auspicious rites and the astrological function which parallel the activities of the classical *brahman* priest. The situation in Burma closely resembles that of Thailand.[1]

The *paahm* in Phraan Muan village is a lay ritual officiant, a householder and a village elder, who performs auspicious rites in some ways reminiscent of the classical *brahman* priest. He is no blood descendant of the court *brahmans* of Thailand, but is in some ways a comparable entity. There is some internal evidence in the content of the *sukhwan* ritual itself to suggest its brahmanical connections.

Consider these features: the offerings are vegetarian and are called *kryang bucha*, which derives from the classical Indian word *puja*. These offerings are made to *thewada* (divinities), who in this ceremony are called upon before the declaration of taking refuge in the Buddha, that is, the deities in this context have a kind of autonomy, while at the same time coming under the Buddhist umbrella. It is true that *ahimsa*—non-killing and non-violence—is a prime Buddhist value, as it is also a critical

---

[1] Shway Yoe (1896) not only documents the presence of *brahman* (*pohna*) 'monasteries' and colonies in Mandalay and other large towns in Burma but also describes the presence of the *pohna* in the villages, where they act as astrologers, playing an important role in auspicious ceremonies like name giving, ear boring (of girls), and marriage. He reports that Brahman priests were originally brought as captives from Manipur in India, and have been employed as astrologers ever since; their descendants have apparently remained 'tolerably pure', are readily distinguishable in their appearance from the *pohn-gyee* (Buddhist monk) as well as by their Indian style of housing, worship of Krishna and twenty-five other deities, the denial to foreigners of entry into their temples, and the practice of great austerities and mortifications. In the village, however, it appears that a Burmese counterpart astrologer to the Indian *brahman* is present, and as in the Thai case, ritual experts and cults take their place within a wider field of religion.

brahmanical value. But the Buddhist ethic does not prohibit meat eating: Buddhist monks eat meat and, more importantly, in Thailand meat is a part of the food offering to the Buddha. Vegetarian offering in the *sukhwan* rite thus directs our attention to a different order of facts, namely the vegetarian/meat eating distinction of brahmanism. Consider also the words in the text which as we saw contain brahmanical ideas of marriage, and invoke the procession of Hindu deities. Yet also note that God Indra, the *Garuda* and the *Naga* are elements of the Buddhist cosmology as well, and that it is therefore possible to formulate a scheme in which the features enumerated, which are reminiscent of classical Hinduism, can also take their place in a Buddhist rearrangement of ideas. (For instance, see the Sakka-Panha Suttanta (Rhys Davids, Vol. III, Part II, Ch. 21, 1910) for the myth of the conversion of Sakka (Indra) to Buddhism.) Finally, we should not forget that *sukhwan* is performed for the candidate for ordination as monk, as well as for the monk himself.

In other words, whatever the historical antecedents, I wish to employ a strategy of analysis which is different from that used in the classical method, which speaks of elements of Hinduism and elements of Buddhism (and also fragments of Animism) co-existing as disparate entities and historical residues in contemporary South-east Asian religions.

My departure from this kind of historical method consists in employing a different approach to the interpretation of the anthropological data. In the village of Phraan Muan there exist today two ritual functionaries— the monk and the *paahm*; one is usually a young unmarried man undergoing an ascetic regimen; the other is an elderly householder invested with authority. If, for the sake of dramatizing the situation, we must employ an historical idiom, here is a case of the *brahman* and the *bhikkhu*, who were *antagonistic* and *irreconcilable* figures in India, co-existing in a Thai village. What is their structural relation and what dynamically links them?

The rest of this chapter is devoted to elucidating the following thesis. There is a differential emphasis, but also a *complementarity* in the roles of both these statuses. Dynamically considered, the Buddhist monk in time *becomes* the *paahm*, *via* service and learning in the *wat*. This dynamic succession is a fulfilment of the life cycle stages in the Thai village, and is the Siamese transformation of the classical Hindu life cycle of four stages. It also illuminates the total systemic character of the religion we are seeking to understand, elements of which are related in dynamic tension. These questions thus take us back to the conclusions of Chapter 8, which dealt with the rewards of monkhood and the career of the literate monk who gives up his robes.

Buddhism and the spirit cults in North-east Thailand

This interpretation, formulated on the basis of village facts, is confirmed dramatically at another level of facts relating to the court *brahmans* of Thailand. Quaritch Wales (1931)—after commenting that, especially in the reigns of staunch Buddhist kings, state ceremonies showed an intensified 'blending of the two religions, Buddhism and Hinduism'—presents this valuable bit of information: 'it is not surprising, therefore, to find that the court *"brahmans"* are also Buddhists, and *that before they can undergo* the *ceremony of initiation* and *wear the "brahman" girdle*, they *must pass through the novitiate as Buddhist monks...*' (p. 57) (italics mine). It is unthinkable in Thailand that a local *brahman* can be outside the Buddhist faith, or that his rites and those of the monk can be mutually exclusive.

We can now deal with the village facts. The *paahm* or *mau khwan*, though a lay ritual officiant, has special characteristics which link him to the institution of monkhood, just as the *sukhwan* rites, although not performed by monks themselves, are clearly allied to Buddhism. The elucidation of these links will also illuminate why the *paahm* is so appropriate as the officiant and the sender of the message at *sukhwan* rites. His social position and moral qualities are an essential ingredient of the efficacy of the message. In Phraan Muan village there were two recognized *mau khwan* (plus an occasional performer). Both were respected elders, ex-monks, and literate in the scripts in which *sukhwan* texts were written.

Literacy, which traditionally was an achievement of only a few, is an essential requirement for the performance of the role. Each *sukhwan* occasion has a special text appropriate for it written on a palm leaf; the text is read at the ceremony, there being no recitation from memory or improvisation of words. The officiants possess collections of texts which they freely borrow from each other, for the texts themselves do not constitute secret knowledge. It is the ability to read that restricts access to them, and it is in part the personal qualities of the literate villager which are crucial for village acceptance of him as an appropriate person to perform the ritual. (See Tambiah 1968a for details concerning texts and scripts.)

The link with Buddhism and monkhood consists in the fact that the *paahm* acquires his literacy during his service in the village *wat* as a novice and monk. Temporary novicehood and monkhood enable the man who spends sufficient time in the *wat* to assume ritual eldership as a layman. This is the most valued 'pay-off' for an ex-monk and it is linked to literacy. In traditional times, that is before the establishment of government schools in the 1930s, the rungs of the ladder of literacy were, first, service as temple boy (*dekwat*), then novicehood, followed by monkhood. Literacy was essential not only for conducting *khwan* rites but also for practising indigenous medicine, the knowledge relating to which is also embodied in texts.

Now, the interesting fact is that both the *khwan* ritual texts and the medical texts were traditionally copied and transmitted by monks. The *wat* and its monks were in fact the library and copyists. While a monk in robes could ordinarily practise medicine, he did not perform *khwan* rites, for they were not considered rites appropriate for him to perform. (The monk, however, may himself be the celebrant in the rite.) The rites are thus not strictly 'Buddhist' ritual, but a monk, in preparation for his lay life, could and did copy texts and could take them away when he gave up his robes. This was quite in order because *khwan* ritual, as we have seen, comes under the umbrella of Buddhism; it is in no way 'antagonistic' or opposed to Buddhism. Thus in a sense it was only the ex-monk who is fit to be a lay ritual elder.

Not every monk, however, becomes literate and able to handle texts; nor does every monk who acquires literacy become a lay ritual elder. Apart from personal interest in becoming one, he must find a practising *paahm* who will teach him the art of performing rites. Finally, it is not until many years after leaving monkhood, when he is in his late middle age and has attained the status of elder, that a man can appropriately perform the *khwan* ritual.

The biographical details of the two widely respected *paahm* of Phraan Muan village illustrate the principles of their recruitment and their passage from monk to village elder.

Phau Tu (grandfather) Phan, over seventy years old, is the village's most celebrated *paahm*; in addition he is village physician (*mau ya*), and one of the lay readers of the Buddhist congregation, whose role is to invite (*aratana*) monks on behalf of the congregation to give precepts, to chant, to give a sermon, and to receive gifts presented by the laymen. Finally, he is also a member of the temple committee, which organizes village temple festivals and looks after the temple finances. This is indeed a remarkable clustering of roles. From the age of twelve to sixteen years, Phan was a novice in the village *wat* and became literate; at the age of twenty-one he was ordained monk and remained in robes for three years. He then resumed lay life and married.

When he was about thirty years old Phan studied medicine from his mother's younger brother, and after his teacher's death began to practise and became very successful. But it was only when he reached the age of fifty that he was invited by a relative of his grandparental generation (and who lived in another village) to learn from him the art of conducting *sukhwan*, since he himself was too old to practise and wanted a successor.

Buddhism and the spirit cults in North-east Thailand

In turn, Phau Tu Phan decided some twelve years ago that on account of his age his ritual duties were more than he could shoulder alone, and therefore picked a distant kinsman, Phau Champi, as his apprentice and eventual successor.

Phau Champi, now fifty-nine years old, is the village's most respected elder. He is a former village headman, had served both as novice and as monk, is a leader of the lay Buddhist congregation and of the temple committee. He was so obviously the right person to succeed Phau Tu Phan as *paahm*.

Champi is a thoroughly literate person and versed in Buddhist lore and village traditions. As a boy, from nine to fourteen years, he had five years of schooling in the village school; at seventeen he became a novice and served in the *wat* until he was twenty, when he was ordained a monk. He gave up his robes after one year as monk. Although literate and learned by village standards, Champi did not commence his ritual activities as *paahm* until he was forty-six, when he was invited to become Phau Tu Phan's apprentice. He had by then become a village leader. He assisted Phan at *khwan* rites for some time before he began to perform the ceremonies himself.

To sum up the structural relationship between the *paahm* and the monk: the *paahm* invariably has been a monk in his youth, and it was in the temple that he acquired his literacy; he invariably is also a leader of the Buddhist congregation. Although the practice of *khwan* rites (and medicine) requires literacy, only a few ex-monks become *paahm* in subsequent lay life. Traditionally the art has to be learned from an existing practitioner, and succession, although it may depend partly on kinship factors, is more importantly associated with the achievement of a position of eldership in the village, which is attained through piety and leadership in Buddhist worship and temple activities.

We have seen that a way of capitalizing on the experience of temporary monkhood is to become a lay ritual elder of the *paahm*, or *mau khwan*, type. Literacy is critical for both monk and *paahm* because language in itself plays a crucial role in Buddhist and *khwan* rites. But words do not play the same role in Buddhist chants as in the recitations of the *paahm*. The Buddhist monk recites sacred Pali chants which are largely not understood by the congregation, nor indeed by many of the temporary monks themselves; however, their recitation *per se* is supposed to confer blessings and protection. The Pali words are sacred and effective because they are the words of the Buddha and are recited by ascetic, disciplined monks who lead a religiously valued life. The *paahm* or *mau khwan* recites texts, the words of which are necessarily in the local language.

Co-existence of 'brahman' and Buddhist monk

The words are expected to achieve their effects in the listener through a charging of morale and a conveying of confidence and support by the assembled village elders. I shall later, when I analyse the rites of affliction connected with malevolent spirits, carry further this comparison of the use of words by indicating still another use.

Monk and *paahm*, young man in robes and elderly householder, Buddhist rites and *sukhwan* rites, all stand in a relation of reciprocity, which in my view is an important interpretative point to be made in the study of village religion. This ritual reciprocity is intimately connected with village social structure. Seen in terms of their refraction in this social structure, the institution of monkhood and the ritual proceedings in mortuary rites represent the services of the junior generation to the senior generation, of *luug-laan* (children and grandchildren) to *phuu thaw* (elders of parental and grandparental generations). The *sukhwan* rites, on the other hand, represent the reciprocity by which the elders perform vital ritual roles *vis-à-vis* the junior generation, their successsors in the social system.

The reciprocity may be elucidated as follows: village youth become temporary monks before marriage to make merit for their elders and community members. In effect, then, the older generation persuades its youth temporarily to renounce its vitality and sexual potency and undergo an ascetic regimen. In a sense it is the sacrifice of this human energy that produces ethical vitality which can counter *karma* and suffering. The young are appropriate agents because they are not yet householders. They are the agents of merit-transfer to the old, who are facing imminent death. And after the death of the elders, they continue to perform the same role of transferring merit to them.

While the young are going through monkhood it is the elders and householders who support them and who play the leading lay roles in Buddhist rites. Although monks are segregated from their families, yet it is their elders who mainly support them through gift giving. Womenfolk cook and serve them food, and continue to nurture their brothers and sons who are monks. Male elders organize collective rites and act as lay ritual leaders in most village rites, except in the case of mortuary rites in which the filial generations (*luug-laan*) are called upon to play the major ritual roles, for it is they who will succeed the elders and it is they who will remember the dead.

In the life-affirming *khwan* rites, the *phuu thaw* perform a vital ritual service to their *luug-laan*. Here the parental generation initiates the young into various statuses and helps them assume the role of successful house-holders. They in fact transfer their protective power and authority to their successors. There is a power in old age which the young must rely upon in order to enjoy a prosperous life, just as much as there is a vitality in youth which the old must transmute into *bun* (merit), long life and good rebirth. I have documented in Chapter 2 the details of the pervasive system of ordering of the village society in terms of five generational categories which are extended to all persons: *pu-ya-ta-yai* (grandparents), *phau-mae* (parents), *phii-naung* (older/younger siblings), *luug* (children) and *laan* (grandchildren). We saw that these generational divisions are collapsed into two hierarchical categories, *phuu thaw* (elders) and *luug laan* (children/grandchildren), with the middle term sibling (*phii-nuang*) or own generation being implicit. The conspicious feature of both kinship and ritual obligations in the village is that they are phrased in terms of these three generational concepts, which simply reduce for any adult speaker into the superordinate and subordinate relationships indicated as *phuu thaw* and *luug-laan*.

The pattern of participation of kin and neighbours in *khwan* rites closely resembles household rites of a Buddhist merit-making kind in which monks participate. Behind this formal similarity, however, there is a difference in expressive idiom concerning assistance and giving of gifts, which will be elucidated now.

MATERIAL TRANSFERS AND THE IDIOM OF TRANSFER

In terms of social participation, all *sukhwan* ceremonies are occasions for the assembling of bilateral kin and neighbours, especially those of *phuu thaw* status. A prime example in the village is the marriage ceremony. The pattern of attendance here is similar to that in mortuary rites, which have been described earlier. Both proceedings include the giving of small gifts of cash by guests, and both are highlighted or concluded by collective feasts. In a general sense, both illustrate the values of reciprocity and mutual help, and the universal merit-making ethos of the village, though there is a difference of emphasis. The ordination rite neatly combines both emphases.

It is useful to compare the transactions at a marriage ceremony and those at a Buddhistic merit-making household rite to bring out the scale of participation, the economic implications of material transfers, and the idiom of such transfers.

Marriage prestations have an important economic dimension. Typically the groom's parents have to make a unilateral payment or price (*khadaung*) to the bride's parents at the wedding ceremony. (This is balanced out by the bride's parents entertaining guests and giving initial residence rights to the couple in their household, and by the prospective land inheritance of the bride according to the bilateral inheritance system of the village.) Elders, we have seen, act as witnesses and intermediaries; they customarily give small cash gifts (of 1–2 *baht*) to the couple (*ngoen pukkhan*) and the parents (*ngoen phaudaung*). These are looked upon as gifts that must be returned on a strict reciprocity basis when the givers are the hosts at some other ceremonial. All guests are feasted by the bride's parental family. No monks participate in the usual wedding rites. Let me illustrate the economic aspects of marriage expenditure by reference to two actual cases.

Case 1: bride from Baan Phraan Muan, groom from another village. At the wedding there were twenty-eight guests from the bride's side, and twenty-seven from the groom's. *Khadaung* (brideprice) was 1,000 *baht* (about £20). Elderly guests gave the couple 88 *baht* and the parents of the bride 34 *baht*. The bride's parents spent about 250 *baht* on food, liquor and tobacco for the guests.

Case 2: groom from another village, bride from Baan Phraan Muan. *Khadaung* paid was 809 *baht*; money contributed by elders to the couple was 180 *baht* (*ngoen pukkhan*) and by the bridegroom's parents 150 *baht* (*ngoen somma*). (The first is paid when elders bind the wrists of the young couple (*sukhwan* rite), and the second is optional.) The bride's parents spent 327 *baht* on feasting the guests; this sum did not include the rice, which was drawn from household stocks.

As an example of a household's merit-making rite I choose the *prasaat peueng* ceremony, which I have described in Chapter 11. This rite is either conducted on the third day after cremation when the mortuary rites are concluded, or it may be done at any time as a special merit-making for the dead. The essence of the rite is the carrying of gifts in a *prasaat peueng* or 'wax palace' to the *wat* and presenting them to the monks (on behalf of the dead) after first feasting them. The economics of this ritual are illustrated in the following two cases.

Case 1: the headman of the village held a ceremony on behalf of his mother, who had died unnaturally some years previously and had therefore been buried. This ceremony was then part of the delayed 'normal' mortuary rites.

On the day the *prasaat* was constructed eighty persons (excluding children) congregated at his house; thirty-three of them were his 'kin' (*yad*). Guests made cash gifts amounting to 79 *baht* (which of course would be 'repaid' later). The headman spent 250 *baht* (£7) on gifts for the monks (robes, clothes, mat, pillow, etc., and 140 *baht* on cash gifts to the officiating monks). His expenditure on food and drink for the guests and monks was 499 *baht* (£10); he spent another 210 *baht* on entertaining the village at night by engaging a *maulum* troupe (folk opera). His total expenditure thus was 1,023 *baht* (approximately £20).

Case 2: this is a *prasaat* ceremony on a more modest scale conducted by an ordinary village household three days after the head's wife died. Forty-four 'helpers' were present at the construction of the *prasaat* and they contributed 34 *baht*. The household spent 81 *baht* on purchasing gifts of robes, cushions and cosmetics for the monks, and spent 228 *baht* on food and drinks. Total expenditure was 309 *baht* (£6).

Thus a merit-making ceremony conducted by individual households is also a social event in which kinsmen and neighbours participate and fulfil obligations. Although the pattern of village participation is similar in marriage and mortuary rites, the former is conceived of as a context in which elders come together, witness the event and give it legitimacy, while the latter is conceived of as an occasion when community members come together to give help and make merit in so doing.

Ritual and material transactions in rites of passage like death and marriage, and at collective cosmic rites at the *wat*, stand in contrast to contexts wherein villagers have dealings with supernatural agencies such as the male guardian spirits of the village or female agents connected with agriculture (goddess of the earth and spirit of rice). This is the subject matter of the following chapters.

15

THE CULT OF THE GUARDIAN SPIRITS

The guardian spirits that concern us in this chapter have village as well as regional significance, and the cult associated with them comprises a ritual complex that has an important place in the totality of religious behaviour of the villagers. It is the phenomenon which some writers have called 'animism' and which with pseudo-historical conjecture they have identified as pre-Buddhist. Moreover, they have variously treated it both as incompatible with, and as combining with, Buddhism. In actual fact its relationship to Buddhism is not simple but complex, involving opposition, complementarity, linkage, and hierarchy.

This chapter sets out the beliefs, rites and practitioners connected with the guardian spirits, first at the level of the village and thereafter in regional scope. The cult is in one sense a totality when viewed in relation to other cults. But scrutinized from inside it is differentiated. It constitutes a spectrum and also portrays contrasts, according to context. This double-viewing in terms of spectrum and internal contrast (Conklin, in Dell Hymes (1964)) illuminates the category distinctions, linkages, and hierarchy both within the cult and between it and Buddhist ritual. Analysis proceeds at three levels: the linguistic level of verbal concepts, the distinctions implicit in behavioural details, and the dialectic between them.

GUARDIAN SPIRITS

The category term *phii* refers to spirits to which are generally attributed powers over human beings. It includes a wide variety of supernatural agents ranging from those who are a permanently existing category of supernaturals to those who are transformations of dead human beings. In the widest sense the *winjan* (soul or consciousness) of every human being turns into *phii* at death; in fact a corpse is referred to as *phii khon raaw*.

In Baan Phraan Muan there are two supernatural agents who, though they fall into the category of *phii*, have an elevated status. They are called *Tapubaan* ('grandparent' or ancestor of village) and *Chao Phau Phraa Khao* (*chao* = honorific title, *phau* = father, *phraa khao* = monk or holy man dressed in white). Both may be referred to as *chao phau*, and in village conception and attitudes they are as much a respected deity as *phii*. They are different from a number of malevolent and capriciously

263

acting *phii*, from whom they are distinguished. On the other hand, certain category distinctions separate all *phii* from *thewada* (supernatural divine angels). Thus it may be said that *thewada* are opposed to *phii*, who in turn are differentiated into elevated guardians (*chao phau*) and malevolent spirits (*phii*). Certain important ritual beliefs and acts (systematized cult behaviour) are associated with *Tapubaan* and *Chao Phau Phraa Khao* at community, household, and individual levels.

The villagers in some contexts distinguish *Tapubaan* and *Chao Phau Phraa Khao* as two separate spirits; in other contexts they are treated as a unified conception with dual aspects. The logic of this unity and differentiation follows from their two separate yet also related domains of influence and interest.

Before we describe these domains, let us be clear about one general distinction. In relation to Buddhism, the villagers view *Tapubaan* and *Chao Phau* cults as belonging in a separate and even opposed domain of religious action (just as, at another level, the *thewada* are opposed to *phii*). Thus it is clearly recognized that Buddhist monks do not take part in the *phii* cult, for they 'belong to a separate party' (*hon la heet la khong*). As one informant put it, 'Monks are human beings, *chao phau* are *phii*. Monks never chant for *chao phau*; they are called upon to chant when human beings die' (i.e. to conduct mortuary rites, a major ritual function of the monks). Buddhist religious action is phrased in terms of the ideology of *bun* (merit)—when one gives gifts to the monks or the temple (*wat*) one receives merit; but when one propitiates or placates *Chao Phau* or *Tapubaan*, villagers explicitly consider the transaction as a *bargain*, an offering made to gain a particular favour, generally to remove an affliction caused by the *phii* because of an offence committed (*pid phii*).

But this general category distinction between Buddhism and the *phii* cult is by no means the whole story. If the distinction were a basic dichotomy found in all aspects of ritual action our analytic task would be easy and the theoretical scheme for placing the systems simple. In fact, at other levels there are intriguing connections and interpenetrations, the exploration of which is of critical interest.

Tapubaan is the 'owner' of the village (*baan*); villagers sometimes elucidate this ownership literally in the sense that he was the original founder and owner of the land. *Chao Phau Phraa Khao* is, on the other hand, the guardian of the *wat*. Thus their domains of authority, *baan* (settlement) and *wat* (temple), are important village ecological and socio-religious distinctions. Throughout the region in every village the dual agents, phrased in this manner and called by the same names, are repeated. (Furthermore, there is a regional cult addressed to a superior guardian spirit of the swamp to whom the dual village guardian spirits are sub-ordinate. I shall describe this phenomenon in a later section.) Here let us note that we are dealing with a widespread religious patterning.

From their respective spheres of influence follow other distinctions between *Chao Phau* and *Tapubaan*. *Chao Phau* is the *phii* of a pious man who lived in the *wat*, took the ten precepts (the same as those taken by a novice) and ministered to the needs of the monks. He wore *white* clothes, the insignia of a pious layman (*upasok*). After his death his *phii* continued to live in the *wat*; its place of residence is actually in the *bood* (the most holy place of the *wat*), and there is a wooden statue of him placed beside the statue of the Buddha. *Tapubaan*, on the other hand, wears the ordinary clothes of a layman, and his residence today is a wooden shrine located at the edge of the village in the jungle. He guards the settlement from its boundary and his shrine faces the village.

The offerings the villagers make to the two guardian spirits show another distinction. To *Tapubaan* is offered chicken, pork, liquor, curries and other strong foods: he is meat eating. To *Chao Phau* is offered *only pawan*[1] (rice mixed with sugar): he is vegetarian. This meat eating versus vege-tarian distinction is especially intriguing in this context. For unlike Sinhalese Buddhism, where meat is not offered to the Buddha but is given to the monks (Obeyesekere 1958; Leach 1962), in Thailand meat and rice are normal food offerings to the Buddhist statue, as it is to the Buddhist monks. The Thai villager will say that 'the food offered to the monks is also offered to the Buddha image', which is a perfectly logical statement. But it appears that at another level—in regard to the white-robed pious guardian of the *wat*, as opposed to the secular guardian of the village —Thai villagers have introduced the Hindu-type pure/impure distinction: a distinction that is again reflected in the vegetarian offerings to the *thewada* as opposed to the carnivoral offerings to the malevolent *phii*.

Table 6 gives details of *Tapubaan's* and *Chao Phau's* separate and joint spheres of jurisdiction over the villagers and the kinds of action which call forth their supernatural intervention in the form of affliction and disease.

In the case of *Tapubaan* there are certain special interdictions connected with the vicinity of his shrine (prohibition against cutting wood and gardening near the shrine) and with eating a certain kind of turtle living in the swamp.[2] Human beings must observe their distance from him except to approach him with ritual intent. *Chao Phau* by virtue of residing

---

[1] *Pawan* may be included in the offerings to *Tapubaan* in addition to meat and liquor.
[2] The turtle, called *taw san diaw*, has one 'stripe' on its shell. Turtles with more 'stripes' can be eaten.

TABLE 6. *Supernatural affliction*

Name of spirit (*phii*) acting	Human acts which arouse supernatural action	Kind of illness that results
Tapubaan (owner or guardian of the village)	A. *Norms concerning village citizenship*	[In extreme cases madness or death may occur]
	(i) Extending compound fence on to roads or lanes in the village	
	(ii) Going to live in another village without informing and getting permission from *Tapubaan via* the *cham*	Fever
	B. *Wan phraa taboos* (Buddhist Sabbath)	
	(i) Polishing rice (female task)	Difficulty in child-birth
	(ii) Taking cart into or out of the village (male task)	Any elder of the village may be afflicted with fainting
	(iii) Cutting and carrying fire-wood into the village (usually female task)	
	C. *Tapubaan taboos*	
	(i) Cutting down trees or bamboo, or gardening in the vicinity of *Tapubaan's* spirit house	Stomach ache
	(ii) Eating turtle of a special kind (this is associated particularly with the spirit of the swamp (*Chao Phau Tong Kyang*))	Body pain
Chao Phau Phraa Khao (guardian of the *wat*)	A. *Protection of wat*	
	(i) Urinating in the *wat* precinct	Stomach ache
	(ii) Plucking mango fruits in the *wat* compound, especially by throwing stones at the fruits	Stomach ache
	(iii) Holding any merit-making ceremony at the *wat* (*gnaan bun*) without requesting permission from *Chao Phau*	The abbot will fall sick. Also public brawls or a fire may occur
	B. *Wan phraa taboos* Same as listed above for *Tapubaan* (B)	

in the sacrosanct *bood* is automatically afforded seclusion from careless lay approach.

Apart from these interdictions *Tapubaan* is primarily associated with norms concerning village citizenship. He acts as a disciplinarian. Common village property rights, as expressed in public roads and lanes, must not be infringed by villagers. Secondly, a man cannot change his village membership and residence without a ritual statement to *Tapubaan* before-hand and getting his permission. This ritual statement is mediated through the *cham*, who is 'elected' by being possessed by *Tapubaan* or *Chao Phau*.

Similarly, *Chao Phau* protects the sanctity and property rights of the *wat*. Villagers should not urinate in the compound, nor plunder its fruit trees. But by far the most important aspect of *Chao Phau's* authority is that no collective *wat* calendrical rite nor any village festival (such as the annual fair) can be held without first informing him at the *bood* and getting his permission. Subsequently permission is sought from *Tapubaan* in his shrine. *Tapubaan's* authority here is secondary, because all such festivals and rites take place in the *wat* compound. Villagers say that if permission is not gained from the *wat* guardian a series of misfortunes may follow—people may quarrel and fight during the proceedings, fire may break out, and the abbot of the *wat* may fall sick. It may also be noted that permission is not requested through the monks but *via Chao Phau's* and *Tapubaan's* elected intermediary, the *cham*. No such permission is necessary for the holding of private or household rituals, which are not village affairs.

In village thought the necessity to get permission from *Chao Phau* to hold Buddhist rituals in the *wat* is not an indication that *Chao Phau* is superior to Buddha, or that his cult is more powerful than Buddhism. *Chao Phau's* authority lies only in his protective guardianship of the temple, and such guardianship is quite common in historical Buddhism.[1] On the other hand, because of his closer association with Buddhism (his piety, white clothes and vegetarian food habits), villagers tend to give *Chao Phau* a formal superiority over *Tapubaan*. In actual fact, of course, their spheres of jurisdiction are both well defined and in some areas unified.

Both *Chao Phau* and *Tapubaan* are directly concerned with certain taboos relating to the Buddhist Sabbath (*wan sil* or *wan phraa*). Village women must not polish paddy on *wan phraa*; villagers must not take a cart in or out of the village, or cut and bring firewood into the village. It is said that *wan phraa* is the day on which the two guardians freely roam about—it is their day of active duty. The taboos, in fact, stress that villagers should not engage in *mundane work* on the Sabbath. The segre-

---

[1] In *Bun Phraawes* ritual, guardianship is attributed to the *Naga*-monk, Phraa Uppakrut (see Chapter 10). It is quite appropriate here to report two incidents in the field. Before the Land Rover in which the field team travelled was allowed to be driven into the *wat* compound, permission was formally sought from *Chao Phau*. During a *wat* festival, when the dynamo we were using in order to show a film failed, a village elder approached *Chao Phau*, apologized for not having let him know about the showing of the film, and requested his permission to show it. The dynamo started working again after some time spent repairing it.

gation of *Chao Phau* and *Tapu*[1] from Buddhist values, however, is seen in the fact that offerings of propitiation and placation to them (especially after the cure of a disease or illness) must be made on *wan pood* (Wednesday), which is special to them. If the Wednesday is also a *wan sil* (*wan phraa*), offerings cannot be made to the *phii* on that day, but instead on the following day or the next Wednesday. This ensures that Buddhist and guardian spirit rituals are segregated in time.

The third column of Table 6 shows the punishment inflicted by *Chao Phau* and *Tapubaan* for infringement of certain norms. Usually the rules apply to individuals and the offending individual is afflicted with illness—stomach ache, fever and body pains being the normal punishments. However, if certain of the Buddhist Sabbath taboos are broken, any village elder (*phuu thaw*) may have a fainting fit. And if a village ritual or festival is held without prior permission, the whole community may suffer either a disturbance of the public peace or damage by fire. In all these matters, then, *Chao Phau* and *Tapubaan* act as moral agents and disciplinarians. They do not act capriciously; they are guardians and custodians of communal property and community interests.

Yet at the same time it must be pointed out that they are not the most important guardians of village morality. The range of rules within which they guard is limited, and to locate the entire range of moral rules other spheres of village religious action have to be considered. The village orientation to *Tapu* and *Chao Phau* is that of a community of children dependent on a guardian or a father figure who has power to grant fertility, rain, individual favours, and to inflict misfortunes.

What has been developed so far concerning *Tapu* and *Chao Phau* is their regulative aspect as guardians, their power to punish. I shall now describe one feature of their positive benevolent and rewarding aspect, which also characterizes their role in a village-wide collective cult. They have the crucial power to ensure agricultural abundance in the village, which is by far the most vital preoccupation of the villagers.

In this agricultural cult *Tapubaan* and *Chao Phau* are propitiated as closely allied dual agents, this time with the former having precedence. I have already mentioned that *Chao Phau* lives in the *bood* and that *Tapu* has a wooden shrine at the edge of the jungle behind the *wat*. In actual fact, this wooden shrine has two compartments—one assigned to *Tapu* and the other to *Chao Phau*. The collective rites to be considered now are enacted at the shrine. In other words, we see that, in this context, the *phii* cult is again spatially and conceptually separated from the *wat* and

---

[1] *Tapu* is the accepted abbreviation of *Tapubaan*, as *Chao Phau* is of *Chao Phau Phraa Khao*.

Buddhist ritual. No monk participates, and the village assembles as a congregation under special ritual intermediaries of the guardians.

Twice a year, before ploughing starts in the sixth lunar month, and again soon after harvest in the first or second lunar month, the villagers assemble to propitiate the guardians. The ritual officiants are the *cham* (intermediary) and the *tiam* (medium). The pre-ploughing ceremony is not as lavish as the post-harvest one which celebrates a successful agricultural season. The purpose of the former is to request agricultural abundance in the coming season, and it therefore is a kind of bargaining or promise that if agriculture is successful, offerings will be made again after the harvest. The typical request made is: '*Luug-laan ja tham raj tham naa ja ma liang haj raksa wua kwai ya haj khon jeb puay*' ('your children and grandchildren are going to cultivate fields and gardens, take care of the buffaloes and don't allow people to fall ill').

The structure and sequence of the two ceremonies are the same. I shall briefly describe the sequence before giving a detailed account of a post-harvest ceremony witnessed in the field.

Each household must in theory provide *gai saung pah* or two sets of chicken (i.e. cooked chicken in two trays), plus liquor as an offering for *Tapubaan* and *pa wan saung pah* (two trays of rice mixed with sugar) for *Chao Phau*. The householders assemble on the day chosen by the *cham*. The *cham* first lights a candle and invites the two guardians to accept the offerings, which are then placed in the shrine. After these collective offerings are made, individuals (*qua* individuals) may make offerings either in order to seek personal favours or as thanks-offering for personal favours granted. This, then, brings out another aspect of the relationship of guardian *phii* to the villagers: in their benevolent aspect they may grant favours to individuals, not as rewards for meritorious conduct, but as the result of a pledge that offerings will be provided if the guardians bestow good fortune. Finally, all the villagers sit together to eat a collective meal of the offerings made to the guardians.

POST-HARVEST OFFERINGS TO THE GUARDIANS: A CASE DESCRIPTION

The ceremony, which is referred to as *liang phii* (offering to *phii*) took place on 24 January 1962 after the rice harvest was completed.

At 9.30 a.m. about fifty villagers assembled at the spirit house (shrine). Each villager was said to be a representative of a particular household; in some cases adult children were sent to represent parents; in other cases villagers represented the interests of householders who could not be present, but who sent offerings through them. The critical requirement was that each household (in cases where junior households lived in the compound of parents to form one economic unit, this can be extended to mean 'compound group') should present or send offerings. (It is believed that failure to make offerings will result in sickness to the members of the offender's household.)

Each householder's offering consisted of a large basket or bowl containing one boiled chicken, sauce, rice in a small basket, *pa wan* (rice mixed with sugar) in a package, betel nut, tobacco, and locally made cigarettes. In all there were 106 such offerings, excluding the three contributed by the officiants, the *cham*, the assistant, and the *tiam* (medium).

The officiants first cleaned the floor of the spirit house, then lit two candles and attached them to the posts. Then with flowers in their hands they squatted in front of the shrine and invited *Tapu* and *Chao Phau* to receive the offerings. The offerings themselves comprised different categories. One called *pa derm*, represented the collective offerings of the village, and were in fact presented in sets sequentially. First, the three offerings of the *cham*, his assistant and the *tiam* were placed inside the shrine, with the rice basket and the liquor bottle open. The *phii* were invited to receive them. After a lapse of a few minutes, half of the chicken and a lump of the offered rice were put in a bowl and placed inside; some of the liquor was poured into a vessel and placed similarly. The left-overs were returned to the three donors.

The next offering consisted of seven sets. The same procedure was followed, and the words said by the *cham* by way of invitation were: '*thang mod ched pa, nimon chao phau rab nam luug nam laan*' ('altogether seven sets of offerings, made by children and grandchildren, inviting honorific father to eat'). In the next sequence eleven other sets of offering were made, and so on until the collective offerings were exhausted.

The collective offerings were followed by another category called *pa ba*, which were made by individual persons soliciting favours from the guardians. In this ceremony four men solicited favours—one requested that a sick pig be cured; another, whose daughter was employed as a bus conductor, asked *Tapu* to protect her from accidents; the third and fourth, both young men, requested physical safety while doing national service and success in a forthcoming examination, respectively.

The next set of offerings (*see pa*) were again made by four persons; these were in gratitude for favours solicited and granted.

The final ritual sequence was the summing up by the *cham* and his assistant: holding five pairs of flowers (*kan ha*) placed in a bowl, they said that 106 offerings, excluding the three made by themselves, had been made by village householders. Let those who paid the guardians respect be rewarded. A promise was made that in the fifth or sixth lunar month (*dyan ha fa hog*) offerings would be made again. (This refers to offerings before ploughing in the next rice cycle.)

The ceremony was concluded by a meal, all those assembled eating the portion of the offerings returned to them. The offerings left in the shrine were later taken by the ritual officiants as their due.

RITUAL SPECIALISTS

There are a large number of specialists in the village who are able to cure disease and communicate with the supernatural. Most are called by names which have the common prefix *mau*. Thus we have *mau song* (diviner/diagnostician), *mau du* (or *mau lek*) (astrologer/fortune teller), *mau mau* (discoverer of lost property), *mau ya* (physician/'herbal' doctor), *mau ram* (medium of *phii fa*), *mau tham* (exorcist of spirits), *mau khwan* (intermediary for *khwan* or spiritual essence, who is also called *paahm*).

In this chapter we are primarily concerned with the cult of the guardian *phii*, and the specialists who figure in this are three: *mau song* (general diviner or consultant), *cham* (spirit intermediary), and *tiam* (medium). The latter two specialists are connected exclusively with *Tapubaan* and *Chao Phau*.

The general procedure when illness befalls a person is that he goes to consult (or he invites to his home) the *mau song*. He is concerned with diagnosing, first whether the illness is caused by spirits or not. If spirits are not involved, then the inference is that it is ordinary organically-produced illness and the patient is sent to the *mau ya*, who treats with medicine. If the illness is supernaturally produced, then the diviner also names the particular spirit that is affecting the patient and the kind of offering that must be given to placate it. Village theory of disease is explicit that a supernaturally caused disease cannot be cured by ordinary medicine (although a patient may combine medicine with supernatural placation in the actual cure).

If the diviner finds that the illness is caused by *Tapubaan* or *Chao Phau*, the two guardian *phii*, then the patient must go to the *cham* (intermediary) of these spirits in order to carry out the rest of the proceedings. (The word *cham* is used exclusively for the intermediary of the guardian spirits.) The first sequence is *kuad khaw phii*, inviting the *phii* to go out of the patient. After the cure, the promised fee offering is given at the *phii* shrine on a Wednesday (*wan pood*). The *tiam* comes into the picture for disease cure only in extraordinary circumstances.

Having stated these preliminary facts, we can now examine various facets of the roles of *mau song* and *tiam*, especially as they figure in the cure of disease.

'Mau song' (*diviner/consultant*)

There were in 1962 at least four individuals who practised the art of *mau song*. The word *song* means 'to seek' and therefore *mau song* may be described as belonging to the category of consultant, diagnostician or diviner. The *mau song* only diagnoses; in that role he does not cure, either through medicine or supernatural action. His role is *conceptually* distinct, although any one person may be *mau song* and also dabble in other special techniques. When he performs other roles he is called by the appropriate name.

There is no standard technique of diagnosis or divination. Individual diviners practise their special mode. I shall briefly mention four techniques current in the village, and then examine in detail two of them. One diviner uses an egg into which he looks and observes the appearance of supernatural agents; another looks through a paper funnel and sees certain marks which stand for different supernatural agents; the third studies the pattern made by the contents of a broken egg and merely tells whether the disease is fatal or not; the fourth uses a mirror and sees in it the appearance of supernaturals in the manner of the first diviner.

The pre-eminent diviner in Baan Phraan Muan was a middle-aged man called Wanthong. Another (Bunsi) who was prominent as *cham* also practised as *mau song* as a secondary activity.

Wanthong, the village diviner: Wanthong's father was himself both *mau song* and *mau ya*, who learned his arts from a man in Laos with whom he had dealings in cattle. Wanthong began to learn the art of *mau song* from his father at twenty-five, and after being an apprentice for seven years became a fully-fledged diviner at thirty-two. Thus is the art of divination learned, and quite young men of the village can fill the role.

Wanthong observed certain food taboos which are required by his divining work. During his apprenticeship he had to avoid eating certain delicacies such as *khaaw pun* (or *kanom jeen* in Central Plain language), which is similar to Chinese noodles, and *khaw tom*, a sweet made of rice, coconut milk and banana steamed in banana leaf. He also had to avoid walking under banana and coconut trees bearing fruit, as well as under clothes lines on which were hung women's garments. His technique of divination is as follows.

A patient wanting to consult him must first offer him *kaj*. This consists of an egg, flowers, a candle, a piece of cotton fluff, rice grain, and 1 or

1½ *baht* of money. This in fact constitutes his fee, but it has ritual importance inasmuch as these are the objects used in the divination. They represent a part of the patient, they are vehicles through which diagnosis is made, and they are a gift to the diviner. An expression used in the village for these ritual objects is *kryang jang hai klab baan* (literally: 'instrument given to return home').

The objects are placed on a plate, the candle is lit and fixed on the rim of the plate. Wanthong first worships (*waj*) in Buddhist fashion three times before the *kaj*. He then invites (*pao sagkhe*) the divine angels (*thewada*) to enter the egg, for it is with their help that he will summon the spirits (*phii*). Next he takes up the egg and holding it in front of the candle says magic words (*katha*) to summon the spirits. According to one version given by him, spirits of all kinds appear in the egg and he questions each whether it is the cause of the illness. If it is not the cause, it goes away; if it is, it answers.

Actually there is no explicit theory of what he sees or should see. For on another occasion, while looking at the egg during a session, he said 'paddy field, house, garden, *Tapubaan, chata khon raw...*' The words referred to the pictures that presented themselves to him.[1]

It is interesting to compare Wanthong's technique with that used by another *mau song*. This diviner puts the ritual offerings (*kaj*) into a paper funnel and looks into it. He sees certain signs which are interpreted according to the following code:

	Interpretation
Sign seen	(cause of illness)
1. a blot of black ink	organic illness (*pa yaat*)
2. red spot as in fire	*phii naa* (spirit of the rice field)
3. a red fire with brighter flames than 2	*Tapubaan* (guardian of village)
4. white lines like thread	*phii seua* (ancestral spirit)
5. glittering points of light	*phii fa* (spirit of the sky)

What then the diviner concludes from looking through the ritual object (egg or funnel) is which one of many sources of illness is at work in the case in question. A named spirit or an astrological danger or simply an organic disease is diagnosed as the cause.

Any one type of spirit from a large array may be the agent. If a guardian spirit—either *Tapubaan* or *Chao Phau Phraa Khao*—or the spirit of an

---

[1] The *chata khon raw* refers to a somewhat obscure astrological system of seven 'lines' (*sen*) which each person has, and if all of them do not appear in the egg, the diviner attributes disease to their absence. The cure requires a long-life ceremony (*sut chata*) for the missing lines to be restored.

ancestor (*phii phau phii mae*) is at work, the implication is that some wrong has been committed by the patient, but the moral aspect of the business of finding the cause is not the primary object here. Rather the attention is focused on actual procedures for removing the action of the supernatural agent. If the cause is some malevolent spirit, rather than guardian or ancestor, then by definition it is a capricious amoral agent, and no question of moral breach is involved. The *mau song* tells the patient what offering must be given to the afflicting spirit. In most cases offerings are standardized.

We now turn to the ritual officiants connected with the guardian spirits. Before seeing how they conclude the proceedings initiated by the diviner, it is appropriate to examine their mode of recruitment and relationship to each other.

Cham

The *cham* is the intermediary of the guardian spirits; the *tiam* is their medium. In theory a *medium* is superior to the intermediary, who assists the former. In practice there are some complications. Every village in the vicinity of Baan Phraan Muan has a *cham*, but not necessarily a *tiam*. The *cham* is initially chosen by the guardian spirit by possessing him; thereafter he is never or rarely possessed. He makes the offerings to the spirits either to cure illness, or to propitiate them as in the collective agricultural rites discussed above. The medium is also chosen by possession, but he experiences it on subsequent occasions when he is called upon to divine in curing ceremonies of an exceptional kind. He also plays a major role in the rain-making ceremony, which will be described later. Mediumship is rarer than the role of intermediary because it requires special psychological attributes. While the *cham* of Baan Phraan Muan is well established and publicly recognized as such, there is doubt among the villagers as to whether their medium is the genuine product. The *cham* is an intermediary of both *Chao Phau Phraa Khao* and *Tapubaan*, and in talking of his mediation both *cham* and villagers refer to the guardian spirits (*Tapu* and *Chao Phau*) as interchangeable entities. The mode of recruitment of the *cham* and the (doubtful) *tiam* indicate certain interesting features.

Bunsi, now in his late forties, became *cham* at the age of thirty-one, which again emphasizes the point that the ritual specialists we are considering here gain recognition in early adulthood. It is relevant to note that he had never been a Buddhist novice or a monk. He stated that before possession by *Chao Phau Phraa Khao* he had no particular interest in the guardian spirits. (Village theory is that *Chao Phau* or *Tapubaan* simply come into any person they choose; the choice is unpredictable beforehand, and so is the logic of the choice.) He also stated that his first possession was totally unexpected. He was sitting one day in his house when giddiness overtook him. He felt bodily tremors and lost consciousness. Those who were with him (the witnesses) reported that in this fit he spoke with a strange voice which declared itself to be *Chao Phau* and said that it wanted Bunsi as his *cham*. He was told all this when he regained consciousness.

But probing into the matter and piecing together what the villagers said, we see that the time was ripe for the recognition of a new *cham*, although it is not possible to say why Bunsi was the right candidate.

Bunsi's predecessor was a man called Beng. It was clear that he could not continue as *cham*. Apparently certain misfortunes indicated his loss of power. It is said retrospectively that his wife died because he failed to respect *Tapubaan* by not making offerings on *wan phraa*. The village concept in such a case is *pid phii* (a fault against the spirit which arouses his anger). It is also said that *Tapu* did not communicate with him any more. Village gossip also had it that he was too old to be *cham*, that he was a drunkard and was not assiduous in his duties. These may have been vital reasons for wanting to find a new *cham*.

It was in this context that the man who made claims to being the medium (*tiam*) had one of his possessions, in which *Chao Phau* speaking through him declared that he did not want Beng to be his *cham* any more. Soon afterwards Bunsi experienced possession by *Chao Phau* in the manner described earlier. After this he fell sick and had many bouts of dizziness. Beng, the *cham*, was called to treat him but he refused. The villagers were certain that the illness was caused by *Chao Phau* and that Bunsi was the chosen new candidate.

The dismissal of an existing incumbent and the recognition of a new one is a tricky business, given the theory of election by possession. For a *cham* cannot simply resign his office. He must be given permission by *Tapu* or *Chao Phau* to do so. As an informant put it: 'If the *phii* sees that the *cham* is tired, that he has been working for a long time and should be replaced by another person, then he may be allowed to give up his work. If he is not allowed, he cannot.'

To become the publicly recognized *cham* of the village, it is not enough to be possessed by the guardian spirit, for possession as such might denote either an affliction verging on madness or an ecstatic state by virtue of election. The village must decide whether election by *Chao Phau* or *Tapu* is genuine or not, whether the illness signifies a chosen representative or an affliction of a malevolent kind. Thus the village public is the final legitimizer of cult office.

In Bunsi's case, his installation was made by village decision simultaneously with the deposition of the former incumbent. A meeting of villagers was called by the headman (*puyaibaan*) and village elders, and the information was circulated that the incumbent *cham*, Beng, wished to resign his office and that therefore it was necessary to appoint a new one.

At the meeting, which was held at the *sala* (preaching hall) of the *wat*, both the outgoing and the succeeding *chams* were present. A village elder —a pious Buddhist lay leader and a *maukhwan* as well, the most respected leader in the village—first invited the *thewada* to attend the ceremony as witnesses (*pao sagkhe*) and then called upon *Tapubaan* to choose one of the two candidates as his *cham*. Bunsi alone experienced a possession by *Tapubaan* and was therefore clearly chosen. The village headman made an announcement that henceforth Bunsi would be the village *cham*. It should be noted that the Buddhist monks, who do not normally participate in the cult of the guardian spirits, were present as *necessary witnesses*. They did not, however, perform any chanting nor did they confer blessings on the proceedings, thus adhering to their segregation from the cult of the *phii*.

It came as a surprise to me, as an anthropologist, that the *cham* observed no special interdictions associated with his mediating role; nor did he prepare himself in any special ritual manner for a ceremony. In this sense he is different from the village's foremost diviner (*mau song*). I realized later that the *cham's* lack of association with special interdictions is consonant with the theory of possession: from the villagers' point of view it is completely arbitrary in that the guardian *phii* choose whomever they want, and the chosen are not distinguished by special virtues or characteristics.

Tiam

The *tiam* (or *chao phuu tiam*) is the medium of *Tapubaan*, the village guardian, and *Chao Phau Tong Khyang*, who is the spirit of the swamp, but who, in Baan Phraan Muan, is identified with *Tapubaan*, just as the latter is identified with *Chao Phau Phraa Khao* in certain contexts.

In the cult of the guardian spirits a true *tiam* is in theory given precedence over the *cham*. In Baan Phraan Muan the present *tiam* has a rather ambiguous position: in 1962 he was regarded as *tiam*, but in 1965 when I made a visit to the village his professional position was in question. This change possibly bears on village social relationships and politics. Chanla, the *tiam*, is not a respected leader, whereas the *cham*, although not himself a leader, is a more established citizen of the village. His daughter, moreover, is married to the son of the most respected leader of the village. There is enough latitude in the principles of validation of *cham*ship and *tiam*ship for villagers to question (if it seems necessary) the authenticity of one or the other. In 1965 the idea was current that Beng was not a true medium (i.e. *Tapu* did not possess him freely as his chosen representative) but that by use of magical formulae he was able to coerce spirits to enter him. This is the distinction between a medium, who is freely possessed, and an exorcist—or in village terminology, a *mau ram*—who has a guardian spirit whom he can control through magic words (*katha*) and with whose aid malevolent spirits are made to submit.

In 1962, however, the role of the incumbent *tiam* was less ambiguous in the village; three years later public opinion was divided as to whether he was *tiam* or *mau ram*, but he continued to play the role of *tiam* in certain contexts. So in what follows I shall bring out the features of Chanla's role under the aspect of mediumship.

Chanla experienced his first possession (*phii ma soon*) by *Chao Phau Tong Khyang* at the age of thirty-eight years. His possession in fact followed the standard pattern as described for *cham* Bunsi. His version is as follows: one evening while working in his house *Chao Phau* entered him. Others who were present in the house later told him that he had begun to cry and to shake. He himself had lost consciousness. On being questioned by the witnesses *Chao Phau* (through the voice of Chanla) revealed his identity. When asked the purpose of his entry into Chanla, *Chao Phau* answered that 'the village was not making progress' (*baan myang baan charoen*) because the villagers were not united, and that he had come to take Chanla as his *tiam* in order to bring about village unity. When the witnesses accepted these conditions the *Chao Phau* left Chanla.

As in the case of the *cham*, Chanla also denied that before possession he had shown any particular interest in *Chao Phau*. He had never made offerings to him at the biannual agricultural rites because his wife's father represented the household.

The possession was followed some days later by a meeting of villagers at the house of the village headman, who informed them of the possession and requested them to agree to Chanla being recognized as the *tiam*. Thus both *cham* and *tiam* must gain village recognition of their possession as signifying genuine election by the guardian spirits. The guardian spirits' election and rejection of their agents follow a standardized cultural pattern.

SPIRIT CURING BY 'CHAM' AND 'TIAM'

We are now in a position to pick up the thread and follow the procedure of spirit healing.

In most cases, if the *mau song* diagnoses that one or the other of the guardian spirits is responsible for the disease, the patient then automatically goes to the *cham*. The procedures he must follow are in two sequences, which manifest important category distinctions.

The first sequence, *kuad khaw phii*, is concerned with the 'invitation'[1] to the *phii* to leave the patient (*choen phii org*). For *kuad*, the patient or his representative has to take to the *cham* certain standard offerings (*kaj*): two lumps of rice, flower, candle, betel nut and tobacco. These objects are called *khong jang mun nee*, meaning 'things given to make it (*phii*) go away'. The *cham* uses these objects at the spirit shrine to invite the spirit to leave the patient; the invitation has a strong element of bribe and bargain, for further offerings are promised if the spirit consents to leave.

On recovery the second transaction takes place, which is the payment of the fee and a thanks-offering (*liang phii*) to the spirit which has removed itself. The offering is *pa wan* (rice mixed with sugar) if the spirit concerned is *Chao Phau Phraa Khao*, and chicken, rice and liquor if it is *Tapubaan*. As stated earlier, this payment of the fee must take place on a Wednesday.

In the usual minor procedures of spirit healing the *tiam* has no part to play, for the *cham* is sufficient to make the necessary offerings at the shrine on behalf of the patient. Minor illnesses get cured in a relatively short time.

But some illnesses become critical in the course of time or are major illnesses from the start. In the first case, if cure is not forthcoming, doubt may arise as to whether the *mau song's* diagnosis of affliction by guardian spirit is correct, or if it is, whether he has been able to determine exactly what offering is required before the spirit will leave the patient. Thus in persisting illness, if the *mau song* and *cham* have failed to effect a cure, the *tiam* (medium) is called in to make a fresh diagnosis through possession.

The medium, the *cham*, and the *cham's* assistant are invited to the patient's house. As in the case of the procedure above for approaching a *cham*, the patient's household must prepare *kaj* for the guardian spirit, but in the present instance it is more elaborate than before. Either five pairs of flowers and five pairs of candles or eight pairs of each (*kan ha*

---

[1] I wish to emphasize the linguistic connotations of *kuad*, 'invitation', which stands in direct contrast to the technique of exorcism of capricious malevolent spirits, which is called '*laiphi*' or '*kaphi*', meaning 'chasing' or 'forcing out' the spirit.

kan paed) must be provided. Other required articles are one or two pieces of cloth, an upper garment of the patient, an egg and a bottle of liquor.

The *tiam* now undergoes possession. Sitting down with eyes closed and holding the *kaj*, he invites *Chao Phau* to enter him (*phii ma soon*). This sequence is called *tiam kaj*. When the *Chao Phau* enters him he feels tremors and waves his hands (*nang ram*). He is said to lose consciousness, and while he is in this condition the *cham* and his deputy question him to find out whether it is *Chao Phau* who is afflicting the patient. Sometimes the *tiam* refutes the previous diagnosis by saying that it is not *Chao Phau* but some other spirit that is at work, or that the disease is not spirit-caused but an organic one which has to be treated by the physician (*mau ya*). If *Chao Phau* admits his responsibility, then further questions are asked to find out what he wants in the way of offerings. The action which had aroused his anger (*pid phii*) may be any of those listed in Table 6.

While chicken and liquor are the usual offering demanded, in cases of major illness, when the patient is feared to be dying, *Chao Phau* requires a more expensive offering on recovery. Chicken is replaced by one or two pigs' heads which are called *muu dam muu daeng* (black pig, red pig). This offering is expensive because normally two pigs will have to be killed.

It is said that the *kuad* (invitation to leave and promise of offering made after the diagnosis) is performed by the *cham* and his assistant with four elders as witnesses. Of course the promised offering is made only if the patient recovers.

To sum up this section on ritual specialists involved in spirit healing: the *mau song* (diviner) is not recruited by possession—he learns his craft. He plays a critical role because he is vital for the diagnosis and for the channelling of patients to the relevant experts involved in curing. The successful *mau song* is also likely to be a respected leader in the village, and may be a pious Buddhist lay leader. But the craft of *mau song* is an open and competitive one, and many specialists with widely differing techniques may exist in the same village. Baan Phraan Muan had one pre-eminent *mau song*.

The *cham* and *tiam* are recruited through possession; the former does not experience subsequent possession, the latter does. In regard to the guardian spirit cult, there can be only one *cham* and one chief *tiam* (and other subsidiary mediums) for the village, and their final recognition depends on public acceptance and validation. The *cham* and *tiam* of Baan Phraan Muan are not leaders in the village nor are they as literate as other ritual experts, especially the *mau khwan* or *paahm*, who are the respected elders of the village and often ex-monks. The *cham* and *tiam* showed little interest in Buddhist worship at the *wat*, and were not involved with the administration of *wat* affairs and the organization of Buddhist calendrical rites.

THE REGIONAL CULT

Tapubaan as guardian of the village settlement and *Chao Phau Phraa Khao* as guardian of the village *wat* are to be found in every village of the region. All these individual village expressions are pulled together in a wider comprehensive cult focused on the guardian of the largest swamp in the region, called Byng Chuan. The villages situated around this swamp participate together in propitiating this guardian.

These facts dictate an observation which I wish to emphasize: just as Buddhism finds a local representation in each village through its *wat* (which at the same time attracts devotees from many other surrounding villages to its festivals and grand merit-making occasions), and again at another level portrays a regional (or wider) participation when devotees from a whole region or country are drawn to famous common centres of worship and pilgrimage, so here in the cult of the swamp guardian we witness both regional and lower level village identities. Clearly, then, we must view the guardian spirit cult as a collective phenomenon *in some respects* comparable in scope to Buddhism, provided we keep in mind the more localizing aspect of the former—for example the domain of the village guardian shrine is a settlement of people within a small area, and that of the swamp guardian a region composed of such settlements in a specified territory; in contrast Buddhism, while it has similar structural components, cannot be exclusively defined in the same way. In so far as these two complexes are collective religious expressions we must discard that formulation which only sees Buddhism as a collective religion, organized as a 'church', while spirit cults are by comparison 'magical' and pertain to individual clients—an erroneous formulation that goes back to Robertson Smith and Durkheim and has been surprisingly revived by some contemporary anthropologists. My viewpoint will have more weight when we see that the guardian cult is characterized not only by formalized ritual but also by complex mythology.

I shall describe the cult centred around the Byng Chuan swamp, in which our village of Phraan Muan traditionally participated as a member, and how it is refracted in individual villages.

Figure 2 in Chapter 2 plots the location of the Byng Chuan swamp and the settlements in its vicinity. Some sixteen of these settlements are said to participate in propitiating the swamp guardian, who is called *Tapu*

Cult of the guardian spirits

Byng ('grandfather' or 'founding ancestor' of the swamp) or alternatively *Chao Phau* ('respected father') *Tong Khyang*.[1] The shrine to the swamp guardian is built on piles in the very centre of the swamp.

The collective propitiations addressed to the guardian are very similar to those made to the guardian spirits in village shrines—that is, biannual offerings made before ploughing and after harvesting—with these differences: the participating units are villages and not households, and the offerings made to the swamp guardian precede in time and also take ritual precedence over those made to the village guardians. Thus the regional community, constituted of village settlements, takes precedence and propitiates in advance of the individual village communities composed of households.

The offerings to the swamp guardian follow a three-year cycle. The one made before ploughing (which begins with the onset of rains in the sixth lunar month) is annual and consists of cooked chicken. The post-harvest offers, made in the second lunar month, follow a different pattern. For two consecutive years cooked chicken is given, but every third year a large offering (*liang yaai*) consisting of a buffalo sacrifice is made. Money for buying the sacrificial buffalo is collected from the member villages, and the buffalo is sacrificed at the shrine, cooked and eaten by the ritual representatives of the contributing villages.

I have already noted, in the section on *tiam*, that while villagers distinguish the swamp guardian from the village guardians, they also fuse them as a single manifestation. When distinguished, the swamp guardian is the superior; thus, for instance, *Tapu Byng* is said to be the father-in-law of *Tapubaan*. But often both are said to be one, just as within the village the village and *wat* guardians are, according to context, separated or fused. And the ritual officiants as well are seen as agents of both levels of spirits, again according to context. Above all, the swamp guardian represents, on a regional scale, what the village guardians represent at the level of local settlement, namely, the guarantors of rain, agricultural prosperity, the good health of humans and their domestic animals, especially the buffalo. It is perfectly understandable that in this dry, arid region of North-east Thailand, swamps, rivers and streams should not only be conspicuous landmarks but also symbolize rain, and the fertility of crops, and the well-being of human beings.

[1] The villages named by informants are Naabua, Hua Bueng, Naapu, Khao, Men, Ton Yaai, Ton Naui, Daun Taeng, Ngaui, Daun Yuad, Pok, Chieng Pin, Naakwang, Pong, Chieng Yuen, Sang Paen, and Phraan Muan. (All villages have the prefix Baan.) These are in fact the larger and long-established villages in the area, and on the map a square symbol (blank or containing a dot in a circle) is beside the names of those I was able to identify.

Buddhism and the spirit cults in North-east Thailand

The functionaries connected with the swamp spirit are many in number and the pattern of their differentiation allows us to bring into relief certain features in a way we could not do when describing the situation in the village of Phraan Muan. Two villages, Baan Naapu and Baan Hua Bueng, are the cult centres for all the sixteen-odd villages that participate in the cult. These are said to be the oldest villages in the area; they are also, in fact, the ones closest to the Byng Chuan swamp, with their fields stretching to its banks. Each of these two villages has a chief medium (*tiam*) of the swamp guardian who is, and always should be, a male. Of the two mediums, the one resident in Baan Naapu is considered the senior. The two function as the chief officiants of the regional cult at its biannual offerings and each acts as the chief officiant at his village shrine. Each has an assistant, the *cham*, who assists in the rites but is not the agent through whom the guardian spirit speaks. This distinction and relative position of *tiam* and *cham* was not evident in Phraan Muan village and in many other villages, for a good reason. A medium has to be 'chosen' by the spirit and should be able to experience repeated possessions by it. The appearance of such a person may occur infrequently. While a resident medium is a luxury and can be dispensed with by a village—for its residents can consult the medium of another village when exceptional circumstances require it—a *cham* is a necessity for the making of frequent offerings. Thus all villages have an appointed *cham*, even if they have no *tiam*.

The rather complex situation that arises may be stated as follows. In addition to the two chief mediums resident in the cult centres, and the subsidiary mediums randomly distributed in the region, there is in every village an appointed male intermediary (*cham*), who normally makes the offerings to the village guardians at village shrines, collects money and food offerings from village members, and acts as the representative of his village in the biannual rites addressed to the swamp guardian at his swamp shrine.

Whereas at the cult centres and at the swamp shrine the prime officiants at rites of propitiation are the *mediums*, assisted by the intermediaries, in villages other than the cult centres the intermediary tends to act as officiant, with the medium, if present in the village, figuring mainly in divination procedures in severe cases of affliction.

Now we can deal with the interesting phenomenon of the subsidiary mediums. They are usually *female* but not exclusively so. As in the case of Phraan Muan village, they are sometimes male. It is not at all strange that the female mediums are concentrated in the cult centres. In the village of Naapu there were three and at Hua Bueng one, all four subordinate to the chief male mediums. Their main role is to deal with individual cases of affliction by the swamp or village guardian spirits, who, apart from their communal significance, act punitively to cause illness in individuals. In such instances, the female mediums, serving as oracles of the guardian spirit, inform the victim and his family whether the spirit is responsible for the illness and, if it is, what offerings it requires as expiation. The subsidiary mediums also have a wider divinatory role, for the guardian spirit of the swamp, in his capacity as benevolent protector of humans and being superior to lesser, capricious spirits, can also reveal which malevolent spirit is causing a particular affliction and what placatory offering would be efficacious. Thus the guardian spirit, in his benevolent aspect, serves to combat the ravages caused by lesser, capricious and malevolent agents.

The sex composition of the mediums of the guardian spirits, their mode of recruitment, and their ritual techniques, open up important questions of comparison. All mediums are recruited through possession, and the distinctive features of their rituals are ecstatic possession and dance, and oracular statements—which characteristics are altogether different from those exhibited by monks and the *paahm* who conduct *sukhwan* rituals. Linked with these features is the fact that, although the chief mediums of the cult are male, the majority of subsidiary mediums are female. Here, then, for the first time in village religion we see an opening for *female* functionaries associated with a certain kind of religious expression.

This correlation is manifestly recognized by villagers. Women are by temperament prone to possession and the spirits possess them because they are soft and penetrable; therefore they are effective hosts. (Although we are here interested in female mediums, it is appropriate to note that this logic is extended to possession by evil spirits and ensuing illness; as we shall see later, women are said to be the commonest victims of attack and subjects of exorcistic cure.) Such ideas are perhaps more finely elaborated in North Thailand, where mediums are called *maa khii*, that is, 'horses ridden' by spirits. Usually such mediums have suffered attack by the spirit (expressed as illness, fits, or certain states of dissociation) and were 'cured' only when they agreed to subject themselves to the authority and sovereignty of the spirit and thus became his medium; that is, the cure consists in redirecting the illness itself to a positive and culturally acceptable use. We may thus state that the guardian spirit cult, in so far as it is associated with afflictions resulting from attack by the guardian spirits, has a special kind of female functionary who through possession acts as their vehicle. This is the only sphere in which females have a dominant ritual role to play.

Buddhism and the spirit cults in North-east Thailand

While the role is not confined only to females, it emphasizes a 'feminine syndrome' of behaviour. Both males and females who act as the vehicles and whose position is that of mediator between humans and the guardian *phii*, adopt a ceremonial dress and engage in behaviour that is somewhat ambiguous. The costume consists of a black waist cloth or skirt, and a blouse, head cloth, and handkerchief all red in colour. If these are worn by a male, he resembles a female; if worn by a female, she resembles a man. That is to say, the mediator assumes somewhat of a transvestite appearance, and engages in an unrestrained ecstatic behaviour in which liberal consumption of liquor and smoking tobacco is an element. The transformation is especially conspicuous in a female medium who, in addition to all these features, speaks in a male-like voice.

For reasons of insufficient data and competence I must conclude the discussion on this note, a discussion limited to the reporting of cultural conceptualization of the mediums' characteristics and observed role behaviour, and not venture into the possible motivational and psychological aspects of the medium's personality. Spiro's (1967) discussion of these aspects in respect of the Burmese *nat kadaw* (*nat* wife), who conventionally is a female medium of the *nats* while in fact, as in our case, a small number of males also assume the role, seems to be echoed here, but I am unable to confirm his interpretation.

16

MYTH AND RITE: THE 'NAGA' SYMBOL AND THE ROCKET FESTIVAL

In the previous chapter I described the beliefs and rites associated with the two guardian spirits of the village, and indicated how they link up with the regional cult pertaining to the guardian of the Byng Chuan swamp. This in turn led us to consider the place and significance of natural phenomena such as swamps and rivers in the life, thought, and religious system of villagers.

I shall now explore this question further by describing and analysing the festival called *Bunbangfai*, which is concerned with soliciting rain before the annual paddy agricultural cycle starts and is addressed to the spirit of the swamp and the village guardians. Following this I shall document and analyse a myth which in the minds of the villagers is linked with the *Bunbangfai* festival. The myth has two facets: it relates the story of the origin of swamps and rivers, and it deals with the question of the relation between man and beast, between society and nature, thereby providing a moral and theological basis for the cult of guardian spirits.

In the concluding section of this chapter two linked issues are taken up. One is the relation between Buddhist ritual and the cult of the guardian spirits, and the second the relation between myth and rite. These relationships are elucidated by comparing the grand Buddhist festival of *Bun Phraawes* with the rain-making festival of *Bunbangfai*. Both festivals are composed of myths and rites, the reciprocal relationship between which constitutes a classical problem in anthropology.

Before I describe the festival of *Bunbangfai* it is well to bear in mind the data covered so far. I have indicated some of the ways in which Buddhist rites are kept separate from the cult of the *phii*. I have also demonstrated that there are certain links between Buddhism and the village guardians. *Chao Phau Phraa Khao* is regarded as a pious Buddhist who guards the *wat*; both he and *Tapubaan*, the guardian of the village, are enforcers of rules concerning the Buddhist Sabbath. The distinction between Buddhism and the *phii* cult is most marked at the level of ritual behaviour; monks do not participate in the biannual collective agricultural rites addressed to the guardian spirits, nor are they concerned with the healing of afflictions caused by *phii* which act as moral punishing agents or as capricious malevolent forces. Category opposition is conspicuous in regard to religious office: the monk, subject to an ascetic regimen and rigorous self-control, stands opposed to the ritual officiants of guardian spirits, the *tiam* and *cham*, who are recruited not because of their moral worth but arbitrarily through possession by the spirits. They do not practise the disciplined life of the pious layman (*upasok*), and their ritual techniques are ecstatic. The contrast reaches its extreme formulation in the association of mediumship with females.

These comparisons, however, are not the end of the story, as we shall see from events enacted in the festival.

THE FESTIVAL OF 'BUNBANGFAI'

Bunbangfai means literally the 'merit of (firing) rockets'. The rockets in question are made locally in the village by packing 'black powder' (nitre) into bamboo sections, which are then reinforced with rope. A 'tail' is attached to the rocket which is ignited by lighting a wick. Each rocket is decorated gaily with ribbons and streamers. The rockets go up a fair distance and the mark of good craftsmanship is their straight upward trajectory.

Bunbangfai is a ceremony of regional importance, and is directly associated with the guardian spirit of the Byng Chuan swamp and the guardian spirits of the village. The rocket ceremony, it is said, is addressed to the powerful guardian spirit of the swamp, *Chao Phau Tong Khyang* (or *Tapu Byng*); it is performed to pay him respect, and to request him to confer prosperity and good health and to send rain ('*tham haj ju dii mii haeng, kho fa kho fon*'). It is in fact primarily a rain-making ritual; if the ceremony is not performed the swamp guardian spirit will be angry, rains may not fall, and he may withdraw his protection so that both villagers and their buffaloes will fall ill.

But unlike the propitiations to the guardian spirits before ploughing and after harvesting, which are conducted both at a regional level in the swamp shrine and in each village at the *Tapubaan* shrine (which I have described earlier), the rocket-firing ritual is conducted by each village separately. It is not merely a propitiation but is also a festival whose proceedings take three days. It is comparable with the Buddhist *Bun Phraawes* festival, which is conducted by each village separately as a post-harvest thanks-offering (Chapter 10); in fact these two festivals are, as we shall see, linked in a complementary fashion.

In Baan Phraan Muan, as in other villages, the ceremony is addressed both to the guardian spirit of the swamp and to the two guardian deities of the village (*Tapubaan* and *Chao Phau Phraa Khao*). I have already expounded the logic by which the villagers sometimes merge the two village guardians—of the *wat* and of the village—in the single concept of *Tapubaan*, and the latter in turn with *Tapu Byng*, the guardian of the swamp. Thus in each village it is the Buddhist temple (*wat*) and the *Tapubaan* shrine (*hau tapu*) which are the foci for the rites. The bringing together of the temple and the spirit shrine in a ritual sense is paralleled by a spatial link between them. In many villages of the region the *Tapubaan* shrine stands in the compound of the Buddhist temple, often a few yards from the *bood* (or *viharn*). The shrine is simple, small, crudely made of wood, and faces the village and thereby guards it; the *bood* in contrast is the most imposing and magnificent piece of stone architecture in the village, and faces east. What values are expressed in this juxtaposition, which is at the same time a startling comparison? Traditionally, the temple and the spirit shrine belonged together, like the *vihare* and the *devale* in Buddhist Ceylon. Nowadays, some villages, Baan Phraan Muan among them, have separated them, possibly under ecclesiastical pressure, and have placed the shrine at the back of the *wat* compound.

One of the problems that the festival of rocket-firing poses is the pattern of the complex integration of Buddhism and the guardian spirit cult in the *same* ritual. There are two major sequences to the festival: first, monks are ordained, and in some years a monk 'promotion' ceremony is also held at the same time (see Chapter 7); following this Buddhist sequence is the ecstatic procession, the paying of respect to *Tapubaan*, and the firing of the rockets. Superficially it looks as if the 'opposed' sequences have been tacked on together; yet the situation is not as simple as this because the role of the monks themselves in the festival is complex—they take part in some sequences and segregate themselves from others. This fascinating festival has puzzled some observers. For instance, one writer (Faure in Berval 1959) has called the festival, witnessed in Vientiane the capital of Laos,

dichotomous...since important religious ceremonies and profane rejoicings follow one another in turn, and without the least transition; the people attending them both passing effortlessly from the deepest piety to the most exuberant merriment...It cannot be denied that it is a religious festival since its foremost object is to glorify the Buddha, His Birth, His Doctrine and His Death...and for this reason it includes both a procession of the whole of the Buddhist clergy, piously followed by the Crown, and by a public Buddhist ordination ceremony conducted in order to elevate to higher office, monks already ordained. But it is also a profane festival, which in many respects, may be compared to our carnival and which affords participants an opportunity for fancy dresses, dances, songs and lively puppet shows whose undisguised realism carry their audiences to the very opposite of the procession and sacred rites. (p. 273.)

Although the festival performed in the village is not as grand as that staged in the capital of Laos, its structure and pattern are revealed more clearly in the village performance. Faure makes the oft-repeated mistake of identifying only Buddhist rites as 'religious' and the ritual sequences directed to fertility and fecundity as 'profane' because of their 'excessiveness'. Nor is it valid to describe the festival as 'dichotomous', if by this word is meant the tacking together of incompatible parts. I shall argue, and such an argument is a central thesis of this book, that the festival portrays a 'necessary' linkage between Buddhism and the guardian spirit cult and that it highlights how the two ritual complexes relate to one another in a logical and orderly fashion. Before describing the sequences of the rocket-firing festival as staged in the village it is necessary to comment on two problems, one relating to the timing of the festival and the other to its name, especially the prefix *bun*.

At the regional cult centre of village Napu it was reported that the festivities were held every year in the middle of the 6th lunar month (*dyan hog peng*) from the 14th to the 16th, with the 15th being the crucial day. This coincides with the full moon of May. Faure (*ibid.*) reports that in Vientiane the festival takes place on the 15th day of the waxing moon of the 6th month. According to the Buddhist calendar this is the day of Visakha Bucha, the day on which the Buddha was born, the day on which he achieved *nirvana*, and the day he died. Because of this synchronization of Visakha and the rocket festival, it can be argued that the first part of the festival centring on ordination and promotion of monks is the Buddhist part, for it is an appropriate day for glorifying the Buddha and his doctrine.

But this association does not appear to hold for Baan Phraan Muan, where the date on which the rocket festival is held varies according to the exigencies of the agricultural cycle. It is held at any time between the 6th and 8th lunar months, in theory on the 15th day of the waxing moon, but in fact on any convenient day in the waxing period. (In 1966, for instance, the rocket-firing was on the 11th day.) There is no recognition in the village that the ceremony is in any way associated with Visakha, which occasion we have seen is not important for the village calendar of temple festivals (Chapter 10). The chief consideration for the villagers in choosing the day is the calculation of when rains will fall so that the rice agricultural cycle can begin.

However, the name of the festival, *Bunbangfai*, poses a linguistic puzzle; it has the Buddhist concept of merit, *bun*, as its prefix. Villagers, applying their usual category distinctions which separate Buddhism from the cults relating to *phii* spirits, are explicit that '*Bunbangfai* has nothing to do with Buddhist monks; it is not related to Buddhism; it is a matter concerning *phii*'. We shall, however, see that the monks are both involved and not involved in curious ways, and that what the villagers are saying is that *Bunbangfai* is not a Buddhist festival at which monks officiate, not that there is no link with Buddhism whatsoever. Furthermore, we have seen that the Buddhist festival of *Bun Phraawes* which precedes *Bunbangfai* is also to some extent concerned with rains and agricultural prosperity. Indeed, there are some fascinating links between the two ritual complexes which we must explore and illuminate.

'BUNBANGFAI' IN BAAN PHRAAN MUAN

Some days before the festival, preparations are made for the making of the rockets. Money is collected from every householder in the village for buying 'black powder'. The amount collected depends on how many rockets are to be made, and this is governed, as we shall see shortly, by another important consideration. A point to note is that the rockets are made in the *wat* by monks and villagers. The participation of monks in rocket-making is a general feature in all villages, and indeed monks are considered the experts at this craft. The rockets are then stored in the *wat*.

There are two rockets—one called *bang tawai* (rocket for paying respect) and the other *bang siang* (wishing rocket), both intended for *Tapubaan* the village guardian—which are made every year and are necessary ritual articles. In addition other rockets are made, the number depending on the scale of the festival. The scale of the ceremony varies according to the occurrence or non-occurrence of an event which critically relates *Bunbangfai* to Buddhism, namely ordination of novices and monks, which is ideally the first phase of the proceedings. If the rocket-firing is to be immediately preceded by the ordination of Buddhist novices and monks, then it is characterized by the making of a large number of rockets (about ten to twelve), with the two ritually important rockets being especially large, and the holding of a village fair at night with much merriment and drinking. In the absence of ordination only two small rockets are made and there is no fair. Since it is only in exceptional years that no ordination takes place, my description will be that of a normal festival.

The festival divides into three sequences: ordination (and promotion) of monks (*bun buad*), the rocket procession (*hae bangfai*), and the firing of the rockets.

In the following discussion I shall describe mainly the festival staged in 1964. (In the appendix to this chapter, I describe briefly the highlights of the same ceremony performed in the village of Napu, the cult centre for the region.)

Ordination

In 1964 in the evening of the 11th day of the 8th lunar month, three novices were ordained at the beginning of the festivities. This ordination was sponsored by the entire village. On the previous day, called *wan hoam* (the day of collecting), the ritual articles necessary for the ordination were brought to the *wat* by the villagers, and the *sukhwan nag* ceremony (calling the spirit essence of the ordinands) was held by the elders in the afternoon; after ordination on the following day the resident monks chanted *suad mongkhon* that night. These sequences the reader will recognize as the usual ones connected with ordination. Hence the question arises, what is the relation between this special ordination associated with *Bunbangfai* and the annual ordination of village youth before the Lent season? The answer is that a varying proportion of the youth, sometimes all the candidates, ordained in a particular year are ordained on this occasion.[1] Thus it is clear that the timing of ordination with *Bunbangfai*, which is explicitly recognized as a rain-making ritual, has very important implications for our understanding of how the institution of monkhood is related and adapted to village interests.

How is ordination, which is strictly a Buddhist institution, related to the propitiation of the guardian spirits of the swamp and village? As I have already reported, villagers who are explicit that '*Bunbangfai*' has nothing to do with Buddhist monks (an important 'first response' to the anthropologist's question) explain that the word *bun* (merit) appears in the name of the ceremony because novices and monks are ordained in order to make merit for and to transfer merit to the guardian spirits. Transference of merit by the living to ancestors and by humans to deities and spirits is, we have seen already, an important reciprocity mechanism in Buddhist religious action.

Even more significant for the issue under discussion is the monk promotion ceremony conducted on the same day, which, although exceptional in occurrence, is nevertheless very telling. I refer the reader to the details of the water-pouring ceremony, by which a monk is elevated to *Somdet* (described in Chapter 7). Monks and villagers pour water into a wooden receptacle in the form of a snake (*Naga*) and the water flows through the head and throat on to the monk's head and body. When the promotion

---

[1] By Canonical law the maximum number that can be ordained in one common ceremony is three.

ceremony does occur, it is often conducted together with the ordination rites preceding the *Bunbangfai* festival. It is clear that in this ceremony the *Naga* is seen as a friend and guardian of Buddhism; at the same time, since he is associated with rain and fertility, the ceremony connotes the sacred *Naga* enhancing and cleansing the monk who is being honoured. Since this drama is staged at a rain-invoking festival we are justified in asserting the equation: just as the *Naga* pours water on the monk to increase his sacredness, so may rain fall on the fields and increase their agricultural fertility. But note the paradox: in the case of the monk it is his non-sexual sacredness that is increased; in the case of the layman their material prosperity and fertility. The resolution of the paradox is the one I have argued previously. The monk is a mediator and vehicle, and it is precisely his access to sacred life-renouncing power that is transformed and transferred into life-giving powers for the layman. What is of interest to us in the ceremony is that it is the *Naga* that acts as the vehicle for transferring sacredness.

'Hae bangfai' (the rocket procession)

The rocket procession constitutes the second phase of the *Bunbangfai* festivities. In 1964 it was held in the afternoon of the day following the ordination (i.e. on the afternoon of the 12th day of the 8th lunar month).

The procession was formed with the *tiam* (medium), dressed in his clothes of office (red shirt and blouse and handkerchief tied on the head), the *cham* (intermediary) with *kanha* (offering of flowers and candles), and his assistant at the head. These ritual officiants of the guardian spirit cult danced as they led the procession. They were followed by the village elders, carrying the rockets which had been placed in a crudely constructed palanquin. It was said that all those villagers who had previously been cured by one of the guardian spirits also danced, because *Tapubaan* or *Chau Phau* was acting upon them. According to the theory, during the procession possession is experienced both by *Tapubaan's* officiants and those he has cured (the latter of whom may be described as the 'community of sufferers', to borrow a phrase from Victor Turner). In fact, all participants drank great quantities of liquor and their behaviour was dionysiac and uninhibited, this contrasting sharply with the processions in Buddhist festivals.

An important feature to note is that monks did not take part in this procession, even though it formed in the *wat* compound. After leaving the compound, it wove in and out of the village settlement, and then made its way to the *Tapubaan* shrine. It circumambulated the shrine three times, and then the intermediary with offering in hand addressed a prayer to the guardian spirit, saying: 'Please give rain, good health and prosperity, and prevent our oxen, buffaloes, pigs, ducks and chickens from falling sick.' The rockets were dedicated, and the rocket named *bang tawai* (rocket of offering) was fired. The procession then returned to the *wat* and circumambulated the *sala* (preaching hall) three times; the remaining rockets were taken into the *sala* and stored for the night.

That night the fair was staged in the *wat* compound. Before the entertainment started, the monks chanted *suad mongkhon bangfai* (blessing chant on behalf of the rockets) in the *sala*. Thus we note that here the monks participated for the first time in the proceedings connected with rockets: they did not participate in the propitiation of the village guardian, but they now chanted Buddhist sacred words of blessing, thereby supplementing and reinforcing the proceedings in the Buddhist mode. Once again the Buddhist sequence is separated from the guardian cult propitiation; yet they are complementary and supplementary.

The entertainment at the fair consisted, as in most village fairs, of *ramwong* (dancing), *maulum* (folk opera), and, as in recent years, a film show. A fair of this proportion is held only when the *Bunbangfai* is accompanied by ordination of monks and novices, and it is marked by the dedication of a large number of rockets to *Tapubaan*.

The firing of the rockets

On the following morning the rocket-firing festivities took place. First of all the monks were feasted at the *wat* by the villagers in order to make merit, and then all the remaining rockets were carried to a launching site near the fields.

Next followed what is ritually the most important sequence—the firing of the wishing rocket (*bang siang*), which actually will foretell the outcome of the wishes made to *Tapubaan*. If the rocket flies straight and high the omens are auspicious. The intermediary (*cham*) first addressed the guardian spirit thus: 'If there is to be prosperity, health and rain, let the rocket rise high, if there is not to be prosperity...let the rocket fail.' Then the rocket was fired; its trajectory was declared to be auspicious.

There is some looseness of interpretation by the villagers concerning the symbolism of the two rockets thus far ignited, the first on the previous evening and the second just described. Some informants held that the rocket of offering (*bang tawai*) is also a wishing rocket and that it represents the wish for rain, while the rocket fired the next morning expresses the wish for the good health and prosperity of the villagers and their buffaloes. It would seem that this interpretation would act as an insurance against the possible failure of using a single rocket as a prophesying agent. Since the chances are that both rockets will not fail, the prophecy can be manipulated in favour of the villagers.

The firing of the second rocket gave way to proceedings whose character can only be described as ritual licence. Virtually the entire village congregated, *including the monks and novices*. The remaining rockets were fired in a spirit of competition. If a rocket either failed to take off or did not go high, the unsuccessful firer was subjected to mud-throwing. This punishment was meted to everyone without distinction, *including monks and village elders* (*phuu thaw*), both of whom participated in the firing. Thus it is clear that the ritual licence allowed dissolves the two most important hierarchical statuses in the village—the Buddhist monk, who normally is highly respected and socially distinct, and the lay elder, who by virtue of his generational superiority and headship of the compound clusters is respected, wields a certain amount of authority, and occupies a position of leadership in the village. *Bunbangfai* represents the one occasion in village life when such extreme privileged joking is allowed. During *Songkran* (New Year) festivities a certain amount of licence is allowed. Young people throw water on everyone indiscriminately. Throwing mud is, however, a more disrespectful and insolent act in normal circumstances.

The ritual licence is regarded as 'fun'. Games were played, cockfighting was staged, as well as 'buffalo fighting' with young men impersonating the bulls. Young men devised ways of extracting money from the spectators for buying liquor. One such is to carry around to houses an evil-smelling vulture tied to a rope; money was given quickly to get rid of the odour.

Let me recapitulate and summarize what seem to constitute the dominant features of *Bunbangfai*. It is a cult addressed to the guardian spirits, who are invested with power to grant rain and good health to the village. As such they are concerned with basic and vital interests. In propitiating them the villagers see them as elevated deities, not malevolent spirits. They are approached as children approach a powerful father figure who grants his favours as a result of wishes expressed in the right manner. The approach has, however, an element of bargaining, characteristic of the approach made to them for the cure of illness and in the biannual agricultural rites, analysed earlier. Thus for instance in 1965 the village ritual was made on a relatively minor scale, but at the ceremony a promise was made that if there was copious rainfall the villagers would make bigger rockets the following year.

In so far as monks do not participate in the procession to the shrine nor in the propitiation, the guardian cult is segregated from Buddhist rituals such as *Bun Phraawes*. *Bunbangfai*, nevertheless, has important links with Buddhism which are woven into the texture of the festivities while certain category distinctions are kept clear. The monks help in the making of the rockets, which are stored in the *wat*. In the first sequence of the festival monks and novices are ordained in a strictly Buddhist ceremonial; but at the same time, one of the chief purposes of the ordination is to transfer merit to the guardian deities. And also connected with the ordination is the occasional monk elevation ceremony.

The propitiation of *Tapubaan* and the firing of the wishing rockets are, however, among the sequences in which Buddhist monks do not participate. These sequences express the category opposition between Buddhism and the guardian spirit cult, for no Buddhist monk can worship or propitiate a spirit. But we note at the same time in a separate sequence, after the rocket procession is over, the monks on that same night chant *suad mongkhon* on behalf of the success of the rockets. Here the Buddhist sequence is supplementary and reinforces the wishes of the villagers for rain and fertility. At the same time that the villagers propitiate *Tapubaan* for rain and fertility they are also making merit in the Buddhist way to double their chances of success. The essential requirement is that monks should not propitiate *Tapubaan*, whereas the villagers can have two strings to their bow—they can practise Buddhism and also propitiate the guardian deities.

The structure of the *Bunbangfai* festival shows an arrangement whereby the Buddhist sequences in which monks participate are kept separate from those in which the officiants of the spirit cult participate, and order is obtained by fusing the sequences without confusing them. Only in the final sequences are all distinctions of social and religious hierarchy temporarily dissolved in ritual licence, as a prelude to beginning a new agricultural and religious cycle.

Having described the *Bunbangfai* festival, I shall now proceed to consider two versions of the myth associated with it.

THE MYTH OF PHADAENG AND NANG AI

Version 1 (related by Phau Nu, a village elder)

Thao Pangkee was once upon a time the 'hired child' (*luug chang*) or servant of a rich couple who in due course gave their daughter Nang Ai in marriage to him. One day Pangkee and his wife went into the forest and there found a wild fig tree (*ton mai ma deua*) bearing fruits. Pangkee asked his wife to climb the tree to pick fruits, which she did, but when she descended she found her husband missing. She searched for him without success, and in the course of the search she came to a river. She then vowed by the bank of the river that in her next life she would not meet a husband like Pangkee, who had deserted her. After their deaths Pangkee was born the son of a *Naga* ruler[1] named Sirisutho, and Nang Ai was born the daughter of Phaya Korm, the ruler of Naung Haan.

Thao Phadaeng, the ruler of a city called Pha Pong, courted Nang Ai and they became lovers. Nang Ai's father, Phaya Korm,[2] proclaimed his intention to hold the rocket festival called *Bunbangfai*, and Phadaeng and Phaya Chieng Han, another ruler, decided to compete in it. Pangkee, the *Naga* prince, also heard the news about the rocket festival and since he had heard about Nang Ai's beauty he wanted very much to see her. So he transformed himself into a human being and attended the festival but he failed to see Nang Ai. The winner of the rocket competition was Phaya Chieng Han; Phadaeng's rocket failed to take off.

Pangkee returned to the *Naga* city, but he still yearned to see Nang Ai. So he solicited permission from his parents to go up again to the human world. They agreed, unwillingly, and sent their *Naga* army to accompany him. When they emerged from the water, Pangkee took the form of a white squirrel (*gahog daun*) and jumped from tree to tree. The accompanying *Naga* soldiers transformed themselves into birds and followed him.

Nang Ai, in her palace at this time, felt uneasy and fretful (*mai pen sug*). She felt she did not want to stay inside, so she went and sat outside in the garden. There she saw the squirrel at the foot of a tree; it was a beautiful animal with golden bells round its neck and a melodious voice. She wanted to possess it and asked her maids and pages to catch it, but they were unsuccessful. She thereupon sent for a hunter who had a cross-bow (*na seeng*). The hunter said that it was not possible for him to catch the squirrel alive but that he could kill it. Nang Ai agreed, and the hunter shot the squirrel. Before it died, it said farewell to its *Naga* parents. Phra In[3] came down from heaven and daubed the squirrel's body with perfume (*kreuang haum*).

The meat of the squirrel filled 8,000 wagons and was distributed to all the citizens except old widows, because they did not help in the work (*mai chuay gnaan*). The hunter was given a leg and he too distributed the meat to several others.

The *Naga* army returned to their city bearing the sad news to Pangkee's parents. The parents became very wrathful and, leading their army, burrowed underground, churned up the mud and attacked the human settlements, which sank into the ground. This is how Naung Huan and Byng Chuan became large swamps.

[1] *Naga*, as noted earlier, may be translated as water serpent or dragon.
[2] Korm means Khmer. He was thus a Khmer (Cambodian king).   [3] God Indra.

Meanwhile Phadaeng, who had been away during the killing of the squirrel, had come to visit his sweetheart, Nang Ai, but his journey was obstructed by logs on the ground. (These logs were the *naga* who had thus transformed themselves.) When he met Nang Ai he inquired what building was going to be constructed, since he had seen so many logs. Nang Ai told him about the killing of the squirrel. She then set out food for him, but he did not eat the meat because it was so sweet-smelling. He asked Nang Ai 'Why did you eat this meat? Are you not afraid that the city will sink?' They went to sleep, but before dawn they heard the noise of the earth cracking (*pandin lun*). Phadaeng fled with Nang Ai on horseback, and they took with them the regalia of the city (*prachum myang*), namely the gong (*kong*), the drum (*glong*), and the ring (*waen*).

The horse found galloping heavy going because of the mud, so the riders threw away the gong, and the place where it fell was called *Baan Nam Kong*; next they threw away the drum, and the place where it fell was called *Baan Naung Glong*. Finally the ring was thrown away, and the place where it fell became *Baan Non Waen*. Phaya *Naga* kept pursuing them, caught up with them, lashed out with his tail and swept Nang Ai from horseback. Phadaeng alone escaped.

Version 2 (related by Phau Champi, village elder and leader)

There was a ruler of a city called Myang Naung Haan and his name was Phraya Korm.[1] He had a daughter called Nang Ai and she was exceedingly beautiful.

Phraya Korm decided to hold a rocket-firing competition in the sixth lunar month (*dyan hog peng*), and ordered his subjects to make the necessary preparations. Phadaeng, who lived in Myang Pong (and who was in love with Nang Ai and she with him), made a rocket in order to participate; so did Phraya Siang Hian, the ruler of the city of Siang Hian Fa Daed. Phraya Korm also decided to be a competitor, and offered the wager that the person whose rocket went up highest would be the winner and would be awarded his daughter, Nang Ai; if his own went highest, Nang Ai would not be awarded to anyone.

On the day of the competition, Thao Pangkee, the son of the *Naga* ruler, came up (from his subterranean residence) to witness the competition and he saw Princess Nang Ai and fell in love with her. Pangkee and Nang Ai were in a previous life husband and wife, but Pangkee had not been attentive to her (*mai liow lae*) and so they had separated. In this life in turn Nang Ai did not pay any attention to Pangkee.

The results of the rocket-firing were as follows: Phraya Korm's rocket

[1] As stated earlier, Korm means Khmer.

exploded and did not go up; neither did Phadaeng's. Siang Hian was the winner but since he was already married he did not take Nang Ai. Both Phraya Korm and Phadaeng were depressed by the failure of their rockets, for this was a bad omen and they feared that their subjects would not enjoy prosperity and good health.

Pangkee, the *Naga* prince, still in love with Nang Ai, took the disguise of a white squirrel (*gahog daun*), wearing a collar with a bell attached. He was most beautiful to behold. He climbed up to the top of a tree. Birds crowded round him because of his beauty. Princess Nang Ai saw the squirrel and wanted very much to have it. A hunter was called to shoot the squirrel, and he shot it. The squirrel fell down from the tree and as it lay dying said in its last gasp to Nang Ai: 'Why do you want to eat the white squirrel's meat? Are you not afraid that the kingdom will sink into the ground?'[1]

Phraya Korm and Phadaeng, and all the people, also heard the squirrel's last words. When the people cut up the squirrel, its meat filled 8,000 carts. All came to take away the meat except an old widow (*mae mai*) who was late in coming. Phadaeng was surprised and apprehensive about the squirrel's words, so he ordered Nang Ai to go away with him on a horse, whose name was Bak Saam. He told her to bring with her the 'good things' (*khong dee dee*)[2] of the city, namely ring (*waen*), gong (*kong*), and drum (*glong*). They sped on horseback towards Phadaeng's town of Pha Pong.

Soon after they set out, the earth behind them cracked and sank down. Phraya Korm's town was submerged and became the swamp Naung Haan. The island in the middle of the swamp was the house of the old widow who did not eat the meat. The hill is called *noon mae mai*. The citizens who lived where the swamp Byng Chuan now stands, when they heard about the squirrel meat, tried to persuade (*chuan*) one another to go and take a share. While they were doing so, their town sank and became the swamp Byng Chuan. The people of another town doubted (*sang*)[3] as to whether they should or should not go to take some meat: their town sank and became the swamp Byng Sang.

Things happened to Phadaeng and Nang Ai as they were fleeing. After some distance the horse, Bak Saam, became very tired and fell down and died. This place was called Huay (tributary) Saam Paad. Phadaeng and Nang Ai then started to walk, carrying the regalia with them. Because they were heavy, Phadaeng asked Nang Ai to throw away the ring (*waen*), the

---

[1] According to another version recorded in a pamphlet printed in the town of Kon Kaen, Pangkee made the dying wish to God Indra that his meat should increase in quantity and that all people, except widows and divorcees, should eat it.
[2] The regalia of the town and kingdom.
[3] In Central Thai the equivalent word is *song sai*.

Buddhism and the spirit cults in North-east Thailand

gong (*kong*) and the drum (*glong*): the place where the ring fell was called swamp Naung Waen, and where the gong and drum fell Huay (tributary) Nam Kong Glong Si. All these geographical features are in Kumpawapi District, Udorn province.

ANALYSIS OF THE MYTH

I have presented the myth as related to me by two Phraan Muan village informants. The myth is well known throughout the entire North-east, and while there are variations of detail as told in different parts of the North-east, the main plot and structure of the myth remain the same.

The myth has two associations for the villagers of this region. It tells of the origin of the various swamps and rivers in the region. Clearly one of the concerns of the myth is to relate the origin and naming of these ecological phenomena which are of such vital interest to villagers living in a dry land. The swamps, for instance, connote perennial water and symbolize rain. In different regions of the North-east the geographical details of the story, such as the names of rivers, swamps and lakes, are changed to correspond to the phenomena of the local region. In presenting the 'social geography' of the region, the myth serves to give a sense of regional identity to the people, as well as a sense of history in that in the mythical past their territories were parts of kingdoms whose capitals were cities, like Sakorn Nakorn, which still exist today.

The villagers view the myth as also related to the origin of the rocket festival (*Bunbangfai*). The myth itself includes a rocket-firing competition, and villagers, after relating the myth, are apt to say, 'This is why we fire the rockets', referring to the competition. The anthropologist, however, notes that the *Bunbangfai* rite has no direct relation to the details of the myth; it is not a simple reflection of the myth.

Apart from these conscious associations, the observer senses an underlying theme, ostensibly presented as a conflict between man and the dragon of the water, but in fact stating a complex relationship between man and nature. This will emerge as the details of the myth are analysed. Since the two versions of the myth agree on essentials, I shall treat them together.

The myth is constructed around a triangular contest. Pangkee, the son of the *Naga* (embodiment of water and the underworld), is opposed to and in competition with the male human protagonist, Phadaeng (who is a ruler of human beings), for a prize represented by a female character, Princess Nang Ai.

The relationship between the three figures is a balanced opposition.

In a previous life, Pangkee and Nang Ai were husband and wife, but

Pangkee was a bad husband and abandoned Nang Ai. In the later life Pangkee falls in love with Nang Ai but she rejects him, and by virtue of her vow is bound to destroy him. We note that in the previous life, Pangkee deserted Nang Ai while she was up a tree picking figs; in the later life Pangkee himself was shot, at Nang Ai's instigation, while he in turn was up a tree.

The relationship between Phadaeng and Nang Ai also carries an element of stalemate. While the two return each other's love, Phadaeng fails to win her legitimately when he loses the rocket competition. It is the losing of this competition by Phadaeng and also by Nang Ai's father through the failure of their rockets, which signifies impending disaster and leads to the next stage of the drama. On Pangkee's side, his persistent and unrequited love for Nang Ai also serves as the catalyst for the movement of the plot.

The myth reaches its climax when Pangkee, a creature of the underworld, takes the form of an attractive trickster, a white squirrel, an arboreal creature. He is killed and his meat, which is inexhaustible, is eaten by all the people except old widows and the hero Phadaeng. The manifest meaning of the story is that the killing and eating of the squirrel results in the disappearance of human settlements and their transformation into swamps. I would suggest that the latent meaning is that the eating of the meat represents the union of man and nature. The swamps and lakes containing perennial water are the product of this union. They contain portions of the *Naga* prince eaten by human beings; his dismemberment also accounts for his multiple presence in individual swamps. The swamps in turn represent ancient submerged human settlements. Thus, while the plot of the myth overtly predicates an antagonism between man and nature, the underlying message is the resolution of the relationship between them in terms of fertile union and sharing of common properties. It is relevant to note that old widows, being barren and useless, were excluded, and escaped the disaster because they did not eat the meat.

The same message comes through in the last part of the myth which describes the attempted escape of Phadaeng and Nang Ai on horseback. Whereas earlier the dismembered portions of the flesh of the *Naga* are seen as acting upon human beings and their settlements, in this sequence it is the cultural products of human beings and their symbols of ordered society—the regalia—which are seen as acting upon nature to produce (or to name, which is the same thing) swamps and tributaries. The significant aspect of the attempted escape is not the uncertain survival of the human actors but that they abandoned the regalia and the horse. The overt meaning is that nature captured those emblems which validate and make possible ordered society. The latent meaning is that the swamps and rivers are the repositories of ancient regalia that give legitimacy to human settlements. Thus, while one level of meaning represents again the opposition between nature and society, and the futility of this conflict for nature is stronger, at another level it is resolved by the implication that the natural phenomena which contain the regalia validate the human settlements around them because of this possession.

In brief, while the sinking of human settlements as a result of humans having eaten *Naga* meat represents *naturalization* of human society, the incorporation of human cultural products by nature represents the *humanization* of nature. It is this balanced equation that the myths portray.

We are now ready to tackle two problems concurrently. The ethnographic problem is the relationship between Buddhist ritual and the cult of the guardian spirits. I propose to consider it by comparing the grand Buddhist festival of *Bun Phraawes* and the myths concerning Uppakrut who figures in that festival (described in Chapter 10) with the rain-making festival of *Bunbangfai* and its related myth. From this ethnographic discussion we can abstract a formal problem which is of theoretical interest to anthropology, namely the relation between myth and rite.

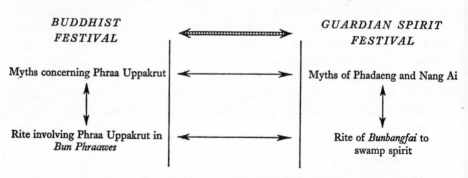

Fig. 4   Diagram showing the relationship between two festivals

The arrows in the diagram indicate the relationships we have to examine in order to arrive at answers to the two problems set out above. The relevant ethnography has already been presented and therefore has only to be brought into focus here. We have at hand Buddhist myths and an associated ritual, and another body of myths (or, rather, variants of a single myth) and an associated ritual devoted to the guardian spirits, *both complexes relating to a common village preoccupation*. It is hoped that analysis will bring out the formal relations (1) between myth and its associated rite, and (2) between two related complexes of myths and their associated rites, which derive their orderly meaning precisely because of their co-existence within one cultural and social universe.

I treat myth and its associated ritual initially as two separate phenomena, each with its own logical structure and message contents, and examine the nature of the 'correspondence' between them. The extension of this comparison to two complexes of myths and rites will allow me to make a further statement about formal structural relations and the configuration of meanings within a single universe of religious thought and action.

The underlying feature that gives coherence to the analysis is the *Naga* symbol. In Buddhist ritual, a good example of which is the *Bun Phraawes* festival, is represented a cluster of features of the *Naga* as a servant of Buddhism and as the life over which the Buddha achieved conquest. In the cult of the guardian spirits, of which the *Bunbangfai* is an apt representation, we have another aspect of the *Naga* emphasized, namely its autonomous status and its power as a force of nature in its own right. In this second aspect, human beings propitiate it as a deity and express their submission to and reconciliation with it.

To recapitulate some of the main conclusions reached in respect of the *Bun Phraawes* festival: it is the major festival of the village performed after harvest at a time of plenty. It is a grand merit-making ceremony in which the villagers make liberal gifts to the monks and the *wat*, listen to the most celebrated story of Buddha as Phraawes engaging in acts of selfless giving which represent the ultimate in self-sacrifice, and by analogy and transfer they acquire merit. Structurally the *Bun Phraawes* festival divides into three sequences. First comes the invitation to Phraa Uppakrut, the swamp monk, to attend the festival; he is associated with protecting the village and ensuring rains. I interpreted this as man's communion with and the taming of natural forces. The second phase is the invitation and propitiation of the divine angels (*thewada*), who are regarded as benevolent agents of Buddhism. This phase represents man's reunion with the upper benevolent spirit world. Uppakrut mediates with nature, the *thewada* with the divine. The ideologically central part, enacted in the third phase, is merit-making and recitation of and listening to the great story (*Lam Phraawes*). This sequence recalls and enacts Buddha's life in this world: it recalls a heroic past and allows present-day humble humanity to participate vicariously in that past. The three structured sequences represent a hierarchy of values in which the lower world of nature and the upper world of divine angels take their place in the service of Buddhism.

How do the myths concerning Phraa Uppakrut relate to the ritual enactments of *Bun Phraawes*? I reported three stories or myths concerning

Phraa Uppakrut. In one he is seen as a product of the incorporation of Buddha's semen by a mermaid: he is thus part Buddhist agent and part of nature, a union that combines both elements. As mermaid's son, or as *Naga*, he represents beneficial water in the never drying pond. In the second story he is seen as nature's powerful agent who allies with human beings against their mortal adversary, Mara, who is death. In the third story he is represented as an ascetic who is superior to temporal power and who defends Buddhism by reconciling theological differences in the *Sangha*.

The intriguing point is that the myths, by exploiting certain thematic oppositions, produce a resolution by which Uppakrut or *Naga* becomes the servant and protector of Buddhism. But the rite addressed to Uppakrut in the first sequence of *Bun Phraawes* (the procession to the swamp in order to 'invite' him) does not dramatize the myths; rather it essentially enacts the conversion and enrolling of the services of the *Naga* in the service of Buddhism. The ritual articles carried in the procession are conspicuous symbols of monkhood—the begging bowl, sandals and robes. He is persuaded to leave the swamp and climb the sedan by showing him the Buddha images, and by the sprinkling of puffed rice. Cries of victory and the chanting of the victory blessing by the monks express the success of his conversion and the assured success of the battle against Mara with him as ally. In a sense then, the myths and the rite stand in an inverse relationship. The myth says that Uppakrut is an agent and guardian of Buddhism; the rite enacts his conversion into an agent. Thereafter his role is that of protector and guardian of peace and order, and the festival itself is regarded as ensuring rain, long life, good health, and absence of conflict in the village. It might be said that at the *Bun Phraawes* festival Uppakrut takes over the role of the village and swamp guardians, while the guardians themselves, in their non-Buddhist aspect, remain intact and separate.

Now when we compare the rocket festival (*Bunbangfai*) with the *Bun Phraawes*, we see a different pattern. This festival is in theory unambiguously directed to the soliciting of rain, prosperity and good health from the village guardians, who are elevated *phii*. But the sequences of the festival show a complex weaving in of Buddhist sequences without confusing category distinctions, and how the guardian spirit cult is linked to Buddhism.

The first sequence described was the ordination of novices and monks. A major reason why ordination takes place at this time is that part of the merit acquired is transferred to the swamp and village guardians. This expresses not so much the conversion of the spirits into Buddhist agents (as *Bun Phraawes* does with Uppakrut) but that the human actors as Buddhists transfer some of their moral worth to the spirit guardians as an offering in order to solicit favours. The ceremony for the elevation and honouring of monks occasionally performed together with ordination embodies rich meaning: the monk is purified by water which flows through the *Naga's* throat. Here the *Naga* is distinctly conceived as a Buddhist agent, and the analogy is that just as the *Naga* in this ritual context purifies a monk, so may the swamp and village guardians fertilize the fields.

The second phase of the festival, which consists of the procession to the *Tapubaan* shrine and the firing of the 'rocket of respect', excludes the participation of monks. The villagers, under the leadership of the spirit guardians' own officiants, enact their collective submission to and dependence on the guardians. The categorical opposition between Buddhism and spirit cult is clearly expressed here. However, that same night the monks in turn chant *suad mongkhon* and bless the rockets at the *wat* according to the Buddhist mode, thereby doubling the chances of success. The third and final phase is the firing of the wishing rocket, followed by ritual licence and competitive rocket-firing. In this final phase all take part, both monks and laymen. All distinctions of social and religious hierarchy are temporarily dissolved in ritual licence as a prelude to beginning a new agricultural and religious cycle. This licence is the very converse of *Bun Phraawes* which concludes with the day-long listening to a moving and austere sermon.

The comparison between *Bun Phraawes* and *Bunbangfai* reveals that two ritual complexes stand in opposition and complementarity, and state a dialectical relationship between two quite different positions taken by the villagers in regard to man's relationship to nature and the divine. The first as a Buddhist ceremony and the second as a *phii* cult bring out the following contrasts. *Bun Phraawes* is staged in terms of the pious Buddhist ideology of merit-making; in this festival the two main categories of actors are monks and lay elders, who occupy the most important statuses in the village. Merit-making is accompanied by a grand fair, thus combining the moral pursuits of monks and elders with the pleasure derived by the youth. The festival concludes with a day-long recitation of a moving story of the Buddha's acts of charity and sacrifice. *Bunbangfai* is staged in terms of the ideology of the guardian spirit cult, in which favours are sought in exchange for offerings. The ritual officiants—*tiam* and *cham*—practise ecstatic techniques. Possession represents the descent and entry into men of powerful supernatural agents in order to aid them. The ceremony concludes with ritual licence in which village statuses and the respect hierarchy are dissolved temporarily before the next agricultural cycle starts. The targets of such licensed behaviour include monks and elders. The entire community participates, the desire for rain being a collective wish without grade or distinction. In this sense and in this context, monks are members of the village like anyone else. When rocket-firing concludes in competitive play, those who fail to fire rockets successfully are greeted with mud because they have failed to represent the wish adequately.

Now to compare the two sets of myths. Placed against the legends concerning Uppakrut, the myth of Phadaeng and Nang Ai states a counter-proposition to the Buddhist statement which is that the *Naga*, representing nature, is a power in his own right with whom man has to come to terms. At one level the Phadaeng and Nang Ai myth portrays conflict between man and *Naga* and the latter's superior powers of destruction. But at a deeper level the myth establishes a relation between society and nature in the form of a resolution in which both participate in each other: the swamps and rivers give an historic stamp to the human settlements around them. The myth validates the power of the *Naga* as swamp spirit, and more importantly asserts through a story of conflict the necessary union of man and nature so as to secure ordered social life.

In the rocket festival as rite, the conflict sequences of the associated myth are not enacted. The guardian spirit of the swamp (*Chao Phau Tong Khyang*), symbolizing rain and fertility, is propitiated by humans in their capacity as subservient children. Here in the rite the guardian spirit embodies the conclusion or resolution of the myth, and unites in one person the twin values of benevolent nature and orderly society. The rockets, which are vehicles of competition in the myth now in the shape of the two *bang tawai* and *siang* rockets, express in the rite the human attitude of respect to the spirit and the wish for rain and good health. They carry these wishes up into the sky in an attempt to reach the inaccessible. It is only at the end of the festival that the remaining rockets are fired in a spirit of competition and ritual licence. There is thus a dialectical inverse relationship between the Phadaeng myth and the rite of *Bunbangfai*, paralleling a similar relationship discussed earlier between the Uppakrut stories and the *Bun Phraawes* rite. It is therefore time to examine the formal relations between myth and rite.

MYTH AND RITE

Malinowski (1948), in arguing against certain scholars who concerned themselves solely with disembodied paper versions of myth, carried his point of view to the other extreme by stating that the meaning of a myth can only be seen in terms of its cultural function, its pragmatic role in social life, its integration into the full context of social life. Myth was related to belief, rite to action, but they were not at different levels of behaviour. Malinowski in fact merged them and talked of an organic whole, which itself fused into the total social context. He wrote:

The union is very intimate, for myth is not only looked upon as a commentary of additional information, but it is a warrant, a charter, and often a practical guide to the activities with which it is connected. On the other hand the rituals, customs and social organisation contain at times direct references to myth, and they are regarded as the direct results of mythical event. (p. 85.) The...reality of myth lies in its social function...the reconstruction of the full meaning of the myth leads you to the full theory of native social organisation. (p. 94.)

Malinowski's reluctance to grant myth a separate existence was linked with the basic view he held about religious phenomena, especially magic and, therefore, ritual. Ritual was grounded in *emotional* wishes and was an emotive reaction with pragmatic interest in the face of the uncontrollable and unforeseen. This means that for Malinowski myth had no intellectual or symbolic content; its primary purpose was not to make things intelligible. Myths do not explain, they are not 'an intellectual reaction upon a puzzle', they have 'emotional colouring and pragmatic importance'.

But despite this overall position curious anomalies are to be found in Malinowski's actual treatment of myths and rites. To cite an example from his essay 'Myth in Primitive Psychology' (Malinowski 1948), let us look at the myth concerning how humans lost their power of rejuvenation by sloughing their skins (p. 103 *passim*). The story revolves around three persons, mother, daughter and granddaughter, and the loss of eternal life is presented in terms of conflict between grandmother and granddaughter. The grandmother cannot remain as young as the granddaughter, and death is represented in terms of the succession of alternate generations. Compare this with another myth. The myth which Malinowski explicitly connected with the annual feast of the dead (*milamala*) recounts the permanent removal of the dead to Tuma. The denial of the right to continue to live in the village after death is represented in terms of the rejection of mother by daughter and solidarity of grandmother with grandchild—a reversal of the former story with the same elements (p. 110). While the myth, then, deals with the separation of the dead from the living, the *milamala* as ritual is staged once a year to bring the dead to the living for a short period of time, for prosperity depends on their continuing interest (see Malinowski 1948, 'Baloma: The Spirits of the Dead'). Thus the myths which clearly are variations on a theme state

305

the necessity of death and the necessity of separation of the dead from the living in terms of succession and replacement, while the ritual establishes communion between the dead and the living.

The dialectical relation between the *milamala* myths[1] and rite may be expressed as follows. Myth sets out an original ideal state of affairs and after presenting a set of inherent contradictions poses resolutions leading to dynamic present time. Rite, on the other hand, starting from the imperfect present, attempts to achieve the ideal conditions set out in original mythic time. Thus the myths, beginning with the time of the co-existence of three generations, state the necessity of death and of separation of the dead from the living in terms of succession and replacement, while the ritual establishes contact and communion between them.

Malinowski's major theoretical assertions were about the relation between myth and magic in the Trobriands. Myth did two things in respect of magic—it validated the 'sociological claims of the wielder' of magic and gave him a pedigree, and it 'served as a foundation for a system of magic', shaping the ritual and vouchsafing for the truth of magical belief (*ibid.* p. 119). There was a reciprocal relation between myth and magic: 'myth has crystallised into magical formulae and magic in turn bears testimony to the authority of myth' (1960, p. 303).

Looking at the role of myth from the standpoint of magic, Malinowski asserted that myth appeared in the magical rite in the form of mythological allusions in the spells. The pedigree of the magician and the charter for the magic were expressed chiefly in the *u'ula*, the foundation or the first part of the spell. Frequently, references to mythical events were made and the names of mythical ancestors, who in succession had used the formula since its creation by the founder of the magic, were recited. Sometimes the magician identified himself with the mythical ancestors, uttering their names as in the first person.

But when we look at the relevant myths and rites, we find that Malinowski was misled by his prior assumption that myth and magic were indissolubly linked, each reflecting and giving legitimacy to the other. He did not inquire, although the evidence pointed that way, whether myth and rite may say and do different things precisely because they are separated as well as connected. We would digress too much if we examined the facts in detail. Suffice it to say here that a close examination of the myths relating to the flying canoe, Kula, and agricultural magic, and of the corresponding rites, show that there is an interesting discrepancy and inversion between them. The myths, dealing with the heroes of ideal

[1] In my view the two myths, since they belong to a single set, bear a similar connection to the *milamala* ritual.

time, explore certain inherent contradictions in the logic of morality as acted out by persons of varying and permuted kinship statuses, and the final message of the myths is that magic of the fantastic kind is irretrievably lost and what remains is magic of a limited kind. In the rite, however, the magician living in present-day historical time, with its limitations and imperfections, claims to impersonate and approximate the ideal state and conditions of mythical time.

Thus in effect once again the relationship between myth and rite appears as an inversion, or reversed progression, or paradox. This paradox is not different from the pattern that emerged from my analysis of Thai data. What I am suggesting, then, is that myth and associated ritual may in fact provide frameworks for stating the two sides of an insoluble paradox, and both may attempt the alternative kinds of mediation allowed by the paradox.

With Lévi-Strauss (1963, Ch. XII) we get a further extension of the theory of the relationship between myth and ritual. Rejecting the views that myth is an ideological projection of a rite or that, in reverse, the ritual is a kind of dramatized illustration of the myth, he advocates that their relationship be seen in dialectical terms 'accessible only if both have first been reduced to their structural elements'. While Lévi-Strauss's method of revealing the logical and symbolic structure of myth and ritual is indeed stimulating (see also 1963, Chs. X and XI), one is not sure of the plausibility of his demonstration. A case in point is his imputation of a dialectical relationship between a Pawnee myth and the ritual of *another*, *alien* society (Ch. XII) whose connection with Pawnee society is asserted in an arbitrary manner.

Following Lévi-Strauss, I have attempted to analyse the structures of myth and ritual as separate entities and then to examine the nature of their relationship. I think my demonstration of the relationship is plausible because I am fairly confident of having observed Malinowski's dictum that we must see myth and ritual within their 'live' social and cultural context. The following are the implications of the analysis.

First, a particular myth (and its variations) within a social universe can be seen to have additional meaning when compared with another myth, as long as the latter is a contrary within a larger universe of meaning. I have tried to demonstrate that Phraa Uppakrut and *Chao Phau Tong Khyang* belong to the same universe of meaning, as aspects of the *Naga* symbol and as representing community interests in rain, good health, and order in society. But the two sets of myths state counter-propositions; they represent two attitudes regarding man's relation to nature. In one, Uppakrut as *Naga* is represented as a Buddhist agent; in the other, *Chao*

Phau is an independent powerful entity with whom villagers have a separate relationship.

A second implication of my analysis concerns the relation of myth to ritual as represented in the ethnography treated here. There is no simple correspondence, one does not directly reflect the other. The myth does not validate the rite in Malinowski's terms. The stories about Phraa Uppakrut represent him as a monk, a product of the union of the Buddha and a mermaid, and a force ranged on the side of Buddhism against Mara, the demon of chaos. In the associated rite—the ceremony of invitation—he is tamed and converted into a Buddhist agent whose protection is all-important. This conversion is the prelude, the first stage, in the merit-making rite, which then proceeds to communicate with the *thewada* before the sermon is preached. The myth concerning Phadaeng and Nang Ai has no direct connection with *Chao Phau Tong Khyang*, to whom the rite of *Bunbangfai* is addressed. *Chao Phau Tong Khyang* is an end result of the story in that he comes to embody or symbolize the spirit of the swamp, which represents the union of nature and man. The myth underlines the power of nature, symbolized as *Naga*, and the necessary collaboration of man with it if man is to experience prosperity. The associated rite of *Bunbangfai* is a simple one of propitiation of and bargaining with the spirit of the swamp and the guardian deities who embody the resolution made by the myth. The rockets which in the myth represented competition between men for a prize, for which the *Naga* was ineligible, become in the rite the vehicles of wishes communicated by man to the guardian spirit, who has transcended the opposition and encompasses the co-operation of nature and society. Whereas *Bun Phraawes* accents the status of monks and elders as ethical merit-makers, *Bunbangfai* erases this form of social structure and reduces all villagers to the status of *Chao Phau's* children, equal in relation to one another. The *Bunbangfai* rite, then, dramatizes the subjection and dependence of all villagers as children *vis-à-vis* their guardian *phii*.

In formal structure the two myths and the rites associated with them show a pattern in which one is the mirror image of the other. In the Buddhist myth and rite, the *myth* validates the religious status, authority and power of the swamp monk, who represents nature; the rite enacts just the opposite—his domestication and subjection to Buddhism. The myth says he *is* a Buddhist agent; the rite *makes* him so. The myth and rite connected with the guardian *phii* show opposite oppositions. The myth is only incidentally concerned with *Chao Phau*, for he is the residue or resolution of a devastating conflict portrayed in the myth between man and nature. The rite expresses the simple dependence and subjection of man to the guardian spirits, whose superior position and powers are not in question. The myth describes the conflict, the rite simple dependence.

This pattern, then, demonstrates a particular formal relationship not only between a myth and its associated rite, but also between two complexes of myths and rites which stand in 'dialectical' association within the larger universe of religious behaviour. These formal relations derive their content, in the present ethnography, from the particular ideology and idiom of Thai village religion which poses its religious conceptions in terms of basic logical operations. The ideology of Buddhist ethical ritual conduct is that man should surmount his normal sensory nature in the service of spiritual self-improvement: the ritual of Uppakrut expresses this in the idiom of taming. The ideology of Buddhist mythology, on the other hand, is that supernatural deities were incorporated into the Buddhist pantheon as benevolent moral agents. The myth and the ritual thus represent the two co-existing ethical attitudes. The idiom of the ritual propitiation of guardian spirits is that of bargaining with and appeasement of a 'father' by villagers who are his 'children'. This is a relationship of dependence and of authority. The ritual expresses this relation. The myth expresses the ideology of a superior power invested in natural forces which gain their guardianship status through conflict with man and the latter's subjection or fusion with nature. It states in fact that man confronted by nature must accept the facts of life and accept its power to harm as well as to reward. The myth and the ritual of *Bunbangfai* express this double relation.

To sum up. The Buddhist theology and mode of ethical action is one kind of proposition concerning man's orientation to the world. The theology and ritual of the guardian spirits phrase the counter-orientation. In the Thai context both appear as necessary and inevitable. Whereas the idiom in which each is phrased is Thai, the formal pattern they present is that of the human use of logical operations in terms of opposition and complementarity, paradox and its alternative mediations.

APPENDIX TO CHAPTER 16

'BUNBANGFAI' FESTIVAL AT NAPU VILLAGE (1966)

The village of Napu, situated on the banks of the swamp Byng Chuan, is the centre of the cult associated with the guardian of the swamp, *Tapu Byng* or *Chao Phau Tong Khyang*. It is therefore worthwhile to describe the *Bunbangfai* staged there; the documentation will provide a comparison with and a confirmation of the account given of the festival staged at Baan Phraan Muan.

In one respect Napu village is more orthodox than Phraan Muan. Its shrine to the village guardian, *Tapubaan*, is situated in the *wat* compound right next to the *bood*. This is a spatial expression of the complementarity between Buddhism and the cult of guardian spirits. Furthermore, Napu, as the cult centre, has the chief medium (*tiam*) of the swamp guardian, three subsidiary female mediums, and an intermediary (*cham*) who is the assistant of the chief medium. All these religious personnel participate in *Bunbangfai*.

Bunbangfai is, it was claimed, always staged in the middle of the 6th lunar month (full moon of May). The ceremony is compulsory and held every year. But its scale varies as in Baan Phraan Muan. As the *tiam* of Napu put it: 'In a good year when there has been a good harvest, a big ceremony is held; in a lean year only a small ceremony.'

The sequence of the festivities celebrated in 1966 is as follows: on the 14th day of the 6th lunar month, which is called *mue hoam* (time for bringing things together), villagers got ready the articles necessary for ordination of monks. In the afternoon the *sukhwan nag* (ceremony for recalling the spirit essence of the postulants) was held in the *wat*, conducted by the *mau khwan* (lay officiant). In the evening, after the monks had chanted *suad mongkhon* (chant of blessing), began the fair. Entertainment consisted of *mau lam* (folk opera) and *ramwong* (dancing).

On the afternoon of the following day (15th) ordination took place. It is important to note that the villagers of Napu said categorically: 'Bunbangfai *follows* ordination', thereby asserting their sequential relationship. In some years the ceremony for elevating and honouring monks to the status of *Somdet* is held, but in 1966 it was not.

After the conclusion of ordination, on the same afternoon, the procession with rockets (*hae bangfai*) took place. Before the procession started, the *tiam* (medium) took to the shrine of the village guardian (*Tapubaan*) candles, flowers and his costume, and made offering (*tawai*) and paid his respects (*karava*) to *Tapubaan*. Then he dressed himself in the costume of the *tiam*, which consisted of: *panung dam* (black waist cloth or skirt), *sya daeng* (red blouse or shirt), *pha kian hua* (head cloth), *pha kard eo* (waist band) and *phachedna* (handkerchief). The last three items were also red. The hallmark of a *tiam's* costume is its red colour, especially the blouse and head cloth. The subsidiary female *tiam* also wear these same colours. The *cham* (intermediary) wears ordinary clothes.

The 'procession with rockets' was formed in the following order: it was led by the male medium; behind him came the three female mediums and the intermediary. All of them danced. The musicians—drummers and bamboo flutists—came next, followed by the other 'dancers', most of whom were persons who had been cured of illness by the medium. These latter are referred to as *luug tiam* ('children of the medium') and it is required that they take part in the procession and dance. The palanquin bearing the rockets (fifteen in number) was carried behind the dancers; the carriers consisted primarily of male village elders. The rear of the procession was brought up by male and female village elders (*phuu thaw* and *maethaw*), and youth of both sexes (*phuubaw* and *phuusaw*).

The procession went three times around the *bood*, and then proceeded to the shrine of *Tapubaan*. The *medium* climbed up the ladder to the shrine, dedicated the rockets and made a prayer, saying, 'If the village is good let the rocket go up high, if it is not, let the rocket explode'. Then the *bang siang* (rocket of wishing and foretelling) was ignited and it was launched successfully.[1] The procession, carrying the remaining rockets, then returned to the village and stored them in village homes.

The procession was formed again on the third morning (16th) and the rockets were carried to the *wat*. There the monks were feasted, after which the rockets were carried out of the *wat* to an open space located toward the east (an auspicious direction). They were then fired, and there was much competitive play and ritual licence of the type described earlier for Baan Phraan Muan.

[1] There is a difference in the proceedings as compared with those at Phraan Muan. In Napu only one rocket (*bang siang*) was fired whereas in Phraan Muan two (*bang tawai* and *bang siang*) were fired, the latter on the following morning. But as explained on page 292 of this chapter, villagers tend to see the *bang tawai* as also a wishing rocket of the *bang siang* type. In Napu one was considered adequate.

17

THE AFFLICTIONS CAUSED BY
MALEVOLENT SPIRITS

The concept of *phii*, elucidated in the previous chapter, refers to a wide range of spirits which affect human beings; within this class I distinguished the guardian spirits of the village and of the swamp from the free-floating malevolent and capricious spirits. This chapter deals with the latter, describing the various types, how they are seen as affecting humans, the ritual experts who deal with them, and the idiom of the ritual. The rites and beliefs and practitioners associated with these malevolent spirits will also be shown in relation to the Buddhist rites, and to the cult of the guardian spirits. I shall begin by comparing the rites concerned with malevolent spirits with those addressed to the guardian spirits, for clearly it is to the latter that they stand in a contiguous and contrasting relation.

We have seen that the guardian *phii* have an elevated status of honoured ancestor or father (*Chao Phau/Tapubaan*, etc.), that they are guardians of village interests and moral values, and that they act as disciplining agents. To them are addressed two annual collective village rites associated with agricultural prosperity and rain. Malevolent spirits are not guardians of moral values; to oversimplify somewhat, they attack capriciously or with reasons of self-interest when humans intrude into their marked-off domain. They are ritually communicated with only when they afflict humans, never are they propitiated outside of the context of attack nor in order to solicit favours. They are agents whose contact with humans must be severed rather than actively sought.

But, nevertheless, another set of facts brings the cult of the malevolent spirits somewhat closer to that of the guardian spirits. The guardian spirits, apart from their benevolent and disciplinary community role, not only grant individual favours but also punish and afflict individual villagers for reasons which are sometimes inscrutable. Affliction is dealt with by first consulting the diviner (*mau song*), then placing the matter in the hands of an intermediary (*cham*), who strikes a bargain with the guardian spirit and subsequently makes an offering when the cure is effected. In more serious cases of affliction the services of the *medium* (*tiam*) of the guardians may be solicited. He will validate or refute the diviner's diagnosis and as the guardians' vehicle directly voice their wishes as regards offerings.

Afflictions caused by malevolent spirits

Somewhat similar, where the afflictions are of a minor order, is the technique of purifying when malevolent *phii* afflict humans. The same diviner (*mau song*) diagnoses, and an intermediary (*mau phii* or *mau lek*) makes a bargain with the *phii* and later pays the fee if the bargain has been honoured. It is relevant to note, however, that the two intermediaries —*cham* and *mau phii*—are distinguished by title and the roles are performed by different persons. And whereas the *cham* is the sole village-ratified intermediary of the guardian spirits, there can be many *mau phii* in a village who are qualified to make the offerings.

In more extreme cases of spirit possession (indicated by serious organic and psychological symptoms) different kinds of practitioners enter the scene. The most dramatic of these is the medium *cum* exorcizer (*mau tham*) who, fortified with the superior powers of his teachers and of the divine angels (*thewada*), combats and exorcizes the afflicting spirit from the patient. This diviner–exorcizer is thus very different from the *tiam*, the medium of the guardian spirits, who acts as their vehicle. For in the *mau tham's* case the superior powers of the divine angels are used to expel violently the offending malevolent spirit possessing the patient. Here we see the *thewada* as a supernatural category conspicuously opposed to *phii*. The *mau tham* is a prototype exorcist of evil spirits, while the *tiam* is a vehicle of moralistic guardian spirits.

It is clear that the *mau tham*, as exorcist, practises an art which can be described as healing ritual. The expressive symbolism and the communication structure of these rituals are thus of special interest. These will be analysed in the next chapter, and the idiom and social significance of the exorcism ritual will be compared with the parallel features of the *sukhwan* rites, which we have seen are also used for therapeutic or prophylactic purposes.

This chapter will be concerned with the various categories of malevolent *phii*, relating them to the theology of death and elucidating their sociological correlates.

DEATH AND SPIRITS

I have discussed in Chapter 11 the concepts of normal and abnormal death in relation to mortuary rites, which are in one sense Buddhist rites *par excellence*. Persons who die normally are principally those who have reached the status of elders (*phuu thaw*); their mortuary rites are conducted by monks, whose role is to lead the *winjan* to heaven thereby ensuring the transition from malevolent spirit to ancestor. Persons who die abnormal deaths are principally those who have died in the prime of life, without completing their life cycle and the orderly succession of statuses. The causes of such deaths are violence, sudden disease or epidemic, and unsuccessful childbirth. The dangers generated by such deaths are reflected in the funerary rites: hurried, unceremonious burial so that the earth may absorb impurity, and subsequent disinterment and cremation conducted by monks.

Now this dichotomy reflected in Buddhist mortuary rites appears again in respect of *phii*: ancestral spirits versus the malevolent spirits of those who died violent deaths. In Buddhist ritual, merit is transferred to dead parents and ancestral spirits (*phii phau phii mae*) (*phii yaad phii sua*); this transfer, we have already seen, is a major theme in the activities of merit-making. A comment is called for in respect of the social-structural underpinnings of the notion of ancestral spirits. The concept *phii yaad* simply means 'spirits of dead kin': that is, it is a general category term for dead relatives. More specifically, *phii phau phii mae*: 'spirits of (dead) father and mother' lumps together both parents under one compound label, thus emphasizing the filial relationship rather than distinguishing a separate paternal and maternal existence after death. Thus beyond dead parents, who receive a collective specification, there is the diffuse category of dead kin (*phii yaad*). All these spirits are believed to be capable of attacking living humans.

The notion that the spirits of parents and grandparents form a kind of pool of the dead, and the fact that there is no firm genealogical structuring or individual remembrance of persons beyond the parents, are both consistent with the bilateral kinship system of the village and its emphasis on relations between generations. (This situation is far removed from descent-based lineal societies, where the father and mother are seen in the dogma regarding conception as contributing different spiritual and bodily substances to children, where paternal and maternal ghosts are differentiated, and where, if ancestor worship is institutionalized, the particular line of ancestors emphasized not only provides a charter for genealogically ordered social structure, but these ancestors are also commemorated and propitiated by name (Fortes 1965, pp. 123–4).) Also consistent is the fact that whenever in the village an affliction is diagnosed as the act of parental or ancestral spirits, no effort is made to determine *which* spirit is the agent.

Whenever ancestral spirits impinge on the lives of living descendants by causing illness they are regarded as *phii* (maelvolent spirits), who are then propitiated in a manner consistent with the theory of spirit affliction and without recourse to the ritual services of monks. It is believed that when descendants (*luug-laan*) fail to transfer merit to the dead, ancestral spirits cause minor illnesses such as headache and fever. When children quarrel over inheritance of parental property, the *phii* of parents may cause difficulties in child-bearing to the women of the families of descendants. These two reactions, we can readily see, are typical ancestor manifestations: ancestral spirits act when they are in danger of being forgotten, and when the unity of their children is threatened. Thus these ancestral spirits, although malevolent, are not capricious but are moralistic agents. While in the Buddhist context they are regularly remembered and commemorated as a general category of the dead (and, apart from parents, not as individually named ancestors), in the sphere of spirit propitiation they are placated only when they make themselves felt in a malevolent manner. Once they have been divined as the agents of affliction, the oldest *luug-laan* (oldest child or grandchild) present in the village makes the usual offerings of cooked fish, roasted or steamed rice, betel nut, tobacco and flowers.

The victims of sudden death, as a distinct category, are generally called *phii tai hoeng*. From the standpoint of comparative ethnography, the Thai characterization of them is the same as in many other societies. They are aptly described in Bradbury's words as the unincorporated dead as distinct from the incorporated parents and elders (Bradbury 1966). Sudden or violent death can of course overtake the old as well as the young, but village fears crystallize around the young woman who has died in childbirth, especially with a stillborn child, or the young man who, in full possession of his physical and mental powers, has died by accident or violence. Their unfulfilled and clinging interests in and attachment to life in this world makes them doubly malevolent, and they assume the existence of free-floating evil. Thus we get an interesting inversion. While parents, when they die, are put in the path of rebirth and can act as moral and disciplinary spiritual agents, the youthful on the other hand become capricious and powerful *phii*, relatively difficult to control and to immunize, and are removed from the channels of rebirth.

This inversion takes on a fuller sociological meaning when seen in relation to the mortuary rites and the rites for calling the *khwan* (Chapter 13). The mortuary rites emphasize the duties of living descendants to dead parents and elders, and in the *khwan* ceremonies the elders reciprocate by installing the youth in statuses and charging them with morale and morality. It is thus understandable why ancestral spirits afflict their children if the latter neglect them. It is also evident that the spirits of the young man who dies a victim of violent death and of the pregnant woman who dies at childbirth are malevolent and uncontrollable, since they are precisely the persons whom the elders have been unable to initiate and install into the ordered sequence of community statuses. They have unnaturally escaped society. An extreme manifestation of this is the unborn child in the womb of a dead woman (*phii prai*).

Human ingenuity, however, finds a way of putting *phii tai hoeng* to use. An expert in spirits (*mau phii*) may manage to tame and look after such a spirit, and use its power to achieve either good or bad. This is the basis of one kind of mediumship which benefits the living, or of sorcery which harms them. No such agent or cult was encountered in the village of Phraan Muan. Where it occurs in other parts of Thailand it tends to be a peripheral cult which borders on the ecstatic and dangerous. Moreover, while the ideas concerning abnormal death are reflected in the village mortuary rites, no named *phii tai hoeng* nor any rituals addressed to them were encountered. (The one exception, an instance of *phii prai*, will be described below in this chapter.) The belief in the violent spirit is thus a magnified and dramatized conceptualization of a free-floating malignant force which, however, does not find expression as systematized cult behaviour. It represents the theoretical extreme of the concept of an unfulfilled life, the concept being transformed into the notion of uncontrollable evil.

AFFLICTION BY NATURE SPIRITS

There is also the large category of highly miscellaneous spirits which reside in mountains or rivers, or are allotted to particular locations, that is, they are nature spirits. Thai imagination is prolific in the creation of free-floating malevolent spirits; there is no standard collection of them, and any one of them may be divined on circumstantial evidence as the cause of a particular affliction. There are, however, certain kinds of *phii* in this category which are most frequently named as agents of misfortune.

Within the sphere of intra-village activities, *phii rai phii naa* (spirits of the rice field) are said to attack villagers. The belief is that each owner's field has a resident spirit, and it is not unusual for farmers to set up shrines for them in their respective fields. There is no systematic thinking as to why field spirits may cause affliction to the owners and their family, or to any other person walking on or near the field.

The field spirits are essentially the guardians of the fields, and farmers dutifully make offerings at their field shrines before ploughing and after harvest. Field spirits are in this respect secondary and individualized counterparts of the guardian spirits of the village, who protect the collective agricultural interests of the entire village and are propitiated before ploughing and after harvesting. The offerings to the field spirits by individual farmers are made immediately after the collective offerings to the village guardians. Thus in a sense the *phii naa*, as spirit owners of fields, are *guardians of household property rights*, who are promised and given their fees for their protective function.

But clearly they are not moral agents when they cause individual afflictions, for they are seen as acting capriciously when they cause them. To achieve a cure the owner of the field secures the services of the *mau lek* (astrologer, fortune teller) and together they promise an offering and invite the spirit (*kuad*) to leave the patient; after he is well, they offer chicken, boiled egg and cooked rice, provided by the patient or his family.

There are many spirits which a man may encounter while he is travelling outside his village. For example, *phii pu loob* is a spirit that lives on the mountain and afflicts passers-by with fever, stomach ache and headache. Often a particular tree at a particular spot is known as the location of a spirit, and villagers will pay their respects to the spirit as they go by. If it afflicts a person it is placated in the manner described above for a field spirit.

Sometimes a returned traveller who falls sick is diagnosed as having been afflicted by a pair of spirits, male and female, *chao phau san* and *nang keo*, who are guardians of the east and the west. Their names suggest that they are powerful and elevated guardian spirits. I have not witnessed a ritual performed for them, but villagers say that on recovery expensive and 'strong' offerings have to be made to them. The offerings named were opium, liquor, an uncooked chicken, tobacco, and betel nut—plus a male organ (lotus flower—*dogbua*) for the female spirit and a female organ (turtle shell—*daung taw*) for the male spirit. These are placed under a tree, pointing in the correct east–west directions.

It must not be thought that the threatening presence of malignant spirits in trees, forests, streams and mountains prevents villagers from travelling and visiting other villages, markets, and Buddhist temples. Nevertheless villagers view their own village as a more secure universe than the outside world. As we saw earlier (Chapter 13), one of the situations the *sukhwan* ritual is concerned with is the departure and return from long trips; this ceremony is essentially directed to the charging of morale, and to emphasizing to the traveller his membership in the village before he departs from it, and his reincorporation into it upon his return. When a traveller actually falls ill and when this is interpreted as caused by malignant external spirits who reside in nature, then placation takes place, and the outside agent's influence is removed. In a sense, then, *sukhwan* rites and spirit placation rites are complementary, the former seeking effects on the mind, the latter physical cure. This point will be developed further at the end of Chapter 18. A returned traveller may undergo both sets of rites without incompatibility: they are performed separately, by different officiants, in totally different ritual idioms.

POSSESSION BY SPIRITS

There is no village concept of witchcraft as such, but the anthropological concept is partially recognizable in the nature and activities of a spirit called *phii paub*. In village classification *phii paub* is one type within the general category of malevolent spirits. But it is distinctive for several reasons. First, removal of *phii paub* affliction usually requires the services of an exorcist (*mau tham*), whose procedure is entirely different from the placation technique. (The steps in the latter technique are: first invitation to leave, then payment of a fee offering.) The placation technique applies to ordinary spirit illness in which a spirit causes affliction but is not thought to enter and reside inside the patient. Secondly, *phii paub* can be hosted by some *living* human beings, whereas all the *phii* we have examined so far are disembodied spirits of dead humans. However, there are some complications which blur the lines between witchcraft and spirit attack, and between witchcraft and sorcery.

The agent (*phii paub*)

Phii paub can be hosted by either a male or a female living person. In everyday life, such people cannot be distinguished because they are like other normal, ordinary people (*pen khon thammada*). The human host becomes known only in the course of the exorcism procedure after a victim has been possessed.

Village theory is that a man or woman who is a *mau wicha*, an expert in the magical arts of love magic, or protective magic (such as making amulets that make the wearer bullet-proof), or control of epidemics (like cholera), is the person who is prone to harbour a *phii paub*, if he acts immorally or contravenes taboos associated with his dangerous but potent art. Since his special powers derive from this secret knowledge of charms and spells, it is said that under certain conditions these spells themselves turn into *phii paub*. Typical circumstances that lead to this transformation are: (1) if a *mau wicha* discontinues his practice; (2) if he uses spells immorally by causing diseases in people rather than curing them, or if he exploits his patients by charging excessive fees (the accusation here being that he himself sends disease in order to extract fees); (3) if he fails to respect and propitiate his teacher; or (4) if he breaks food taboos associated with his profession.

318

Afflictions caused by malevolent spirits

To comment on 3 and 4 first. The teacher–pupil relationship is emphasized not only among monks but also among all village cult specialists, especially those connected with the malevolent spirits. Sometimes a patient becomes a practitioner after his cure, learning the technique from his curer. In this case there is a double bond: patient–curer, pupil–teacher. A spirit specialist must pay homage to his teacher at the beginning of each ritual; some practitioners say that it is the spirit of the teacher which enters them and gives them the power to make their spells effective, or if they are exorcists, it is the teacher's spirit that possesses them and enables them to combat the spirit possessing the patient. Hence the failure of a *mau wicha* to propitiate his teacher is a serious ritual mistake.

All controllers of magical powers (*mau wicha*) and all exorcists (*mau tham*) are said to have special food taboos associated with their practice. Thus for instance, a *mau wicha* must never eat the placenta of a cow (*rok wua rok kuay*) which is ordinarily eaten by villagers: if he does he will become host to a *phii paub*. The association here appears to be an analogy between, on the one hand, a cow and its placenta (a 'kind of' calf) and a woman and her placenta at childbirth, and on the other hand, the human host and the *phii paub* which resides inside it. The *phii paub*, moreover, usually attacks and penetrates women who appear to be the most frequent victims of *phii paub* attack. However, in addition to the similarity between *phii paub* and placenta, there are also differences. Thus the *phii paub* inside a person and the placenta of a cow or a woman are both analogous and opposed, because the latter represents the innocuous remains of life-giving pregnancy and birth, while the former connotes disease-producing internal growth.

Implicit in 1 and 2 above—that the practitioner of magical arts must not discontinue his practice, nor must he on the other hand misuse it—is an ambivalence in value judgments about those who deal with spells and charms and exercise extra-human powers. Such powers have their use in the society and must be kept available for those who need them. But, at the same time, such powers are in themselves dangerous; they are a double-edged sword, cutting both ways. He who dabbles in them in order to control spirits is in danger of becoming their victim or agent. Thus a man who learns to control disease through spells may himself sometimes send or cause disease; a man who gives love magic to earnest lovers may himself come to fornicate with village wives; the man who exorcizes malevolent spirits may himself become a sorcerer sending spirits to possess his enemies.

The ambiguous structural position of the *mau wicha* and the *mau tham* exorcist is a reflection of this ambivalent evaluation of their ritual roles and the rituals they conduct. In the hierarchy of evaluation of the different cults and their practitioners, they are not accorded anything like the respect and approval the monk enjoys, nor are they looked upon as prestigious village elders and leaders as *mau khwan* are.

Now village theory attributes the historical origin of *phii paub* to the transformation of spells into an evil force inside a magical expert, be it man or woman (the latter are sometimes said to dabble in love magic), who uses spells to achieve supra-human effects. But when it comes to the persistence of *phii paub* after the death of the original human host the theory takes two directions. One possibility, it is said, is that before the host dies, he or she transfers the spirit to his or her son or daughter. It is important to note that this is a case of transference, not automatic inheritance at birth. The ageing host, before his or her death, transfers to one child only. The mode of transference is poorly articulated:[1] it is said by some that the parent spits saliva into the mouth of a loved child, or on to its skull.

But there is another mode of spirit persistence which does away with the need for a living human host. Village theory asserts that when a man or woman who has *phii paub* dies, the spirit (*phii*) itself does not die but will be free-floating and wander in the village and attack one person after another. Here the *phii paub* is seen as capable of existing apart from any human owner. When a person is attacked by a *phii paub* one part of the exorcism ceremony consists of getting the patient to name the person in whom the spirit resides or from whom it emanates. In the case of a disembodied spirit it is said that the patient may name the host who, although dead, has returned to the village in spirit form.

This kind of malevolent disembodied spirit shades into another type which also attacks humans, especially mothers at childbirth. The spirit in question is called *phii prai* and is generated in a pregnant woman dying with the child inside her. It is said that when she dies the child inside her turns into a *phii prai* and consumes the mother's blood. The dead mother is taken to the cemetery, a 'surgeon' is invited to cut the womb and extract the child's corpse, and the mother and child are buried separately so that the child will not go on existing as a *phii prai*. For if the child is not removed and separately buried, it will grow into a monster which sucks the blood from other mothers at childbirth, or from victims of physical injury who bleed profusely. Thus the notion of *phii prai* is centred around violent and sudden death, especially the death of pregnant mothers. Profuse bleeding at childbirth is a symptom of *phii prai* attack, and may provoke the holding of an exorcism ceremony to stop it.

[1] In North Thailand, where witchcraft notions attached to women as hosts are well developed, the theories of transference are more exact.

Afflictions caused by malevolent spirits

The victim

It is clear from village description that it is women, both married and unmarried, who are the most common victims of *phii paub*. Children of both sexes may also be victims. Adult men are rarely or never attacked. *Phii paub* afflictions have been on the decline in recent years: the last appearance, according to villagers, was around 1960 in a nearby village. But there are in the village women who were previously possessed and have been cured.

The symptoms of affliction are that the victim cries out or laughs loudly and, when addressed, hides her face. These appear to be hysterical symptoms. The patient may also complain about lack of attention, that she has not been given the food she has asked for. Such complaints appear to signify unfulfilled wishes and a demand for attention, and probably come to a head or are culturally permitted at the time of pregnancy and impending childbirth. The villagers describe the affliction as a mental disturbance, and when actual cases occur they readily diagnose it as *phii paub* possession. Sometimes the possession takes place right at childbirth, in which case in addition to the behaviour described the patient also bleeds profusely. Here the *phii paub* is described as sucking the mother's blood, and behaves like the *phii prai* (the spirit of the dead child in a dead mother's womb) which I have already described.

The exorcist

In the case of a minor spirit affliction resulting in a relatively minor illness, the spirit concerned—whether it be ancestral spirit, nature spirit, spirit of a young person who has died a violent death, spirit of the fields—is not interpreted as possessing the victim, but as causing an illness through attack. The mode of treating such illness, we have seen, is diagnosis through divination and placation through paying a fee.

Any of these malevolent spirits, however, may cause more serious illnesses which are accompanied by 'mental' symptoms. This is interpreted as *spirit possession*. The spirits most commonly associated with such possession are *phii paub* (which is reminiscent of witchcraft) and *phii prai*. In such instances, the exorcist (*mau tham*) takes over, performing both the identification of the afflicting spirit and its exorcism from the patient. His training and technique are very different from those of other ritual experts I have so far examined. Yet at the same time his art is in a subtle way an inversion of the arts of the others. The exorcist's true colours emerge in full view when he is compared with the other specialists and when he is placed in relation to classical Buddhist doctrine.

Buddhism and the spirit cults in North-east Thailand

I shall argue in a novel fashion that the exorcist is both a caricature and an inversion of the orthodox Buddhist monk. He uses Buddhist sacred words for purposes diametrically opposed to those of the monk; the latter chants sacred words in order to teach morality and to transfer merit and blessings, whereas the exorcist uses the sacred words to frighten spirits and drive them away. The exorcist has a ritual relationship with his teacher (*achaan*) which is reminiscent of the monk's relationship to his *upacha* (preceptor and ordainer). He treats primarily diseases of women whereas the monk assiduously keeps his distance from them. There is thus a mock affinity and an inversion between monk and exorcist.

The name *mau tham* literally means expert in reciting words from the Buddhist sacred texts (*Dhamma*); *tham* has also the second meaning of 'straight' or 'upright', that is one who observes the five Buddhist precepts. One set of connotations is then that he is a pious and learned Buddhist. The *mau tham* of Phraan Muan village considers himself a Buddhist and goes to the Buddhist *wat* for worship, but he is neither pious nor well-versed in Buddhism and the sacred texts. How then do we resolve this paradox that a *mau tham* is both a pious Buddhist and his opposite? The resolution lies in the fact that Buddhist sacred words carry power. Whereas they are normally chanted by monks, here we have the very antithesis of a monk using the words for different purposes. Yet this employment of the words requires that he be a kind of 'mock' monk. (Furthermore, there is one trend or development in Buddhism itself in which supra-natural powers are sought and the *mau tham* is not alien to this tradition: of this, more later.)

These statements will become clearer if I describe the characteristics, recruitment and equipment of one of two exorcists in the village. Nai Sarlee, forty-nine years of age (in 1966), was born in another village (Baan Naabua) in the region, and has been residing uxorilocally in Baan Phraan Muan for twenty-two years. He is virtually illiterate, is a small farmer, and he has no position of leadership in the village. He is in fact considered somewhat eccentric and is certainly not a village elder.

Nai Sarlee learned the art of exorcism from a travelling teacher from another province (Sakorn Nakorn), who arrived in the village and was prepared to teach the art for a fee. Three candidates enrolled. The period of teaching was three successive *nights*. The teacher was given an 'offering' (which constituted his fee) before the studies began. The offering consisted in the main of the ritual articles we have repeatedly noted in village *khwan* and guardian spirit rituals, but it was more substantial. It consisted of *kanha-kanpaed* (5 and 8 pairs of candles and flowers), white cloth 1 metre in length, 160 pairs of small candles, 10 pairs of big candles each of 1 *baht* weight, 1 pair of *bajsi* (ceremonial flowered structure) and 25 *baht* in cash (about 10 shillings).

The first sequence in the instruction was the finding out of whether the candidate was suited to practise as an exorcist. Suitability here means the ability of the candidate to go into a trance (*khaw song*), and to tremble (*thua sun*) and lose consciousness (*khaw charn*) when Buddhist sacred words are recited. It is here that we get a simulation and a parody of Buddhist ordination.

The candidates sat cross-legged before the teacher and his assistant, with the hands in the *waj* (worship and showing respect) position. The teacher then chanted the sermon which is normally chanted at the ordination of a monk. On hearing these sacred words those who were capable of study began to tremble and lose consciousness. (Two of the three candidates passed the tests.) Then, while they were in the trance state, the teacher questioned the candidates as to what they wanted to learn. Nai Sarlee said that he wanted to learn the *gatha* (sacred verses) for driving away spirits. The spirits he mentioned were: *phii paub, phii prai, phii fa* (spirit of the sky), which are the three possessing spirits *par excellence*, and several other less malevolent spirits, some of which have been mentioned before: *phii naa* (spirit of the field), *phii pong* (spirit of the forest), *phii sya naam* (mermaid or spirit of the water), and *phii saeg sao hyan* (spirit of the house-posts).

The appropriate formulae were written down on paper in the alphabet of the local dialect but composed of words in the Korm (Khmer) language which is one of the sacred languages for Buddhist texts. The words as such were and still remain *totally incomprehensible* to Nai Sarlee, but he believes them to be *gatha* from Buddhist texts. On the following two nights, while in a trance, he was taught to recite the words and how to conduct the exorcism ritual. There was an interval of one year before he was authorized to practise—during this time he was expected to memorize the verses. Nai Sarlee was also enjoined to observe certain food taboos which are called 'ten kinds of flesh': cat, snake, dog, horse, elephant, two kinds of monkey, tiger, human beings, and turtle. All except turtle are taboo to all villagers; however, the candidate is also prohibited from drinking liquor, which is liberally taken by other mediums. If he breaks any of these food taboos, the spells he makes are likely to turn into *phii paub* inside him, the very spirit which is his arch enemy and which he combats and exorcizes in his patients.

There is also a Buddhistic twist to his role commitment. Since his spells are supposedly derived from Buddhist *gatha*, he is required to worship the Buddha at the private shrine in his house every evening.

(In contrast, it is not incumbent on him to be a pious worshipper at the temple.) Nai Sarlee alleged that sometimes in the course of worship he fell into a trance. We shall see later on that not only does he follow the practice of all ritual experts by invoking the Buddhist Trinity at the exorcism ritual, but he also, like a Buddhist monk, administers the five precepts to the exorcized patient. All this reminds one of the Black Mass.

Let me now make a digression. Although I have so far described the exorcist as in some ways acting like a 'monk' but in a manner and for purposes totally different from those of a village monk, yet it is also true that the art of exorcism by using Buddhist verses actually stems from or has precedents in one rather unusual development in Buddhism itself. Although none are to be found in Phraan Muan village, there are elsewhere literate exorcists who possess, read and use written magical texts, and who have acquired their esoteric knowledge and techniques from famous extraordinary monks who have been their *guru* and who themselves have been famous healers and exorcists. It is important to note that these monks have used their special powers and knowledge for curing and not for nefarious purposes such as sorcery. Village exorcists often claim that they themselves have learned under some famous abbot. It is thus possible that the enacting of some of the monk's attributes and his religious role by the village exorcist may be an imitation of the behaviour and techniques of the monk–exorcist.

The link between this phenomenon and classical doctrinal Buddhism is as follows. Buddhism shares with traditional Hindu Yoga the notion that when a monk (or *yogin*) attains a particular stage of meditational discipline and control over thought and physical desire, he automatically acquires 'mystic powers' (*siddhi/iddhi*) such as the ability to fly in the air, to know the mental states of other men, etc. In Chapter 3 I discussed the Buddhist conception of the *arahat* and the mystic and extraordinary powers he has access to. (There is the analogous Hindu belief that 'By virtue of renunciation, of asceticism (*tapas*), men, demons, or gods can become powerful to the point of threatening the economy of the entire universe' (Eliade 1958, p. 89).) Doctrinal Buddhism, however, deplores the use and exhibition by the *arahat* of his miraculous powers, in the same way the *yogin* is admonished to resist the temptation of magic, and encouraged to reach a higher stage of spiritual enrichment. The point I am making here, in regard to monks and their miraculous powers, is that the notion of renunciation having the capacity to give the ascetic extraordinary powers is the basis for some monks and ascetics actually taking to the practice of doctrinally devalued but tempting magical techniques.

Tantric Buddhism contains certain ideas and distinctions that are germane to our problem. Adepts in occultism are differentiated as those who follow the 'right-hand path' and those who follow the 'left-hand path'. Evans-Wentz (1960) likens the right-hand path to 'white magic' and the left-hand path to 'black magic'. The former is used for beneficial purposes, for invoking the appearance of deities, and for proceeding upwards to final emancipation, whereas the latter employs the *mantras* to call up and command inferior orders of spiritual beings and is often used for nefarious purposes.

It is most interesting that the distinction appears at a different level in Burmese exorcism. The hierarchical distinction made in relation to exorcists—who are usually not monks—is between *athelan hsaya*, 'master of the upper path' and *aulan hsaya*, 'master of the lower path' (Spiro 1967). The *athelan hsaya* is committed to Buddhist discipline and aspires to become a *weikza* (reminiscent of the *arahat*), belongs to a *gaing* sect, and practises alchemy. The inferior *aulan hsaya* tries to control harmful supernaturals. The remarkable aspect of Spiro's description is that the *athelan hsaya* uses Buddhist *gatha* prayers, the monk's *paritta*, and invokes the Buddhist Trinity in his encounter with the possessing spirit: 'the purpose of the ceremony is to enlist the support of Buddhist power, for it is the power of Buddhism, not the power of the exorcist...which overcomes the evil power' (Spiro 1967, p. 199). Not only this, but another statement of Spiro's has relevance for a formulation made by villagers in our Thai village: the power of the exorcist is morally ambiguous and the power to heal can also be abused to do harm, and in the eyes of some Burmese villagers the two kinds of practitioners are therefore not distinguishable.

The point I wish to make is that, rather than viewing the exorcist and exorcism as un-Buddhist deviations or antitheses to Buddhism, we shall increase our understanding by placing them in relation to it. The classical Buddhist distinction is between the true *arahat* who renounces the use of his mystic powers for worldly ends and transports himself to a higher plane, and the ascetic who does not; the Tantric distinction is between the mystic who employs them ethically and the one who does not. Similar distinctions occur in Burma at the level of exorcists who are also Buddhist laymen. The lay exorcist's powers are derived from Buddhist techniques and words, as are the monk's, but are used for different purposes. Thus in Burmese village Buddhism the distinction is re-established between the monk, who is engaged in higher pursuits and must have nothing to do with spirit (*nat*) cults, and the exorcist who, while subservient to Buddhism, is rigorously separated from the monk because of his lower pursuits. Similar distinctions can, I think, be discovered in Thailand. The distinction is again paralleled at another level between normal death and bad death, and the rites and officiants associated with them. It therefore makes great sense to view the exorcist both as a 'mock' monk and as the 'inversion' of a monk, a viewpoint which will become clearer after we view the exorcistic ritual.[1]

[1] My interpretation differs from Spiro's in that he pictures the exorcist as standing midway between monk and shaman and occupying an interstitial position between Buddhism and Animism. Whereas Spiro's view arises out of his theory of two diametrically opposed religions co-existing in Burmese society, mine postulates a field of religion in which various cults are arranged according to principles of complementarity, hierarchy and linkage.

18

EXORCISM AS HEALING RITUAL

In the extreme case of possession by *phii paub*, recognizable from the hysterical symptoms of the patient, the drama of exorcism moves through certain sequences. My concern here is to view exorcism as a healing ritual and to discern the way in which it seeks to achieve its effects. We can then compare this healing ritual to the *sukhwan* ritual analysed in Chapter 13.

When dealing with the *sukhwan* ritual I used as the framework of analysis four dimensions: the occasion for the ritual, the specification of the receiver of the message, the role and position of the sender of the message and the supporting cast, and, finally, the message itself. While this same framework is appropriate for viewing exorcism ritual, there is one important difference. The victim of possession is seen as not being in contact with society, or, more specifically, with his or her family and kinsmen. The ritual as such relies on shock therapy in which the exorcist and patient confront each other directly; family members, kinsmen and neighbours play, in comparison with the *sukhwan* ritual, a less conspicuous role as supporting cast; they devote their attention mainly to preparing the ritual articles and acting as helpers.

The following are the main sequences in the exorcism ritual.

1. *Invitation of the exorcist*: when a patient is seen to be possessed, someone from his or her family must go to the exorcist and 'invite' him (*nimon*). The verbal solicitation is accompanied by the offering of a pair of candles and flowers (*tian khu dogmai khu*). The exorcist then comes to the home of the patient, where the latter's family have prepared the ritual articles (*thang kaj tham*), which the exorcist offers to his own teacher (*khruu* or *achaan*). In theory the *kaj* presentation should be the same as the articles which the exorcist himself presented to his teacher as an offering when he first learned his art as a pupil. The 'teacher' in question is not only the particular teacher who taught him, but through him the whole line of teachers extending back to the mythical *guru* or *rishi* who was the first teacher. This same offering with which the exorcist pays respect to his teacher also constitutes the exorcist's own fee. The standard fee in the village is *khanpaed* (8 pairs of candles and flowers), 160 small candles, 20 large candles of one *baht* weight each, 1 *phakoma* (waist cloth), 2 metres of white cloth, and 12 *baht* cash. The cash fee may be increased in multiples of twelve and collected later. It is a graduated fee, charged

according to the affluence of the patient's family and the difficulty of curing (usually given an empirical index in terms of the number of days during which the curing ritual is repeated).

2. *The exorcist goes into a trance*: the exorcist sits before the ritual articles and, facing the propitious east, first worships the Buddha, the *Sangha* and the *Dhamma* (the Trinity), and then chants sacred words (*gatha*) in order to pay his respects to his teacher (*waj khruu*) and to invoke the power of his teacher to enter and enable him to combat the patient's possessing spirit. In effect then the teacher's spirit possesses the exorcist. The theory is that, along with the teacher, the divine angels (*thewada*) are also invoked to come into the exorcist; it is the teacher and the *thewada* who, through the vehicle of the exorcist, wage battle with the possessing spirit. Here we see that the *thewada* are categorically opposed to the malevolent *phii*; also that while the *thewada* and the teacher are voluntarily solicited to descend and take possession of the exorcist, the patient has, by contrast, been invaded and possessed by an intruding and unwanted spirit.

From the standpoint of the actual technique by which the exorcist reaches the ecstatic state of trance and trembling, what the observer sees is an increase in the speed with which the unintelligible magical spells are repeated, accompanied by the waving and shaking of arms which also increases in tempo, until the whole body shakes so as to bring the exorcist to his feet. He then exhibits a frenzy of physical movement and a violent change in voice which produces a distorted flow of words. The exorcist is now speaking with the voice of divine angels and his teacher; they are within him; he is they. This process is called *tham soon*, which has two meanings: to make the teacher and the divine angels 'come into him'; to 'become angry'. The exorcist is indeed now in a state of fury, as he rushes to confront the malevolent spirit within the patient.

3. *Making the possessing spirit reveal itself*: the exorcist shakes and jumps, and kicks the persons present, but it is the patient who bears the brunt of what may be called shock therapy. The exorcist frightens the patient, whips him with a rattan stem with a top made of white cotton, or with a fern. In extreme cases he may use a tiger's tooth and pierce the patient, extracting blood and eliciting howls. At the same time he verbally threatens the afflicting spirit thus: 'Are you afraid of me? I'm a representative of *thewada*, I've come from heaven to drive you out.'

The theory, as I have said before, is that the *thewada* and the power of the teacher confront the malevolent spirit. If the patient's body is attacked it is not he but the spirit who feels pain. If the patient cries and talks it is the possessing spirit which does so. The strategy of this therapy is to make the spirit reveal its identity. In the case of the *phii paub* the revelation is that of its living or dead human host. The admission of its identity by the spirit automatically signals its defeat, and the therapy can then move towards its expulsion.

I interpret the implications of the revelation of the possessing *phii* thus: Culturally, the manifestation of the patient's violent hysterical and psychosomatic symptoms is interpreted as due to spirit intrusion and possession. The patient himself is out of touch with reality and lives in a world of hallucination. The strategy of therapy is to re-establish through shock-effects the patient's contact with the world (both through pain and by confronting him with a magnified fearsome figure in the form of the exorcist) and to force him,[1] by *naming an external agent as the cause, to formulate in concrete terms the nature of his malady*. The hysterical patient is in a state of emotional lesion; the problem is to make him conceptualize and identify the nature of his condition. In spirit possession the cultural definition is that an external agency is the cause, not the internal condition of the patient. Once the patient has identified an external agency, he has also automatically expelled the offending disease. The remarkable thing about this theory of mental and physical disturbance is that the victim is not blamed for his condition; he bears no guilt because the illness is not generated internally.

The drama is over when the patient has identified his persecutor. Both patient and exorcist are said to become quiet if the therapy has been successful. The therapy now progresses to the purification of the patient and his reincorporation into normal life.

4. *Purification*: the purification of the patient consists of reciting charms and lustration with and drinking of charmed water, administered by the exorcist at three locations: outside the house at the foot of the ladder, on the threshold platform of the house, and finally inside the house at the place called *huean naui* (small house) where guests are entertained. This orderly progression of words, purification with water, and house categories expresses forceful meanings.

The exorcist first makes lustral water by chanting sacred words (*seek namon*) into a bowl of water prepared by the inmates of the patient's house:

(*a*) then the patient is made to sit on the ground beneath the house-ladder while the exorcist stands on the top rung. He chants sacred verses called *gatha lai* (verses to chase away) into the water and pours it on the head of the patient. This sequence is called *rodnamon tai khan dai* (pouring sacred water under the ladder);

---

[1] I shall hereafter use the generalized masculine to indicate either sex. The patient is more likely to be female.

(*b*) the exorcist now forms an arch with his left leg at the top of the ladder and the patient creeps through this arch and enters the open threshold–platform (*saan*). The exorcist thus appears to stand guard at the top of the ladder, giving entry to the exorcised patient but not to the malevolent spirit. The use of the leg in this fashion would be highly insulting in everyday life, and perhaps symbolizes the power of the exorcist;

(*c*) the next sequence takes place on the platform and is called *laang sanyed* (washing away bad things), which consists of sacred water again being poured on the patient at this place;

(*d*) the patient is then led to the *huean naui*, the place for entertaining guests. The exorcist 'blow spells' (*gatha seek*) into a small bowl of water which is then drunk by the patient. This sequence is referred to as 'washing the inside to come out' (*laang khanai org ma*). Thus after external purification, internal purification is performed;

(*e*) the next sequence, also performed at the *huen naui*, is called 'protecting at five places' (*cham haa prakaan*): the exorcist binds the neck, wrists and ankles of the patient with cord to prevent the spirit from entering his body again;

(*f*) the patient receives from the exorcist the five Buddhist precepts (*rab sin haa*). This is indeed a remarkable sequence, for normally it is the Buddhist monk alone who gives the precepts. This adds weight to my argument that the exorcist is in some respects 'impersonating' the monk;

(*g*) lastly, the exorcist gives the patient *khan haa* (five pairs of flowers and candles) which he must place at the head of his bed inside the *huean yaai* (the large house, i.e. the sleeping quarters). He must not remove them until he is fully cured. The patient may subsequently visit the exorcist a couple of times for more sacred water to be poured on him to help the convalescence.

The purification procedure exhibits two noteworthy features. First, the external and internal cleansing with water is accompanied by verses chanted by the exorcist; these are secret spells, the contents of which are not heard by the patient or bystanders except as murmurings and which clearly do not communicate a verbal message to the patient as do the words in the *sukhwan* ritual. They are, however, perceived as powerful in themselves. We have noted that in Phraan Muan the village exorcist himself did not know the meaning of the words, so that for him too they were powerful spells because they were believed to be taken from the Buddhist texts.

Secondly, the orderly progression of lustration from the foot of the house-ladder, then to the house-platform (which is normally looked upon as unclean and at which guests entering the house must wash their feet), then to the *huean naui*, the place for entertaining guests and kin, and finally the placing of ritual articles in the private and sacred sleeping quarters (*huean yaai*), embodies a set of meanings which are clear in terms of the values attached to different parts of the house elucidated in Chapter 2. The patient starts as an 'outsider', then climbs up to the open platform which is the unclean threshold to the house and is purified externally there; he then enters the room where guests are entertained and undergoes internal cleansing; and finally, cured and protected from the malevolent spirit, he enters the private part of the house where at night he will sleep, guarded by sacred objects given by the exorcist. The progression is a neat dramatization of progressive reincorporation into normal family life. The melodrama of exorcism in its final phases, when it enacts the return of the patient to normality and the resumption of his place in family life, utilizes the simple but powerful symbolism of the social values attached to different parts of the house.

THE ACCUSED AND HIS FATE

We have seen in the case of possession by *phii paub* that the exorcism procedure is to force the patient, or more accurately the possessing spirit, to reveal and identify itself. Village theory is that the *phii paub* may reside in a living person, or may belong to a dead host who is revisiting the village.

In terms of the ongoing social relations of the village, there is no complication if the *phii paub* confesses its association with a dead human. But if a living person is named, then of course an entirely new dimension is introduced. What are the sanctions against the living witch? Are accusations of witchcraft symptomatic of structural strains and stresses in the social structure?

I am unable to tackle these questions systematically, because possession by *phii paub* and therefore exorcism rituals have in recent times declined to the extent that they are considered extraordinary. In the circumstances, I was only able to record details of cases that occurred in the village in the past. While it is relatively easy to study the theory of spirit possession and the ritual procedures from the experts, it is more difficult to get, concerning actual cases of possession, the circumstantial details necessary for a sociological analysis. Any statement of a sociological order based on hearsay is necessarily unsatisfactory and incomplete.

It would appear that when living hosts of *phii paub* were named, they were usually of three types: (1) a *mau wicha*, a practitioner of powerful disease or love magic, who was suspected of using this knowledge unethically, or more usually, who had become a *phii paub* host because the spells had turned bad inside him (or her) as a result of breaking taboos; (2) an outsider, male or female, who had come to reside in the village by virtue of marriage; (3) a stranger who had passed through the village.

It is clear to the anthropologist, from his knowledge of village attitudes and of social relations in general, that the villagers of Baan Phraan Muan would be prone to view malevolent agents more as disorderly forces emanating from the unpredictable external non-human world or the world of the dead than as originating amongst their living contemporary fellow-villagers and kin. And if in the case of *phii paub* possession a living person is named, then he or she is likely not to be a close kinsman but either a peripheral person or, as in the case of the *mau wicha*, someone who is unlike the ordinary villager by virtue of consorting with dangerous forces.

The sanctions traditionally applied against the witch appear to be consonant with this view that *phii paub* possession and accusations were on the whole a 'peripheral' phenomenon, in two senses of the word. First, the accused were, if living persons, marginal to the village community; secondly, the experiencing of possession and the rituals of exorcism were in incidence and in terms of their significance for the entire field of religion and ritual of somewhat minor importance. Village religion is dominated by Buddhism, *khwan* ritual, and the cult of the *guardian phii*; the malevolent spirits figure as breaches in this ordered world. Thus I consider *phii paub* possession and exorcism to be peripheral in the sense I. M. Lewis referred to spirit possession among the Somali as 'peripheral' in the spectrum of religious experience and action (Lewis 1966).

Villagers say that when a living resident of the same or of another village was named, ordinarily no action was taken against him. The ritual concentrated on the exorcism rather than on the accused host of the spirit. But if there was a sudden wave of possessions in the village and the victims named the same person as the *phii paub* host, extreme action was taken in the face of these cumulative accusations and evidence, whereby the accused was asked to leave the village or was simply forced out by stone-throwing and threatened violence. In extreme cases, then, witchcraft accusations had serious implications for village life, and the offender was summarily expelled. Thus repeated and cumulative accusations were resolved by expulsion of the accused from the village rather than by making an attempt to heal relations. Sanctions against witchcraft ranged from ignoring the accused to his expulsion. This system of sanctions accorded with the fact that accusations had little to do with the key social relations in the village social system.

To report now three instances of *phii paub* accusations in the past.

Exorcism as healing ritual

A woman was accused in the village, some thirty years ago, of being a *phii paub* host. A number of victims had over time named her as the person harbouring the spirit which entered them. At the time of the accusations, this woman was thirty years old, had two children, and had come to the village from outside and taken up virilocal residence. The village exorcist and all the villagers were convinced she was a *phii paub*. Villagers stoned her house at night. The village elders solicited the aid of an elderly monk from a neighbouring village, who poured sacred water on her, and told her on behalf of the villagers to leave the village. It is said that the woman confessed to the monk that she was a *phii paub*. The village in fact drove her away with her family, including her husband. After she left, the epidemic of spirit attack subsided. The woman moved to her natal village of Baan Chiang Yuen, only a few miles away, and is apparently still alive and leading a normal life there.

Nang Uan is an elderly mother living in the village. More than ten years ago she was afflicted with spirit possession. She cried and she mourned and did not open her eyes. Her husband and fellow villagers diagnosed the affliction as *phii paub* possession and invited the exorcist to deal with her. She was given the shock therapy I have already described and upon questioning identified the *phii paub* host as a stranger from the village of Baan Khao (in the same *tambon* as that to which Phraan Muan belongs); while he was passing through the village, the spirit had entered her. The spirit was successfully exorcized; the accusation itself was unimportant. Nang Uan has never been afflicted again.

Nang Sai, a young married woman of the village, died in childbirth some ten years ago. Her child survived. Her delivery was difficult and she behaved like a woman possessed. An exorcist was sent for but he did not arrive in time. After her death, a diviner was consulted and he diagnosed the death as caused by *phii paub* possession and identified Phau San as the perpetrator of the crime. Phau San was not a native of the village; he came from another province (Mahasarakam) and had settled here uxorilocally. He is reported to have studied *wicha ha khom* (magical control of epidemics) and was widely suspected of letting loose disease in the village in order to earn money through treating patients. It was suspected that he did not observe the taboos of his profession. Hence the diviner's diagnosis merely confirmed village opinion. Phau San was driven away from the village by the usual recourse to nocturnal stone-throwing. It is reported that he went south to get 'cured' but was unsuccessful and died some years later. His wife and children separated from him and went away in another direction: their whereabouts are not known.

EXORCISM IN RELATION TO OTHER RITUALS

The exorcistic ritual reveals very interesting features when placed in relation to Buddhist rites. Let us keep in mind certain features and inferences already stated concerning the monk's rites, especially the three-dimensional character of the Pali sacred words (which derive their power because they are related to the Buddha, the *Dhamma* and the *Sangha*), and the ritual transaction by which monks transfer grace to laymen who have previously asserted their adherence to the precepts and the Trinity, and have demonstrated their right intention through gift-giving.

In spite of the overall differences, the exorcistic ritual manifests some remarkable parallels. The trinity of features which give efficacy to the exorcistic ritual can be clearly seen.

1. The exorcist demonstrates his filiation to his teacher (*guru*) and through him to the line of ascending teachers culminating in the supreme *guru*. The sacred words gain their authority through this impeccable derivation, and in the ritual situation the spiritual power of these teachers is present in the officiant. This assertion of a genealogy has an added feature in rituals employing *mantra*. *Mantra* are *secret* formulae, jealously guarded, revealed and taught by the teacher to his initiated pupil.

2. We have seen that the spells of the exorcist, which he recites esoterically, are said to be derived from Buddhist *gatha* and *paritta*—perhaps distorted and adapted—which are publicly and audibly recited by monks. Not only this, but the exorcist at the beginning of the rite pays homage to the Buddhist Trinity, worships the Buddha statue and his teacher, invokes the *thewada*, and even administers in the course of the rite the Buddhist precepts. Clearly this is a use of Buddhist procedures with a twist and an inversion.

3. The third basis for the efficacy of the ritual stems from the special properties of the exorcist himself—who theoretically has been trained in the proper intonation of the words, observes food and liquor taboos in the service of bodily purity, and undergoes certain acts of preparation.

These three features are paralleled in the monk's rites, especially in respect of the three-dimensional character of the Pali sacred words. But the formal similarities must not be allowed to obscure the differences in the transactions. In the Buddhist case, monks publicly and audibly transfer grace through sacred words to laymen who support the faith. By contrast, in the exorcistic rite the exorcist is a protagonist confronting a malevolent antagonist, and uses spells which are esoterically muttered to magnify his power and to master and dominate the enemy.

Thus, from this point of view, it is clear that the monk and the exorcist, the Buddhist religious action and the rites addressed to malevolent spirits (especially the exorcism procedure), are strongly contrasted. The first is devoted to the achievement of merit whereas the latter is concerned with the removal of unwanted supernatural contact. The monk in theory has no contact with malevolent spirits; the higher and purer religious pursuit is insulated from contamination by the lower pursuit. Nevertheless, the hierarchy of village religious values is expressed in the fact that the exorcist is a Buddhist and relates himself to Buddhism while practising his doctrinally devalued art. Everyone in the village is a Buddhist first and foremost. But most intriguing is that the exorcist is in some ways a 'mock' monk who uses the sacred words of the monk in a manner which is apparently antithetical to the use made of them by the monk. There is, then, an interesting inversion and a link between the ascetic monk and the dionysiac exorcist which is partly traceable to the notion of miraculous powers (*iddhi*) in doctrinal Buddhism itself, to the use made of sacred words in all ritual as embodiments and carriers of power, and finally to the notion of normal and abnormal death reflected on the one hand in the mortuary rites of Buddhism, and on the other in the spirit cults in the form of guardians and ancestors versus victims of sudden or violent death.

The contrast and link between the malevolent spirits and the village guardian spirits, and their respective rituals and specialists, are of a different kind. The major contrast is that guardian spirits have a collective village significance as controllers of agricultural fertility and rain, and in this respect the cults addressed to them have a territorial and communal aspect. The malevolent spirits only act capriciously against individuals, and the rites addressed to remove their influence primarily concern the victim and his household, not necessarily the wider kinship group or the territorial community. The ritual specialists of the guardian spirits are either their intermediaries who propitiate them or mediums through whom they verbally communicate with human beings. The exorcist is also an intermediary and a medium, but of the power of divine angels and his teacher, and he makes combat with the malevolent spirit who is his enemy. While these contrasts are clear, there is some overlap, however, in the fact that guardian spirits can also punish individuals and are in such instances propitiated in a manner similar to that adopted when malevolent spirits cause minor illnesses and are placated (not exorcized). But even here there is a contrast: when guardian spirits cause individual affliction they are seen as acting not capriciously but as upholders of moral values. The relation between the exorcism ritual and the *khwan* ritual warrants special comment. The *khwan* ritual is a prophylactic (and healing) ritual; the exorcism ritual also is a healing ritual. The situations they deal with, the techniques of therapy and the expressive symbolism and communication structures of the two systems are therefore of analytical interest. At the conclusion of Chapter 13 on *Sukhwan* rites, I formulated a hypothesis which I indicated might be confirmed after the data in this chapter had been presented.

The *sukhwan* ritual, we saw, is built around the notion of *khwan*, a man's spirit essence, the presence of which is considered essential to well-being and which is believed to leave the body and escape into the outside world, usually the forest. The flight of the *khwan* is most likely to occur in certain situations, especially before undergoing rites of passage or preliminary to integration into village society (and its constituent groups) or at moments of actual or potential departure from it. Village elders recall the escaped essence and aggregate it to the body, thereby charging the celebrant with morale, and restoring his sense of wholeness and well-being.

The exorcism ritual represents a different therapeutic situation, in which the exact reverse of the elements in *sukhwan* ritual is represented. Here a person is mentally and physically ill because an alien external agent has entered him, which produces in the patient an alienation from society. The ritual technique here consists of persuading the patient to define his illness by naming the attacking agent, thereby enabling the patient to re-establish contact with society. The remarkable aspect of this theory of mental illness and the therapy for it is that its cause is externalized and objectified in an outside force or agency. The patient thus is not held responsible for the illness; nor is it seen as being caused by events or processes generated inside the human organism. He does not carry the burden of guilt or personal responsibility. I must emphasize that these statements describe culturally defined and conceptualized notions of disease and curative procedures. From the clinical or psychotherapeutic point of view, it may well be that what the healing ritual does is change 'idiosyncratic conflicts and defenses to culturally conventional conflicts and ritualized symptoms', and that the cure achieves a 'social remission' for the patient. (See Ari Kiev 1964, p. 27.)

The *sukhwan* and exorcism rituals are, from a comparative point of view, expressions of two explanations of disease causation commonly found in many societies: loss of vital substance from the body (soul loss), and introduction of an external and harmful substance in the body, this including spirit intrusion or possession. In the Thai case, loss of spirit essence may be likened to a state of diffuseness in the person; the ritual by charging morale re-establishes concentration of mind and achieves moral commitment to status requirements. Intrusion of a foreign spirit results in the opposite state of over-concentration on (preoccupation with) oneself and withdrawal and alienation from society. Normal relations with society are re-established through expelling the cause of abnormal behaviour.

19

A KALEIDOSCOPIC VIEW OF
THE RELIGIOUS FIELD

Thus far four ritual complexes have been examined, both independently and in respect of their mutual links. The ritual complexes are: Buddhist ritual (i.e. rites conducted by monks), *khwan* rites, cult of the guardian spirits, and rites addressed to the malevolent spirits. The aim of this chapter will be to co-ordinate the salient features of these complexes in order to present the totality as a *field*.

There are several possible ways of presenting the distributional features of the total field. We might view it as a spectrum in which the four ritual complexes arranged side by side form a succession of dominant colours which, however, overlap at their margins. Or we could view the field as a circle divided into four sectors, each representing a ritual complex. The sectors could again be divided into segments to represent the components of the complex, and these segments of the same order could be contrasted.

Ideally, a total field is best displayed in terms of the linguist's notion of hierarchy, which is made up of successively larger units at more comprehensive levels (e.g. a lexical hierarchy ranging upwards from morpheme to word to phrase or sentence, etc.), or a taxonomic hierarchy of successive inclusion of units. This kind of representation cannot be achieved with our data. One primary reason for this may be that anthropology has not discovered as yet the kind of universal categories of ritual from which by transformations the higher levels are built. But there is also another reason why the empirical data, as identified now, do not quite build up into a neat hierarchical scheme. The ritual complexes not only portray oppositional features but also share similarities and complementarities. Hence they cannot be neatly pigeon-holed, and their contrastive features have to be displayed on several frames of a shifting character.

It is indisputable that the ritual complexes exhibit patterns of contrastive features and it is therefore worthwhile to display their distribution on several dimensions. I have frequently used, in previous chapters, concepts such as opposition, complementarity, linkage and hierarchy (in the sense of differential evaluation) to describe these contrastive features. I shall attempt now to present them in a concise and formal manner.

337

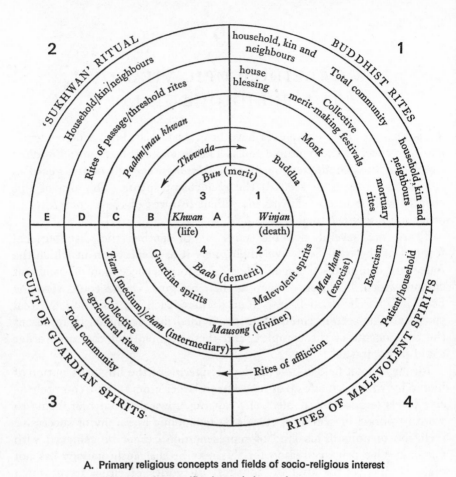

A. Primary religious concepts and fields of socio-religious interest
B. Supernatural personifications relating to A
C. Ritual specialists associated with B
D. Rites conducted by C
E. Scale of social participation in D

Fig. 5   The religious field

Figure 5 essays a picture of the total field using the circle and sector mode of representation. It is composed of five concentric circles divided into four sectors. Each sector represents a ritual complex (1-4), which is named at the rim of the outermost circle. It is convenient to treat each concentric circle as a band (A, B, C, D, E). Thus each of the 4 sectors (ritual complexes) has 5 segments or portions of bands, which are its components, and which if systematically compared will provide us with the contrastive features.

Band A is the innermost circle and is used to represent the primary religious concepts of the villagers. *Bun* (merit) and *baab* (demerit), *khwan* (spiritual essence associated with the maintenance of life) and *winjan* (spiritual essence that persists after death), are two pairs of primary religious conceptions which are diagrammatically represented as two axes. Their intersection provides four quarters which may be viewed as these dominant foci of religious action:

1. *good death and good rebirth*, which is the domain of Buddhist ritual *par excellence*;

2. *bad death and bad or delayed rebirth*, with which are associated the rites directed towards capricious and malevolent spirits;

3. *prosperity and orderly progression in life*, which is the domain of *khwan* rites;

4. *protection and fertility*, which are the themes of the guardian spirit cult.

Band B lists the supernatural personifications or entities which figure in religion. Their positions signify their relation to A.

Band C names the ritual specialists who deal with the supernaturals listed in B.

Band D lists the rites which are conducted by the specialists in C.

Band E gives details of the scale of social participation in the different rites in D.

The diagram is only a rough guide for making sense of the variety of religious phenomena. To avoid misunderstanding, it must be stated that it is not a conscious model on the part of the villagers; rather it is a composite picture derived from several analytical procedures. The starting point is the category distinctions made by the actors themselves. Apart from their verbalized religious concepts, the villagers, as we noted when we described their rites, made distinctions concerning the supernatural agents, kinds of offering to them, the types of ritual specialists, and the ritual idiom itself. The analyst, however, strives to go further. Having systematically worked through the beliefs and rites, he is in a position to present a total picture of the field wrought both from the conscious categorizations of the actors and from the patterns and structural features embedded in the rites which may be unknown to the actors.

Few villagers, if any, are faced with the need to contemplate or visualize the many aspects of their religion as an intellectual puzzle. A villager tends to act according to situation and context. He is aware that each religious context requires him to behave in a stipulated manner. The systematic arrangement and structuring of the religious field as such has to be sought not at the level of the individual actor but elsewhere—at the level of collective representations composed of religious ideas and formalized rituals.

The distinction I am making can be stated in a different way. If a villager is suffering from a misfortune, he may conduct a merit-making ritual for the monks and he may, at the same time, go to the diviner and on his instructions propitiate a guardian spirit. This does not mean that he is confusing Buddhist ritual with the spirit cult; it simply means that the misfortune may be interpreted as a consequence of lack of merit or as spirit affliction, or as both working in conjunction. From the point of view of the individual actor there are many strings to his religious bow, and furthermore, the different theories of mystical causation are not mutually exclusive in operation.

But if we view this same situation from a different perspective, from the standpoint of Buddhist ritual and the cult of the guardian spirits as ordered phenomena, we can see that, although a layman may resort to them simultaneously, their procedures are different. They represent different ethical ideas and different approaches to the supernatural; their ritual functionaries are separate and cannot intermingle roles; the grammar of their rites is not the same. As structured ritual complexes they are separated, segregated, and yet complementary. It is in this sense that they are separate collective representations within a single field, and the analyst tries to understand the logic of their differentiation in terms of underlying distinctions and relations.

CATEGORY DISTINCTIONS IN RITUAL OFFERINGS TO SUPERNATURALS

The following are the major classes of supernatural agents to whom village ritual action is addressed:

1. the Buddha image (and let us also include here the monks who, though not supernaturals, are associated with the same transaction);
2. *thewada* (divine angels), including Nang Thoranee (earth goddess);
3. *khwan* (spirit essence of human beings (and of rice));
4. guardian spirits of village, *wat* and swamp (*Tapubaan, Chao Phau Phraa Khao* and *Chao Phau Tong Khyang*);
5. malevolent and capricious spirits (*phii*).

There is a single linguistic index pertaining to food offerings which tells us that villagers reduce these five classes into two groups. All offerings to classes 1, 2 and 3 are referred to as *kryang bucha*, while those to 4 and 5 are called *liang phii*.

Kryang bucha: *bucha* is derived from the Indian word *puja*, which means 'propitiation' or 'ritual worship'. The Thai concept is used only in respect of certain supernaturals.

Offerings to the Buddha statue are called *kryang bucha khaw phraa*, that is, offerings presented to the Buddha statue in respect. There is no notion that the statue partakes of the essence of the food offered. It is relevant to note that the same type of offering is made to the monk in an attitude of respect (*pha khaw tawai phraa*). Food offered to the Buddha and the monks may consist of rice, meat and fish (*non*-vegetarian) but excludes liquor. Typically *bucha* offerings also include candles and flowers and joss-sticks.

Now, although offerings made to divine angels (*thewada*) are also called *kryang bucha*, they are typically vegetarian. This is interesting in view of the inclusion of meat in offerings to the Buddha (and the monks). An historical conjecture is that the brahmanical value of vegetarianism may be preserved in respect of the deities which originally belonged to the Hindu pantheon and were later brought within the fold of Buddhism. *Thewada* are both witnesses in Buddhist rites and an independent category opposed to *phii* (malevolent spirits), and their vegetarianism may be a contrast to the meat-eating character of *phii*. However, such speculation is not important to the orientation of the actors, for whom the overall *bucha* concept is dominant.

The food offerings in *sukhwan* ritual are also referred to as *kryang bucha*, although there is a more specific ritual item called the *phakhwan* which is a ceremonial conical structure filled with lumps of rice, bananas, boiled egg and flowers. Divine angels are invoked as witnesses and homage is made to the Buddhist Trinity in *khwan* rites, and therefore the linguistic extension makes sense.

Liang phii: this contrasting term, which means offerings to take care of spirits, is used in the case of both the guardian spirit cult and the rites addressed to malevolent spirits, thereby indicating that in this sense they comprise a common class. A common feature emphasized by the concept of *phii* is that guardian spirits and miscellaneous malevolent spirits alike may cause affliction to individuals and have therefore to be placated, or in the case of 'possession' driven out. In rites of affliction other than 'possession' which requires exorcism, we have seen that there are two sequences: (1) *kuad*, which means 'inviting' the spirit to leave with an opening offering; and (2) *pai karav*, which is a larger thanks-offering given after the spirit has removed its bad influence. In exorcism, however, instead of invitation to leave, we have *lai phii*, 'chasing away of the spirit', but the placatory offering made to the spirit after its expulsion is still called *liang phii*. This offering stands in contrast to that made by the exorcist to his teacher and the *thewada* at the beginning of the rite; it is a *bucha* type offering called *kaj*. Thus, the exorcist's ritual which deals with both *thewada* and *phii* clearly expresses the *bucha* and *liang phii* distinction.

We have seen before that there is an internal differentiation between the guardian spirit of the village, who is meat-eating, and the guardian spirit of the *wat*, who is vegetarian. Offerings to both, however, are *liang phii*. All malevolent spirits, as well as the guardian of the village (*Tapubaan*), are offered rice, varieties of meat, liquor, betel and tobacco—articles of a 'stronger' character than those employed in *bucha*.

In sum, then, the distinction between *bucha* and *liang phii* expresses a basic difference as to the form of communication and reciprocity between man and the supernatural. Offerings to the Buddha and the divine angels as well as the monks, are in formal ideology given as free gifts and to honour and pay respect to them. In the *phii* affliction rites, offerings are made in terms of a bargain and a fee if recovery is achieved. The same logic is carried over to the guardian spirit rituals of a collective nature conducted to solicit ample rain and good harvests.

It is this fundamental difference in the idiom of gift giving and making offerings that assigns Buddhist norms and action a higher place than those associated with spirit cults, in the hierarchy of values and acts that comprises the universe of religious action. The Buddhist idiom of selfless giving of gifts, control of passion through asceticism, and renunciation of worldly interests is an idealization and extension of the social norm of reciprocity. On the other hand, the coercive relationship of bargaining with spirits, their placation or subduing, is again a statement of power relations which are an extension of socially manipulative behaviour. Ethically the first ranks above the second, as purity above power; hierarchically the cults are similarly ordered. The social existence of the people of Baan Phraan Muan is inevitably fraught with moments of harmony and disharmony. Religious action devoted to the securing of the former and the elimination of the latter is modelled on the possibilities of social relationships ranging from altruism to naked power. However ethically valued, both are stubbornly present in real life—and if either should gain supremacy life would be heaven on earth or pure hell; both are improbable.

The religious field: kaleidoscopic view

CONTRASTIVE FEATURES OF RITUAL FUNCTIONARIES

1	Monk	conducts Buddhist rites
2	*Paahm, mau khwan*	village elder, ex-monk, who performs *khwan* rites
3(*a*)	*Mau Song*	diviner who channels patients and is primarily concerned with spirit affliction
(*b*)	*Tiam*	medium of guardian spirits
(*c*)	*Cham*	intermediary of guardian spirits
4	*Mau Tham*	exorcist

The four broad categories of ritual experts relate to the four major ritual complexes.

1. The Buddhist *monk* is the only ritual expert in the village who practises his vocation as a full-time occupation as long as he is in robes. The office of monk expresses the value of asceticism for male youth. The monk has access to sacred words in Pali which, when recited, transfer prosperity to laymen. He is chiefly (but not exclusively) engaged in collective merit-making and mortuary rites. He receives gifts, transfers merit, and mediates between life and death. His ritual procedure is controlled, austere and non-ecstatic. While in robes a monk has nothing to do with spirit (*phii*) rites, but he can be the celebrant in *khwan* rites.

2. The *paahm* or *mau khwan* is typically a village elder, householder (*phuu thaw*), ex-monk, and a literate. There is no contradiction between *khwan* rites and monkish ritual. *Khwan* rites are primarily concerned with initiation into new statuses at birth, marriage, ordination, and with various threshold situations. The *paahm's* ritual procedure also is non-ecstatic and puts emphasis on public recitation of words. Like the monk he transfers grace, but the procedure is symbolized as restoring to the celebrant his spirit essence (morale), which has escaped him. The monk/ *paahm* relation involves a co-existential relationship within the same society of the classical *bhikkhu* and *brahman*, who were antagonists in the parent country (India). In the village context there is a direct reciprocity between elders as *paahm* and their children or grandchildren (*luug-laan*) on the one side, and on the other, between monks as *luug-laan* and elders to whom merit is transferred. In fact, a number of reciprocal oppositions hang together and may be summarized as follows:

Gift giving	Asceticism
Paahm/householder	Monk
(Normal) Secular life	(Abnormal) Sacred life
Elders (*phuu thaw*)	Male youth (*luug-laan*)

These features can be read both vertically and laterally as forming inter-connected sets.

3(*a*). The diviner (*mau song*) is of an intermediate status in this comparison of ritual experts. He plays a bridging role as diagnostician in the curing of disease. He is never called to office by a spirit but becomes diviner through mastery of a technique, and is not directly associated with the propitiation of spirits. His technique verges on the ecstatic. He is distinctly separate from *paahm* and no one person performs in both capacities.

(*b*). More clear-cut are the contrastive features of medium (*tiam*) and intermediary (*cham*) of the spirit guardians. They acquire their powers through possession by the spirit guardians and their techniques are ecstatic, expressing extraordinary and idiosyncratic mystical powers. These ritual offices are not tied to village leadership as the office of *paahm* is. Furthermore, the fact that women can and frequently do become mediums points up an underlying male/female distinction embedded in the Buddhist and *khwan* rites (whose functionaries are male) which does not prevail in the spirit cults.

4. The exorcizer (*mau tham*) is employed when a malevolent spirit 'possesses' a patient. The exorcist coerces or chases out the spirit, a technique that sets him apart from *tiam* and *cham*. By virtue of the secret knowledge of charms (which are said to be Buddhist *gathas*) he exercises control over afflicting spirits with whom he communicates, not as a medium but as a master invested with more potent power. His technique is ecstatic like the medium's. In all these respects the exorcist stands in opposition to the monk, in relation to whom, however, he is an 'inversion'. When compared to the *paahm*, we see that whereas the exorcist displaces an unwanted external spirit which has entered the patient, the *paahm* replaces an escaped spirit substance internal to the patient.

CONTRASTS IN THE SCALE OF SOCIAL PARTICIPATION AND SIGNIFICATION

We need now to view the four ritual complexes within the framework of social groupings and scale of social participation, in order to appreciate their spheres of relevance from the standpoint of social structure.

The social groupings are divided into three broad levels ranging from (1) individual/household/compound; to (2) bilateral kin (and neighbours); to (3) community. We shall see that Buddhist rites and the cult of the guardian spirits span all these levels while *khwan* rites and rites addressed to malevolent spirits are more narrow in their scope.

The religious field: kaleidoscopic view

Individual, household and compound

At this level rites conducted by Buddhist monks are concerned with such threshold ceremonies as house-blessing and housewarming (*khyn huean mai*) and with merit-making by the members of a household or compound (*thambun baan*). Such rites are of small importance in the whole spectrum of rites in which monks participate. The chief recipients of merit are the household and compound members, although the attendance may be wider.

In contrast the *khwan* rites have primary significance at this level of social structure, for example pregnancy and childbirth, marriage (i.e. recruitment to and establishment of families and households), and situations concerned with the economic interests and prosperity of households and compounds. In such events, the wider community is interested in the fortunes of its smallest constituent units.

There is a further narrowing in the case of spirit rites dealing with the afflictions of individual patients. Here the patient and the intermediary are the major parties involved, and the occasion (illness) has little relevance outside the household and compound. The rites in question involve propitiation of malevolent spirits and exorcism to remove misfortunes and illness.

Bilateral kin (and neighbours)

Monks are importantly involved in mortuary rites, whose significance extends to bilateral kin and neighbours. Death is an event at which institutionalized Buddhism directly participates in the family and kinship networks of villagers. Thus the juxtaposition of Buddhist mortuary rites, which deal with lesions or ruptures of the social structure and which mediate between death and rebirth, and *khwan* rites, which are concerned with initiation into statuses and with incorporation into village social life, provides us with a clue to their social significance: the reciprocities between the parental generation of elders (*phuu thaaw*) and their successors (*luug-laan*).

The cults relating to spirits (*phii*) have little significance at this intermediate level of social structure.

Community

While *khwan* rites and spirit affliction rites have no collective communal significance, both Buddhist rites and the cult of the guardian spirits have village and regional significance. The entire village and representatives from surrounding villages participate as a single congregation in the calendrical *wat* festivals. The guardian spirit rituals have a similar representative feature—in fact, signified more distinctly than Buddhist rites as solidarities of people associated with territory, both village and region—which is expressed in the biannual agricultural rites and rain-making festival.

Our conclusion is that in certain conspicuous ways Buddhism and the guardian spirit cult have a symmetrical and balanced position in village and regional life. Both are congregational: Buddhism draws together human beings in its temples, located in villages, in which their sons and grandsons serve as monks; the guardian cult assembles village communities (collections of households) and regional communities (collections of villages) together as territorial bodies under the protection of guardian 'fathers' whose 'children' human beings are. Furthermore, Buddhism and the guardian cult intersect at one point which is of primary interest to all peasants—the ensuring of rains and agricultural fertility and prosperity.

I regard the complex relationship between Buddhism and the cult of guardian spirits examined in previous chapters as a major contribution of this book and a corrective to that kind of formulation which has phrased their relation in classical terms—as religion versus magic, expressive action versus instrumental action, church versus client. Their complex relationship can be seen differently and more illuminatingly if we regard them as separate, opposite, complementary and linked foci of religious action within a single field.

THE GRAMMAR OF RITUAL TRANSACTIONS

Let us forget for the time being the meanings and associations that global concepts like Buddhism, Animism, and Spirit Worship have for us and seek in a different manner the principles of ordering and differentiation exhibited by the variety of rituals examined here. We might use the notions of particles or units, sequences of particles, and the grammar of these sequences to uncover this order.

In the rituals described we saw that villagers identified and labelled discrete sequences which broke up into smaller sequences or particles. It might be said that a progression of certain particles of activity produced a ritual sequence, and a set of finite sequences the complete rite. The identification and contrasting of these various 'emic' units and sequences will enable us to say something of the lexical structure and meaning of the ritual transactions. Since I have already analysed in great detail the form of these rituals, I shall here merely contrast the general features of some major classes of rites.

346

The religious field: kaleidoscopic view

Three rites can be chosen to represent the variety in Buddhist rites: a simple house-blessing ceremony, a mortuary rite, and the *Kathin* festival.

(*a*) *Major sequences in house-blessing rite*

(Following)

Evening chanting ———→ Morning chanting ———→ Feasting of monks
(*suad mon yen*)   (*suad mon chaw*)   and giving them gifts

This rite has three major sequences. In the evening the main body of *paritta* chants are recited to 'charge' the house and its inmates, and holy water is made; the next morning the monks return to chant the victory blessing and to sprinkle the lustral water; finally the monks are given their morning meal (and other gifts) and they chant the *anumodana gatha* (acceptance with blessing).

(*b*) *Major sequences in mortuary rite*

This is a more complex and prolonged ritual and the major sequences are best set out as happenings on different days:

First day   ———→   Second day   ———→   Second night and two
(Chanting by monks to   Funeral procession and   successive nights
desacralize corpse and   cremation of corpse   Chanting to purify
presentation of food to   house and inmates
them)

———→   Fifth day   ———→   Conclusion (same day)
          Bone collection and   Presentation of *prasaat peung*
          effecting the passage   of gifts and food by the
          of the dead man's   bereaved to monks in order to
          winjan to heaven   transfer merit to the dead man

(*c*) *Kathin festival* (a collective festival)

First day

    Morning   Evening
    Feasting of monks and ———→ Suad mongkhon chanting, that is,
    assembling of gifts   collective purification and
                              protection threshold ceremony

Second day

    Morning
    Villagers receive ———→ Kathin procession ———→ Monks give
    5 precepts from   and presentation of   blessings and
    monks   gifts to monks   sermon

                  Evening
     ———→ Fair and funmaking

The festival demonstrates well the ideology of voluntary gift giving for purposes of merit-making. Gifts are made *first* and monks reciprocate

347

later. The ideal Buddhist transaction occurs: the presentation of gifts as a voluntary act and in proper spiritual state precedes the transfer of grace by monks. In the mortuary and house-blessing rites, however, we see that the monks first chant and perform their ritual service and are rewarded *afterwards* with food and gifts. Yet this reward is very definitely conceived as a gift, though the sequences are suggestive of payment for specialist service, a service that receives explicit formulation in the spirit rites, in which monks do not participate.

Let us now contrast the Buddhist transactional idiom with that of the collective guardian cult.

(*d*) The sequences in the rain-making festival (*Bunbangfai*) are slightly different from those of the Buddhist festival.

First day ⟶	*Second day* ⟶	*Third day*
Merit transferred by villagers to the guardian deities by ordaining sons as monks	Procession to shrine, presenting food, firing of rocket of respect	Firing rocket of request for rain and promise of larger offering in the following year

⟶ Ritual licence and fun making

The festival combines elements of respectful propitiation of a deity through offerings, and elements of a bargain to be followed on fulfilment by the payment of a fee. The latter element is the more dominant theme and is unambiguously expressed in the biannual agricultural rites which show two major sequences.

(*e*)	*Before ploughing* ⟶	*After harvesting*
	Minor offering of food, request for a good yield and *promise* of a large offering after harvest	Fulfilling of promise, large offering, and expressing of thanks. Also request for good yield in the following year

The element of bargain and promise of later payment is given its most explicit statement in the dealings with malicious spirits which cause illness. The transaction with the supernatural is paralleled by that with the specialist: he, too, is given an opening fee and a completion fee.

(*f*) The transactions in the *khwan* rites, in which elders conduct rites of passage and of status assumption for their successors, are cast in an idiom that is different from that expressed either in Buddhist ritual or in spirit rites. Here the officiant, who is an elder, backed by a supporting cast who are village elders, transfers by chanting and ritual acts morale to the celebrant(s), and at the end instead of receiving a gift or a fee, he and the elders make gifts to the celebrant(s). Ritual service and gifts *go in the same direction* as demanded by the logic of the ritual context. It is clear that the idiom of the *khwan* rite is closer to the Buddhist than to the spirit rites.

The three modes of ritual transactions that inhere in the rites are paralleled by three different uses of language in the same rites.

THREE USES OF SACRED WORDS

Throughout this monograph I have attempted to view the various rituals as culturally structured systems of communication which transmit messages, and have stated that the effects sought rely on transference in which the sender of the message, the receiver, and the supporting cast all occupy meaningful positions in a ritual situation or context. I have also indicated that to understand the mechanism of transference it is not enough to decode the language of non-verbal ritual acts, but that we must also investigate what the 'sacred' words say and how they are used in conjunction with ritual acts to effect the transference. My conclusion is that in the three ritual complexes in which sacred words figure importantly the words are used differently, and that their distinctive roles can be understood fully only in terms of the total religious field.

One use of sacred words—in this case Pali chants—by monks in Buddhist ritual has received detailed treatment. Pali chants are recited at various occasions; they are by and large not understood by the audience; the words, however, are viewed as charged with power and listening to them in itself confers merit. The sacred power and authority of the words derives from a threefold relation expressed in the Buddhist Trinity, and the semantics of the ritual consists of a metaphorical use of words linked with a metonymical manipulation of objects and corresponding acts. The monks in fact at the close of chanting confer blessings of a this-worldly kind on the laity. The mechanism involved in this transference has to be seen in terms of the relation between monk and layman, of village monastic institutions and their integration with village interests and life. Through proper ritual procedures the monk, who is an ascetic, partly aggregated to the world of death, transmutes Buddha's conquests (through non-violence, compassionate love, and restraint of the dangers and sufferings inherent in human existence), expressed in sacred words, into prosperity and mental states free of pain and transfers these blessings to the laity, who are ethically inferior and rooted in this world. In effecting this transference mere access to the sacred Pali words by the monk is not enough; two crucial conditions are right conduct and discipline on the part of the monk and right intention, merit-making and liberality expressed by free gift giving on the part of the layman. The monk's mediation is effective because he is an apt mediator.

In the case of the *sukhwan* ritual the words recited by the officiant in fact comprise the major part of the ceremony. This ritual is structured as a prophylactic and therapeutic device. The words, which significantly are expressed in the local language rather than in a sacred and unknown language, are meant to transmit a message that is intended to alter the orientations of the celebrant. While the non-verbal part of the ritual shows only small variations, the words are changed to suit particular occasions. The ritual's effectiveness depends on the role of village elders, whose representative the officiant is, and who act as supporting witnesses in the initiation of youth into statuses. The ritual texts are by no means secret; they are in theory accessible to all who can read; but the efficacy of the words partly derives from the fact that it is a venerable elder acceptable to the village community who, supported by village elders, plays the role of officiant. The *sukhwan* ritual often resembles a teaching situation, which becomes all the more effective inasmuch as it is dramatized as a grand mythological event in which the chief participants are invested with elevated attributes.

The third use of sacred words is exemplified in the exorcism ritual. Sacred words are again important in this therapeutic ritual but play quite a different role from either of those in the other two contexts. There are certain formal similarities with the monk's ritual in that the exorcist's words are thought to derive their efficacy from a three-dimensional relation (authority of the original teacher, the power embedded in the words themselves, and the special characteristics of the practitioner). But the exorcism ritual is a shock therapy. The exorcist as the protagonist in the ritual, combating the possessing spirit, shows in dramatic form the supra-human powers of the supernatural agents whose vehicle be becomes. Significantly the charms and spells he recites are believed to be taken from the Buddhist sacred texts, but a vital difference is that their knowledge is secret, and the words have been transformed into powerful spells which are uttered esoterically. The exorcist as a mock, dionysiac monk coerces the patient into revealing the identity of the intruding malevolent agent. It is not the monk's ethical power that the exorcist wields, but rather the dangerous power acquired through secret instruction by a *guru* and the ability to induce and experience an abnormal state of mind.

20

THE PARADE OF SUPERNATURALS

It might be thought by those who have an 'elevated' view of religion that I am being frivolous in concluding an exposition of a religion with a myth and a rite concerning rice, the staple food of the villagers. In doing so, I do not want to argue that religion is a metaphysical projection of the rumblings of the stomach. On the contrary, I use rice as a point of reference in order to suggest that the primary and basic interest of the villagers—the production, consumption and distribution of food—is so impregnated with moral and ethical conceptions that this myth and rite provide a miniature view of the universe in which nature, society and the deities combine and play their parts. It should cause no surprise that one of the idioms in which Thai villagers express their ethical values is in terms of the language of food transactions. The myth I deal with is not a summary of all their myths, nor does it encompass all their religious conceptions. It is, however, a comprehensive one, which reflects from one vantage point the major religious ideas and brings into perspective the cults of the village. It gives us a vivid suggestion of the moral and emotional ambience of village religion; it is a rainbow refraction of the religious prism; and it places in focus other pictures which have come into view in the course of previous analysis. Moreover, at the beginning of this book I gave a brief account of a cosmology that is inscribed in the written treatises of the grand Buddhist tradition. It is therefore appropriate that at the end of the monograph I should show how this same cosmology comes alive in the social life of villagers as they pursue their ordinary tasks of living.

The supernatural actors whom we have witnessed playing their parts on the village stage now parade before us in this myth to take their curtain call. They belong to one troupe. But in the rite associated with the myth, man also makes his ultimate declaration of his role in the drama, and states the dignified manner in which he confronts the supernaturals.

MYTH: THE STORY OF NANG PHRAKOSOB
(THE FEMALE SPIRIT OF RICE)[1]

In the time of Phraya Wirupakha[2] rice grew by itself in his garden. The rice stalk was big in girth—seven times the size of the human fist. The

---

[1] This myth is written down in an ola-leaf manuscript; it was read to us by a villager. The following is a free translation of the recording, with some abbreviations.

[2] Wirupakha (Virupaksha) is the King of the *Nagas* and is one of the four world guardians (*lokapala*) presided over by God Indra. See details in Chapter 3 on Cosmology.

351

rice plant had many stalks with many heads of paddy on them. The circumference of each grain of paddy was five times that of the fist; its length was five finger spans. The grain was as bright as silver and it had the fragrance of coconut and cow's milk. Human beings were attracted by these qualities in the rice and so brought it to Chao Rathi,[1] who informed them that the rice belonged to Phraya Wirupakha, who lived in heaven and came down to earth in the company of Phraa Chao Kakusantho[2] to eat it. Human beings then cut the rice, cooked and ate it. In this way life was sustained, and they built a barn to store the rice. Ever since then rice has been their food.

Phraa Chao Kakusantho,[2] when he was reborn in Chompoo (India), brought rice with him in order to feed (human) life and religion. He lived for 10,000 years. He said that religion (Buddhism) would last for 8,000 years. At this time rice kept its original fragrance.

Next, Phraa Gonagamano[3] was reborn in this world, and he had much supernatural power. In his time the rice grain was already becoming smaller—its circumference was four times that of the human fist and its length was four finger spans. This Lord Buddha lived on this kind of grain. He said that religion would last 7,000 years. The rice preserved its fragrance, people did not starve, and there was no death caused by starvation.

At this time there lived an old widow who had been married seven times. She had neither children nor grandchildren. She decided to build a barn, and while it was being built her merit caused rice to grow by itself under her barn. The paddy was plentiful. She was annoyed with this profusion of growth, and so she hit the rice grains with a stick. The grains broke into pieces, both big and small, and these pieces flew up into the sky. The big pieces fell in the jungle and took root there. This variety is called *khaw doy* (mountain rice). Other pieces fell into water and grew there. This rice was called Nang Phrakosob,[4] and she lived in the company of a fish by the name of Toloptalan. Rice became angry with people and did not return to them. Thus people starved for 1,000 years.

There was the son of a rich man who went into the forest to earn a living. Unfortunately he lost his way one day and therefore had to spend several nights in the forest. During his wanderings he came to a swamp, and

---

[1] King or ruler of the kingdom (Chao Rata).

[2] According to Buddhist mythology, there have been four Buddhas in this present era. The first is Kakusantho; the second is Gonagamano, the third is Kassapo, the fourth is Gotamo. The fifth to come in the future is Maitreya. All five are mentioned in this myth. See Chapter 3 on Cosmology, p. 42.

[3] See note 2 above.

[4] *Nang* means Lady. Thus rice is identified as a female 'deity' or spirit.

because he could not go any farther, he sat down and cried. A fish called Plaa Kang, who heard the weeping of the young man, came and addressed him in sweet and gentle words. The fish told him that it would bring Nang Phrakosob to him, and that if a person eats Nang Phrakosob he will be cured of fever, stomach ache and abscess, and will derive many other benefits. She lived in a cave in the forest, and the elephants, lions and tigers which lived in the forest paid homage to her because she was virtuous. The young man was told to take Nang Phrakosob back with him to feed life and religion.

The fish told the young man where Nang Phrakosob lived and he went there intending to take some grains to grow at his home. On his approach, Nang Phrakosob flew to meet him, he caught her by the leg, and her fragrance spread in all directions, even up to Indra's heaven. She protested that she did not want to return to her previous abode among humans, for the old woman had badly beaten her. The rich man's son, glad that he had met Nang Phrakosob, tried to persuade her again and again that she should accompany him, but she refused.

Now there were two *thewada* (divine angels) who sympathized with the fish's (Plaa Kang's) plan. One changed into a golden deer (*suvanna mika*) and the other into a parrot (*nog kaeg tao*). They endeavoured to help the fish, and tried to persuade Nang Phrakosob with sweet words. The fish said, 'Dear Nang Phrakosob, please return. Don't live with fishes in this manner, go back to feed human life and religion.' Then the wise deer said, 'Dear Nang Phrakosob, please return home. Don't live in the forest. Go and sustain life and religion.' And the parrot also told her that she should go and support religion; it was not the right thing to remain in the forest. The Buddha would return to be reborn, and she would be praised more than before.

When Nang Phrakosob learned that she was being asked by *thewada* in disguise, she agreed to accompany the rich man's son. When she returned to the town she still smelled fragrant and she sustained people and religion. The gratitude of the rich man's son was great beyond measure. This was the time of Phraa Chao Kassapo (the third Buddha). The rice grain had diminished in size again—its girth was thrice as large as the human fist and its length was four finger spans. It smelled as fragrant as before, and the Buddha lived on the rice. Phraa Kassapo lived for 4,000 years and entered *nirvana*. It was said that religion would last for 6,000 years.

It was now the time of Phraa Chao Sakkyamuni Godhom,[1] who was considered the most excellent being in the world. Phraya Mara[2] had been

---

[1] Gotama Buddha, the known historical Buddha.
[2] Mara, the demon enemy of the Buddha.

defeated by him. The rice grain had again grown smaller—its circumference was $1\frac{1}{2}$ times that of the human fist and it was $2\frac{1}{2}$ finger spans long. It was sweet-smelling and the Buddha lived on the rice. When Phraa Sakkyamuni was eighty years old he entered *nirvana*.

One thousand years later there lived a man of high rank (Phraya) whose heart was filled with jealousy. He never made any meritorious acts; he committed demerit. He ordered his men to build a barn to store rice in, and he sold the rice. Nang Phrakosob took umbrage again because she was being sold. She threatened to go away, but she did not know where to go, because wherever she went there would be human beings who would find her. She therefore went to stay with Chao Rathi at the mountain called Hin Nong Tho. As a result of her departure people died of starvation and this continued for 320 years.

There was at this time an old couple called *pu yer-ya yer* ('grandparents'). They were feeble because they suffered from hunger. They tried hard to clear the land in search of rice but it was in vain. *Thewada* (divine angels) brought them before Chao Rathi.[1] The old couple prostrated before Chao Rathi, who thought to himself that people were dying of starvation because they did not follow religious precepts. Chao Rathi sent for Nang Phrakosob and offered her to the couple and told them to take her and grow rice in order to feed lives and religion. Nang Phrakosob protested that she wished to stay with Chao Rathi in order to feed his children, and that once before she had been beaten by an old widow, and that she now feared she might be sold. Chao Rathi, however, was not pleased with her protest. He gave the old couple some *gatha* (sacred verses) and asked them to memorize the words, which would prevent misfortune befalling Nang Phrakosob. These *gatha* are: Pancha, Ekha, Apicha, Hathayum, Sahum.[2] He also taught the old couple how to keep rice attached to religion for ever.

The sacred words made Nang Phrakosob feel that she wanted to go with the old couple. Chao Rathi then caught her by her wings and tail and thus the rice grain broke at the middle. Then he directed Nang Phrakosob to divide herself into varieties of rice: *khaw kam* (dark rice), *khaw khao* (white rice), *khaw chao* (ordinary rice), *khaw niow* (glutinous rice), *khaw pee* (annual rice), and *khaw dyan* (monthly rice). She did as instructed and then she held her breath and died. Her flesh and skin turned into stones. When religion is about to end Phraa Ariya Mettai

---

[1] The same mythical ruler mentioned in paragraph 1 of this chapter.

[2] These are all Pali words, here signifying names of magical verses. Pancha means 5, Ekha means 1, Apicha means 'super knowledge', Hathayum means 'hand', and Sahum stands for the final sound made at the end of a *gatha* (just as Om is the opening sound).

(Maitreya) will be reborn in this world, and rice will also be reborn as *khaw sali* (wheat) to feed life and religion.

The old couple grew the many kinds of rice they had received and obtained much yield. The best seeds of *khaw niow* and *khaw chao* were chosen for growing in the succeeding season. When they planted the rice they solicited help from *phii* (spirits) to secure ample harvests and in return they promised offerings such as liquor, duck and chicken, rice, betel nut, water for bathing, clothes, and jewellery such as bracelet, anklet and ring. They constructed a shelf at eye-level height, put all the offerings on it, and asked *phii* to render help. Rice grew abundantly, yielding bountiful harvests, because of the assistance of *phii* and because of the efficacy of the sacred lustral water, which was sprinkled on the plants. The lustral water was made by chanting the sacred words taught by Chao Rathi.

The old couple distributed rice near and far, to different peoples in different countries. Among the recipients[1] were the kingdoms of the *Naga* (mythical water serpent), of *Krut* (mythical sky bird *Garuda*), of Jetawan (a locality in India associated with the origins of Buddhism), of *Chatoom* (the heavenly kingdom of Wirupakha, the King of the *Nagas* and one of the four world protectors) as well as Chompoo (India) and Langkha (Ceylon). Each of these places got 100 heads of rice. But countries and peoples nearby received 134 heads—namely, the Kula (Khmer of Cambodia), the Jeen-Jum (Chinese), *brahmins* (Hindus), the Thai, Lao, and Vietnamese. People brought their buffaloes and carts to collect and take away their share of the grain.

When the old people died, people transferred merit to them and they went to heaven. At mealtime, both morning and evening, people paid their respects to them and invited their *khwan* to come and partake of the food. After the old couple's death, rice yields became smaller and smaller.

From that time, the method of growing rice has been well known to people who have cultivated it for themselves. The jungle is first cleared; then several tools like the plough are made; the buffalo is used to draw the plough; and then rice is planted. A month later heads of paddy appear. Later they are harvested, tied into bundles, and piled up on the threshing floor. *Khaw haeg* ('first paddy') is selected, tied into bundles, and placed on the top of the pile. At an auspicious day and time, permission is asked from Nang Phrakosob to beat the rice or to have the buffaloes trample on it.

[1] I give in parentheses in the text the identification of proper names. The *Naga* and *Garuda* are mythical 'opponents' in Buddhist and Hindu mythology. It is interesting to note that Jetawan ('where the *sasana* existed'), Chompoo and Langkha are treated as mytho-historical places in the same vein as other mythical places, such as heavens. The class of peoples noted last as receiving 134 heads are actually known peoples.

After threshing is completed, the *sukhwan khaw* (calling the spirit essence of the rice) is performed at the threshing floor.[1]

All of us, males and females, do not grow much rice any more. We have handled the harvested rice and we have made a seven-tiered *bajsi* (ceremonial structure), in which we have placed white cloth, candles and joss-sticks.

I invite all good things like *ya gao* (old grandmother) to enter and reside in the *bajsi*. The good teacher is also invited to confer blessings on the paddy, beautiful long-headed paddy, and to summon together all the *khwan* of the paddy. *Khwan* which stay on the top of the mountain, under the water, at the mouth of the cave, and on the big mountain are invited to come together today. We have got together several gifts—cloth, food dishes in pairs, fish and pork. Also various kinds of flowers, clothes, bracelet, ring, comb and water for bathing.

Then *gatha*[2] (verses) are recited like this: *Khwan* of rice, you may have gone to live in the *Naga* town, come back if you are aware; you may have gone to stay in Chetawan (Jetawana) jungle, the Himmaphan (Himalaya) jungle, come back if you are aware. *Khwan* of rice, you may be in Chatoom, in Langkha (Ceylon), please come back; you may have gone to Chompoo (India), please come back.

When the *khwan* hear this calling out, they come from several places—from the town of Than (heavenly creators), from *Naga* town, and from Langkha. When they arrive they are invited to eat yam, taro, betel nut, and other foods. They are invited to climb up to the house with a wooden floor and a thatched roof. Inside the house several kinds of fruits are laid out—such as pomelo and tamarind. These fruits cure diseases like rheumatism.

Rice is both excellent and costly. Lord Buddha and rice were born at the same time. Rice came along with religion. Phraa Achaan (the teacher) has given praise in verses, saying that through the possession of rice can be achieved transcendent virtues (*bahranee*). When one eats rice its results spread out...one can wish to be Indra, Brahma, rich man, ruler...one can wish to enter *nirvana*, to possess an excellent *winjan* (soul), to be reborn as Phraa Pachek Pothiyan (Pacceka Buddha)...

ANALYSIS OF THE MYTH

The myth links the arrival of rice and its subsequent vicissitudes with religion, in this case Buddhism. If human civilization owes its sustained existence to the domestication of rice, so is religion associated from the

---

[1] The myth proper appears to end at this point, but the text goes on to include a sort of commentary made from the standpoint of present-day villagers.

[2] The *gatha* in this paragraph are in Pali language.

beginning with ordered human life. The myth reiterates again and again that rice was given to man in order 'to feed life and religion', that 'rice came along with religion', that 'Lord Buddha and rice were born at the same time', that if human beings starve, then religion too is in jeopardy, and conversely, that if religion is not cherished then people starve.

It would appear that the unfolding of the story betrays a tragic vision of humanity. The protectors of heaven and earth (*lokapala*), particularly the king of the *Nagas* (serpents), gave rice to human beings as a boon but man was unworthy of it, and this led to a progressive deterioration of his life and also his religion. The rice gets smaller and smaller in size, less prolific in yield, less fragrant. Concurrently, the life span of Buddhism, beginning as 8,000 years, gets progressively shorter. The history of the Buddhist religion is dated in terms of the five Buddhas, the fourth being the historical Gotama Buddha, and the fifth being the Buddha-to-come, Maitreya, with whose appearance a new religious cycle starts and wheat replaces rice. This view of humanity is, of course, in line with both Hindu and Buddhist cosmological ideas—the succession of the four cycles of time (*yuga*), the present era being Kali Yuga, the dark and destructive age. According to Buddhist tradition it is said that Gotama Buddha predicted a finite period of existence of 5,000 years for Buddhism, ending with its final decline. The myth thus incorporates classical Buddhist cosmology and eschatology as set out in Chapter 3, p. 47.[1]

Nevertheless, such a tragic vision—while no doubt a product of Indian experience and formulation of that experience, and while it is embodied in the doctrinal texts of philosophical Buddhism—is, however, mitigated by the belief in the golden age to be initiated in this world by Maitreya, the expected Buddha. It is also patently contrary to the existential orientations of the villagers, for whom religion is an affirmation of life, and for whom ethical conduct will bring its returns in the here and now. In fact, the last paragraph of the commentary to the myth is in a way a triumphal counter-statement of the villagers' point of view. Although human existence is not blessed with material plenty, rice is still a precious human possession, and it is a vehicle for fantastic acquisitions of power, wealth, and spiritual aims. Orthodox, purist Buddhists might consider the concluding sentences blasphemous: 'When one eats rice its results spread out...one can wish to be Indra, Brahma, rich man, ruler', enter *nirvana* and even be reborn as a Pacceka Buddha. The purist might be more understanding if he were to appreciate that the villagers are here postulating that rice, which has a precious value, is both a basis and a vehicle for higher aims; around it cohere religious actions and ideas.

[1] Some features of this recorded village myth have precedents in the early Buddhist origin myth related in the *Aggañña Sutta* (see Rhys Davids 1957).

Anyway, the highest achievement stops short at the Pacceka Buddha who is concerned only with his salvation and cannot teach the way to others.

These preliminary remarks lead us to a closer examination of what the myth says. Looked at sequentially, the myth brings into focus the kinds of religious activities or cults that comprise the field of village religion. The connections between rice cultivation and religion are pervasive: not only does rice support Buddhism, but also the various attitudes towards rice expressed in the incidents relating to the old widow, the rich young man, and the old couple (who are archetypal ancestor figures) contain ethical statements about meritorious conduct as propagated by Buddhism. In fact these sequences are central to the understanding of the myth in structural terms.

We note that in the incident of the rich man's son the *thewada* (divine angels) help man: they are mediators and witnesses at auspicious happenings, a role they play in most village cults. Next we note, in the sequence relating to the old couple, that Chao Rathi taught them sacred verses (and the necessary ritual) so that Nang Phrakosob, the spirit of rice, would remain with man and be protected from any misfortune that might result from man's mishandling of rice. Thus is introduced the *sukhwan* ritual that will be performed by man to keep the essence of rice with him for ever. So delicate and fragile is the spirit of rice that man has to handle her with care; if she flees away she must be propitiated and persuaded to return.

We are then told that when the old couple planted the rice they solicited the help of spirits (*phii*). The kind of approach made to them signifies their special relationship to man, different from that of the supernaturals mentioned so far. Man solicits the help of *phii* in order to ensure ample harvests, and promises offerings in return. The *phii* help man on the understanding that man rewards them—this, then, is reciprocity phrased in the idiom of bargain and equivalence.

Thus we note that around rice cultivation cohere particular manifestations of most of the religious cults of the village—Buddhist rites, the invocation of divine angels (*thewada*) who are benevolent mediators, the propitiation of the original 'ancestral' couple who are in actual life transformed into village guardians (*Tapubaan*), *sukhwan* rites for recalling the spirit essence of rice (and in other contexts of human beings themselves), and finally a relationship of conditional reciprocity with *phii* (spirits), whose character contrasts with that of *thewada*. These are the cults that have engaged us in this book.

I now employ the method of structural analysis to discover the major category oppositions and the attempted mediations in the myth, and the messages it conveys.

(*a*) First, let us examine the theme of the progressive diminution in the size of the rice grain and the size of the yields, and the periodic cycles of starvation faced by human beings. This theme is worked out in terms of the proper/improper attitudes of man towards the life-giving food. In the beginning rice grew by itself in the land of an *old barren widow* who had been married seven times. As a result of her bad temper she beat the rice, which then crumbled into pieces and flew away. The result was the first period of starvation which lasted for 1,000 years.

Rice was next given to the grateful son of a rich man, but it passed into the hands of a *man of high rank*, who, being greedy and full of sinful conduct, stored it and sold it commercially. This again violated the spirit of rice, which therefore deserted man for a period of 320 years during which starvation again prevailed.

Rice was then given to an *old couple*, 'grandparents', and it was they who were taught the ethics of a moral relationship to it. They were taught the proper rituals. The proper attitude to rice is then demonstrated in the myth by their *free distribution* of rice to peoples in different countries, which include mythical kingdoms of the *Naga* (underworld) and *Garuda* (sky), kingdoms in India and Ceylon, and finally all the peoples in Thailand and its neighbouring countries. It is this free gift (valued highly in Buddhism) that is seen to enable the sustenance of civilization on a universal scale. The old couple were beatified and remembered regularly by their descendants.

At one level, then, the message is that to beat rice and to be ill-tempered towards it brings calamity; to sell rice in the interests of profit like a merchant does the same; to grow it with proper care and distribute it freely is the basis of continuing prosperity. At another level, however, the incidents and their implications highlight the exigencies of practical existence which necessitate 'wrong' actions. If man is to harvest and thresh rice in order to consume it, he must beat rice and harm it. But one should not do so in the manner of an old barren woman. Secondly, rice must be sold to others or bartered away in order that man can acquire other necessary things in life—but here again the example of a rich acquisitive merchant is not the best model of imitation. Essentially, then, like the old couple, farmers must take ritual precautions, help others, and control callous attitudes and acquisitive aims.

(*b*) The second theme susceptible to structural analysis is that concerning the ways in which rice came to man, as expressed in the three sequences relating to the old widow, the son of the rich man, and the old couple. These sequences imply oppositions and mediations (and also a scheme of progressive resolution) in the relationship between nature and culture. The stages in the history of rice thus given are:

1. rice, which initially grew in the garden of Phraya Wirupakha, a protector of heaven and earth, was divine food which also gave sustenance to the first Buddha. Human beings discovered this food, at which time rice is represented as 'growing by itself'. Thus when human beings first found it, it was in a divine as well as a wild state;

2. from here begin the three sequences. During the time of the *old widow*, rice grew spontaneously and profusely under her barn, that is rice in its *wild* and *undomesticated* stage, a product of nature;

3. we then come to the story of the fish, the golden deer, and the parrot, animals which are respectively of water, of land, and of the air or trees. Rice lived in the water and in the forest, and the animals played the role of mediators who persuaded rice to go with man. Rice was equally the food of animals and of man, which postulates a commonality between the animal and human worlds. Rice was thus delivered by animals to man, which represents its passage from nature to culture, from a wild plant to a cultured plant. This sequence of the passage of rice from the animal to the human world sets up not only the dichotomy between nature and culture, between animals and human beings, but also the categories of human habitation or village (*baan*) as distinct from forest (*paa*), a distinction still observed in village thought and ritual;

4. in the third sequence, the old couple are said to receive rice from Chao Rathi, the ruler over man, and he teaches them the cultural devices for cultivation, which include proper relationship to the supernaturals and to the spirit of rice itself. In other words, rice is represented in its *domesticated* stage, when it is controlled and properly cared for by the arts of man, both technical and religious.

Thus the stages are a progressive statement of the passage of rice from its wild to the domesticated stage: first as growing in a divine garden on earth and being food of the gods (and men), then as wild in the forest and water unavailable as food for man, and finally as food for all varieties of human beings under the aegis of culture and human effort. Rice was first of all a divine product and a boon to man; it was also a product of nature and was relinquished to man by animals; it was finally gifted by the ruler of men on condition that men organize themselves properly in relation to other men, deities, spirits, and nature. The categorical oppositions that emerge in the myth are deities/human beings; nature–animals–forest/culture–human society–village; spirits (*phii*)/human beings; first ancestors (grandparents)/descendants; ruler/subjects; Thai people/others (Chinese, Hindus, Laotians, Khmer, Vietnamese, etc.).

(c) A third theme, also concerning rice, can be isolated in the myth. Although from one perspective the story moves through the vicissitudes of immoral human behaviour to a final moral harmony, it is at the same time these human actions that lead progressively to the emergence of varieties of rice from its original undifferentiated state.

At the time rice grew in Phraya Wirupakha's divine garden, a grain of rice was a very large object. When the old woman beat the rice the fragments dispersed and then crystallized into two varieties—wild mountain rice of the forest, and rice in the cave of the fish, Plaa Kang, that is swamp rice. Then after its domestication, Chao Rathi further fragmented the rice into other varieties—dark rice, white rice, glutinous rice, monthly and annual rice, etc., which with their different flavours, textures and growing periods are the actual varieties known today to the villagers and cultivated by them. (In the actual *sukhwan* ritual, which I shall take up next, we see that rice varieties are metaphorically divided into still others, but these are poetic descriptions and not actual varieties.)

THE RITE OF 'SUKHWAN KHAW' (CALLING THE SPIRIT ESSENCE OF RICE)

The commentary at the end of the myth of Nang Phrakosob described how, since the time rice-growing has been well known to villagers, a certain technology of cultivation is practised, and how after threshing the ceremony of *sukhwan khaw* (calling the spirit essence of rice) is performed. It described how offerings are got together for the spirit essence and verses are recited to call the *khwan* dispersed in mountain, cave, water, and in the jungles of India and Ceylon.

The rite of *sukhwan* related to the myth is performed today by the villagers. In Chapter 13 I described the rite as it is conducted for human beings. Here I shall relate how it is performed for rice and examine how, as a rite, it is related to the myth.

From the moment the paddy grain begins to form in the fields, villagers address rites to Nang Phrakosob, the female spirit of the rice, that is the *khwan* (spirit essence of rice). The rite of *plong khaw* is performed before threshing, at which time permission is asked of Nang Phrakosob to 'beat' her, that is to thresh. This is followed by *sukhwan khaw*, which is performed by each cultivating household separately when the newly harvested grain is stored in individual household barns. The officiant at the rite is the *paahm* or *mau khwan*. The members of the household are present at the barn when the rite is performed.

The essence of the rite is the calling of the dispersed *khwan* of the rice to enter the barn and to reside with the grain. The belief is that if the ceremony is not performed, the grain will be exhausted quickly and that, moreover, the yield in the following year will diminish. Elaborate offerings of meat, liquor, the tops of banana trees and sugar cane plants, and sweets made in the shape of buffaloes are placed in the barn, and the *paahm* recites a fairly long text written on palm leaves. After the recitation, the rite ends with the *paahm* pouring paddy into a basket—which is described in Thai as 'pouring paddy for children'—and making a final plea for good yields in the future.

As in the ceremony for humans, here too the recitation of the text is the most important part of the ceremony. Therefore it is necessary that we scrutinize the content of the words recited before we attempt to relate the rite to its associated myth. I give below an English translation of the complete text read by the village *paahm* at the ceremony for the spirit of rice.

Text read by 'paahm' at 'sukhwan khaw': 'Saykhe charupe okasa okasa'[1]

When the fifth lunar month ends and the sixth begins, it thunders and it rains, and the ploughing of fields begins. People go into the jungle with a sharp axe and cut *mai paniang*[2] wood and bring it home to make a plough. The plough is carried to the field; a yoke is made and placed on the buffalo's neck; the rope is drawn tight, the buffalo walks and the plough tills the earth. Ploughing takes many days. Then paddy is sown. When the seedlings have grown well, they are pulled out and tied in bundles. After their leaf-tips are cut, the bundles are put together in a heap. The field is then harrowed and the bundles of seedling are divided into parts and transplanted according to the customs of up-country folk. In the tenth lunar month during the period of the waxing moon, the rice plants grow heads of paddy; the heads bend but the leaves stand straight. It is a beautiful sight to see them sway back and forth in the breeze. We all try to drive away the small birds—*nogkrachib* and *nogkrachaab*[3]—which come to eat the grain. It takes a long time for the grain to ripen. When they do so, the leaves turn yellow. The sickle is used to harvest the rice. The harvested paddy is left in the sun for three days, and then carried and heaped together on the threshing floor. Then the beating of rice begins; sometimes we use the buffalo to trample on it. A branch of a tree is used to sweep away the straw, and then the grains are collected.

---

[1] These are Pali words inviting the *thewada* to attend the ceremony. They are recited in all *mangala* (auspicious) ceremonies officiated by monks, as well.

[2] A kind of wild tree with edible fruits.

[3] *Nogkrachib* is the name for various kinds of small birds which eat paddy in the rice fields; *nogkrachaab* is also a small bird which eats growing paddy. These rice birds, together with the sparrow (*nogracang*), are the most ubiquitous predators of growing paddy and therefore are frequently alluded to in this ceremony.

All of us then invite a wise *achaan*[1] to come and be seated on a mat to officiate at the *khwan khaw* ceremony. *Si si*, today is a good day, it is full of good luck. The offerings prepared by all of us and placed in the *pha khwan*[2] are: food, fruit, betel nut, *khaw tom* (a kind of dessert made of rice); those placed in the tray are: young banana leaves, tender leaves of sugar cane, *bai koon*,[3] boiled egg and boiled chicken. Other articles are *maikan haab* and *kanlao* (pointed sticks for carrying bundles of threshed rice). We have laid a white cloth on the tray and have also placed in it one pair of candles, thread (*fai sai sin*), and four *namtao* (water vessels made of gourds). Four *taleo*[4] have been woven in the shape of a cow's head and they have been placed at the four corners of the threshing floor. In the middle of the floor a mat has been unrolled and a wise *achaan* has been invited to sit on it and celebrate the *khwan* of rice.

Si si, today is an auspicious day and I am going to perform the *sukhwan* ceremony for the rice plants in the field. When the plants are transplanted and when the heads of paddy grow erect, we refer to them as *khaw makkok*; the plants which are transplanted on the sides of the bed are called *khaw makkeua*; plants whose grain are shaped like the *makgleua* tree are called *khaw kajmak*; plants which have a cluster of many grains are called *khaw plong saeng*; plants which have many grains are called *khaw makpoh*; plants which bear many heads of grain are called *khaw leb chang*.[5] From the plants which bear good grain are selected the seed paddy for the next year.

Om! Rice grown on the upland field, you are asked to return today at this moment. Rice planted in the wet-land fields and which are now growing in Myang Lan Chang,[6] you are requested to come today at this moment. Rice spilled from the basket which fell sideways because its string was broken, is asked to return today. Rice spilled while it was being carried on the shoulder-pole is asked to come today. Rice which was carried away by the rice birds (*nogkrachib* and *nogkrachaab*) is asked

---

[1] Teacher, here meaning one versed in ritual.

[2] A tiered ceremonial structure made of flowers and leaves. Offerings to the *khwan* are placed on it.

[3] *Bai koon* literally means 'leaves of prosperity'. The tree in question bears yellow flowers which are considered auspicious and are used in ceremonies; sometimes leaves are substituted for the flowers. In Central Thai the tree is called *chayapreung*.

[4] Taleo (*chaleo* in Central Thai) is made by folding and crossing thin bamboo strips in the shape of two equilateral triangles, which are then interlaced to form a six-pointed star, or other figures.

[5] All the names given to paddy (*khaw*) are metaphorical. *Makkok* is a kind of tree that bears edible sour fruits. *Makkeua* is a tree that bears fruits which are cooked and eaten as 'vegetable'. *Makgleua* is a tree bearing dark fruits from which a black dye is obtained; villagers use the fruit as a purgative. *Plong saeng* means a cluster growing out of an erect stem. *Makpoh* refers to the fruit of the sacred bo (banyan) tree; the fruit has many seeds. *Leb chang* is a reference to the toes on an elephant's foot.

[6] The name of a region in northern Thailand.

to return today. Rice which fell into the elephant's mouth, into the tusked boar's mouth, rice stolen by the horse, rice eaten by the rabbit which lives near the field is asked to return today. Rice which went waste in the partridge's (*nogratah*) beak, in the yellow-headed rice bird's beak is asked to return today. Rice which was in the parrot's (*nogkaeg*) beak, in the beak of the rice bird, *nogkrachib fyang* (which lives in the fields), is requested to come today. Rice which fell into the peacock's beak is asked to come today. Rice eaten by the mouse (*nuu*) and by the crab (*puu*), rice which was destroyed in the fish's mouth is asked to come today. Rice eaten by worms and insects is asked to return today. The tops of rice plants eaten by cattle and buffaloes, elephants and horses are asked to return today.

Red gold, liquor and egg have been laid out for all *khwan* which come from every field, from every place. Come and reside in the pile of paddy. Let the barn remain full, even after paddy has been taken for consumption for ten years. When paddy is taken out, let it flow back into the barn like the flow of the Ganges River and the ocean. Come, *khwan*, come and stay in the barn which has a wooden floor, which is roofed with elephant grass (*ya faeg*); come and sleep on the bed made with hardwood (*maj kaen*). When you are taken out to be pounded,[1] please be replenished again; when you are taken away for consumption, please, *khwan*, be present. When we strike a wedge in the barn, or pound the mortar, please don't be frightened. May you rice grains entwine as *naga* (serpents) do; may you embrace like young lovers; may you protect one another.

Anyone who eats this rice, may he have a long life, may he become as wise as Phraa Chao Mahosot[2] and be as patient as Phraa Mettai.[3] Let everyone's wishes be fulfilled as I have said.[4]

The message of the ritual text

The text begins with the invitation to *thewada* (divine angels) to be present to make the proceedings auspicious. It then proceeds to give in prosaic terms an account of the paddy cultivation cycle practised in the village: the sequences of preparing land, ploughing, transplanting, harvesting and threshing, up to the point when the paddy is ready to be stored in the barn. One may wonder why the villagers, for whom the growing of rice is an everyday occupation, need to have recounted these humdrum details of their technology.

[1] Pounding here refers to the removal of the paddy husk by pounding in a mortar.

[2] Mahosot (Mahosatta) was Buddha in a previous incarnation as described in *Jataka* tales. He was a *bodhisatva* renowned for his wisdom.

[3] Mettai (Maitreya), the Buddha-to-come, is associated in this text with patience.

[4] In the North-east, it is customary for elders to bless the young in this manner, invoking the wisdom of Mahosot and the patience of Mettai.

The text then describes the preparations for the ceremony: the invitation of the officiant, the offerings got together. This is a description of the way a ceremony should be conducted, recited in the course of performing the actual ceremony, a statement of details of staging while the drama itself is being enacted.

The main body of the recitation is the lengthy calling of the *khwan* of rice. (The metaphorical descriptions of rice—the comparisons with various fruits and with the toes of the elephant—are a good example of the villagers' poetic sense.) The respective and sonorous, yet compelling, calling of the *khwan* is worthy of attention. In reconstituting the dispersed spirit-essence of rice, rice from the various fields, rice spilled or left behind, rice eaten by various birds (of which the small rice birds get repeated mention), by elephant, deer, boar, fish, crab, mouse and insects, by the stubborn buffalo, are requested to return.

Finally, after the spirit of rice has been recalled, it is invited to enter the barn, and to replenish the store of grain despite continual consumption. The final blessing is in terms of the highest Buddhist aspirations—may he who eats the rice become as wise as Phraa Mahosot and as patient as Phraa Mettai.

The text illustrates certain points already well known in information and communication theory. The actual description of rice technology and the details of how the ceremony is performed as embodied in the text may be said to be a store of information. In a sense, a man who reads the text finds in it the necessary instructions to perform the ceremony. The compelling repetitive calling of the *khwan* is akin to 'redundancy' in that it is meant to ensure the message gets through emphatically to the listeners.

Nevertheless, the message contained in the ritual text expands in scope when placed in relation to the *myth*.

MYTH AND RITE

Myth can, of course, exist apart from rite; conversely, many rites performed have no associated myths. But in this case myth and rite are so clearly linked that a challenge to interpret their relationship is posed for us.

We have seen that the myth of Nang Phrakosob contains certain category oppositions and their attempted mediations. Three aspects of the way in which rice came to man are stated. Rice was divine food, it was found by man in its spontaneous wild state. Rice was given to man by animals, which represents its passage from nature to culture, from wild state to domestication; we note here that animals are seen to co-operate with man, to act benevolently on his behalf. Finally another mode of its coming into the possession of man is stated—man maintains rice permanently through the art of magical control taught him by a ruler over men.

The sacred words of the rite itself, however, do not simply say the same things as the myth, nor is the myth a simple charter for the rite. I posed the question above why rice-growers should prosaically have their technology described in the rite. The answer is that the villagers are saying in the rite that rice-growing is a man-made activity which is characterized by hard work and meticulous attention. The harvest is a culmination of this activity, and there is a point in the listeners reliving and recounting the effort they put into cultivation.

Related to this is the insistence that rice which was taken away by predatory birds and animals must be retrieved from them. This, then, is the second inversion of the myth. In the myth the fish, animal, and bird co-operated to persuade rice to leave its natural wild state and become the food of man. Here in the ritual, the animal world and the human world are represented as being antagonistic as well as separated. Man must keep the animal world at bay if he is to retain the fruits of his labour. The rite is essentially concerned with maximizing and perpetuating the stock of rice gathered after harvest.

While these are not necessarily the only links between this myth and this rite, what has been indicated does confirm the proposition made previously that the relation between myth and associated rite in the Thai village is not a simple parallelism or isomorphism, but an inversion or a statement of the two sides of a paradox which in combination portray the complexity of man's ideas about and solutions to central problems. In this instance the preoccupation is the origin of rice, the meaning of rice cultivation as a human activity, and how to handle and treat this precious substance which sustains life and which is a vehicle for expressing man's relation to other men, to nature, and to divine beings.

The myth and the rite express two opposed propositions, which together compose a complex totality of ideas and values. The myth says that rice was given to man in a manner which shows his dependence on gods, animals (nature), and his rulers; in the rite man affirms that rice-growing is a human activity which requires effort and care and that rice must be protected against the predations of nature—animals and birds. At the same time, the spirit of rice, reflecting Buddhist moral and ethical values, is fragile and elusive and must be persuaded to stay with man.

21

THE PAST AND PRESENT IN THE STUDY OF RELIGION: CONTINUITIES AND TRANSFORMATIONS

In Chapter 19 I gave a synchronic structuralist outline of village religion based on analysis of the distinctive and contrastive features of four ritual complexes. But this book has also been concerned with another analytical perspective. The village rituals and festivals have a demonstrable past and are linked to the grand Buddhist tradition, especially the literary tradition, much of which is common to many countries of South-east Asia. Thus wherever it was relevant, when I engaged in elucidating the symbolism of ritual acts and the message contents of ritual words, I referred back to cosmologies, myths and doctrinal texts of the literary tradition of Pali Buddhism shared by such countries as Ceylon, Thailand, Burma, Laos, and Cambodia. And referring to this domain of facts has contributed an additional dimension of meaning to my presentation.

In this concluding chapter, therefore, it is appropriate and necessary to state systematically what I see as the relation between grand literary Buddhism and village religion, and the methods I have used in linking them. This particular problem and its solution have a direct relevance for cognate issues: the relation of the present to the past, the relation between synchronic and diachronic procedures, between anthropology and history, between anthropology and Indology, between the anthropologist's observations about a small-scale universe and the facts pertaining to the wider stage of the total society.

There have been in recent years two approaches toward resolving the classical question of how the anthropologist's field observations relate to the religious tradition represented in the literary texts. Both refer to India, but their formulations have wider implications. One is the Chicago school represented by Redfield and his associates. McKim Marriott's essay 'Little Communities in an Indigenous Civilization' (Marriott 1955) is a fine example of this approach, and I would include Srinivas' concept of Sanskritization as constituting a parent idea in the development of this approach. Opposed to them have been the views of Dumont and Pocock as expressed in *Contributions to Indian Sociology*; their distinctive view of Indian sociology has at its heart the problem of how India's past (however selectively that past may have been defined) relates to its present. We are wiser now than when Marriott's pioneering thoughts were set down, and I concur with the criticisms of them made by Dumont and Pocock: to conceive of the problem in terms of the village versus the great tradition of civilization is a false opposition because the village as such is not the unit of social life and therefore it has little sociological reality; the postulated processes of universalization and 'parochialization' that describe the exchange between village and wider civilization relate to disembodied elements of religion and not to the structure of the religious system itself.

There is another criticism that can be made: Marriott's own analysis led him to realize that the little tradition/great tradition distinction is not at all coterminous with the village/civilization distinction. The great tradition is a major component of village religion and what is unique to a village is truly residual. We should keep this qualification in mind.

How differently have Dumont and Pocock approached the problem? In *Contributions to Indian Sociology* a critical axiom for them, in fact the cornerstone of their approach, is that India is one and that its unity lies in reiterated *relationships* (rather than isolated elements) which can be discerned in different areas of Indian life. Now Dumont and Pocock, like Marriott and Srinivas, employ for some purposes the notion of two levels of Indian culture: the traditional higher Sanskritic civilization (which demonstrates that India is a unity), and the lower or popular level of culture and Hinduism (Contributions no. I (1957), p. 9; no. III (1959), pp. 7–8). We should note, however, that they are fully aware of the complexity which prohibits a simple reduction to these two levels. Thus Popular Hinduism (i.e. the religion of the Hindu people as it is observed today), strictly speaking, 'forms only a part of, or consists of only one level of Hinduism' (Contribution no. III, p. 7). Nor does literary Hinduism comprise all of Hinduism, for there is a great deal that is not codified which yet belongs to Hinduism. Some idea of the complex nature, the levels and constituent units of Hinduism is conveyed by Dumont in his essay 'World Renunciation in Indian Religion' (*ibid.* no. IV, 1960), in which he contrasts observed Hinduism and Brahmanism, discusses the influence of the philosophy of the renouncers on Brahmanism, and concedes that a place must be found for Tantric Hinduism, for Bhakti worship, and for sects.

Despite these qualifications, it is nevertheless the case that Dumont and Pocock have by and large substituted for Marriott's problem another one, formulated as the relevance of Sanskritic Hinduism for Popular Hinduism, and the relation between them. The importance of the higher Sanskritic level is proclaimed in their manifesto, 'For a Sociology of India' (*ibid.* no. I, 1957): 'In our opinion, the first condition for a sound development of a Sociology of India is found in the establishment of the proper relation between it and classical Indology.' A sociology of India is seen as lying at the point of confluence of Sociology and Indology, and it is necessary for the sociologist to be acquainted with Indian literature and the works of classical Indology.

But Dumont and Pocock also affirmed that as anthropologists and sociologists they take their 'point of departure from life itself, not from texts, from rites and belief, not from speculation and philosophy' (*ibid.* no. III, 1959, p. 7). This, of course, is not to mean the disregarding of brahmanical literature nor ignoring the intimate relation between religion and speculative thought.

Where Dumont and Pocock thus differ from Marriott is first on how to demarcate the two levels and secondly on the nature of the relationship between them. They rightly repudiate Marriott's notion of village religion as made up of great-traditional and little-traditional elements. As far as the villagers are concerned there are not two traditions but simply one, 'which is their life'; for them village tradition is not conceptually separable into different elements. Thus for the sociologist little tradition is not a residual category of festivals not found in other villages, but is the whole cycle of festivals studied in their social context.

What, then, is the relation between popular religion (that which the anthropologist studies and observes in the field) and Sanskritic literary Hinduism? On this question Dumont and Pocock have made no sustained systematic statement, but they make several *ad hoc* assertions which are brought together below:

1. An important and challenging idea is that the lower (popular) level has 'to be taken as being in some way *homogeneous* with the higher one' (italics mine). Elsewhere they say that there is 'constant interplay' between the levels and 'some degree of homogeneity between what we know from direct observation and from the literature' (*ibid.* no. I, 1957, pp. 9, 15). To put it in slightly different words, what they are stating is that homologous structures of ideas and relationships can be discovered at the two levels, though their idiom may be different. If there is some homogeneity between popular practice and literary disquisitions, then '"Sanskritization" does not consist in the imposition of a different system upon an old one, but in the acceptance of a more distinguished or prestigious way of saying the same thing' (*ibid.* no. III, p. 45). I suppose the point they are making is that the three basic complementary relationships in Hinduism: the pure/impure distinction, the double relationship to the divine through

priesthood and possession, and the distinction between male and female deities in cults are reflected both at the level of Sanskritic literature and in everyday Hindu ritual action.

2. Another and rather different relation is postulated as well between the two levels. A guiding premise for discovering the underlying similarity of relations is the following statement: 'The Indian sociologist must keep his attention upon a constant interaction between a general idea and the local working out of that idea' (*ibid.* no. III, 1959, p. 25). One suspects that in this statement primacy is being given to the general ideas propounded in the texts, the field situation being seen as a concrete manifestation of these ideas. This formulation, by the way, is not dissimilar to Marriott's 'parochialization' process. It is not at all clear how this conforms to the previous assertion that as anthropologists they take their point of departure from actual life, not from the texts.

3. Dumont and Pocock also postulate a third kind of relationship between the two levels, signified as that between the past (represented in literary texts) and the present (represented by the anthropologist's data). They say that 'the set of relations of "structures" discovered in the present can be fruitfully applied to the understanding of past evidence' (*ibid.* p. 15). An example which Dumont cites is how contemporary prestigious and non-prestigious marriage forms in South India throw light on the concept of mixed unions in the old law books. This method of using the present to understand the past, 'an operation that demands a critical approach', might be regarded by the fully-fledged historian as problematic if not questionable. Yet looked at more closely the implications of the procedure are perhaps no different from those contained in Croce's view that all history is contemporary history, and Collingwood's view that 'The past which a historian studies is not a dead past, but a past which in some sense is still living in the present'. I think Dumont is right that one of the contributions an anthropologist can make is to illuminate by analogies drawn from the living present the obscurities of ancient texts; most of such work, however, will be at the level of inspired guesswork.

While one admires the stimulating assertions of the editors of *Contributions*, one can, I think, partly on the basis of my study of Thai village religion, advance further in some respects than the editors managed to do.

To begin with, the very idea of two levels in religion—the higher Literary and the lower Popular—and the attempt to uncover their links can be criticized as being in some respects static and profoundly *a-historical*, inasmuch as the notion of Sanskritic or Literary Hinduism is posited as a single uniform category or level, when the fact is that the texts range over vast periods of time and show shifts in principles and ideas.

Continuities and transformations

The idea of Sanskritic Hinduism (which in other places he called 'philosophical Hinduism', 'All India Hinduism') came to us originally from M. N. Srinivas in *Religion and Society Among the Coorgs of South India*. How did he represent this phenomenon in his book? On close scrutiny it turns out to be a hodge-podge made up of the Vedas, the Upanishads, and early philosophical thought; of mythology, especially the *Ramayana* and *Mahabharata* epics, and the Puranas (which are the Scriptures of a later, more exuberant Hinduism); of feasts, fasts, pilgrimages, the sacred cow and sacred geography; of ethical and religious ideas such as *karma, dharma* and *moksha*; of practices such as vegetarianism and teetotalism; and finally of rituals such as worship of trees, rivers and mountains. (See Srinivas 1952, pp. 213, 220, 226, 227.) Similarly, if 'Pali Buddhism' were thus decomposed it would be seen to consist of highly miscellaneous, varied and non-contemporaneous elements. Srinivas' notion of Sanskritic Hinduism violates history in that it is all-embracing and includes everything from the early Vedas to the Puranas of later times. No meaningful entity exists in fact (except in the sense of a library of diverse works). It is a fabrication of anthropologists which they have bequeathed to the modern Indian consciousness. Nor can the mythical Sanskritic Hinduism be equated with All India Hinduism, which again is neither a real entity in the consciousness of Hindus, nor a useful analytical concept, because it simply stands for the lowest common denominator of shared Hindu religious beliefs and customs.

I submit that the idea of two levels is an invention of the anthropologist dictated not so much by the reality he studies as by his professional perspective. By definition an anthropologist goes into the field to study live action, and from the observations made over a short period of time he tries to derive a systemic pattern or order. He takes for granted that the piece of reality he has studied is both an autonomous and a meaningful universe capable of exhibiting order. Because he is already committed to an anthropological level of reality and social facts, the anthropologist who works in complex 'historical' societies is likely to view the literary culture of that society as constituting another 'level' or order equivalent to the level of 'live action' he has managed to record. Moreover, this static view of the literature and recorded history may be an inevitable result of the fact that an anthropologist is not primarily interested in them; they are the province of the Orientalist or the Indologist and the historian. An anthropologist is first and foremost preoccupied with the problems turned up by his own field data, and sometimes their solution may lead him into the realm of literary tradition and recorded history. When this happens, there is the danger that he may walk around the library in cavalier fashion

371

and pick out at random those documents that are apt for the interpretation he wants to make.

Embedded in the anthropologist's notion of two levels is the serious danger of the past civilization represented in the classical literature being imagined as a static and consistent whole expressing clear-cut principles. The historian may well find this orientation naïve: for him there are periods, eras, continuities and changes, not a single unbroken tradition. To demonstrate an overall unity in the literature ranging through the Vedas, Upanishads, Brahmanas and Puranas, would be an impossible intellectual feat, even for a *brahman* dialectician, whether Kashmiri, Madrasi, or Bengali. Such an anthropological perspective may well postulate a *theological* view of the society in terms of a timeless architecture, whereas an historian tuned to an open-ended future and a dynamic perspective may think of India as essentially diverse, a diversity that is the result of unevenness in society and the unequal play of competitive forces, in themselves a result of antecedent events.

Perhaps the most important criticism that can be made of the analytical usefulness of the two levels—higher literary and lower popular religion—stems from my study of Thai religion, which is that the distinction is frequently inapplicable to the anthropologist's field data and experience. It is surely inappropriate in the case of an Indian village to talk of popular Hinduism and Sanskritic Hinduism as separate levels, when the local Brahman priest and perhaps educated members from other castes with literary traditions are active members in the local community and are using texts and orally transmitted knowledge which are directly or indirectly linked to the classical forms. It seems to me that if anthropologists in India had been oriented to the collection and recording of ritual texts and the literature used by rural specialists, they might have formulated the question differently.

We have seen that in our remote and humble Thai village the ordinary Buddhist monk preaches sermons the words of which are taken from and relate to the *suttas* and the *Jataka* tales; he chants *paritta* verses which are adapted and elaborated from similar source texts; he recites fortnightly, preferably from memory, the *Patimokkha*, which is an old classical statement of the rules of monastic discipline; he is to some degree formally indoctrinated in the rules of the *Vinaya*, with elaborate commentary on discipline; finally in one way or another the village monk of some duration of service may deal with secondary elaborations of doctrine, and with myths, local and classical. That even the lowliest village monk has some kind of access to the corpus of Pali literature of Buddhism is due to the fact that the monk's practice of his vocation demands some knowledge of this content, and to the fact that the local village *wat* (temple) is a place where literacy in the sacred language is acquired and sacred knowledge is transmitted.

The spread of Buddhist doctrinal knowledge and sacred lore is not uniform among the monks placed at various levels of the society just as it is unevenly spread among the lay social strata. At this point I must depart from the village to take account of the entire Thai society. If one wants to plot the distribution of religious knowledge among the monks in Thailand one has to take into account at least three hierarchies: (1) the formal ecclesiastical hierarchy, from the patriarch and the council of ministers to village abbot and monk, which is mainly related to the exercise of administrative authority but partially correlates with learning; (2) the historically older hierarchy relating to the distinction between royal *wat* and commoner *wat*. The former not only enjoyed royal patronage but were the agencies which carried out the king's sponsorship of programmes for reviving and promoting religious zeal, for translating and editing classical Pali texts, etc.; (3) the third hierarchy relates to the differences between and stratification of *wat* as institutions of learning and repositories of knowledge. In Thailand today one can progress from the lowly village *wat* to provincial centres of learning and from these to national centres in Bangkok, culminating in universities for monks. A network of learning exists, with channels for geographical, intellectual and social mobility for monks.

In short, what needs to be emphasized is that anthropologists dealing with complex literate societies should pay greater attention to the role of literacy and the traditional networks of learning and transmission of knowledge. Important to understand are the institutional arrangements for the production of literate specialists who retain certain kinds of knowledge, mediate on behalf of non-literate masses, and in some respects hold the total society together within a common framework. If we had proper knowledge of this, we would be less confident in holding naïve views about literary versus popular religion. In a complex society like Thailand or Ceylon or India, various kinds of written sacred literature have a referential basis for the whole society, even for the unlettered masses; hence the need to understand the mode of transmitting this knowledge and the manner in which the literate specialists are recruited and trained. This is an issue to which I have given some attention in Chapter 8, but primarily only as it is manifest in a single village.

This might be the place to pay homage to Hocart who, if he thought in terms of kingship and court culture and distinguished it from peasant culture, did so to show the influence of the former on the latter and their affinity at deeper levels. Some decades before anthropologists discovered 'Sanskritization', Hocart had proposed a notion equally as important and which portrayed a contrary process. Hocart propounded the concepts of 'nationalization' in his book on *Caste* (1950) and of 'centralization' in *Kings and Councillors* (1936), to describe the process by which certain customs and styles of life became diffused in society. The notion of nationalization is an elitist view: '...every new custom or idea begins with the leaders whether kings, priests, professors or merchants, and spreads to the crowd' (1927, p. 157); or again, 'The King's state is reproduced in miniature by his vassals...' (1950, p. 68).

While Hocart no doubt overworked and exaggerated his thesis that there was a prototype form of kingship which by diffusion spread to different societies and became particularized in each, it was by no means inappropriate for depicting *some* historical processes in the Indianized kingdoms of South-east Asia, where certain customs, styles and rituals, originating with the court appear to have spread in ever-widening circles to the outer margins of the society. The value of Hocart's version of the relation between high and low culture was that he specified the *political structure* of the society as providing the grid and the channels of transmission, a view superior to later formulations of diffusion and 'parochialization' because it was sociologically well grounded. And the fact that the high or elite cultures from Burma to Indonesia share conspicuous patterns and themes, and that in the societies of this belt the high culture was and is a yardstick for the peasantry tempts us to look for similar underlying processes which they may also share.

Let me, in the concluding paragraphs, return to the problem of levels, taking note of the criticisms already made and building on the shoulders of the writers cited. In the study of religion in societies like Thailand I would make a distinction between *historical* religion and *contemporary* religion without treating them as exclusive levels. Historical Buddhism would comprise not only the range of religious texts written in the past, but also the changes in the institutional form of Buddhism over the ages. Contemporary religion would simply mean the religion as it is practised today and should *include* those texts written in the past that are used today and those customs sanctified in the past that persist today and are integral parts of the ongoing religion.

Thus, if the question of the relation between historical and contemporary religion interests us, we should look for two kinds of links, namely *continuities* and *transformations*.

Continuities are evidenced in contemporary Buddhism by the use of *suttas*, *Jatakas*, and liturgical texts in rituals. Furthermore, as we have already seen, there are many aspects of contemporary monastic life (*Vinaya* rules, the basic form of the ordination ceremony, the observance of Lent (*Vassa*), the recitation of the *Patimokkha* confessional, etc.) which have been handed down from the classical past, and as such exhibit a structural logic inhering in southern Buddhist monastic institutions that tends to persist through time.

Another kind of continuity that we witnessed was the conspicuous role of symbols like the *Naga* (and the *Garuda* and *hamsa*) both in grand art and mythology, and in village ritual, artifacts and legends. The *prasaat* and the *chedi* and the seven-tiered umbrella of kingship, and the monumental Buddhist centres of worship, also play their role in village life, even if they are only materialized as palaces and palanquins of coloured paper and bamboo strips.

But there have been important transformations as well. One kind stems from the great historical change in Buddhism: the change in the way of life of most monks from that of homeless wanderer to one of monastic habitude; from that of personal salvation quest without obligations to society to one in which the laity have been allowed to cultivate the *Sangha* as a 'field of merit'. All these transformations finally add up to the double relation in which the *bhikkhu*, on the one hand in theory is not of this world and has cut himself loose from its ties, pleasures and passions, whereas the layman, on the other, is positively in this world and aspires to be born again in more sumptuous circumstances. Thus are world renunciation and world affirmation conjoined in institutionalized Buddhism.

A fascinating chain of historical changes leads us to the present-day structural relationship, in the form of the co-existence in the village of the monk (*bhikkhu*) and the *paahm* (*brahman*). The Theravada monk made his way from India to Ceylon and thence to Siam;[1] the court *brahman* of Thailand came by a different route—from India *via* Cambodia to Siam. The classical *bhikkhu* and *brahman*, antagonists in their home of origin in India, co-exist in Thailand in a transformed state.

There is another set of transformations, the evidence for which is not to be found in historical treatises but is the discovery of anthropological study of contemporary social life. This book has in several places displayed these gems sifted from the muddy facts of everyday life. For instance, we have seen that, although the office of monk and the norms of monastic life can be referred to the past, there are nevertheless a number of features which derive their logic from the interwovenness of classical Buddhist

[1] I am here referring to the fact that the Thai who gained political pre-eminence in Siam in the thirteenth century, although already exposed to Theravada Buddhism *via* the Mons and Burmese, consciously espoused Sinhalese Buddhism.

religious values and the social structure, the religious values thereby in a sense owing their *maintenance* to the institutional logic of village life. Thus, in Baan Phraan Muan the *sociological* transformations are to be detected in the union of monkship (renunciation) with the concept of filial obligation and merit transfer, the union of lay sponsorship of religion with parental support of sons in robes, and the union of temporary monkhood with the exigencies of a life cycle rooted in this world.

It is this perspective which permits us to appreciate how the classical distinction between monk and layman has been transformed, the two roles now being dynamically linked in a life cycle during which a young man shifts from ascetic monkhood to marriage and family life and then becomes an increasingly pious layman who in old age begins to approach monkhood again. (And this product is not so dramatically different from the classical Hindu formulation of four stages.) Furthermore, the dynamic integration of religion and lay life is revealed in the rewards of monkhood and in the preparation of the monk for leadership in lay life by means of his acquisition of literacy and of ritual knowledge for use in domestic rites.

There are certain circumstances in which classical ingredients exposed to the fire of contingent human life and its needs synthesize into intriguing compounds. The metaphorical and metonymical basis of the monkish use of sacred words, especially the *paritta*, and the sociological basis for the congregation's belief in the power of sacred words is an absorbing problem which engaged my attention. Or again it is tempting to see the exorcist, in the light of the classical concept of mystical power (*iddhi*), as the inversion of a monk; but we must also take the precaution of going beyond this and examining the effectiveness of the exorcist's art in terms of the logic of the ritual itself as a communication device in a living social context.

Having so far distinguished continuities from transformations, both historical and sociological, let me now deal with instances of their co-existence and simultaneous manifestation—primarily as homologous structures at different *levels* of culture and civilization. We have seen how seemingly bizarre cosmological schemes developed in theological tomes come to life in village myth as a parade of supernaturals and a succession of Buddhas. Or again, ideas expressed in abstract verbal form in the texts are activated in ritual through a sequence of events with metaphorical import and through the manipulation of concrete objects invested with symbolic properties. Thus cosmic ideas of the three forms of existence or worlds make their poignant point in a mortuary rite as three circum-ambulations, or the throwing back and forth of funeral cloth over the coffin; they find their theatrical expression in the three phases of a *Bun Phraawes* festival, played by humans turned into cosmic actors. The distance that separates the highly sophisticated and verbalized *Tibetan Book of the Dead* and the cruder village mortuary ritual is not so great as appears on first sight. Finally, in myth and its associated ritual we see a dialectical relation between two modes, one expressed in language and the other in action.

Village religion is expressed in rituals and these rituals in turn clothe abstract philosophical ideas. The underlying rationale of ritual is that the ideas so represented and made concrete can be manipulated realistically in an instrumental mode. In this perhaps lies the difference between ritual and philosophy.

I conclude with a gloss on the remark made earlier that the anthropological study of the present can illuminate the past. There is a preeminent advantage in studying a phenomenon in its live social context. The trouble with old texts is that they are fragmentary; and since in addition they accumulate over time, the student is hard put to reconstruct what the total field of religion at any point of time was, how the constituent cults and rites related to one another, what weight one belief or practice had in respect of another, and when if ever a particular myth or sermon or discourse was brought to life by association with a ritual. The virtue of a synchronic structural account of contemporary religion is that this is what it precisely accomplishes—the construction of a total field. And the structural relations of hierarchy, opposition, complementarity and linkage between Buddhism and the spirit cults arranged in one single field in contemporary life can therefore give insights into the historical processes by which Buddhism came to terms with indigenous religions in its march outwards from India. The relation between the rocket festival addressed to the guardian spirit and the festival of *Bun Phraawes* may well be the model of a general process of durable, if not timeless, mutual accommodation between Buddhism and the spirit cults.

BIBLIOGRAPHY

Alabaster, Henry (1871). *The Wheel of the Law. Buddhism, Illustrated from Siamese Sources.* London: Trübner and Co.

Ames, Michael (1963). 'Ideological and Social Change in Ceylon'. *Human Organization,* vol. 22, no. 1.

(1964). 'Magical-animism and Buddhism: a structural analysis of the Sinhalese religious system', in *Religion in South Asia* (ed. E. B. Harper). Seattle.

Ariyapala, M. B. (1956). *Society in Medieval Ceylon.* Colombo.

Berval, René de (1959a) (ed.). *Kingdom of Laos, The Land of the Million Elephants and of the White Parasol.* Limoges: A. Bontemps Co., Ltd.

(1959b). 'The Boun *Bang-Fay*' (Rockets Festival, 6th month), in *Kingdom of Laos, The Land of the Million Elephants and of the White Parasol.* Limoges: A. Bontemps Co., Ltd., pp. 272–82.

Blanchard, W. *et al.* (1958). *Thailand: its people, its society, its culture* (Country Survey Series, ed. Thomas Fitzsimmons). New Haven: HRAF Press.

Bode, M. H. (1909). *The Pali Literature of Burma.* London: Royal Asiatic Society.

Bowring, Sir J. (1857). *The Kingdom and People of Siam.* 2 vols. London: Parker.

Bradbury, R. E. (1966). 'Fathers, Elders and Ghosts in Edo Religion', in *Anthropological Approaches to the Study of Religion* (ASA Monographs, no. 3, ed. M. Banton). London: Tavistock Publications.

Briggs, L. P. (1951). 'The Ancient Khmer Empire'. *Transactions of the American Philosophical Society,* N.S. vol. 41. Philadelphia.

Brohm, J. (1963). 'Buddhism and Animism in a Burmese Village'. *The Journal of Asian Studies,* vol. XXII, no. 2.

Coedès, G. (1957). 'The Traibhumikatha Buddhist Cosmology and Treatise on Ethics'. *East and West,* vol. VII, no. 4.

(1966). *The Making of South East Asia* (transl. by H. M. Wright). Berkeley and Los Angeles: University of California Press.

(1968). *The Indianized States of Southeast Asia* (ed. W. F. Vella) (transl. by S. B. Cowing). Honolulu; East-West Center Press.

Conklin, H. C. (1964). 'Hanunoo Colour Categories', in *Language in Culture and Society* (ed. D. Hymes). New York: Harper and Row, pp. 189–92.

Copleston, R. S. (1892). *Buddhism, Primitive and Present in Magadha and in Ceylon.* London: Longmans, Green and Co.

Cowell, E. B. (1895) (ed.). *The Jataka or the Stories of the Buddha's Former Births,* vol. II (transl. by W. H. D. Rouse). Cambridge: University Press.

(1905) (ed.). *The Jataka or the Stories of the Buddha's Former Births,* vol. V (transl. H. T. Francis). Cambridge: University Press.

Crawford, J. (1828). *Journal of an Embassy to the Courts of Siam and Cochin China.* London.

De la Loubère, S. (1693). *A new historical relation of the Kingdom of Siam by*

Bibliography

M. de la Loubère, *envoy extraordinary from the French King, to King of Siam, in the year 1687 and 1688, wherein a full account is given of the Chinese way of arithmetick and mathematick learning.* 2 vols. in 1, London.

Douglas, M. (1966). *Purity and Danger.* London.

Dumont, L. (1957). *Une Sous-Caste De l'Inde Sud. Organisation Sociale et Religion des Pramalai Kallar.* Mouton and Co.

(1960). 'World Renunciation in Indian Religions'. *Contributions to Indian Sociology* (eds. L. Dumont and D. Pocock), no. IV.

Dumont, L., and Pocock, D. (1957) (eds.). *Contributions to Indian Sociology,* no. I.

(1959). *Contributions to Indian Sociology,* no. III.

(1960). *Contributions to Indian Sociology,* no. IV.

Durkheim, E. (1926). *Elementary Forms of the Religious Life* (transl. J. W. Swain). Glencoe, Ill.: The Free Press.

Duroiselle, M. C. (1904). 'Upagutta et Mara'. *Bulletin de l'École Française d'Extrême Orient,* vol. 4.

Dutt, S. (1960). *Early Buddhist Monachism.* Bombay.

(1962). *Buddhist Monks and Monasteries of India, Their History and Their Contribution to Indian Culture.* London.

Eliade, M. (1958). *Yoga.* Bollingen Series LVI, Pantheon Books.

Eliot, C. (1954). *Hinduism and Buddhism: An Historical Sketch.* 3 vols. Barnes and Noble, Inc. (first published in 1921).

Erikson, E. H. (1958). *Young Man Luther, A Study in Psychoanalysis and History.* New York: W. W. Norton and Co., Inc.

Evans-Wentz, W. Y. (1960). *The Tibetan Book of the Dead.* Oxford: University Press.

Evers, H.-D. (1967). 'Kinship and Property Rights in a Buddhist Monastery in Central Ceylon'. *American Anthropologist,* vol. 69.

Fortes, M. (1965). 'Some Reflections on Ancestor Worship in Africa', in *African Systems of Thought* (eds. M. Fortes and G. Dieterlen). London: Oxford University Press, for The International African Institute.

Fortes, M., and Dieterlen, G. (1965) (eds.). *African Systems of Thought.* London: Oxford University Press, for The International African Institute.

Geiger, W. (1960). *Culture of Ceylon in Medieval Times* (ed. Heinz Bechert). Wiesbaden.

Gerth, H. H., and Mills, C. W. (1946) (eds. and transl.). *From Max Weber: Essays in Sociology.* New York: Oxford University Press.

Goffman, Erving (1961). *Asylums: Essays on the Social Situation of Mental Patients and other Inmates.* New York: Anchor Books Edition, Doubleday & Co. Inc.

Gogerly, D. J. (1908). *Ceylon Buddhism.* 2 vols. Colombo.

Graham, A. (1912). *Siam: A Handbook of Practical, Commercial and Political Information.* London.

Grant Brown, R. (1908). 'Rain-making in Burma'. *Man,* no. 80.

(1921). 'The Pre-Buddhist Religion of the Burmese'. *Folk-Lore, Transactions of the Folk-Lore Society,* vol. XXXII, no. II.

(1925). *Burma as I saw it.* New York: Frederick A. Stokes Co.

Bibliography

Greenway, J. (1966) (ed.). *The Anthropologist Looks at Myth*. Austin: University of Texas Press, published for the American Folklore Society.

Hardy, R. Spence (1860). *Eastern Monachism*. London: Williams and Norgate. (1880). *A Manual of Buddhism, in its Modern Development*. 2nd edition. London: Williams and Norgate.

Harper, E. B. (1964). 'Ritual Pollution as an Integrator of Caste and Religion', in *Religion in South Asia*. Seattle, pp. 151–96.

Hertz, R. (1960). *Death and the Right Hand* (transl. R. and C. Needham). Glencoe: Free Press.

Hocart, A. M. (1927). *Kingship*. Oxford: University Press. (1936). *Kings and Councillors*. Cairo: Printing Office. (1950). *Caste, A Comparative Study*. London, Methuen and Co., Ltd.

Hymes, Dell (1964) (ed.). *Language in Culture and Society: A Reader in Linguistics and Anthropology*. New York: Harper and Row.

Ingram, J. C. (1955). *Economic Change in Thailand since 1850*. Stanford: University Press.

Kaufman, H. K. (1960). *Bangkhuad, A Community Study in Thailand* (Monographs of the Association for Asian Studies). New York: J. J. Augustus Inc.

Kiev, A. (1964). *Magic, Faith and Healing*. Glencoe: Free Press.

Klausner, J. (1964). 'Popular Buddhism in Northeast Thailand', in *Cross-Cultural Understanding* (eds. F. S. C. Northrop and Helen H. Livingston). New York.

Knowles, D. D. (1963). *The Monastic Order in England. A History of its Development from the Times of St. Dunstan to the Fourth Lateran Council 940–1216*. 2nd edition. Cambridge: University Press.

Landon, K. P. (1939). *Siam in Transition*. Oxford: University Press.

de Laszlo, V. S. (1958) (ed.). *Psyche and Symbol: A Selection from the Writings of C. G. Jung*. New York: Anchor Books.

Leach, E. R. (1958). 'Magical Hair'. *J. R. Anthrop. Inst.*, vol. 88, pp. 147–64. (1962). 'Pulleyar and the Lord Buddha: an aspect of religious syncretism in Ceylon'. *Psychoanalysis and the Psychoanalytical Review*, vol. 49, no. 2. (1968*a*) (ed.). *Dialectic in Practical Religion* (Cambridge Papers in Social Anthropology, no. 5). Cambridge: University Press. (1968*b*). 'Introduction', in *Dialectic in Practical Religion* (ed. E. R. Leach) (Cambridge Papers in Social Anthropology, no. 5). Cambridge: University Press.

LeMay, R. (1926). *An Asian Arcady*. Cambridge: University Press.

Lévi-Strauss, C. (1963). *Structural Anthropology* (transl. C. Jacobson and B. G. Schoepf). New York: Basic Books.

Levy, P. (1968). *Buddhism: A 'Mystery Religion'?*. New York: Schocken Books.

Lewis, I. M. (1966). 'Spirit Possession and Deprivation Cults'. *Man* (N.S.), vol. 1, no. 3, pp. 307–29.

Littleton, C. S. (1966). *The New Comparative Mythology, An Anthropological Assessment of the Theories of Georges Dumezil*. Berkeley: University of California Press.

Malalesekera, G. P. (1928). *The Pali Literature of Ceylon*. London: Royal Asiatic Society.

(1960). *Dictionary of Pali Proper Names*. 2 vols. London: Luzac and Co., Ltd.

Malinowski, B. (1948). *Magic, Science and Religion and Other Essays*. Boston: Beacon Press.

(1960). *Argonauts of the Western Pacific*. New York: Dutton.

Marriott, M. (1955). 'Little Communities in an Indigenous Civilization', in *Village India, Studies in the Little Community* (ed. M. Marriott). Chicago: University Press.

Mauss, M. (1954). *The Gift* (transl. I. Cunnison). London.

Mayer, A. C. (1960). *Caste and Kinship in Central India: a village in its region*. London: Routledge and Kegan Paul.

Mendelson, E. M. (1963). 'Observations on a Tour in the Region of Mount Popa, Central Burma'. *France-Asie*, Extrait du no. 179, Mai–Juin.

(1964). 'Initiation and the Paradox of Power, A Sociological Approach', in *Initiation, Contributions to the Theme of the Study-Conference of the International Association for the History of Religions, held at Strasburg, Sept. 17th to 22nd, 1964* (ed. C. J. Bleeker).

Monier-Williams, M. (1890). *Buddhism, in its Connexion with Brahmanism and Hinduism, and its contrast with Christianity*. London: John Murray.

Nānamoli, B. (1960) (transl.). *The Minor Readings (Khuddakapatha). The First Book of the Minor Collection (Khuddakanikaya)* (Pali Text Society Translation Series, no. 32). London: Luzac and Co., Ltd.

Nānamoli, T. (1966) (transl.). *The Patimokkha, 227 Fundamental Rules of a Bhikkhu*. Bangkok: Social Science Association Press.

Nash, M. (1965). *The Golden Road to Modernity, Village Life in Contemporary Burma*. London: John Wiley and Sons, Inc.

(1966) (*et al.*). *Anthropological Studies in Theravada Buddhism* (Cultural Report Series, no. 13, Southeast Asia Studies). New Haven: Yale University Press.

Noss, R. B. (1964). *Thai Reference Grammar* (Foreign Service Institute). Washington, D.C.: Dept. of State.

Obeyesekere, G. (1958). 'The structure of Sinhalese ritual'. *Ceylon Journal of Historical and Social Studies*, vol. I, pp. 192–202.

(1966). 'The Buddhist Pantheon in Ceylon and its Extensions', in *Anthropological Studies in Theravada Buddhism* (M. Nash, *et al.*) (Cultural Report Series, no. 13, Southeast Asia Studies). New Haven: Yale University Press.

(1968). 'Theodicy, Sin and Salvation in a Sociology of Buddhism', in *Dialectic in Practical Religion* (ed. E. R. Leach) (Cambridge Papers in Social Anthropology, no. 5). Cambridge: University Press.

Pachow, W. (1951). 'A Comparative Study of the Pratimoksa'. *Sino-Indian Studies*, vol. IV, parts 1 and 2.

(1953). 'A Comparative Study of the Pratimoksa'. *Sino-Indian Studies*, vol. IV, parts 3 and 4.

Paranavitana, S. (1959). 'Civilization of the Early Period: (*continued*) Religion and Art', in *History of Ceylon*, vol. I (ed. H. C. Ray). Colombo: Ceylon University Press.

Bibliography

Postan, M. M. (1939). *The Historical Method in Social Science; An Inaugural Lecture.* Cambridge: University Press.

Rahula, W. (1956). *History of Buddhism in Ceylon.* Colombo.

Rajadhon, A. (1961). *Life and Ritual in Old Siam* (ed. and transl. W. J. Gedney). New Haven: HRAF Press.

Ray, H. C. (1959) (ed.). *History of Ceylon,* vol. I. Colombo: Ceylon University Press.

Rhys Davids, T. W. (1899) (transl.). *Dialogues of the Buddha* (Sacred Books of the Buddhists, vol. II). London: Henry Frowde.

  (1963) (transl.). *The Questions of King Milinda,* part I and part II. New York: Dover Publications, Inc.

Rhys Davids, T. W., and C. A. F. (1910) (transls.). *Dialogues of the Buddha, Translated from the Digha Nikaya,* part II (Sacred Books of the Buddhists, vol. III). London: Henry Frowde.

  (1957) (transls.). *Dialogues of the Buddha, Translated from the Digha Nikaya,* part III (Sacred Books of the Buddhists, vol. IV). London: Luzac and Co., Ltd.

Rhys Davids, T. W., and Oldenberg, H. (1881) (transl.). *Vinaya Texts Part I. The Patimokkha. The Mahavagga, I–IV* (The Sacred Books of the East, vol. XIII (ed. F. M. Muller)). Oxford: Clarendon Press.

Satiră-Košes (1960). *Thai Culture and Traditions* (in Thai). Bangkok.

Sharp, L. (1953) (*et al.*). *Siamese Rice Village: A Preliminary Study of Bang Chan 1948–1949* (Cornell Research Center). Bangkok.

Shorto, H. L. (1963). 'The 32 myos in the Medieval Mon Kingdom'. *Bull. of the Sch. of Oriental and African Studies,* vol. XXVI, part 3. London.

Silcock, T. H. (1967) (ed.). *Thailand, Social and Economic Studies in Development.* Durham: Duke University Press.

Spencer, R. F. (1966). 'Ethical Expressions in a Burmese Jatika', in *The Anthropologist Looks at Myth* (ed. J. Greenway). Austin: University of Texas Press.

Spiro, M. E. (1967). *Burmese Supernaturalism.* New Jersey: Prentice-Hall.

Srinivas, M. N. (1952). *Religion and Society among the Coorgs of South India.* Oxford: University Press.

Stevenson, H. N. C. (1954). 'Status Evaluation in the Hindu Caste System'. *J. R. Anthrop. Inst.,* vol. 84, pp. 45–65.

Tambiah, S. J. (1963). 'Ceylon', in *The Role of Savings and Wealth in Southern Asia and the West* (eds. B. F. Hoselitz and R. D. Lambert). Paris: UNESCO.

  (1968*a*). 'Literacy in a Buddhist Village in North-East Thailand', in *Literacy in Traditional Societies* (ed. J. Goody). Cambridge: University Press.

  (1968*b*). 'The Ideology of Merit and the Social Correlates of Buddhism in a Thai Village', in *Dialectic in Practical Religion* (ed. E. R. Leach) (Cambridge Papers in Social Anthropology, no. 5). Cambridge: University Press.

  (1968*c*). 'The Magical Power of Words'. *Man* (N.S.), vol. 3, no. 2, pp. 175–208.

The Pali Chanting Scripture with Thai and English Translation Donated on the Occasion of the Birthday (72) of Mrs. Chaemvijasorn (Phin Niyomhetu), May 17, 1963, Bangkok.

Bibliography

Thomas, Edward J. (1951). *The History of Buddhist Thought*, London: Routledge and Kegan Paul Ltd.

Thompson, V. (1941). *Thailand, the New Siam*. New York.

Vella, W. F. (1955). *The Impact of the West on Government in Thailand* (University of California Publications in Political Science, vol. 4, no. 3). Berkeley: University of California Press.

Waddell, L. A. (1912/13). 'The "Dharani" Cult in Buddhism, its Origin, deified in Literature and Images'. *Ostasiatische Zeitschrift*. Erster Jahrgang.

Wales, Quaritch H. G. (1931). *Siamese State Ceremonies*. London: Bernard Quaritch, Ltd.

(1965). *Ancient Siamese Government and Administration*. Paragon Book Reprint Corp. (First published in 1934 by Bernard Quaritch, Ltd.)

Weber, M. (1958). *The Religion of India: The Sociology of Hinduism and Buddhism* (transl. H. H. Gerth and D. Martindale). Illinois.

(1963). *The Sociology of Religion* (transl. E. Fischoff). Boston.

Wells, K. E. (1960). *Thai Buddhism: Its Rites and Activities*. Bangkok.

Wijewardene, G. (1967). 'Some Aspects of Rural Life in Thailand', in *Thailand, Social and Economic Studies in Development* (ed. T. H. Silcock). North Carolina: Duke University Press.

Wood, W. A. R. (1924). *A History of Siam*. London.

Yalman, N. (1964). 'The Structure of Sinhalese Healing Rituals', in *Religion in South Asia* (ed. E. B. Harper). Seattle: University of Washington Press.

Yoe, S. (1896). *The Burman, His Life and Notions*. London: Macmillan and Co.

Young, E. (1907). *The Kingdom of the Yellow Robe*. London: Constable and Co.

Zimmer, H. (1946). *Myths and Symbols in Indian Art and Civilization* (ed. J. Campbell) (Bollingen Series VI). New York: Pantheon Books.

INDEX

agriculture
holdings, 9
expansion of, in nineteenth century, 9
marginal land, 9 f.
1963 *Census*, 10
land ownership, 23 f.
role and rituals of the guardian spirits in, 268–71
field spirits, 316 f.
myth of the rice spirit, 351–66
Alavaka (the demon), 204, 216
Anawrata, King, 27
Angkor, 25, 38, 252
Angulimala, the robber, 204, 216, 221
animism, 41, 263, 326 n.
Anuradhapura, 32, 174
arahats (ascetics), 42, 47–51, 210, 222, 324
Asoka, King, 33, 169 f., 176
asuras (demons), 38
Ayudhya, 25 f., 28–31, 77 f., 252

Baan Phraan Muan
the legend of Muan the hunter, 6
situation, 6–8
administration, 8
settlement pattern, 10 f.
social structure, 10, 14–23
age distributions, 12
household composition, 12–14
Baka, the Brahman, 204, 216
Bangkok, 25, 31, 110, 137, 150, 191, 254, 373
Bodhgaya, 47
Borom, Khun, 29
Bowring Treaty, the, 9
Brahma, the god, 44, 60 f., 114, 356 f.
brahman, and *bhikkhu*, 64–6, 213
of the court, 74
code, 86, 89
compared with Thai *paahm*, 252–62, 375
Brahmins, 149, 193
Buddha, Gotama, 33 f., 42–7, 49 f., 51 f., 61, 66, 72, 92–4, 107, 111, 113, 126, 158 f., 161 n., 166, 169 f., 170, 173 f., 177, 196 f., 203 f., 210 f., 214, 216–18, 288, 301, 340 f., 357
Buddha-to-be (*bodhisattva*), 38, 42, 46, 200, 219 f.: and kingship, 46, 48, 74, 253; Maitreya, 38, 43, 46–8, 61, 66, 94, 165, 177, 355, 357, 364; Pacceka, 66, 356–8

other Buddhas, 42 f., 48, 203, 217, 352 f., 357
Buddhagosa, 47, 92, 196
Buddhism
in Thai history, 26–30
Mahayana Buddhism, 26, 28, 48, 62, 199 f.
Hinayana Buddhism, 27, 48
Pali Buddhism 27 f., 252, 371
Sinhalese Pali Buddhism, 27 f., 29, 32 f., 265
Theravada Buddhism, 29, 48, 62, 69, 74, 82, 97, 197, 199, 375
doctrinal concepts, 34 f., 39–42
the anthropological approach, 41 f., 62
Burma, 25–8, 30 f., 35, 38, 41, 44, 46, 48, 51, 57, 62, 68, 74, 76, 90 f., 119, 175, 192 f., 253 f., 284, 325, 367, 374
Upagotha in, 176–8

calendrical rites, 144–6, 152–68, 190, 267, 269–71, 285–311
(*in chronological order*)
Songkran (New Year), 152–4, 293
Wisaka (birth of Buddha), 154
Khaw Phansa (entering Lent), 154, 155 f.
Bunbangfai (the rocket festival), 156, 286–94, 298, 300–4, 308–11, 348, 377
Phansa or *Vassa* (Lent—the rain retreat), 28, 69–71, 103 f., 118, 125, 154–7, 205
Bun Khaw Saak (merit with rice), 156
Org Phansa (end of Lent), 125, 126, 157, 160
Bun Kathin (presentation of robes), 28, 157–60, 347
Bun Phraawes (harvest festival), 61, 160–8, 289, 293, 300–4, 377
Cambodia, 25, 28 f., 31, 33, 38, 74, 119, 175, 252–4, 355, 367, 375
Candima or Canda (the moon god), 221
Ceylon, 27 f., 31–5, 37–9, 44, 46, 48, 56, 60, 62, 67 f., 71, 73–6, 90, 93 f., 174, 192–4, 211, 252, 287, 355 f., 359, 367, 373, 375
Chakri dynasty, 31
Chiengmai (Lan Na), 25, 27, 29 f., 119
Chinese, 20, 26 f.
Christian monks
compared with Buddhist, 87–9
morality and salvation, 95
Cincamanarika, 204, 216

385

Index

Coorgs, 193
cosmology, 32–52
  the planes of existence: *kama loka*,
    36–9; *rupa loka* and *arupa loka*,
    39–42

dagoba, the, 46
death
  normal, involving mortuary rites, 22,
    180–8, 339, 345, 347: chants in, 205 f.;
    collection of bones, 186 f.; cremation,
    183–6; funeral procession, 182 f; im-
    plication of, 191–4; kinship participa-
    tion in, 189; laying out the corpse,
    180–2; *prasaat peueng*, 186–8
  the dead visit the living, 154, 156
  abnormal, 179, 189 f., 313, 315 f.
  transferring merit to the dead, 190 f.
  death and spirits, 313–16
devas (the gods), 38–40, 43 f., 52, 202
Dharmasastras, the, 27
Dhrita-rashtra, 37
directions of the compass, symbolism of,
    21, 180–3
Dvaravati, 26

eclipse, myths of, 221
education
  of village children, 11, 97 f.
  examinations, 78, 80
  of novices and monks, 120–8
  uses of literacy, 129–34
Europeans, 31
exorcism, *see* spirits

Fa Ngum, 29
Franco–Siamese Treaty (1893), 31

Gandharvas (musicians in heaven), 37,
    204
Ganesh, 254
Garuda (the eagle), 173–5, 219 f., 238, 246,
    255, 355, 359, 375
ghosts, *see* spirits
gift-giving, 212–14, 347 f.

hearing without understanding, virtue of,
    195 f.
hierarchy
  of generations in village life, 16–18,
    189, 260
  of monks, 117; monks and laymen, 142
Hinduism, 27 f., 38, 44, 62–5, 91, 95, 139,
    173 f., 193 f., 213, 252, 255 f., 265,
    324, 341, 355, 357, 368–72, 376
houses
  plan, 19

symbolism, 21–3, 181, 331
household rites, 206, 347

iddhi (*siddhi*), powers, 49 f.
India, Indians, 20, 26 f., 31, 63–5, 74,
    169, 194, 213, 237, 252–4, 355 f., 359,
    367–75
Indonesia, 26, 374
Indra (the god), 37 f., 44, 60 f., 114, 166,
    202, 238, 246, 253, 255, 357
inheritance patterns (of land), 12
Islam, 138

Jains, 63, 86, 89 f.
Jambudvipa, 36
Jetavana, 202, 214

Kallar, the, 193
Ketu (the demon), 38
Khmers, 26–31, 119, 174 f., 252, 323, 355
King, Maung, 176
kingship, 46, 48, 74–80, 110, 253, 374
kinship terminology, 16 f., 189
Kublai Khan, 26
Kumbandas (monsters), 37, 204
Kuvera, 37

Lamphun, 26
languages and scripts, 26–30, 119, 121,
    244, 254
  Pali, 122, 124 f., 128, 195–8, 349
Laos, 25, 28–31, 109 f., 114, 119, 287 f.,
    367
Lavo, 26
Loi Kratong, 169
Luang Phrabang (Muang Chawa), 25, 27,
    29–31, 114
luck, dispelling bad, 226

Maccadevi (the fish princess), legend of,
    176
Maha-dharmaraja, 77
Mahavihara, 32
Malwa, 193
Mara (the demon), 51 f., 158, 163, 169–71,
    173, 176–8, 204, 210, 216 f., 239, 245,
    302, 308, 353
marriage
  residence, 12
  endogamy, 15
  regulations, 17 f.
  ceremony, 22 f.
  sukhwan rites, 224, 227 f., 230–4, 237 f.:
    text of, 245–8
'medicine'
  practice of, 48, 133, 136, 257
  chants for curing illness, 206–8

Index